Creation
—An Ecumenical Challenge?

Creation
—An Ecumenical
Challenge?

Reflections issuing from a study
by the Institute for Ecumenical Research
Strasbourg, France

by Per Lønning

PEETERS

MERCER

*Creation
—An Ecumenical Challenge?*
Copyright © 1989
Mercer University Press, Macon GA 31207 USA
All rights reserved
Printed in the United States of America

The paper used in this publication meets
the minimum standards of American National Standard
for Information Sciences—Permanence of Paper
for Printed Library Materials, ANSI Z39.48-1984. ∞

Library of Congress Cataloging-in-Publication Data

Creation—an ecumenical challenge? : reflections issuing
from a study by the Institute for Ecumenical Research,
Strasbourg, France / by Per Lønning, 1928–

viii + 272 pp. 6 × 9″ (15 × 23cm.)
Includes index.
ISBN 0-86554-356-9 (Mercer : alk. paper)
1. Creation. 2. Creation and Christian union. 3. Cre-
ation—History of doctrines. I. Institute for Ecumenical
Research. II. Title.
BT695.L66   1989   89-35703
231.7′65—dc20   CIP

Contents

Preface

In terms of content and method (but not of thematic orientation) this book is somewhat different from the author's original intention. It was foreseen as a documentary report of a study project organized by the Institute for Ecumenical Research, Strasbourg, France, on ''Creation—An Ecumenical Challenge?,'' to include a comprehensive analytical reflection by the author—the leader of the project—in light not only of the Institute's study as a series of organized events, but also of a broad personal observation of contemporary ecumenical events and publications relevant to the overall topic.

However, as the manuscript started to take shape it became increasingly clear that it was not easy to combine this broader reflection on the theme with a ''report'' giving a comprehensive review of the various project events and do justice to the contributions of the wide range of participants involved. Two separate publications had, therefore, to be foreseen. The Department of Communication of the Lutheran World Federation (LWF) graciously offered to include the documentary part in its *LWF Documentation* series (no. 27, 1989).[1]

How, then, does the present book relate to the Strasbourg project? Without intending to give a presentation of the project as such, it makes heuristic use of the organized project events in order to: 1. reflect how questions related to a new and obviously promising field of ecumenical studies did and do arise from actual encounter; and 2. collect arguments and considerations that help to provide the solutions to such questions. Basically, references to project-related events will oc-

---

[1] ''Creation—An Ecumenical Challenge? Documentation from a Study by the Institute for Ecumenical Research,'' ed. Per Lønning, *LWF Documentation* no. 27 (October 1989). Also to be published in German.

cur in order to shed light on the theme, not on the research process. A summary account of the project strategy is included (§1.5) only in order to provide a general idea of the character and the bearing of the observations made. For further information and for assistance in critical assessment, reference will have to be made to the above-mentioned *LWF Documentation.*

Particular gratitude should be expressed to the Institute for Ecumenical Research, where I had the privilege to work for six years and which—without any initiative on my part—invited me to take responsibility for this extremely provocative and stimulating task. In particular, I am indebted to my three research colleagues, the professors Harding Meyer (Director of the Institute), André Birmelé, and Mark Ellingsen, for their valuable assistance in organizing the study project and for substantial discussion of the material that gradually emerged. In addition, Dr. Ellingsen, as my closest day-to-day collaborator on the creation project, has been constantly available for consultation. He made a remarkable contribution to the project as a whole in carrying out a particularly important section of it, the "inductive" study of contemporary church statements on social ethics with regard to the expression of creation motivations.

The Department of Communication of the Lutheran World Federation deserves thanks, not only for undertaking to publish the documentation part of the study, but also for volunteering to put the manuscript of the present volume into a viable form, for controlling the rather imperfect English of the author, and for replacing quotations in other languages by official English translations where such could be traced. In this connection I owe particular thanks to Frances Maher for her extraordinary and dedicated cooperation. It goes without saying that I am extremely grateful to the Norwegian Research Council for Science and Humanities (Norges Almenvitenskapelige Forskningsråd) for the substantial grant that made the publication of the present volume possible.

Per Lønning   Bergen, April 1989

1

Creation and ecumenism —A meaningful topic?

1.1 Asking the question

In the early 1980s rumors started to spread that the Institute for Ecumenical Research was going to launch a project on "Creation—An Ecumenical Challenge," and it was interesting to observe the highly divergent comments. On the one hand, these were rather critical: Why should an ecumenical research institute waste time and resources on such an off-the-trail juxtaposition as this? Creation has never ranked high on the list of denominational controversies, so why push it? On the other hand, one heard: How wonderful that an unconventional step is to be taken to brush up the ecumenical agenda, a step into a domain that is so obviously at the heart of contemporary theology! Since the project was announced in 1982, general remarks have swung more and more in the latter direction, but it has been our experience that it takes some efforts to arouse the awareness of unprepared observers about the issue at stake. A short explanation of the rationale of the project may be in order.

There is no doubt that "creation" and "ecumenism" are both areas of crucial concern, not least toward the end of the 20th century. But it is not immediately recognized that when two areas of concern meet—however stimulating and challenging they may be—new and equally interesting questions arise from the encounter. Needless to say, the expectations at the root of our enterprise will have to stand the test of subsequent observations. Expectations alone will establish no conclusion.

Even without particular observation or analysis, the concerns of "creation" and "ecumenism" face each other in a wide variety of settings and many puzzling and stimulating questions arise from their everyday encounter. The demands of "life" and "environment" pose a new test for Christianity, and such are the new claims being made on the churches that the challenge can only be met ecumenically, setting aside all geographical and denominational limitations. On the one hand, this may give rise to new and refreshing aspects of practical church cooperation. On the other hand, the resurgence of creation theology, resulting very much from the same demands, may open up new avenues to ecclesiological self-understanding, to exploring the unity of the church in light of the unity of humankind and, perhaps no less important, in light of the unity of all creation. This may be important to the future of the ecumenical venture, not only in view of the light thrown on the question of unity, but also—given the intrinsic coherence of theology as a whole—through an unconventional approach to theology at large, opening up new avenues of approach for tackling questions that have traditionally been seen as church dividing.

In referring to our study as new we do not infer that to date creation theology has been void of ecumenical reference, nor that ecumenical conferences, study activities, or dialogues have completely ignored all aspects of creation. It should not, however, require much to demonstrate that systematic theology and organized ecumenism have so far shown little inclination to use the First Article as a key to church unity/disunity. There may be few objections to the program set by Jürgen Moltmann: that a creation theology should consciously use an "ecumenical method," that is, listen to the wide variety of Christian testimonies of creation faith,[1] and this is certainly important. But letting the *oikumene* speak about creation is not sufficient for our undertaking, which is, equally, to let creation speak about ecumenism. As new problems have emerged at the crossroads of "creation" and "ecumenism," the tendency has been to see them as two separate areas of concern rather than to observe the crossroad as such.

However, some ecumenical study projects with an obvious bearing on creation have indicated a wider orientation. At the meeting of the Faith and Order

---

[1]Jürgen Moltmann, *God in Creation: An Ecological Doctrine of Creation,* trans. Margaret Koch (London: SCM Press, 1985). Original: *Gott in der Schöpfung: Ökologische Schöpfungslehre* (Munich: Christian Kaiser Verlag, 1985).

Commission of the World Council of Churches (WCC) in Aarhus, Denmark (1964), three papers from different confessional traditions were presented on the main theme, "Creation and Redemption"[2]—at the request of the 1963 World Conference of Faith and Order in Montreal, Canada. Another working paper, "God in Nature and History,"[3] was approved by the Commission on Faith and Order at its 1967 meeting in Bristol, England. The major ecumenical accomplishment of this document may be its balancing comparison of two theological traditions, the one viewing Christ as the restoration of creation, the other viewing Christ as the perfection of creation. While regretting this historical polarization as such, the working paper gives priority to the latter understanding. However, given the title, it is remarkable to observe how little attention the paper pays to "nature." In terms of content, "nature" can hardly be said to play more than a cosmetic role. Certain aspects of creation were also observed in and integrated into the Faith and Order study "Giving Account of Hope" (1972–1978).[4] Whereas one of the ongoing Faith and Order projects, "The Unity of the Church and the Renewal of Humankind" (1982–), seems to limit creation aspects to an anthropological setting, the parallel project, "Towards the Common Expression of the Apostolic Faith Today," intends to give the First Article its full share of attention within the historical framework of the Creed.[5]

In a socioethical perspective, creation issues have been broached by the WCC Working Committee for Church and Society, especially in connection with the world conference on "Faith, Science, and the Future" (Cambridge, Massachusetts, 1979). This conference was prepared in light of the WCC program "For a Just, Participatory, and Sustainable Society," in which the concept of "sustainability" suggests an important avenue for a new assessment of creation as involving the preservation of some constitutive elements of givenness. A new world conference on "Justice, Peace, and the Integrity of Creation" (JPIC) is planned for 1990 as the highlight and conclusion of a consecutive study project of a similar format.

---

[2]*Kerygma und Dogma* 1 (1965): 1-48.

[3]*Study Encounter* 1/3 (1965).

[4]*Giving Account of the Hope Today,* Faith and Order Paper no. 81 (Geneva: World Council of Churches, 1976).

[5]Cf. *Confessing One Faith: Towards an Ecumenical Explication of the Apostolic Faith as Expressed in the Nicene-Constantinopolitan Creed (381),* Faith and Order Paper no. 140 (Geneva: World Council of Churches, 1987) 28-36.

The wording "integrity of creation" has come in as a rather conscious replacement of "sustainability," underlining some holistic ecological vision rather than the more static perspective of indiscriminate preservation. "There are . . . two features of integrity of creation which . . . will carry it beyond previous ecumenical discussions. . . . The vision of wholeness must be expressed from within a multitude of cultural contexts . . . an urgent need for a universal environmental ethic based on a holistic understanding of ecosystems."[6]

This study project, which is foreseen to comprehend three theological approaches (theology of nature, value of life/life-centered ethic, ecumenical social ethics) will be carried out in close cooperation with Faith and Order and with the WCC subunits on Dialogue, and with great stress on a unified approach to the three key concepts of the JPIC formula.[7]

Among the ecumenical contributions on a regional level, there is particular reason to mention the report of the Bucharest consultation of the Conference of European Churches (CEC), *The Groaning of Creation*.[8] As an important contribution on a national level, one must mention the 1985 report by the theological commission of the United Evangelical Lutheran Church of Germany (VELKD), *Schöpfungsglaube und Umweltverantwortung*[9] and, with a more immediate practical orientation, the 1984 "Manifest zur Versöhnung mit der Natur" by the *Umweltpfarrer* (pastors with special responsibility for their churches' ecological involvement) of the German Protestant churches, the 1985 joint declaration of the German Roman Catholic Bishops' Conference and the Evangelical Church in Germany (EKD), "Verantwortung wahrnehmen für die Schöpfung," and the 1985 memorandum of the Association of Christian Churches in Switzerland, "Menschsein im Ganzen der Schöpfung." An instructive review of important stages in official church involvement in ecology over the years 1975 to 1989 is to be found in Günther Altner's *Fortschritt wohin? Der Streit um die Alternative*.[10]

---

[6]David Gosling, "Towards a Credible Ecumenical Theology of Nature," *The Ecumenical Review* 38/3 (July 1986): 323-24.

[7]*Church and Society Newsletter* 5 (1986).

[8]*The Groaning of Creation: European Christians in Quest of Their Responsibility Today* (Geneva, 1982).

[9]*Schöpfungsglaube und Umweltverantwortung: Eine Studie des Theologischen Ausschusses der VELKD,* ed. Wenzel Lohff and Hans Christian Knuth (Hanover: Lutherisches Verlagshaus, 1985).

[10]Günther Altner, *Fortschritt wohin? Der Streit um die Alternative* (Neukirchen-Vluyn: Neukirchener Verlag, 1985) 160-76.

Important material and valuable suggestions for our own research have been found in these and many other studies. However, as already indicated, the scope of orientation has to be considerably widened. Our particular aim is not to point out concrete challenges in the realm of "environment" or joint strategies for church cooperation in that field (as has been done in so many earlier studies); rather it is our aim to reflect on the importance of such involvements for ecumenism—and the importance of ecumenism for such involvements.

Can a new awareness of creation contribute to a new reciprocal awareness among the churches? Can an authentic ecumenical vision imply a new discovery of God's creation and provide motivation for a joint ministry to that creation?

1.2 The eclipse and resurgence of creation

So much has been said and written in recent years about the alleged *Schöpfungsvergessenheit* (oblivion of creation)[11] in contemporary theology that one gradually starts to doubt it. A forgetfulness so generally observed and regretted can hardly be too dominant—it must somehow belong to the past?

In spite of this general observation, it is true that creation has been "lost" to theology in a rather crucial way and that in our day a remarkable revival seems to be taking place. Even if words like Creator, creation, creature, and createdness have always been frequently used in theological language, this vocabulary has been integrated into Christology or anthropology in such a way that its relatedness to the universe, to nature, to the environment, and to the real phenomenal world to which we belong has become radically restricted. Creation talk tended to be about something different than the realm of the creature! Neither the human "creatureliness" (*Geschöpflichkeit*) of existential theology nor the human "creativity" (*Schöpfertum*) of political theology—the one with utterly pessimistic overtones, the other so optimistic—had a primary focus on creation, that is, the relationship of the Creator to his creature. In a way, the ideas of "creatureliness" and "creativity" are competitive, the one emphasizing that the limitations of human existence are dependent on a creator beyond all human control, the other confirming that human activity is the immediately relevant expression of the wonder of creation. However, in their anthropological restriction they have two decisive things

---

[11]Cf. Pierre Ganne, *La Création* (Paris: Les Editions du Cerf, 1979) 3: "Il y a longtemps que des observateurs attentifs ont remarqué que beaucoup de chrétiens semblent avoir perdu le sens de la Création; il ne savent plus bien ce qu'ils croient en disant: le Créateur, le Père créateur, la Création, sans parler de la créativité."

in common: They overlook the creature in its multiplex concreteness, and they tend to reduce the role of the Creator to that of a qualifier of human existence (be it in a negative or a positive direction) instead of viewing creation as a dynamic, global relationship—Creator: creation—the Creator's action *for, with,* and *through* his creatures.

Taking up a linguistic model from Richard Niebuhr, George S. Hendry in his *Theology of Nature* speaks critically of the three "unitarianisms" of individual articles of the Creed.[12] A "unitarianism" of the First Article has hardly prevailed within mainline church history since the Enlightenment. A "unitarianism" of the Third Article was installed into power through Friedrich Schleiermacher with his emphasis on inwardness and psychological experience. In reaction against the latter, Karl Barth represents a most pointed "unitarianism" of the Second Article, making salvation history the only legitimate frame of reference for Christianity. In the recent upsurge of a more vital creation theology, Hendry distinguishes a hopeful sign in overcoming the various "unitarian" tendencies. This warning was certainly valid, especially in the late 1970s. But, in view of recent developments, there may be reason to ask whether these difficulties are overcome by substituting a "Trinitarian" doctrine of creation. This program seems to be widely accepted today, as demonstrated by the reviews of Jürgen Moltmann's *God in Creation,*[13] and it also seems to set the direction for the WCC Church and Society/Faith and Order studies on the "integrity of creation."[14] The history of modern creation

---

[12]George S. Hendry, *Theology of Nature: The Warfield Lectures 1978* (Philadelphia: Westminster Press, 1980 [1978]).

[13]See n. 1.

[14]Report of the Working Group, Potsdam (July 1986) 21: "The WCC has tended to stress 'Christ' in such a manner that the first and third members of the Trinity become merely functional. We need to interpret the second person of the Trinity in terms of the first and the third, which is precisely what Faith and Order and Church and Society are trying to do in their current explorations of the doctrine of creation." The validity of this Trinitarian orientation should not be questioned. But when adopted as the unchallenged recipe for an ecumenical theology of creation, it will eventually give rise to two problems: 1. The unity of God the Creator can be problematized in such a way that it may have consequences both for the unity of creation and for the polarity of Creator/creation. 2. The understanding of creation can be so exclusively tied up with biblical revelation and a specifically Christian doctrine of God that any possibility for a common human understanding in "the room of creation" is lost.

eclipse has been reviewed fairly frequently in recent literature and shall not be repeated in any great detail.[15]

Sociological factors have certainly been at work. Growing urbanization has detracted the general attention from nature to what has been termed "civilization." The incredible economic achievements of science and technology have given rise to a new attitude toward reality as a whole: from "mystery" to "mastery."[16] The emergence of new sciences, seemingly contradicting established Christian beliefs (including the Bible itself), have led to a series of apologetical disasters that make theology look for safe positions beyond the reach of science. Such a refuge was made possible through new philosophical onsets (René Descartes, Immanuel Kant, Martin Heidegger), which were, in a way, the product of a similar apologetical need—felt by Western culture in general—to protect the humanity of humans against the seemingly totalitarian assault of an emerging natural science. The superiority of the human mind, secured by Cartesian and Kantian philosophy, not only protected humankind from being swallowed up by matter, but also gave a moral justification for subdual of that matter—and of nonhuman nature as a whole—through a rapidly expanding technology. In theology, Pietistic inwardness and otherworldliness combined with the new philosophical trend, which in its fight against "metaphysics" made it rather easy to separate faith from physical events and phenomena. In existentialism, this tendency was reinforced, partly by enabling individual human existence to constitute itself independently of all objective givens, and partly by defining existence as "moment," an event apart from the contextuality of "time" and "matter," and understood as some completely nonobjectifiable "presence."

In recent years Eastern and Oriental Orthodox theology have criticized Western Christendom of having a fatal flaw that dates further back than the breakthrough of modern science. Paul Evdokimov has developed this criticism rather explicitly.

A partir de la fin du XIe siècle l'Occident se trouve à un tournant décisif qui le sépare de l'Orient. Du monde de similitude et de participation, d'une

---

[15]One should bear in mind the well-founded warnings against merely replacing anthropocentric one-sidedness with an equally one-sided anthropofugal perspective. This warning is well stated by Joachim Track in his reflections on "Menschliche Freiheit: Zur ökologischen Problematik der neuzeitlichen Entwicklung," *Versöhnung mit der Natur?*, ed. Jürgen Moltmann (Munich: Christian Kaiser Verlag, 1986) 48-93.

[16]Cf. the terminology of Paul Gregorios in his *The Human Presence: An Orthodox View of Nature* (Geneva: World Council of Churches, 1978) 88-89.

perception synthétique, le passage se fait à un univers de la causalité efficiente, à l'analyse scolastique et à la formation par l'Ecole. . . . A la scolastique en tant que statut de la connaissance religieuse, à sa méthode analytique, et par là de type rationel, l'Orient préfère la connaissance sapientielle où convergent le dogme, la contemplation mystique, la théologie et la philosophie."[17]

And, directing attention still further back:

L'Occident réfléchit surtout sur la grâce et la liberté, sur le péché originel et la prédestination. Ainsi la théologie et surtout l'anthropologie de saint Augustin, plus tard la sotériologie de saint Anselme, la gnoséologie de saint Thomas, sont déjà bien différentes de la théologie de saint Athanase, de saint Maxime, de saint Jean Damascène, de saint Grégoire Palamas.[18]

With particular reference to creation, a similar viewpoint (but with a somewhat different twist) is developed and defended by Paul Gregorios in a booklet made available as preparatory material for the 1979 world conference on Faith, Science, and the Future. Here, the predicament of Western thought is developed in alliance with the 19th-century Russian Orthodox thinker Vladimir Soloviev:

Soloviev saw clearly the two opposing tendencies in Western life, one seeking to glorify man at the expense of God, the other seeking to glorify God by denigrating the human—the conflict between Renaissance optimism and Augustinian pessimism. Between these two spirits the West never achieved a creative synthesis, though there were scattered efforts like those of Erasmus, Nicolaus of Cusa, and St. Francis de Sales.[19]

On the other hand, Gregorios himself is accused of an ecologically detrimental anthropocentrism by H. Paul Santmire:

---

[17]Paul Evdokimov, *L'Orthodoxie* (Paris: Desclée de Brouwer, 1980 [1959]) 17.

[18]Paul Evdokimov, *La connaissance de Dieu selon la tradition orientale* (1967) 9.

[19]Paul Gregorios, *The Human Presence* (see n. 16) 79.

For Gregorios, as the title of his book indicates . . . nature stands or falls with the human presence. He finally ends up by espousing an ethic of mastery over nature similar to [Thomas S.] Derr's.[20]

In his later and more comprehensive study, *Cosmic Man: The Divine Presence*, Gregorios points to Augustine as father of the Cartesian "Cogito"—and thus of a philosophy making the human mind the constitutive foundation of reality[21]— and extends his criticism of the Occidental Augustine in the name of the Oriental Gregory of Nyssa.[22] Western alienation from creation is here seen in dual perspective: on the one hand, there is the epistemological estrangement, which sees the realm of objects as submitted to the human mind; on the other, there is the hamartiological estrangement, which makes nature in itself evil. The latter of these two errors, then, tends to provoke its own opposite: the admiration of the goodness of nature that seems to make a saving divine presence unnecessary.

It is quite remarkable—and as an introduction to the present study it is extremely important to observe—that such challenges from the Eastern to the Western churches (rather commonplace as they have become) have so far elicited less than little response. The 1979 world conference on Faith, Science, and the Future (under the presidency of Paul Gregorios) took up the Eastern accusations and made them its own:

Modern Western Christian theology . . . undergirded the opposition between nature and humanity. . . . Western theology has introduced the . . . opposition even into the interpretation of the Bible: creation and salvation have been separated.[23]

One could imagine that such a response would be of considerable importance for the further development of ecumenical dialogue—whether in the form of an

---

[20]H. Paul Santmire, "Toward a New Theology of Nature," *Dialog* 25 (Spring 1986): 50. The reference is to another official WCC Church and Society publication, namely Thomas S. Derr, *Ecology and Human Liberation: A Theological Critique of the Use and Abuse of Our Birthright*, WSCF Books 3/1 (1973) serial no. 7.

[21]Paul Gregorios, *Cosmic Man: The Divine Presence* (Geneva: World Council of Churches, 1980) xii-xiv.

[22]Ibid., 184, 210-18.

[23]*Faith and Science in an Unjust World.* Report of the WCC Conference on Faith, Science, and the Future, Massachusetts Institute of Technology, Cambridge, USA, 12-24 July, 1979, vol. 2, *Reports and Recommendations*, ed. Paul Abrecht (Geneva: World Council of Churches, 1980) 29, 30.

admission, a refutation, or something inbetween. As a matter of fact, this observation alone should be enough to grant creation theology (with its connecting links to epistemology, anthropology, hamartiology, etc.) a rather visible place on the priority list of ecumenical issues.

It may be somewhat futile to discuss precisely how far back one can date theology's difficulties with creation. As most other issues, it may have its roots in the garden of Eden: the wondering about the Tree of Knowledge being the first question raised concerning creation theology. Tendencies, on the one hand, to extol the integrity of creation and, on the other, to underscore its depravity may have been juxtaposed in unsettled conflict for as long as there has been theological reflection. When Friedrich Schleiermacher bases the dialectic of *Der christliche Glaube* on the heresiological typology of "Pelagianism" and "Manicheism"[24] and states that the task of theological reflection is the overcoming of this confrontation between idolatrous exaltation and irreverent degradation of nature,[25] his concern is basically the same as that of Gregorios—even if, of course, articulated in a different historical framework. In spite of this, there seems to be widespread agreement today that more than anyone else Schleiermacher has contributed to the eclipse of creation in Western theology, not only through translating the Kantian distinction between knowledge of the physical world and human self-cognizance into theological language, but also and equally by allowing the uniqueness of creation to be swallowed up by a general vision of divine providence.

A dialogue between Eastern and Western Christianity is probably the optimal setting for raising the issue as to *why*—and not so much *when* and *how*—the Western churches got into so much trouble with creation. It is obviously not sufficient to refer to the fact that modern natural science arose in the West and not in the East, as that would immediately invite discussion as to why *that* happened. Two factors seem to be dominant in the Eastern image of Western theology: 1. the tension between an undue exaltation and an undue degradation of nature, allegedly caused by an unproportionate emphasis on sin and redemption; and 2. an idea of nature as the object of human domination, allegedly caused by the Scholastic principle of distinction and objectification and reinforced through the following breakthrough of science. These are questions that demand ample reflection and

---

[24]A dialectical scheme that can be traced back to at least the Formula of Concord, Epitome I, III, I, 1577.

[25]Friedrich Schleiermacher, *The Christian Faith,* ed. H. R. Mackintosh and J. S. Stewart (Edinburgh: T. & T. Clark, 1928) §22. Original: *Der christliche Glaube* (Reutlingen, 1828).

certainly cannot be assumed to be clarified before a fairly substantial research has been undertaken.

For several reasons it may be meaningful to make our starting point not one but two philosophers, who through their diametrically opposed responses to one and the same challenge have jointly contributed to framing the modern Western mind, not least with respect to nonhuman creation. To Francis Bacon and René Descartes the more or less simultaneous challenges of Renaissance skepticism and emerging "modern" science demanded a complete purification of inherited human consciousness. Bacon found the answer in a thorough empirically based method for the elimination of all prejudice and the establishment of pure factual observation. Descartes found it in universal doubt as a gate to unbiased consciousness: subjective self-awareness accedes to the universal divine mind, which again establishes the validity of individual observations. Running in opposite directions, the two orientations met at the other end of the racecourse, thus concluding a rather remarkable concurrence. With a certain justification, Jürgen Hübner suggests that Bacon is the forerunner of Descartes.[26] To the latter, humankind is "maître et possesseur de la nature" because of the absolute supremacy of the *res cogitans* (mind) over the *res extensa* (matter). To the former, a comprehensive scientific methodology based on the distillation of unbiased "facts" was a means to reintroduce the complete domination of humankind over nature—as was supposedly the case before the Fall. Consistent subjectivism (rationalism) and consistent objectivism (empiricism) tend to reach the same conclusion: The world of objects is completely in the hands of the human manipulator—whether the latter be conceived as superior mind or as the skilled agent of fact-controlling observation.

It is helpful to note the gravitation of these two diverging yet converging traditions as they have been established by David Hume and Immanuel Kant. In their work the last bridge between observation of nature and natural theology was broken. Hume basically denied the possibility of inferring laws and rules from single observations, and thus also of any given structure of universal meaning that could possibly conflict with the seigneurial exercise of human privilege. With Kant things are somewhat more complex, in that rational order is accepted as a transsubjective reality, albeit only as a function of our own conceptual categories. This means that they open no access to *Ding an sich* (matter in itself). We can know the outward world only as it exists in the explicative categories of the human mind. In addition to the distinction between *Ding an sich* and *Ding für mich* (matter in itself; matter as conceived by me), there is the distinction between theoretical and practical rea-

---

[26]Jürgen Hübner, *Die Welt als Gottes Schöpfung ehren* (1982) 64-65.

son. Cognition relating to the world of observable facts belongs in the theoretical sphere. Practical reason deals not with facts but with moral value, judging concrete acts in the light of universal validity. Practical reason also postulates the existence of God as moral authority but virtually precludes the possibility of immediately relating God to the realm of facts and outward events. God "within the boundaries of pure reason" is not acting upon the phenomenal world as we see it. He is the ultimate source of human values and the guarantee of their triumph in the life hereafter.

The impact of these patterns of thought (especially as developed by Kant) exercised an enormous influence on theology in the 19th and a good deal of the 20th century. For how long it is difficult to say, as there is profound disagreement as to whether the Barthian epoch (the second third of the present century) should be seen as a continuation or as a breakdown of this neo-Protestant domination. The Kantian triumph in theology started with Schleiermacher. In this context, it is of minor importance that Schleiermacher substituted Kantian dichotomy (theoretical/practical cognition) with a seemingly more subtle trichotomy (theoretical/moral/religious),[27] whereas later theology, in the period of Albrecht Ritschl, tended to go back to the simpler Kantian dichotomy. The point is that in both cases religion and the world of empirical facts are basically not seen as being related to each other. Not only does this exclude a "natural theology"—an extraction of knowledge about the Creator from the observation of creature—it excludes at the same time any universally valid knowledge of created phenomena derived from a preconceived concept of creation. "Creation," as confessed by faith, is a qualifier of human existence, resting in an unconditional confidence in God as its ultimate ground. With Ritschl and his school, this position is reinforced through a violent "no" to metaphysics, that is, to any unifying vision of "God" and the physical universe. Statements of faith are seen exclusively as value judgments, not as judgments of fact (*Werturteile* not *Seinsurteile*), which means that in the act of faith the human mind ultimately responds only to God, the fountain of eternal love, not to any element of phenomenal environment.[28]

---

[27]"Religion is neither a knowledge nor a way of acting, but a state of immediate self-consciousness." (Friedrich Schleiermacher, *Reden über die Religion*, 1799, Zweite Rede).

[28]Paul Tillich stands in good continuity with this tradition when he states: "If nothing is an object of theology which does not concern us ultimately, theology is unconcerned about scientific procedures and results and vice versa." (*Systematic Theology*, vols. 1/2 [1968] 21) Cf. on the other hand A.M. Klaus Müller and Wolfhart Pannenberg, *Erwägungen zu einer Theologie der Natur* (1970) 35: "Die

Today there are few theologians who profess adherence to Schleiermacher and Ritschl, and especially to the dual (or triple) approach to reality. Nothing is as universally feared in present Christian reflection as a separation of God and (factual) world. The question is, however, to what extent the teachers of yesterday may have survived in new garbs. To a large extent this is—and has been recognized as such in contemporary debate—a question about the Barthian impulse: How has the widespread influence of Karl Barth contributed to creation theology?[29] To a large extent current tensions in the theology of creation reflect advocacy versus questioning of the Barthian inheritance.[30] This observation may be almost as appropriate with regard to Roman Catholic theology as it is to Protestant theology. The emphatic Barthian "no" to the Schleiermacher-Ritschl tradition is a "no" to understanding the reality of God in terms of human consciousness, insisting instead on the Word as proclaiming a reality beyond the control of self-asserting subjective experience. This "no" remains, however, in the line of that tradition when creation is approached not as the universal basis event objectively extending beyond the reach of the Christian confession, but as "creation in Christ" and thus as a qualifier of Christian existence rather than as the concept carrying our total vision of the world.[31]

Karl Barth's own exposition of creation theology in the third volume of his *Kirchliche Dogmatik* certainly shows no lack of interest in the notion of "creation." And subsequently some of the most striking contributions to the theme of creation have come from more or less proclaimed followers of Barth. In our day it may be meaningful to distinguish three trends of Barthian creation theology.

Unerreichbarkeit für naturwissenschaftliche Kritik bedeutet . . . zugleich die Irrelevanz der theologischen Aussagen . . . für das . . . Weltbild der heutigen Menschheit. Aus dieser Schwierigkeit hilft auch eine auf das Existentielle reduzierte Schöpfungslehre nicht hinaus."

[29]See esp. Karl Barth, *Church Dogmatics*, III/1 (Edinburgh: T. & T. Clark, 1957) §41: "Creation and Covenant," 42-329. Original: *Kirchliche Dogmatik*, III/1, §41: "Schöpfung und Bund," 44-377.

[30]Cf. *Zeitschrift für Theologie und Kirche*, 1986, Beiheft 6, "Zur Theologie Karl Barths."

[31]Also, Barth's emphatic rejection of "natural theology" (cf. the controversy with Emil Brunner on "nature and grace," 1932–1933) must be seen in the same context: the only authentic relationship with God is that of listening, embracing the words of the Bible. No glance at "nature" should be allowed to distract. From about 1950 the Barthian "covenant" approach to creation had good support from the Old Testament school, linked above all with the name of Gerhard von Rad, whose basic vision of Exodus preceding Genesis was hailed with enthusiasm among Barthians.

First, there is the super-Barthian view developed most characteristically by Hans-Joachim Kraus in his *Systematische Theologie im Kontext biblisher Geschichte und Eschatologie,* in which "God the Creator" (§§80-88) is programmatically and emphatically subordinate to "The God of Israel Giving Testimony of His Coming" (§§52-137):

> Nach biblischem Verständnis ist Schöpfung weder fabricatio mundi noch Objekt einer protologischen Spekulation. An Gott den Schöpfer glauben heisst: im freien, weltlichen Raum der Verwirklichung des Reiches Gottes dankbar und hoffnungsvoll die dem Geschöpf zukommende, universale Weltverantwortung wahrzunehmen.[32]

Whereas this must be seen as a vigorous reinforcement of Barth's *Heilsgeschichte* (history of salvation) approach to creation, professed neo-Barthians like Eberhard Jüngel and Christian Link see a need to overcome a certain narrowness in the original Barthian approach by developing a conscious "theology of nature." In attempting to formulate the program of a new "natural theology," Link emphatically rejects "metaphysics" as "inference from certain given 'orders'," denies "nature in its pure objectivity" as a source of intelligence, and focuses instead on the parables of Jesus as examples of a faith actively engaged in shaping reality, a real *credo ut intelligam* (Anselm of Canterbury: "I believe in order to understand").[33] Jüngel's prescription for a new "natural theology" goes very much in the same direction:

> . . . dass die natürliche Theologie dabei als solche in ein die ganze Dogmatik begleitendes, aber nicht durch sich selbst begründetes Moment der theologia revelationis aufgehoben wird. . . . Theologie des Wortes Gottes ist deshalb die gegenüber der sogenannten natürlichen Theologie allemal und ungleich natürlichere Theologie.[34]

Roughly speaking, this means that nature has nothing to say about God, but that the word of God has a good deal to say about nature—not about nature as a realm of reality cognizable prior to faith in Christ, but about "nature" as a new vision of the universe constituted through the event of redemption in Christ.

---

[32]Hans-Joachim Kraus, *Systematische Theologie im Kontext biblischer Geschichte und Eschatologie* (Neukirchen-Vluyn: Neukirchener Verlag, 1983) §85, 216.

[33]Christian Link, *Die Welt als Gleichnis: Studien zum Problem der natürlichen Theologie* (Munich: Christian Kaiser Verlag, 1976) 72.

[34]Eberhard Jüngel, *Entsprechungen* (Munich: Christian Kaiser Verlag, 1980) 177, 197.

The main exponent of a third post-Barthian trend is Jürgen Moltmann, with his comprehensive project of a Messianic theology:[35]

Messianic theology is theology under the presupposition of the presence of the Messiah and the beginning of the Messianic era. On this presupposition, the Messianic understanding of the world is the true natural theology.[36]

As opposed to the other authors quoted, Moltmann does not see that traditional natural theology is contradicted by the theology of revelation; rather, he understands the theology of revelation as a successor to and adaptation of traditional natural theology.

So pure *theologia naturalis* is theology under the conditions of pristine creation . . . in paradise.[37]

Also for Moltmann, creation theology is but one aspect—albeit an integral aspect—of a vision that is totally oriented toward the history of salvation. There is, however, an obvious change in emphasis between his *Theologie der Hoffnung* (theology of hope) of a good 20 years ago and his more recent creation theology. His original point of reference, in addition to Barthian antimetaphysics, was Ernst Bloch's *Prinzip Hoffnung,* in which a basic concern is to liberate biblical apocalyptic vision from the bondage of biblical creation faith. The "Behold, I make all things new" of the Apocalypse is a fiery protest against the "Behold, it was very good" of Genesis.[38] In Moltmann's theology, Bloch's idea of creation as a reactionary principle, committing the believers to authorize the present world as an expression of the Creator's will, is taken over and given a theologically challenging reinterpretation through a new and accentuated Trinitarian approach.[39] Moltmann's Trinitarian doctrine of God refutes traditional monotheism, with its idea

---

[35]Jürgen Moltmann, *God in Creation* (see n. 1) 7-9 (German: 14).

[36]Ibid., 60 (73).

[37]Ibid., 59 (72).

[38]Cf. esp. Ernst Bloch, *Atheism in Christianity: The Religion of the Exodus and the Kingdom,* trans. J. T. Swann (New York, 1972). Original: *Atheismus im Christentum* (Frankfurt: Suhrkamp, 1968) 59-64.

[39]This was developed more explicitly in Jürgen Moltmann, *The Trinity and the Kingdom of God: The Doctrine of God,* trans. Margaret Koch (London: SCM Press; New York: Harper & Row, 1981). Original: *Trinität und Reich Gottes* (Munich: Christian Kaiser Verlag, 1980).

of creation as the work of one allegedly "monolithic" Creator's will. Creation and Godhead are understood in a prominently Trinitarian way, as an interaction of Father, Son, and Spirit, and creation is seen within the framework of an all-comprehensive Messianic event. Although less pronounced than in Moltmann's earliest writings, the emphasis in this Messianic vision of history is still on the *adventus,* on God as the coming giver of future, but his reinforcement of the Trinitarian motif means that more equal weight is given to past and present as perspectives of the ongoing realization of our final hope.

When Moltmann gives his doctrine of creation the subtitle "an ecological doctrine of creation," it is, on the one hand, a sign of present-day involvement, namely that the ecological challenge is the setting for a truly contemporary theology of creation. On the other hand, it suggests a program of ecological awareness as a vision of the interrelatedness of all things. Even the divine, Trinitarian involvement with the world is not an interference from outside; rather it is an involvement *in* and *for* the created world. The most remarkable point about Moltmann's creation theology is probably how different emphases—more than one of which were originally obstructive to a substantial theology of creation—are combined and reinterpreted in light of a serious contemporary demand. The Barthian *Heilsgeschichte* scheme is preserved in principle, but doors are opened not only for an integration of scattered "natural" observations but also for a seemingly pragmatic orientation based on a concern for the preservation of creation, a concern that is not and cannot be derived from a traditional soteriological approach to theology.

Just as striking, but less convincing in terms of integration, is the new creation theology of Dorothee Sölle. Although Sölle was an advocate of the "death of God" theology of the late 1960s, even her creation theology is to some extent a sequel to Barthian theology, inasmuch as the latter resulted from a combination of the "no" to metaphysics and a consistent affirmation of salvation through the historical Jesus event as the only authentic key to human self-understanding. It may be seen as a characteristic sign of the times that Sölle, emerging from a creator-less theology, finds it important to write a theology of creation—and in so doing explicitly admits to earlier neglect:

> It may be that I am homesick for God and have been for a long time. . . .
> Today I find it necessary to ground my early, existentialist *solus Christus* position in a recognition of the source of life itself. . . . I want to reconcile my faith in Christ with my new understanding of God the Creator.[40]

---

[40]Dorothee Sölle, *To Work and to Love: A Theology of Creation* (Philadelphia: Fortress Press, 1984) 5.

However, the book testifies that for Sölle this is merely the beginning of her reorientation and that the way to the reconciliation she seeks may still be long. To her it remains evident that "liberation precedes creation,"[41] and this forms the basis of the whole development of her creation theology. If liberation does not presuppose some already existing entity that can be liberated, then liberation itself of necessity replaces creation. This, in turn, will most likely mean—as analysis proves with Sölle—that one's idea of "liberation" automatically determines one's concept of creation. Creation is understood not as an event but as a qualifier of some event identified by criteria other than creation faith. But even given this basic self-contradiction, the creation theology of Sölle indirectly represents a powerful testimony to the recent attraction of the creation theme, and also to the necessity to face actual threats to life with nothing less than a reflected vision of the meaning of what reality as an inviolable totality of all things "is about."[42]

The somewhat hesitant but ever more evident turning to creation theology on the part of theologians rooted in the tradition of Schleiermacher and Barth (with its profound reluctance to "objectification," "nature," and "natural theology") is in a way as remarkable as the less biased resurgence of creation theology in a new generation of—above all German—theologians who are less dedicated to hermeneutical speculation and more occupied by the challenges of the world around us. Günther Howe's attempt to initiate a new dialogue between science and theology in the early 1950s was a more successful prelude to theological reorientation than that of Karl Heim (probably the first modern Continental theologian recommending science as a vital conversation partner for creation theology) in the 1930s and that of Emil Brunner (probably the first to champion "orders of creation" outside a conservative Lutheran tradition). Likewise, the growing influence of the work of Pierre Teilhard de Chardin among German theologians concerned with creation theology should by no means be underestimated.[43]

In its comprehensive attempt to cross-fertilize theology, natural sciences, and social studies, the Forschungsstätte der Evangelischen Studiengemeinschaft (FEST) in Heidelberg, Federal Republic of Germany, has been one major agent in the rise

---

[41]Ibid., 8.

[42]Already in his *Im Bauch des Fisches: Ökologische Theologie* (1979), Gerhard Liedke could present an impressive survey of "Ansätze des Umdenkens in Theologie, Philosophie und Naturwissenschaft" (85-108).

[43]See Sigurd M. Daecke, *Teilhard de Chardin und die evangelische Theologie* (1967) and, more recently, Günther Altner "Aktuelle und historische Tendenzen im Gespräch zwischen Theologie und Naturwissenschaften," *Evangelische Theologie* 45/3 (1985): 248-60.

of a new climate and a new milieu to cope with the environmental provocation of the 1970s and 1980s. Among the theologians and scientists who have made significant contributions in this area in recent years are such people as Günther Altner, Sigurd M. Daecke, Jürgen Hübner, Gerhard Liedke, Klaus M. Meyer-Abich, A. M. Klaus Müller, and Odil Hannes Steck. Common to these authors is, above all, a strong preoccupation with human responsibility for the whole of creation. In this they resist not only a secularizing division between God and world but also a subjectivizing distance between the human mind and the creature in its empirical givenness. Strong emphasis is placed on a biblical vision of the dignity of the world as God's creation, and reflection moves from this vision and its exegetical foundations toward a broad assessment of information and observations provided by contemporary science. That similar tendencies may be observed in British and American theology is, historically speaking, less surprising. And their occurrence in contemporary Roman Catholic thought, now more inspired by Teilhard de Chardin than by Thomas Aquinas, is less surprising than their evidence in Lutheran and Reformed thinking.

As far as the biblical approach is concerned, one somewhat important reorientation is to be noted. The echoes of Albert Schweitzer's "Ehrfucht vor dem Leben"[44] may be less striking but, as an intermediate, must also be taken into account. There is still a pointed emphasis on the Old Testament, with the understanding that Claus Westermann's interpretation of Genesis has to a large extent replaced that of Gerhard von Rad. Von Rad—and even more so some of his scholars—laid particular emphasis on the observation that *Heilsgeschichte* preceded creation faith in old Israel. Exodus comes before Genesis. To celebrate this discovery was a most welcome opportunity for Barthian covenantal theology, and also for the ensuing "liberation theologies." Westermann's interpretation calls attention to the fact that in the Old Testament creation is not understood as a mere derivative of salvation history (with the inevitable anthropocentric narrowing that such an understanding involves) but as a nonderivable and all-orienting basis of reality.[45]

---

[44]See Albert Schweitzer, *Die Verteidigung des Lebens,* ed. Peter Helbich (Gütersloh: Gütersloher Verlagshaus Gerd Mohn, 1984) 31-32.

[45]"Eine Auslegung des A.T., die dem Reden von Schöpfer und Schöpfung ihre Eigenbedeutung nicht liess, ihre Bedeutung vielmehr allein in ihrer Beziehung zur Heilsgeschichte sah, hat dazu geführt, dass das *andere* Reden von einem *anderen* Wirken Gottes, wie wir es . . . im Reden von Schöpfer und Schöpfung im A.T. finden, nicht mehr sorgfältig genug gehört wurde. . . . Wenn aber die existentiale Interpretation zum ausschliesslichen Prinzip der Schrift-

In the midst of this, the role of the New Testament may have been less constitutive for the reciprocal orientation of creation and redemption than that of the Old—an observation that certainly has something to do with the sparse occurrence of explicit creation statements in the New Testament. Texts like John 1, Romans 1, and Colossians 1 have, however, frequently been quoted as testimonies of a consistently Christological approach to creation. Without any hesitation, Link assumes that it is "the only possible dogmatical consequence" that the New Testament exalts "die neue christliche, durch Christus erschlossene Erfahrung zum Erkenntnisgrund der Schöpfung."[46] But, in fact, the reverse is true in the respective New Testament texts: Their purpose is obviously to state the meaning of the incarnation in the light of Old Testament creation faith, not to communicate a reinterpretation of creation as such! Already in 1973, John Reumann gave a balanced assessment of "exclusionist" and "inclusivist" motifs in the relevant New Testament texts with regard to what he terms the "new interest in creation and new creation."[47] Likewise, Gerhard Friedrich uses a New Testament approach for a conscious attack on modern theological *Schöpfungsvergessenheit.*[48]

The growing interest in creation theology should not least be seen in light of the ecological crisis, which has received increasing general attention since about 1970. Theology—and above all the theology expanding through the communication network of ecumenical organizations and study agencies—was not sufficiently prepared to deal with this challenge. The 1960s had seen a remarkable resurgence of Christian social consciousness and world responsibility on a political level—as testified by the Second Vatican Council and various events of the World Council of Churches, such as the 1966 World Conference on Church and Society in Geneva and the 1968 WCC Assembly in Uppsala. But up to this time the development was predominantly affected by so-called "secular theology" and its ideal of a "church for others." The most striking expression of this theology

---

auslegung wird, verliert das biblische Reden von der Schöpfung der Welt seine Bedeutung. Es verliert seine Bedeutung aber auch dort, wo eine Theologie so einseitig soteriologisch bestimmt ist, dass Theologie und Soteriologie fast oder ganz identisch werden." (Claus Westermann, *Genesis, Kap. 1-11* [Neukirchen-Vluyn: Neukirchener Verlag, 1983] 241-42.) See also the "neo-Barthian" attempt at reconciliation in Christian Link's modification of the two positions in *Versöhnung mit der Natur?*, ed. Jürgen Moltmann (see n. 15) 35-36.

[46]Christian Link, ibid., 37.

[47]John Reumann, *Creation and New Creation* (1973) 12.

[48]Gerhard Friedrich, *Ökologie und Bibel: Neuer Mensch und alter Kosmos* (Stuttgart/Berlin/Cologne/Mainz: Kohlhammer, 1982).

was possibly in *The Secular City* by Harvey Cox (1965), but it was particularly unsuited to deal with the environmental crisis. First, it interpreted biblical creation faith as desacralization, attributing sacredness to the Creator alone and thus leaving a totally disenchanted world in the hands of a human quest for unconditioned freedom. This made it virtually blind to the dignity of nonhuman nature as well as to the values of traditionally established patterns of human fellowship. It also made it praise technological efficiency and urbanization as a means to promote freedom and to prepare for the ''New Jerusalem.'' Second, in sharpening the Barthian ''no'' to religion, secular theology virtually denied any veneration of nature issuing not only from non-Christian religions or religion in general, but also from Christian adoration of God the Creator of the cosmos. Third, through celebrating the Bible as the historical source of secularization, secular theology tended to frown upon any civilization that was consciously based on religious values—such as the great cultures of the East, native Africa, or native America—and in an international perspective could thus be seen as another outburst of Western arrogance in the name of Christianity.

It is no wonder that such a self-glorification of Christianity was harshly criticized by writers such as Lynn White and Carl Amery.[49] If admirers of the Bible claim for it the honor for modern secularization, it certainly also has to carry the blame!

One theological school that was extremely sensitive to the ecological challenge and obviously grew considerably during the 1970s and 1980s was the school of ''process theology,'' which originated in the USA. At first glance, process theology seems to be everything that Barthianism—in all its forms and consequences—is not. It puts creation in the center of interest and defines it through reference to the immanent presence of the Creator in his work, thus understanding reality as a religious totality. It defines reality as becoming, not as being, and thus emphasizes creation as an ever-ongoing process in the middle of which we have to find and understand ourselves. Last but not least, it confirms religion as a universally human source of inspiration, and creation as a perspective unifying all manifestations of life in face of the present-day ecological crisis. In recent years process theology has enjoyed particular resonance in the work of the WCC Standing Committee on Church and Society through the Indian Syrian Orthodox Bishop and Professor Paul Gregorios (its chairperson from 1975 to 1983) and the Austra-

---

[49]Lynn White, Jr., ''The Historical Roots of our Ecological Crisis,'' *Science* 155 (10 March 1967), and *The Environmental Handbook* (1970). Carl Amery, *Das Ende der Vorsehung: Die gnadenlosen Folgen des Christentums* (Reinbek: Rowohlt TB, 1974 [1972]).

lian Professor of Biology Charles Birch (its vice chairperson and subsequent chairperson). The first made no secret of his profound admiration for process theology; the second professed his wholehearted allegiance to the Whiteheadian model of theology.

To date the most remarkable process contribution to creation theology may be the joint work of the biologist Charles Birch and the leading American process theologian John B. Cobb, Jr., *The Liberation of Life* (1981). This book is based on a Teilhardian vision of unified reality (even though there are certain reservations about Teilhard de Chardin's explanation of evolution) and on Whitehead's concept of process, as was made theologically expedient by Charles Hartshorne.[50] The study proceeds toward a unifying concept of "life" based on the notions of "evolution" and "ecology," attempting to show that "life" as the focal expression of reality can be understood only in terms of a comprehensive process of global interaction. In light of this vision, "an ethic of life" is tentatively spelled out, and religion is explained in terms of "faith in life." These general insights are made use of in the latter part of the book for the exploration of certain issues of burning contemporary concern, such as the biological manipulation of human life, a just and sustainable world, economic development versus ecology, and rural and urban development in an ecological perspective.[51]

Here it may be appropriate to refer briefly to the importance of the study by Birch and Cobb as a sign of the times. Already the way in which it effects dialogue between biology and theology—as a solidly unified adventure into a domain that is accepted, quite naturally, as common ground—calls for attention. Even the 1978 Bampton Lectures of the scientist-theologian Arthur Peacocke,[52] in which efforts

---

[50]See esp. *Existence and Actuality: Conversations with Charles Hartshorne*, ed. John B. Cobb, Jr. and Franklin J. Gamwell (Chicago/London: University of Chicago Press, 1984).

[51]Very different from this approach—and from what is usually referred to as "ecological" models in general—is the global challenge to evolution in Gerd Theissen, *Biblical Faith: An Evolutionary Approach*, trans. John Bowden (London: SCM Press, 1984). (Original: *Biblischer Glaube in evolutionärer Sicht* [Munich: Christian Kaiser Verlag, 1984].) The purpose of Theissen's antibiologist approach is to show how true monotheism (and especially the gospel) resists the dehumanizing pressure of natural selection. Without rejecting evolution as such, he sees theology as having a critical function in face of an ethical adaptation of biological models, an orientation rather bluntly opposed to the process vision of Birch and Cobb.

[52]Arthur Peacocke, *Creation and the World of Science* (Oxford: Clarendon Press, 1979).

in the direction of a unified vision of reality are just as apparent, does not reach the same degree of reconciliation. It still moves within dialectical tensions that seem to be close to overcome in the process vision. But this is not the only remarkable thing about the Birch-Cobb undertaking. As important as the reconciliation of faith and science may be, the consistency of the theological vision is equally remarkable. So also is the compliancy of this vision with the practical demands of our time, not only when viewed as popular concerns of the day but also when seen in light of ethical urgencies that are deeply rooted in an obviously biblical view of reality. At the same time, it is easy to see why this vision has been and continues to be under heavy fire. It has been accused of amalgamating the divine with an empirical world process and delimiting ethics to an ecologically justifiable compromise, thus eliminating the I-you confrontation between God and the human being.

> We believe it necessary, on account of the demands of ecology, to work intensively and in a new way at the theology of creation, which must have consequences for liturgical life as well as for theological ethics.[53]

This statement from the report of a consultation of the Conference of European Churches (Bucharest, March 1982) may be representative of a widespread thinking in the churches today. While underlining and wholeheartedly acclaiming it, we cannot but raise the question: "on account of the demands of ecology"— is that *all*? If no ecological crisis had been observed, could we have continued with the creation theology of the 1950s? Certainly not! It is not the crisis that has made our theology inadequate; it is the exposure of a latent inadequacy! Any suggestion to the contrary would reduce creation theology to a historically instructed pragmatism.

Several other observations could have been added on the resurgence of creation in contemporary theology, in contemporary church life, and, not least, in contemporary culture as a whole. What has been brought to the fore is by no means intended to be exhaustive. The aim was to reflect the urgency that is being recognized by more and more responsible people: that of regaining creation not only as a domain in its own right and with its own weight but as a constitutive horizon of theology as a whole. This means that creation should not be seen as a predicative, as a qualifier giving a special tint to any and every theme in theology ("creatureliness," "createdness," "creativity"— everything but creation!); creation should be seen as the basic event determining all other events—their real "root cause."

---

[53]*The Groaning of Creation* (see n. 8) 88.

There seems to be general agreement—and much attention is being given to the fact—that en route something has gone wrong, seriously wrong, with creation in the general awareness of the churches. But *when, where, why,* and *how*? Many answers have been proposed, all of which may be only a faithful reflection of the great complexity of the issue. Some of the culprits are more or less commonly identified. With regard to others, there may be more hesitation, particularly among critics who, based on confessional location or other patterns of historical self-consciousness, are inclined to defend particular heroes or forebears. However, a quick review of these proposals may be useful, not only for the sake of historical identification, but also in order to describe some of the ecumenical dimensions of the problem and to point out the necessity for each of us to approach the problem with a certain modesty in spite of our vested historicotheological "interests."

Who is to carry the blame and who is to be examined with the greatest degree of critical alertness?

—Contemporary *liberation theologies,* inasmuch as they claim, or seem to imply, an ontological priority of redemption/liberation over any created "givenness" to be liberated?

—Yesterday's *secular theology,* inasmuch as it declared the world to be "merely" worldly, delivered from all religiously motivated taboos and demands on mystical veneration?

—*Existential theology,* inasmuch as it limits theological awareness to the isolated act of human decision before God—I-here-now—and excludes "objectified" reality from its vision?

—*Barthianism,* inasmuch as it rejects not only "natural theology" (in principle, a floor open to all) but also a biblical theology that is unwilling to adopt a *Heilsgeschichte* approach to creation?

—*Ritschlianism,* inasmuch as it rejects a factual orientation of religious judgments as "metaphysics" and claims theology to be purely "value"-based?

—*The Schleiermacher school,* inasmuch as it excludes the world—its origin as well as its complexity—to the benefit of mystical human dependence on an abstract divine providence?

—*Immanuel Kant,* inasmuch as he separated "practical" cognition from the observation of facts and threw ethical awareness back on sheer inwardness?

—*Enlightenment "Deism,"* inasmuch as it exiled God to an imaginary site *behind* the nexus of causality, thus leaving the actual world as a network of natural "laws" without any imprint of immediate divine intervention?

—*René Descartes,* inasmuch as he separated mind and matter and metaphysically reconstructed the universe with the human "I" as the all-determining center of orientation?

—*Francis Bacon* and *Galileo Galilei,* inasmuch as, in the way they proclaimed the purity of factual observation as a means to gain control of the world of matter, they made human beings the sovereign ruler of their environment?

—*The Reformers,* inasmuch as their focus on salvation as the human being's personal interrelatedness with God unconsciously screened off the wider setting of creation?

—*Late medieval Scholasticism,* inasmuch as its voluntaristic image of the Creator tended to make creation an arbitrary event without the coherence of a detectable, intrinsic meaningfulness?

—*Classical Scholasticism,* inasmuch as its strictly conceptually ordered universe neglected creation faith—live relationship with the Creator—and prepared posterity for an endless series of controversies with alternative cosmological models?

—*Augustine,* inasmuch as he prepared an anthropological narrowing of the theological vision and a corresponding overemphasis on the corruption of nature, principally seen as an object of human covetousness?

—The *Neoplatonism* of the ancient as well as the modern Greek theological orientation, as it is reflected in the iconic presentation of divine presence in creation, a rather denaturalized concept of transfiguration?

—*Docetism* and *Manicheism,* officially condemned and rejected by the old church (and thus by the entire *oikumene*) but surviving secretly according to the old law: *victus victori legem dat* (the conquered dictates his conditions to the conqueror)?

In various blends and combinations, all of these proposals have cropped up in the present discussion on this topic, but as far as we know they have not yet been brought together in the kind of review we have suggested here. To date, least attention has been paid to the last two possibilities, because the general mood of historical critique (which has frequently come either from the Eastern churches or from Western observers very much in sympathy with them and critical of the West) has been to see Oriental Christianity, in its relative ecological innocence, as the pertinent judge of Occidental Christendom. No objection should here be voiced about the ecumenical appropriateness of such a critical perspective, but there is an objection about its universality. For truly ecumenical encounters it is important that equal standards of critical examination be used in *either* direction and in *all* directions. In the East-West encounter this demand for quality has not always come to pass.

Excursus on ecumenics and "creationism"

Here attention should be drawn to one particular problem, partly of language, partly of substance. It concerns the word "creation" and especially its use in the interdenominational trend usually referred to as "creationism." A creationist movement is particularly strong in the USA, but it has to some extent also spread to other continents and regions, including Northern and Central Europe.[54]

The issue of creationism—the claim that the creation narratives in Genesis are not only theologically indispensable but even scientifically sustainable as cosmogonic accounts—is generally combined with a strict terminological insistence to reserve the word "creation" for a series of primeval events, situated in a distant "past" and prior to and constitutive of all other events. The terminological discrepancy with contemporary mainline theology was clearly demonstrated at the 1985 consultation on "Creation and Culture,"[55] when an official spokesperson of this orientation repeatedly contested the use of the word "creation" to designate the task of that consultation. Use of the word "creation" in the simple "creationist" sense would have resulted in the title of that consultation having a very different (and certainly very restricted!) meaning.

The questions raised by creationism have clear ecumenical repercussions, particularly through the divisive influence of this controversy in the USA, where for the past 60 years it has been the most spectacular issue of division between "Fundamentalists" and other Christians. In part, it has separated Fundamentalists from other churches (a separation that is to some extent to be seen also among churches of a common confessional family); in part, it has caused tensions between groups and/or persons within one and the same church. A study on the roots and repercussions of the "creation" controversy would surely be a meaningful ecumenical task and would have significant practical implications, especially in North America.

---

[54]An instructive survey is given in Conrad Hyers, "The Fall and Rise of Creationism," *The Christian Century* (24 April 1985): 411-15. See also the condensed survey on "Bibel oder Darwin" in Jürgen Hübner, *Die neue Verantwortung für das Leben: Ethik im Zeitalter von Gentechnologie und Umweltkrise* (1986) 193-97, and particularly his critical assessment of Horst W. Beck's *Biologie und Weltanschauung: Gott der Schöpfer und Vollender und die Evolutionskonzepte des Menschen* (Neuhausen: Hänssler Verlag, 1979). From within an American setting, a critique of contemporary "creationism," based on a linguistic approach to Genesis 1 and 2, is presented in Conrad Hyers, *The Meaning of Creation: Genesis and Modern Science* (Atlanta: John Knox Press, 1984). In a comprehensive biblical perspective, the assumptions of "creationism" are strongly contested in Odil Hannes Steck, *Die Herkunft des Menschen* (Zurich: TVZ, 1983). Sigurd M. Daecke concludes his "Gott: Opfer oder Schöpfer der Evolution?," *Kerygma und Dogma* 28 (1982): 230-46, with an unambiguous "yes" to God the "Creator of Evolution" as a facet of recent Continental discussion.

[55]See here, pp. 39, 44-45, 47ff.

If the present study does not address this problem, it is for the following reasons: 1. The "creationist" controversy seems to gravitate toward the authority of Scripture for contemporary Christian existence rather than toward the importance of the First Article. 2. This controversy seems to have little affinity with the traditional patterns of church division—Fundamentalist trends being as characteristic of Protestant as of Roman Catholic and Orthodox "right-wing" orientations—and it is to be expected that an analysis would contribute little to the overcoming of such divisions. 3. It might serve to distract attention from the intended global orientation of contemporary Christian creation commitment, and thus disturb the priorities to be set for a basic and contemporary ecumenical creation study. As a more specialized study it would certainly have a place, but not within the framework of our project.

As is usual in contemporary theology, it is vital to maintain a fairly flexible use of the word "creation," providing the widest possible spectrum for examination of the question: What does it mean to profess faith in God the Creator today, and how does that profession relate to aspects of Christian unity? Creationists are welcome to join in such a discussion, but they are definitely not invited to set (that is, restrict) the agenda.[56]

1.3 Ecumenical studies today

There may be indications that the present age of ecumenical rapprochement is nearing its end and that new patterns of progress will have to be sought. Cer-

---

[56]In his *Pollution and the Death of Man: The Christian View of Ecology* (London: Hodder & Stoughton, 1970), Francis A. Schaeffer, one of the most influential spokespersons of a Conservative Evangelical creation approach, provides a valuable contribution to the general ecumenical self-criticism of his day. (German version: *Das programmierte Ende: Umweltschutz aus christlicher Sicht* [1975].) Schaeffer warns against the influence of Platonic dualism in the Christian tradition (30-31 [German: 46]) and challenges a certain arrogance inherent in traditional Orthodoxy in its approach to nature, an attitude that has invaded and determined the basic orientation of Occidental science. Schaeffer even proposes St. Francis of Assisi as patron saint for a long-needed Christian reorientation toward a more inclusive approach to nature—a reorientation that could finally contribute to a turning away from manipulation and exploitation also on the part of science. Schaeffer's approach shows that the possibilities of an ecumenical exchange (and of practical cooperation!) with regard to creation-based ethical orientation might develop to a not unimportant extent—in spite of the standing "creationism" controversy.

tainly, in the area of bilateral encounters some dialogues are still young, and it may take time to reach the level of understanding attained long ago by the most advanced church-to-church conversations. In the work of Faith and Order (of the World Council of Churches), promising projects such as "Toward the Common Expression of the Apostolic Faith Today" and "The Unity of the Church and the Renewal of the Human Community" are still incomplete. An epoch never ends overnight. The situation facing us can, however, be described in approximately the following terms: The major challenge to the ecumenical movement today is the obvious discrepancy between the ecumenical understanding produced through official studies and dialogues and the lack of practical consequences drawn in and by the churches. This is what is normally referred to as the problem of "reception." To continue the discussion of traditional theological issues of church division is obviously of limited worth as long as the agreements produced tend to pile up in ever-growing numbers waiting for "something to happen." In many ways, the fate of the Faith and Order document on *Baptism, Eucharist, Ministry* (the so-called Lima Document of 1982) may be symptomatic. This comment is written at a time when the "outcome" of the comprehensive ecumenical hearing on that remarkable convergence document is not yet fully known. But it seems to have been evident for a long time that the euphoria radiating from its spell and expressed in the "eucharistic vision" of the remarkable Vancouver Assembly of the WCC (1983) has disappeared, and that joint theological statements continue to be more easily produced on the expert level than they are "received" by the congregations and (N.B.!) church leaders. Obviously, in the years ahead of us, a much larger portion of ecumenical resources will have to be invested in reception efforts. And for quite a while to come there will probably be less means available for the refinement of agreements that have already been reached on the academic level.

Without challenging the importance of more practically oriented studies and a more immediate reception strategy, it should be observed that more fundamental studies of and discussion on questions of faith and theology can provide a vital service to ecumenical progress. However, this presupposes extending the agenda to issues that have so far not been regarded as preeminently "ecumenical." By broadening the agenda of ecumenical theology it might be possible to explore the unity of the church versus the disunity of the churches in a wider perspective. This might open up ways to tackle "authorized" ecumenical issues from new angles and to put the "results" to a new test that might—if they so deserved—confirm them and revitalize their practical impact.

This, again, suggests an integral unity of Christian faith, the understanding of any genuinely theological question involving some understanding of all the others. To mention one very conspicuous example that is extremely relevant in present-day theology: Is it possible to consider a doctrine of the incarnation or a doctrine of the eucharist that does not reflect some theology of creation? Is it not possible to derive powerful arguments in favor of or against a certain position on the basis of its constructive or destructive consequences in relation to other areas of faith?

In part, the present proposal is to select creation as a testing ground for previous ecumenical theology. But that is not the predominant reason. Our primary aim is not to look for the confirmation or refutation of established ecumenical insights. We shall be looking for new ecumenical disclosures in view of the basic importance of creation theology for theology as a whole. It is not necessary to recall the situation of the First Article as the introitus of the Creed. The importance of its revitalization in contemporary theology was already suggested in the previous section. Obviously, in the present context of our ecumenical conversation no major area of theological concern recommends itself for exploration more than the confession of God as Creator of heaven and earth.

As already indicated, the first signs of a new and hopefully expanding awareness of this are now evident in ongoing ecumenical study projects. Above all, this is apparent in the joint Church and Society/Faith and Order exploration of the "integrity of creation," an enterprise that—on the basis of considerations developed above—can only be acclaimed and wholeheartedly supported. However, the Strasbourg project that forms the basis of the present presentation is not a duplication of this research. It moves beyond it in that it is searching not only or primarily for an ecumenically acceptable approach to creation theology and to lanes of practical church cooperation arising from it; its main goal is to explore creation theology as a unifying and/or divisive ecumenical factor and as a point of entry to the whole complex of theological unity/disunity, paying particular attention to the relationship between historically "established" positions and contemporary function. The present project is different from studies that assess creation and carry this out, for some practical reason, in an ecumenical setting, in that it intends to review creation as part of or even constitutive of the ecumenical setting as such.

One objection to this proposal is: Why wake up slumbering ghosts? Ecumenically speaking, isn't it rather risky to invite confrontation in an area in which there has been as good as none for at least 1,500 years? The aim of a new direction of studies is always to seek and, hopefully, find something of interest. But this could also mean that one may awaken controversies in an area in which few or no dividing conflicts have as yet been observed. If the result of an ecumenical study was merely the confirmation of the topic's ecumenical innocence, one would feel one had wasted time and resources. What one has to look for, therefore, is some hidden conflict, or some unexpected and threatening perspective to already established conflicts, which will give ecumenical therapists something more to grapple with. In short, the task is to look for and conjure up hitherto undreamed of confrontation. One has the choice between undertaking either an ecumenically irrelevant or an ecumenically retrogade project.

This is a fairly understandable but remarkably shortsighted argument, the starting point being the rather arid assumption that concord is no more and no less than the absence of discord. Stating a positive accord in one area of faith is more than observing the absence of a disagreement on that point. It may entail the discovery of new and hitherto neglected resources of unity, and thus an exploration of paths leading to the elimination of traditional separations also in other areas. Of course, if an approach to an ecumenically virginal problem leads to the discovery of hitherto unobserved hindrances to unity, this should also be greeted. Detecting problems does not imply the invention of problems. When one uncovers previously hidden problems in a certain area, one may uncover the key to mastering problems of which one was hitherto unaware in another area. A sickness has to be diagnosed as realistically as possible before it can be cured. In this perspective, unpleasant discoveries may be looked upon as encouraging events, even if one should bear in mind the danger that it is possible to make negative observations more fatal and thus more "interesting" than the facts strictly allow. In a way, "negative" and "positive" observations in ecumenical research cannot be neatly separated. For, when viewed in a constructive, ecumenical manner, any disclosure of facts and factual interrelatedness becomes a tool—a constructive tool—for promoting Christian unity.

These considerations should encourage ecumenical studies to look for new fields of observation and, no less, new angles of orientation. The courage to move in a new direction should be all the more determined the more a new field/angle/direction imposes itself by virtue of its importance in contemporary theology in general. Once these criteria are established, there should be no doubt that creation is a promising challenge to ecumenical studies today. But can it also be seen as a promising challenge to ecumenism?

1.4 Creation—Ecumenically relevant!

The decision to study the bearing that creation faith has on church unity was seen as such a watershed that it caused the Strasbourg Institute to pause and reflect once more on the theme. An ecumenical study—what in effect does this mean? Clearly, it is futile to think of ecumenical theology as a neatly segregated field within theological research and education as a whole. Indeed, it may well be obsolete to think of any theological discipline in this way. As the differentiation process within all sciences (including theology) has been accelerating in our century, it is unavoidable that the same points appear in several disciplines, with varying emphases. As a fairly young orientation, ecumenical theology does not eschew the traditional hunting grounds of church history, missiology, symbolics, hermeneutics, dogmatics, ethics, and practical theology. On the contrary, it is deeply involved in them all, and it invites and rejoices in their intervention. It claims no distinctive area of theology as its "own," but sees its particular legacy in a determining focus on Christian unity as its omnipresent orientating concern.

Thus, the main criterion for an ecumenical study project is not: Does this theme definitely belong in our garden rather than in that of one of our neighbors? It is: Is this topic of ecumenical relevance and is that relevance sufficient to recommend this topic over against other obvious study projects?

In the planning of "Creation—An Ecumenical Challenge?" the staff of the Institute for Ecumenical Research spent a good deal of time discussing and clarifying the concept of "ecumenical relevance." Even if not clarified conceptually, ecumenical relevance is the assumption lying more or less at the root of all ecumenical study planning. The general conclusions were as follows:

"Ecumenical relevance" could and should be seen in a triple perspective. It should be ascribed to projects that further: 1. mutual Christian understanding and fellowship in faith, worship, and witness; 2. practical church cooperation in service to humankind and in mutual assistance; 3. a common vision for the authentic interaction of Christian unity and the unity of all creation. As may be expected, there is nothing revolutionary about this statement, but it does make some fairly important departures to common ways of thinking, partly in the third observation and partly in the interrelationship of the three. The first and second could be labeled the traditional starting points of "Faith and Order" and "Life and Work" (bearing in mind the developments and readjustments of the last 60 years!). The third could, strictly, be seen as a derivative of the first and second, but in our age of "dialogue" it should rather be seen as the response to a new challenge, with retroactive influence also on the orientation of the first and second.

Since the first two emphases can hardly be seen to be controversial, it will suffice here to say a few words about the third emphasis and about the interaction of the three observations. With their strong preoccupation with Christian world responsibility, the 1960s coined the concept of "secular ecumenism," the idea that the Christian vision of unity does not relate to the unity of the church alone— or even predominantly—but to the unity of humankind and thus to the unity of human concerns and aspirations as a whole. On the secular level—in politics, economics, and cultural endeavors—unity should be seen as the completion of a truly ecumenical vision. In the 1970s and 1980s this vision has been slightly reoriented in the direction of non-Christian religions and ideologies: The unity of humankind is seen to be more and more religiously based, but it cannot be appropriately consumed by one faith alone. Interfaith dialogue has come forth not only as a means of reconciling one religion with another but also as an efficient tool for world peace and comprehensive human cooperation. Hans Küng typifies this orientation when he seems to witness a "slow awakening of a global ecumenical consciousness" in the present historical situation. He continues:

> Ecumenism should not be limited to the community of the Christian churches; it must include the community of the great religions, if ecumenism—in accordance with the original meaning of *oikumene*—is to refer to the whole "inhabited world."[57]

But this argument is by no means unique to Hans Küng. It has been in use not only in the era of interreligious dialogue (since the early 1970s) but also and already in the day of "secular ecumenism." It contains at least two important observations that can by no means be contested: 1. that problems related to peace, understanding, and the unity of humankind are important to the church and should be given high priority on the agenda of the individual churches and also on the level of international church-wide cooperation; and 2. that the word *oikumene*, with its etymological derivations, stands for the whole inhabited world and thus, symbolically, should serve as a reminder to the church that it can never fence itself in and isolate itself from the surrounding world.

But the use of this argument should be questioned if etymology as such is allowed to govern theological reflection. Stating undialectically and without reservation that "ecumenism" refers to the unity of all humankind irrespective of creed and worship tends to establish the following conclusion: that any issue pertaining to human unity must per se be allowed to orient those endeavors traditionally known as "ecumenism." Therefore church unity should basically and simply be seen as a means to promote the visible unity of humankind and to foster patterns of human cooperation in general. It is not difficult to see how easily "secular ecumenism" understood in this way may become "secularized ecumenism." Even if attention is focused on the relationship between the world religions, it is obvious that unrestricted subscription to the etymological orientation expropriates what has always been the raison d'être of the "ecumenical" movement. Political unification would basically replace the organic unity of "the body of Christ" and usurp the role or prefiguration of the totality of creation recapitulated "in him."

This is not a discussion on "the right meaning" of the word *oikumene*, for discussions on the "right meaning" of a word are somewhat futile if the com-

---

[57]*Christianity and the World Religions: Paths of Dialogue with Islam, Hinduism, and Buddhism,* ed. Hans Küng, Josef van Ess, Heinrich von Stietencron, Heinz Bechert (London: Collins, 1987) xiv. Original: *Christentum und Weltreligionen* (Munich: R. Piper Verlag, 1985) 16.

plexity of its more or less established function is ignored. If, by extending the meaning of the word *oikumene* to mean worldwide human cooperation, we are likely to lose the specificity of the church as the agent of the gospel, the loss would obviously outweigh the gain. But if, on the other hand, it is generally admitted that the specificity of the preoccupation with unity of the body of Christ cannot be lost, and if this preoccupation has so far been given a particular name, then there is no point in changing that name and risk confusing our orientation. A simple etymological backward somersault—as so ostentatiously offered in our quotation from Hans Küng—is certainly out of place.

If it is clear that the unity of the church implies something more than simply serving as a unifying segment of humankind at large, it is also clear that it deserves some proper designation and that an exchange of nomenclature would merely create confusion. A viable proposal for the relationship between ecumenism and world unity at large could be: Endeavors in the direction of increased human cooperation—including conversations between the world religions—should not be labeled "ecumenical." But neither should "ecumenism" be restricted to the concern of the church for the establishment and preservation of its own "ecclesial" unity without regard to a universal legacy. "Ecumenical" should therefore also include the particular contribution of the church worldwide to the human struggle for unity. The church as church has a particular contribution to make to the unity of humankind. It also has a particular impulse to communicate that relates to all practical concerns for the unity of God's creation. To reflect on that contribution in light of the Bible and Christian tradition, to prepare for it, and to coordinate activities aimed at effecting it must also be seen as tasks with an ostensible degree of "ecumenical relevance." For this reason, even if it protests the concept of an "ecumenism of the religions" or of a "secular ecumenism," the present study definitely opts for including "a common vision of our Christian contribution to the unity of humankind" as a third orientation on the list of endeavors that are genuinely ecumenical.

How does "creation" seem to adapt to these standards? Let us start with the easiest part of the question and then proceed toward the most difficult! We will reverse our list of the three types of "relevance" and start with the last: the unity of humankind. Here the forthright relevance of creation is more than obvious. "One God and Father of us all, who is above all, and through all, and in all." Even if formulated in an ecclesiological setting, these words from the letter to the Ephesians (4:6) strongly emphasize how a vision of global unity is rooted in belief in God as the one source of existence. "The God who made the world and everything in it . . . made from one every nation of men to live on all the face of the earth" (Acts 17:24-26). This famous statement from Paul's Areopagus speech also relates powerfully to this issue. And the song of the angels in Luke 2:14 combines the glory of "God in the highest" with "on earth peace among men."

There is no doubt that creation faith—the assurance that other people are God's creatures irrespective of creed and race and the conviction of the importance to preserve the created world—provides a strong Christian motivation for promoting peace and friendly communication beyond all borders, including the borders of religion. The veneration of a divine Creator is widespread, also outside the frontiers of Christendom. This may provide a platform for interfaith dialogue and thus for joint guidance in issues that are important for the survival of the creature. But even where conscious faith in the Creator is not present in a conversation partner, creation faith undauntedly counts on the Creator's "image" in fellow human beings as a sounding board. Creation faith provides the courage to conduct a conversation with people of different credal opinions in the assurance that a latent sensitivity to the inviolability of creation is there and can be addressed, irrespective of how that sensitivity may be explained by a specific person or within a specific culture.

If we now turn to the "Life and Work" concept of Christian unity—churches united for purposes of practical service and cooperation—there is also much to be said about creation. Some tasks are too demanding of resources to be solved by one or the other church. They call for a joint exploitation of resources: personnel, skills, experience, and financing. Apart from the endeavors of witness and proclamation—which have also to be seen in light of the "Faith and Order" concern—there are diaconal and educational projects and commitments to human rights, peace, and justice that call for common initiative. In the history of the ecumenical movement in our century, and especially since the Second World War, there has without doubt been a general tendency to base what could be referred to as the "secular" commitments of the churches on the Second Article of the Creed. If creation faith is more or less screened out from these areas of concern, can it be avoided that political involvement (in the widest sense of the term) is seen in a perspective of salvation that tends to confuse the *roots* of Christian commitment with a certain selection of its *fruits*? Even if it is by no means presupposed that Christian social ethics should be founded mainly in the First Article, it must be assumed that it cannot be properly located without substantial reflection on creation theology.

Finally we come to the "Faith and Order" dimension, that of mutual Christian understanding and fellowship in faith, worship, and witness. Even if this is not isolated from the two perspectives already examined, nor made *the* ecumenical issue per se, it should not be denied that it lies at the base of the ecumenical orientation as a whole. In this setting the role of "creation" may at first glance seem less evident than in the others. Creation has not been in the foreground of ecumenical conversations on Christian unity and to date has hardly been seen as an issue with many church-dividing repercussions. During the German *Kirchenkampf* (church struggle of the 1930s) a certain use of creation arguments was particularly controversial. But this did not occur *between* the confessions; the tensions were *within* one and the same church (possibly with a certain difference in statistical balance, Lutheran/Reformed). In the bilateral dialogues references to creation have to date been somewhat summary and remarkably conventional. In our sketch of the eclipse and reappearance of creation in modern theology, we have seen how in recent years certain Eastern voices have charged the West with having a deficient creation theology. If these challenges have not so far become an issue on the ecumenical agenda, it may be due to a certain persistence of the aforementioned *Schöpfungsvergessenheit,* not least on the part of the ecumenical "top level." As long as the traditional ecumenical agenda is not resolved, why should we make things more complicated by throwing in "additional" problems? As we have seen in our review of present ecumenical studies, this way of thinking (which may be rather unreflected and to a large extent even subconscious or unconscious) is unrealistic in that it fails to observe the interrelatedness of all authentically theological issues. Once a challenge is there (as in the case of the Orthodox criticism), unity is better served through an open exchange than through cautiously sweeping difficulties under the carpet.

If we look at the history of the church, this is not the only area where ecumenical confrontations have touched on creation. The East-West tension we have observed in our own days—pointing to the ancient Thomist/Palamite controversy on the vision of God—has roots back in the ancient church. Other traditional confessionally related doctrines may in part have been dislodged in the course of time, but they are still present at least as parts of a historical inheritance. The actual ecumenical importance of this inheritance has never really been up for discussion: the traditional Roman Catholic understanding of "nature" with its cosmological, anthropological, and ethical consequences; the Lutheran coordination of the "two kingdoms" and the "orders of creation"; the Reformed covenantal approach that integrates creation faith with "salvation history"; the Orthodox and Anglican trend toward a unification of creation/incarnation/sacrament; and in many ascetic, revival, and Free church milieux a certain fear of the realm of creation as being "worldly."

As a real church-divisive force—and not only factor—creation made itself felt in the early church. In the Gnostic movement creation yielded to a hierarchy of emanations signaling an ever-increasing distance between the upper world of light and the lower spheres of darkness. In the name of the gospel, Marcion fought the "Jewish God" of the Old Testament and thus, in effect, the image of a divine Creator. Manicheism accentuated a radical dualism between spirit and matter, the latter being seen as the very principle of evil. Impulses from Iranian dualism met with Platonic idealism and fostered a variety of combinations, many of which mixed with pseudobiblical motifs and tried to invade the church. Characteristically enough, the dogmatic controversies that inevitably resulted from this came to focus on Christology more than on creation as such. The anticreation emphases appeared as alternative ways of salvation and had to be met by nothing less than a full-blooded Christian soteriology. In addition, incarnation presupposes and includes a creation theology, but it cannot be derived from it. A struggle for authentic Christian belief, then, would quite naturally respond to the Gnostic-Manichean creation deficit by questioning its consequences for the faith in Christ incarnate.

It would appear that the doctrinal confrontations in the ancient church—as settled in the decisions of Nicea, Constantinople, and Chalcedon—were still more successfully conquered with regard to creation than with regard to Christology. In the last 1,500 years—with the exception of medieval confrontations with Manichean-influenced sects such as Albigenses, Bogomils, and Cathari—Christendom has never experienced serious divisions that can be immediately traced back to creation theology. The question could thus be raised whether the successful settlement of the complex creation controversy in the ancient church may indicate a recipe for the conquest of other theological divisions.

With regard to creation, for the past 1,500 years there has been something close to universal agreement *in* and *among* Christian churches—not about some solidly unified theology but at least about rejecting all Gnostic and Manichean betrayals of this world as belonging essentially to God the Creator. Contesters of this fundamental consensus have never gained a hold within the churches. They have remained fringe groups like the Anthroposophists and Christian Scientists of our own day. This unity is particularly remarkable when one looks at the complex pattern of divisive differentiations that have developed over the centuries. It should, of course, be seen in light of the unifying role of the ecumenical symbols, and not least the Nicene Creed. This unification is usually thought of in terms of Christology and Trinitology, but the accomplishments in these fields basically rest on an impressive consensus in confessing God as Creator. In a way, it could be referred to the underlying understanding of creation as an elementary consensus, an agreement that has already been reached and is being continuously confirmed as the foundation of all further agreements.

The fact that this foundation has been questioned so infrequently during the past 1,500 years cannot be a sign of mere indifference—except, in a certain sense, for the modern *Schöpfungsvergessenheit* described above—for God's creatorship has played a vital role in Christian spirituality throughout the ages. And already this observation indicates that creation may be a particularly instructive paradigm for an ecumenical solution to problems.

In our day new concepts—such as a "sacramental universe" (William Temple), a unifying "eucharistic vision" (Vancouver 1983), and an increasing urge on the Christological dimension of creation—suggest a new awareness of the theological link: creation-incarnation-sacrament. There seems to be increasing awareness that each of these concepts can be genuinely understood only in an intimate relationship with the other two, and, on the other hand, that each of them essentially contributes to the meaning of the other two. The sacraments have certainly been a (if not *the*) major issue of ecumenical divergence. And Christology has been the focus of ecumenical attention, less as a complex of problems to be resolved than as a resource (sometimes the sole resource) of a, hopefully, emerging Christian unanimity. Creation, on the contrary, has been left aside in the ecumenical deliberations. This is not to say that it has been silenced to death or deprived of conventional mention; rather it has been politely laid aside as dead capital, as a historical treasure that, for good reasons, cannot be turned into ecumenical currency. In the foregoing we hope to have shown why this should no more be so, and why at least some sort of bold attempt should be made to explore the ecumenical vitality of creation faith, also in search of new resources of theological rapprochement and new impulses toward the conquest of existing doctrinal divisions.

1.5 The Strasbourg creation project

As stated in the preface, a description of the rationale and development of the study project "Creation—An Ecumenical Challenge?" will be limited to the minimum required to make meaningful, heuristic use of the now completed project in our present setting of thematical reflection. Basically, the material produced or collected in the course of the organized project events is of no other importance to our reflections than the observations made in current literature, recent conference reports, and more or less "private" contacts and encounters. Their particular importance is that they were specifically directed to opening up viable paths to the new realm of ecumenical investigation here under review. Basically, it is the realm that matters, not the paths. In order to understand the usefulness of the project for such a purpose, a summary presentation of the directions and events will here suffice. Readers interested in more detailed information on the project are referred to *LWF Documentation* number 27.

1.5.1 Orientations

It was obviously useful to the Strasbourg study that certain basic directions— deductive, inductive, and exemplificatory—were immediately established, even if the original idea of seeing them as distinctive working phases or operations had to be modified considerably en route. For the principle orientation of the work, these distinctions remained rather significant, even if the organized events and undertakings could not—as originally foreseen—be qualified as unconditionally serving one direction or the other.

Deductive referred to research operations that presupposed certain theological givens, such as established confessional positions, determinant patterns of tradition, and easily verifiable "schools" and trends of theological thinking, and an effort was made to observe their integration in and influence and interaction on contemporary (church) life.

Inductive referred to designated operations that were geared to observe actual church involvement with the world around it, and from there attention was directed to the possible underlying creation-related theological motivation.

Exemplificatory referred to particular case observations that were intended to concretize or test conclusions emerging from the two previous directions.

From the beginning the "deductive" part of the study focused mainly on a program of international consultations on the importance of confessional and more or less established theological givens in today's world. The "inductive" study was seen to concentrate on creation motivation as it is explicitly or implicitly discernible in contemporary church statements on issues of social ethics. Finally, the "exemplificatory" study was mainly foreseen to encompass a comprehensive review of contemporary theological involvement in the ecological issue.

The first modification to the concept of distinctive "phases" or operations was to integrate the "exemplificatory" ecological considerations into the project as a whole—partly for reasons of methodological convenience, partly in light of the comprehensive initiatives already taken in this field, not least by contemporary German theology. Also, that the indispensable interaction of deductive and inductive considerations would force us to speak of particular "deductive" or "inductive" study events with a certain care became particularly clear in connection with the third study consultation, on "Creation and Culture" (see below). But in spite of these operational modifications, the conscious distinction between deductive, inductive, and exemplificatory orientations of research remained useful to the project as a constant reminder of distinctive, even though closely interrelated, directions of research.

1.5.2 Events and initiatives

Descriptions of the following three consultations have already been made available in *The Ecumenical Review* (World Council of Churches, Geneva) and are being reprinted in *LWF Documentation* number 27.

The first consultation, "The Theology of Creation—Contributions and Deficiencies of our Confessional Tradition" (Strasbourg, October 10-14, 1983),[58]
was attended by 12 participants selected to represent six main confessional orientations (Orthodox, Roman Catholic, Lutheran, Reformed, Anglican, and Free
Church, each confession having one main lecturer presenting his own tradition and
one prereflector commenting on one of the other traditions) and 11 participants
from the staff of various ecumenical organizations and from the two theological
faculties of the Strasbourg university. This consultation was therefore deliberately
structured in a denominational way, with semiofficial church representatives who
were known to identify consciously with their respective churches but were at the
same time known to be open to denominational self-criticism. The six main presentations were on topics selected by the Institute as being of particular pertinence
to the historical positions of each tradition.

> Theosis—The Aim of Creation (Orthodox)
> Nature and Supernature—The Dimensions of Creation (Roman Catholic)
> Incarnation and Sacrament—A Key to Creation? (Anglican)
> Creation and Recreation—Continuity in Discontinuity (Lutheran)
> Creation in Light of Covenant (Reformed)
> "No" to the World as "Yes" to Creation (Free Church)

In addition to the outline offered in *The Ecumenical Review* and *LWF Documentation,* basic orientation on each of the six presentations will be reviewed in the
section on "Creation and Confessional Divisions" (§5) of this present study.

For the second consultation, "Tensions in Contemporary Theology of Creation: Are They Ecumenically Relevant?" (Klingenthal, Bas-Rhin, France, October 15-19, 1984),[59] the 21 international participants (in addition to four of the
Institute staff) were not primarily chosen according to confessional allegiance but
rather in order to secure a maximum coverage of influential contemporary trends
in the field of creation theology. After a comprehensive brainstorming session, in
which the purpose was to bring out as many contemporary creation-related concerns as possible (be they mainly fundamental, dogmatical, or ethical), the consultation was organized around four "umbrella themes," each of which was
introduced by three speakers with as supposedly differing concerns as possible.
These themes were:

> Theological Discourse on Creation—Christian or Pre-Christian?

---

[58]*The Ecumenical Review* 36/2 (April 1984): 204-13.
[59]*The Ecumenical Review* 37/3 (July 1985): 360-70.

Being—Becoming—Actuality: Ontological Implications of the Concept
    of Creation
Creation Faith and Responsibility for the World
Creation—Secularity or Sacrality of the Created?

The burden of this consultation is mainly reflected in our section on "Creation—
Actual Theological Confrontations" (§4).

The third consultation, "Creation and Culture" (organized in cooperation with
Lutheran World Ministries in Burlingame, California, March 18-21, 1985),[60] followed a somewhat different pattern of organization since it was a purely American
consultation. In addition to the short report given in *The Ecumenical Review* and
reprinted in *LWF Documentation,* a more substantial publication contains a description of the event and presents the introductory papers.[61] Among the 17 participants were spokespersons for four North American minority cultures: native
American ("Indian"), black, Hispanic (Mexican), and Asian, who made the following challenging presentations:

Christianity and Indigenous Religion: Friends or Enemies? A Native
    American Perspective
Nature: Sacred or Secular? An Asian-American Perspective
When Cultures Meet: Integration or Disintegration? A Hispanic-Amer-
    ican Perspective
The Bible and Cultural Interaction: A Black American Perspective

In addition, Western participants made presentations on

Creation and Culture—Why?
Doing Social Ethics in Different Cultural Contexts
The Challenge of Indigenous Culture to Western Spirituality
Concluding Reflections: Toward a Theology of Creation

We reflect on substantive observations from this consultation in the section on
"Creation and Culture" (§2).

We also considered the possibility of arranging a fourth consultation on the
ecumenical aspects of "Creation and Science." To this end, contact was established with the group preparing for a "First European Conference on Science and
Religion," and at one stage the Institute actively participated in the planning of

---

[60]*The Ecumenical Review* 37/4 (October 1985): 506-11.

[61]*Creation and Culture: The Challenge of Indigenous Spirituality and Culture to Western Creation Thought,* ed. David G. Burke (New York: LWM Studies, 1987).

this event. But as the general direction developed in a way that became too specialized to comply with our concern (the main theme becoming "The Argument about Evolution and Creation"), it was understood that the Institute should withdraw from any sponsoring responsibilities. To a not unimportant extent, however, the interests of the Institute were taken into account in the selection of topics and speakers, and two representatives of the Institute did participate in the conference, which took place in the Evangelical Academy at Loccum, Hanover, March 13-16, 1986.

Certain contributions at this conference may be said to have had a direct bearing on the Strasbourg project. The topic "Evolution in Different Theological Traditions" was treated by professors Jürgen Hübner (Lutheran), Arthur Peacocke (Anglican), and Karl Schmitz-Moormann (Roman Catholic), and this orientation was pursued and deepened in the working group sessions, when Jürgen Hübner made a presentation on "The Impact of Confessional Traditions on the Interpretation of Evolution" and other working groups reviewed "evolution" in relation to other key words such as "life," "process," "creation," and "selection."[62]

In addition to this official consultation program, the annual International Seminar of the Strasbourg Institute (July 1984) was on "Partners in Creation—Ecumenical Vision and Responsibility." Participants at this seminar were also invited to discuss the progress of the research project on creation.

Several gatherings were also arranged in order to assure a more powerful Third World contribution to the research. Third World participants at the International Seminar held during the Luther Year (1983) were invited to an information evening during which several critical voices from among the audience made refreshing contributions. Also, in cooperation with the LWF Department of Church Cooperation a "Creation Day" was organized in connection with the Third APATS (Asia Program for the Advancement of Training and Studies) Luther Consultation held in Manila, Philippines, in December 1984. From this event there emerged a questionnaire, which was directed to Christians in the Third World and sought to explore thoughts and attitudes with regard to creation in Christian constituencies of different cultural backgrounds. The impression arising from the analysis of this questionnaire could to some extent be considered representative of contemporary

---

[62]The presentations of the conference were published in *Evolution and Creation*, ed. Svend Andersen and Arthur Peacocke (Aarhus: Aarhus University Press, 1988). Of particular interest in this connection is also the recent book by Jürgen Hübner, *Die neue Verantwortung für das Leben* (see n. 54), esp. the chapters on "Theologie und Evolution" (163-87), "Zur Kontroverse: 'Bibel oder Darwin' " (193-97), and "Philosophische Voraussetzungen der modernen Naturwissenschaft und ihre Folgen" (203-17).

creation orientation in the wider *oikumene*, for it represented not only a variety of geographical backgrounds but also contrasting and sometimes seemingly confusing orientations within the same community (and sometimes within the same mind). This particular aspect of the research is referred to in *LWF Documentation* number 27 but is not reflected in any particular section of the present study. It may, however, be assumed to have affected our general image of a creation "crisis."

In October 1986 the present author also had the opportunity to lecture on certain aspects of the creation project during courses offered by the Strasbourg Institute at the Theological School of the Evangelical Lutheran Church of Cameroon in Meiganga and at the joint Faculty of Protestant Theology in Yaoundé, Cameroon. From October to November 1984 and March to April 1987 similar courses were given at the "Theologisches Studienjahr" in the Dormition Abbey in Jerusalem for theological students from German-speaking countries in Europe. The exchanges that developed at all of these occasions were of considerable importance to the progress of the project.

Much of the same all over influence can be traced to the output of the comprehensive "inductive" research carried out by my Institute colleague Professor Mark Ellingsen. Brief information on this will be given in §3 (Creation and the Integration of Ethics), but for a more comprehensive assessment of that important study operation reference should be made to Ellingsen's general review in *LWF Documentation* number 27 and also to his more specialized book on particularly burning socioethical themes, which resulted from the same study.[63] The rather complex interaction of theological premises—whether of a typical creation or a typical redemption pattern of reflection—and the avenues of ethical orientation, which constitute the main findings of his research, have been of basic importance to the reflections offered in this present study.

---

[63]Publication by the World Council of Churches, Geneva, anticipated in 1990.

2

Creation and culture

The four main catchwords directing the thematic presentation of our "findings" will be dealt with in the following order: culture, ethics, theology, confessions. This indicates a movement from the wider, more general orientation of an ecumenical creation study toward the increasingly explicit aspects of discernible ecumenical relations.

The full title of chapters 2 to 5 was intended to be Creation and ecumenism in the light of: 1. Given cultural diversity; 2. Contemporary ethical involvement; 3. Actual theological confrontations; and 4. Traditional confessional divisions. But for the sake of expediency more simplified forms have been used.

The questions discussed in this chapter are in the main those faced by the March 1985 Burlingame consultation. At the same time, the Third World questionnaire (see §1.5.2), with its reflections on a complex interplay of, on the one hand, creation ideas and creation-oriented attitudes and, on the other, cultural variety, will play a not unimportant background role—even if, as already stated, isolated observations from that research should not be given too much emphasis.

The concept of "culture" is somewhat vague and multivocal. It is perhaps necessary to state that attention will not be paid to culture in general, as distinct, say, from "nature," "barbarism," or "primitivism." Rather, what we intend to discuss is the variety of historically given patterns of civilization. The implicit distinction is not that between "culture" and something else, but between "culture" and "culture." Even in an ecumenical perspective, "nature and culture" is an interesting topic. And in certain cases our different understandings of the inter-relatedness of the terms may even reflect differences of theological orientation. Or vice versa? But our present topic should arise from the recently emerging discussion about creation and anthropology: How can we discharge a theology that for too long and too insistently has promoted uncritical human dominion over "nature" (that is, nonhuman creation)?

Right here and now, our question starts with the diversity of "cultures" as this may relate to possible differences in the very vision of creation and differing concepts of "what the world is about." As everyone knows, cultural diversity is a complex phenomenon, ranging from the near total alienation between an isolated tribe in the Amazon jungle and the world as represented by a supersonic aircraft passing miles overhead to insignificant differences between two neighboring villages or two professional milieux within one and the same society. It is generally impossible to give a precise definition of where one "culture" ends and another begins, and for the purpose of our research it is not important to pursue a high level of precision on this.

In my introduction at the Burlingame consultation I referred to two concerns: "creation speaks on culture" and "culture speaks on creation."[1] Obviously, these orientations should not be torn apart, nor should they be confused. In the course of the Burlingame consultation it became clear that there was a need to integrate some dimension of interreligious dialogue. This concern about "religion(s)" did not and does not change the systematic of the issue(s), as it does not add any dimension to the problem that is not already implicit in it. Rather it underscores the comprehensive character of the creation/culture challenge as such. "Religion" as a particular example of and a guide to cultural diversity is certainly not the only—or even most important—aspect of the theology of religions as such. But in our context it is a rather instructive introduction to the whole perspective of creation and culture.

How does creation, as testified in the Bible, relate to cultural diversity? How are the reception and integration of creation faith affected by cultural diversity? How does this faith elucidate—and eventually encourage or restrict—cultural diversity? In viewing "culture" in its interaction with "creation," creation images and creation ideas derived from other sources than the Bible will also have to be taken into account. Even if they should, as far as possible, be distinguished from a biblical concept of creation, they may be integral parts of the "culture" that cre-

---

[1]Per Lønning, "Creation and Culture: Why?," *Creation and Culture: The Challenge of Indigenous Spirituality and Culture to Western Creation Thought*, ed. David G. Burke (New York: LWM Studies, 1987) 7-12.

ation belief directs us to deal with—not only where they may be functional elements in cultures identifying themselves as "Christian," but also as they appear in cultures with a different historical identity.

2.1. Culture speaks on creation

The "environmental crisis," about which awareness began to grow in the late 1960s, very soon led to a questioning of Western Christianity (or even "biblical religion" as such) about its role in a technological civilization based on a simple, instrumental consideration of nature. This was partly a negative echo to the claims of "secular theology" in the immediately preceding period, for example, "Creation as the Disenchantment of Nature," "The Exodus as the Desacralization of Politics," "The Sinai Covenant as the Deconsecration of Values."[2] What the spokespersons of this theology considered to be the immortal glory of the Bible was exposed by the champions of the new ecological awareness as a betrayal of creation and a matchless seduction of humankind. The best-known critics were Lynn White, Jr. and Carl Amery,[3] to whom it seemed clear that the three world religions rooted in the Bible—Judaism, Christianity, and Islam—had been the real agents in the promotion of a secularized vision of the world in that they stressed the transcendence of the Creator in such a way as to leave the earth at the ruthless exploitation of human hands. Most blame, however, was attributed to Christianity by virtue of its dominant political role in the modern world.

In face of this criticism Christian apologists hurried to admit that certain trends in Christian theology, as already pointed out by Max Weber, may well have exercised an exploitative influence, albeit due more to a distorted reading of the Bible—not least with regard to the "Dominium terrae" of Genesis 1:28—than to the Bible itself. Many observers, not least those speaking in the name of the Eastern churches, were particularly concerned to allocate the distortion to the Western

---

[2]Harvey G. Cox, *The Secular City: Secularization and Urbanization in Theological Perspective* (New York: Macmillan; London: SCM Press, 1965) 21, 25, 30. Cf. the critical comments in Ole Jensen, *Unter dem Zwang des Wachstums: Ökologie und Religion* (1977; Danish original, 1976) 52-58.

[3]Lynn White, Jr., "The Historical Roots of Our Ecological Crisis," *Science* 155 (10 March 1967). Cf. *The Environmental Handbook* (1970). Carl Amery, *Das Ende der Vorsehung: Die gnadenlosen Folgen des Christentums* (Reinbek: Rowohlt TB, 1974 [1972]). For reactions to Amery and White, see, e.g., Udo Krolzik, *Umweltkrise: Folge des Christentums?* (1979) and Norman Young, *Creator, Creation and Faith* (London: Collins, 1976).

theological tradition, where a pessimistic Augustinian vision of the corruption of nature was said to have combined with a disintegrative Scholastic overemphasis on conceptuality.[4] The report of the world conference on Faith, Science, and the Future (Cambridge, Massachusetts, 1979) uses a similar language.[5]

The deep veneration for nature that is meant to be at the base of most preindustrial civilizations has found organic expression not only in Eastern brands of Christianity but also, and no less, in the great religious civilizations of the East and the primordial religions of African or North American tribal cultures. A remarkably apt side event at the 1983 Assembly of the World Council of Churches in Vancouver, Canada (under the theme "Jesus Christ—The Life of the World") was the spectacular, semiofficial presence of North American Indians on the campus of the University of British Colombia. The Indians made their presence felt by means of a steady fire on the campus lawn, through an evening of special performances in the large conference tent, and also through the erecting of an impressive totem pole in the middle of the campus as a special gift to the World Council of Churches (subsequently transferred to the Ecumenical Center in Geneva). The most spectacular expression of a Christian reception of North American Indian impulses with regard to the dignity of creation was probably the inclusion of Chief Seattle's famous speech to the USA president (1855) in the liturgy of the 1981 World Prayer Day for Women.[6]

Like the present author, several of the Vancouver participants may have had some difficulties with the theological interpretation of this kind of North American Indian presence. Even given that the majority of the visiting Indians seemed to be church members and that their presence was an expression of sympathy and sharing, their modes of expression reflected a pre-Christian religious civilization to such a degree that some delegates from other parts of the world obviously felt uncertain about how that presence was to be understood. Was it an expression of Christians sharing a joint hope in "Jesus Christ—The Life of the World"? Did it represent fellow human beings testifying to the sacredness of life manifest in a variety of religiocultural traditions?

---

[4]Paul Gregorios, *The Human Presence: An Orthodox View of Nature* (Geneva: World Council of Churches, 1978).

[5]See the section on "Humanity, Nature and God," *Faith and Science in an Unjust World*. Report of the WCC Conference on Faith, Science, and the Future, Massachusetts Institute of Technology, Cambridge, USA, 12-24 July 1979, vol. 2, *Reports and Recommendations,* ed. Paul Abrecht (Geneva: World Council of Churches, 1980) 28-38.

[6]Cf. Jürgen Hübner, *Die neue Verantwortung für das Leben: Ethik im Zeitalter von Gentechnologie und Umweltkrise* (1986) 207.

In an interesting introduction to ecological theology,[7] Ole Jensen draws special attention to the North American Indian thinking and its almost visionary integration of the human person in a globally perceived reality—even though he concludes with a rather weighty question about the aptitude of that thinking to conquer suffering and death. Obviously, the historical confrontation with Christianity in the wider North American area developed more harmoniously than one might have expected from the violent clashes widely characteristic of the encounter between red and white. That the Indians—irrespective of the not too convincing behavior of Christian intruders—widely accepted Christianity (or at least, in manners partly enigmatic to the white world, integrated it into their own patterns of religious conduct) may be due to a general quest for a unified vision of reality that was particularly receptive to a biblical vision of Creator and creation.

That native American tribes and communities have generally accepted Christianity with little explicit credal reservation should hardly be seen as a sign of the harmonious integration of cultures. The present sociological and theological trend to revalorize cultural (including religious) autochthony in Latin America obviously gives new self-confidence to the traditional Roman Catholic attitude of cultural accommodation. Where it has developed more or less spontaneously, "syncretism" is now generally seen to be less alarming, in a theological sense, than it was a few years ago.[8] In North America the ecological challenge calls attention to the situation of the aborigine population in two ways: first, as an example of communities that, against their wishes, have had their "way of life" ruined through an ecological revolution; second, as heirs of a primeval wisdom that may well be of importance to agents of the dominant majority culture. The famous speech of Chief Seattle, in which he mildly but urgently challenged his white neighbors about their lack of veneration of the natural environment, has more or less become a reader in environmental theology.

In a much more aggressive way, a similar point was made at the Burlingame consultation by Dr. Vine Deloria. His aggressiveness was not the result of bad temper but of a rather careful reflection. After training as a Christian (Lutheran) theologian, he concluded that there was a basic irreconcilability between Christianity and the tradition of his people—and opted in favor of the latter. Deloria

---

[7]Ole Jensen, *Unter dem Zwang des Wachstums* (see n. 2) 92-95.

[8]Particularly indicative of this new trend is Harvey G. Cox, *Religion in the Secular City: Toward a Post-Modern Theology* (New York: Macmillan, 1984) esp. 240-61.

concluded with a series of antithetical oppositions that may raise incentives for our further reflection.[9]

Tribal Religions	Christianity
THE NATURE OF THE UNIVERSE	
Nature is good, or at least benign.	Nature is evil, or at least fallen, because of the historical disobedience of human beings.
Animals are good, have a place in nature, have personality and knowledge, and each takes a part in a natural process.	Animals and other forms of life are brutes, designed for people's pleasure, and are subservient to humans.
People are part of the universe and have a role to play, for humankind and for other forms of life.	People are above creation, set aside in a special creative act, and then cursed for disobedience, taking creation down with humankind.

Conclusion. The tribal idea of nature is a tapestry or symphony—creation cannot be completed unless every entity plays its part. The Christian idea of nature is loneliness and alienation. Humankind can never enjoy companionship with other life forms and has been pitted against nature since the expulsion from the Garden of Eden.

THE NATURE OF HUMAN EXPERIENCE	
Life is communal—for all species. Social contract is a covenant of duties, not of rights.	Life is individual. God comes to individuals, who are then supposed to constitute a community. Social contract articulates rights and assumes responsibilities, but does not outline them.
Culture is a function of religion and all things ultimately derive from revelation.	Religion is a function of culture and all religious ideas ultimately derive from social interaction—prophets.
All powers and talents are a gift.	An institutional hierarchy affirms and confirms the exercise of corporate power and allocates corporate talents.

Conclusion. Christianity promotes an adverse social milieu. Tribal religions promote an advocacy milieu. Tribal religion must change before

---

[9]Vine Deloria, "Christianity and Indigenous Religion: Friends or Enemies? A Native American Perspective," *Creation and Culture* (see n. 1) 31-43.

tribal culture gives way; Christian culture must change if Christian religion is to have an impact on people.

THE NATURE OF RELIGION

Religion is healing and balances human lives.	Religion is commemorative.
Revelation is always ahead and open.	Revelation is closed: when God stopped writing the authorized books of the Bible, he stopped communicating.
Religion is communal.	Religion—as salvation—is individual.
Social shame and responsibility are inhibiting factors in ethical behavior.	Cosmic, eternal guilt is an inhibiting ethical factor.

Conclusion. Tribal religions are living religions in the sense that new revelations and ceremonies are still possible. Christianity is dead insofar as God has said everything he wants to say. Tribal communal activities are consonant with the nature of creation—communal. Christian individual salvation is a fraud in that it suggests the possibility of a completely isolated individual.

ATTITUDES TOWARD LIFE

Tolerance for other religious traditions.	Intolerance.
Maintain a balanced universe.	Salvation from this world.
Equality of gender and recognition of age differences.	Masculine world with no age differentials.
Responsibility to present life on earth.	Responsibility to the next world.

Conclusion. Tribal religions show by example; Christian religion uses many tactics to demonstrate its validity—but primarily it is a religion of force and oppression. Tribal religions are at home in the world and are designed to solve its problems; Christianity cannot live in the world with any competitor next to it, for fear it would be revealed as a fraud.

The Burlingame consultation did not undertake a critical examination of these statements; nor did it discuss their value as a balanced description of tribal religion vis-à-vis Christianity.[10]

---

[10]Eloi Messi Metogo, *Théologie africaine et ethnophilosophie: Problèmes de méthode en théologie africaine* (Paris: Editions l'Harmattan, 1985) presents a frontal attack on the method of comparing indigenous culture and Christianity as two more or less static entities. Accusing what has been a main trend in African

In different settings, there may be a legitimate function for characterizations on different levels: (a) an "ideal" level—a description of how a movement understands its own vocation; (b) a "factual" level—a description of the same movement seen in its empirical complexity; and (c) a polemical level—a description with selected observations made by some opposing partner. When, as frequently happens, a comparison between two rival movements is made in terms of a level (a) description of the one opposing a level (c) description of the other, the juxtaposition may provoke more objections than reflections. However, this does not rule out that such a challenge might be a useful invitation to critical self-examination by the opposing partner, especially when it is a question of a culturally and economically oppressed group challenging its oppressors. In such circumstances, such a reversal of the customary self-idealization of the dominant culture may be precisely what is required to provoke a healthy and critical self-examination on the part of the culprit.

Although it was not explicitly spelled out, the representatives of the majority culture at the Burlingame consultation generally seemed to perceive the challenge in this way, and readers should be encouraged to do the same. We cannot here gauge Deloria's challenge against the yardstick of balanced "objectivity"—this may well have to be postponed until such a time when it is so universally recognized that it informs the theological agenda of the day. It should also be underscored that his critical comments are not mentioned here only with regard to the North American aboriginal culture. At Burlingame, certain aspects of it were also echoed in the presentations of the nonautochthonous minority cultures. And similar questions and accusations are frequently heard on the world level.

In several ways, "tribal religion" is a fairly diffuse and diffusive phenomenon when viewed in the perspective of cultural geography. And especially in contemporary Africa the ways in which Christianity and elements of tribal religions meet and frequently combine is a complex and often fascinating story.[11]

---

theology for about 30 years, this Cameroonian theologian writes: "La culture n'est pas un dépôt, mais un échange permanent entre l'homme et son milieu naturel et social. . . . Le théologien africain fait fausse route quand il assimile la culture africaine à une collection d'objets, à des pratiques et usages en voie de disparition reconstitués avec plus ou moins bonheur par l'ethnologie. . . . A moins de choisir l'insignifiance et l'inefficacité, la théologie africaine ne peut plus ignorer la critique de l'ethnophilosophie." (115-17)

[11] An interesting supplement to the observations in this section may be found in the book of Kwesi A. Dickson, *Theology in Africa* (London: Darton, Longman & Todd, 1984). In underlining the importance of "The African Religio-Cultural Reality" (47-73), the author is very concerned to relativize the established dis-

In several cases, it is precisely the lack of a measure of comparable conceptuality that seems to make a confrontation between a literate and an illiterate religion easier than that between two literate traditions. It is, however, universally observed that tribal religion—not only on the world level but also in a regional setting—has little chance of speaking on behalf of itself. Since it lacks the structures and media to interpret its own cause, it has to rely on researchers trained in a completely different cultural context to voice its concerns. Even though Deloria's presentation focused mainly on the North American scene, it could well be seen as an invitation to Christians to practice self-criticism on a world scale. Indeed, it may be fruitful to take it as a more or less universal digest of accusations in recent years concerning an alleged Christian "betrayal" of creation, since these accusations come as much from tribal religion in Africa as in America and, of course, to a no lesser extent from the great religions of the East (which, at least, have more possibilities of making themselves heard in a worldwide setting than the tribal religions). It has come to the fore in a Western, ecologically founded criticism of Christianity (Lynn White, Carl Amery) but also to some extent in Oriental Christian correctives to the West. It may be symptomatic that in Burlingame the Orthodox respondent to Deloria's paper (Dr. Emilie Dierking Lisenko) immediately accepted the relevance of his criticism with regard to (nota bene) Western Christianity, but said that the Orthodox integration of creation and restoration would not be vulnerable to this critical approach. She referred, for example, to a wide-ranging difference in behavior in Alaska on the part of Russian Orthodox and Protestant missionaries with regard to respect for indigenous traditions versus a rather harsh inculturation.

It may therefore be justified to see that Deloria's comparative study has more than a regional validity, but at the same time one must be aware not only of the purport of the questions raised but also of their bearing in the context immediately

---

tinction between "polytheism" and "monotheism" in that he calls attention to the fact that in African tribal religion "God's self-sufficiency is never in doubt" and that "there is almost continent-wide agreement that . . . God is . . . Creator" (59). In reporting the actual confrontations surrounding a more inclusive approach to ideas and practices inherent in traditional religiocultural patterns, Dickson adopts a basically comprehensive line as opposed to an evangelical (B.H. Kato) and Barthian (H. Hässelbarth) purism (120-24). He also observes a somewhat dialectical relationship between "African theology" and "South African Black Theology" (as represented by Manas Buthelezi). These two may converge in their opposition to indigenization as an external mixing together of received Christian teaching and elements of African culture. They also agree on the actual political consequences of Christian faith. But they disagree on the theological bearing of cultural commitments in general (127-40).

under observation. It is now time to make the questions heard and prepare for a comprehensive and responsible discussion and handling of them, but it is still too early to suggest final answers. First of all, we have to hear and respond to the "questions behind the questions."

And what are these "questions behind the questions"? They may be traced through the following observations. 1. Even if one may question a somewhat "romantic" description of tribal religions as being, at best, oversimplified, such a description nevertheless contains basic elements that have such a universal echo—also within Christendom!—that it must be appropriate to clarify the concern for the advocacy of creation in relation to biblical creation faith. To phrase the issue in as challenging a way as possible: Can tribal religion—or "natural religion" in general—serve as an introduction to basic truths of the Bible that have to a large extent been forgotten? 2. Even if the unilateral presentation of a denaturalized Christianity may be dismissed as not echoing the theology of creation that is generally taught in the churches today, it does confirm impressions that are sufficiently widespread and observed by theological self-criticism and raises the question as to how established "Christian" ideas and practices do in effect relate to a biblical vision of creation. Can the encounter with extrabiblical adaptations of creation contribute toward detecting contemporary Christianity (or segments of it) in possible deviations from biblical creation faith?[12]

---

[12]In his *Theology of Africa* (see n. 11), Kwesi A. Dickson includes a special section on "Cultural Continuity with the Bible" (141-84), in which he finds convergence between biblical and African ideas concerning "The Theology of Nature" (160-66), "Spirit possession" (166-70), and "The Individual and the Community" (170-84). At the same time, he admits that "the African understanding of land is closer to . . . the Canaanite view . . . in that Africans consider the land to be a divinity" (166) and that "Israelite prophecy was able to be critical of . . . institutions in a way that prophecy in Africa has not" (170). It may well cause some reflection when Dickson openly states that "the cultural approach being urged in this study necessitates" the question whether "other sources of the life and work of Christ deemed unworthy of being canonized by the early church" could not "be found more satisfying spiritually in the light of the Africans' religiocultural and other circumstances" (183). Where, here, is the center of normative gravitation?

Another distinctive attempt to approach African and Hebrew culture is Modupe Oduyoye, *The Sons of the Gods and the Daughters of Men: An Afro-Asiatic Interpretation of Genesis 1-11* (Maryknoll NY: Orbis Books, 1984). This approach rests on a linguistic-etymological method that may be rather difficult to assess. Even if its attempts at demonotheizing biblical creation myths and extending the "imago Dei" also to the nonhuman creature (16-87) may well be debatable, several observations pertaining to fellowship in ecological orientation seem to be rather striking.

One general hermeneutical observation should be made to give immediate substance to these questions. However evident it may be that no extrabiblical vision can claim a priori authority as a guide to the Scriptures, it should be equally evident that—even though our understanding would still be restricted by our own historicoconceptual horizon—the introduction of differing perspectives would powerfully assist our reading of the Scriptures in that it would open up new horizons and thus stretch our imagination in the way we listen to the Bible. We make the simple hermeneutical presupposition that every communication is comprehended by means of and in relation to concepts that are already ours and—to a much greater extent than we tend to realize—depends on presuppositions proper to our own cultural setting. New observations are internalized through adaptation to the knowledge that is already there. Even as readers of the Bible we are determined by our own cultural milieu.

The question is, then, to what extent impulses from other cultural milieux, in their involvement with creation, may open up alternative visions to those that seem self-evident in our own given situation—visions that could legitimize themselves by disclosing new and convincing aspects of the biblical message itself. One should certainly admit the possibility of recognizing that some extrabiblical vision not only corresponds with but helps us toward an awareness of biblical orientations hitherto neglected in our own ecclesial environment. And it does no harm to the conviction that the Bible is the supreme source of truth, because it ultimately refers us to no other authority than the Bible itself. It simply relativizes given human understandings of the Bible by admitting God's sovereign freedom to speak through the Bible or to the Bible also through the mouths of agents outside the established space of Christendom. It goes without saying that what is maintained here applies a fortiori to visions developed in segments of Christianity that are culturally different from the dominant North Atlantic quadrisphere.

Two observations should be added, one of a more epistemological, the other of a more theological character.

1. If Western Christianity has tended to stray away from a genuinely biblical vision of creation, it is due to the idea of human mastery over nature, an idea that has found expression and—simultaneously—reinforcement in modern science and technology. The growing technological exploitation of the earth—now being extended to more and more of the universe—and a consumerist vision of reality are intertwined in an almost incalculable pattern of reciprocal promotion. Critical opposition to the Western concept of progress in the name of creation draws inspiration from preindustrial cultures that are based on limits set by nature itself and that stress the family and the local community rather than large-scale structural efficiency. This refers also to the voices of Eastern Orthodoxy—even though some emanate from highly industrial societies—because the Orthodox vision of reality

is so emphatically embedded in tradition and has been so little concerned about making a theological response to the questions arising from modern society. However, this means that we are concerned here with voices that speak from cultural contexts that are much closer to the original "world of the Bible" than the dominant Western culture can claim to be. Could this not imply that they are also at a closer listening distance to the old texts than those nations that have for centuries had the decisive voice in the world of Christian theology?[13]

2. The second observation is of a more straightforward theological character. Under what conditions can biblical creation belief endorse the statement: "Culture speaks on creation"? A full answer can only be made in light of the inverse statement "creation speaks on culture," to which we shall soon proceed. But a few remarks may be in order. We have already suggested the possible role of various cultures—irrespective of religious affiliation—for the discovery of biblical creation commitments. Communicating with the Bible is immediately cross-cultural communication, and, if not carefully assessed and criticized, our own cultural presuppositions are likely to exercise a narrowing and even a deflective influence on the reception. That they may also open up stimulating avenues for further discoveries is another matter, which can be meaningfully confirmed only on a more advanced stage of critical reflection. For this reason, one culture needs the assistance of others in listening to the Bible. In theory, much more than in practice, it is generally admitted that there is no such thing as one given normative Christian culture with which all attempts at interpreting divine revelation have to comply. In order to understand the language of the Bible and the "world" reflected in it, it is always useful for the various cultures to be ready to listen to each other. This enables them to get a better grasp of and make a better readjustment to their hermeneutical orientation.

The question is, however, whether this observation applies to creation faith in a more immediate sense than, say, to salvation. In dealing with salvation history, and thus with divine revelation, as a contingent historical event, it is obvious

---

[13]We are fully aware of the rather diffuse comprehensiveness of the question posed here. This applies not only to the complex choir of critical voices to which we have referred, but also to the complexity inherent in talking about "the world of the Bible," a term that could be used only in the plural in a meaningful historical analysis. The more than millenium-long genesis of the Bible reflects a series of changing and partly competitive "cultures," each of which is in only limited correspondence with another. A tense exchange between different cultures on, say, creation should be seen as much as an intrabiblical event as as a postbiblical event. How Genesis 1 and Genesis 2 relate to each other in this perspective may already be an extremely instructive question.

that there is but limited assistance to be drawn from extrabiblical resources with no immediate link to the history of the Bible. Extrabiblical observations have no direct bearing on the substance of faith, even though general observations concerning human understanding, or relating to historical and cosmological circumstances as such, are relevant to the work of theology. So far, nothing positive has been said about one article of the Creed that does not also have bearing on the others. The issue is whether creation faith goes beyond this and is ready to recognize testimonies from other than biblical sources—not, certainly, in addition to or as a corrective to biblical faith in the Creator, but as thematically valid statements of a truth that is common to Christians as well as to people of whatever religious allegiance may profess truths that seem to open up avenues toward the biblical vision of creation. Can authentic creation faith arise or exist outside a biblically informed community? And should Christians in this domain of faith listen to the testimonies of others with a different kind of attentiveness to the one demanded in light of the second and third articles of the Creed? This question should be borne in mind as we proceed to the relationship between culture and creation in the reverse order.

2.2 Creation speaks on culture

"Creation" in this setting definitely means "creation faith" in the sense of a biblically founded faith in God the Creator. Our question is as follows: What light does a biblical vision of reality as created throw on the variety of human interpretative communities? To what extent does it confirm and to what extent does it restrict such communicative variety?

In biblical creation belief there lies a fundamental proclamation of the unity of the created world. In recent years an ostensibly growing emphasis has been laid on a long neglected theme: that the vision of creation is not restricted to the unity of humankind; it encompasses the whole of the creature in its common createdness. There is no reason to elaborate on this basic perspective, which we wholeheartedly sustain. In both the creation accounts of Genesis (1 and 2) the formation of humankind is solidly integrated in that of the world as a whole. In the Old Testament wisdom literature animate and inanimate being indiscriminately reflect the Creator's design. And in the Psalms the whole universe, all its elements and occurrences, all its inventory and inhabitants, are called to praise the Lord (Psalm 148).

This being said, it more or less follows that creation is the ultimate source of human unity and community. God "made from one every nation of men to live on all the face of the earth, having determined allotted periods and the boundaries of their habitation" (Acts 17:26), "one God and Father of us all" (Ephesians 4:6). The account of the tower of Babel (Genesis 11:1-9) gives a different assessment of human unity/diversity: Not all kinds of organized human cooperation are pleasing to the Maker: humans associating for the promotion of their own power and glory promote the divisions of egoistic self-exaltation. In this case, the divine intervention would immediately look like a "no" to human togetherness and like the ordination of cultural (linguistic) plurality as punishment for a too ambitious quest for universal human fellowship—an understanding that could easily be adopted by nationalist or racist ideologies. Once we discover that God reacts not to human togetherness but to the purpose of that togetherness—"Come, let us build ourselves a city, and a tower with its top in the heavens, and let us make a name for ourselves" (Genesis 11:4)—then we also see how a human get-together can be the exact opposite of authentic unity, a massive self-assertion whereby individual dignity and individual responsibility are swallowed up in self-celebrating mass intoxification. Accordingly—and paradoxically—the seemingly alienating effect of the diversity of language serves real fellowship, even when and while encouraging humankind to "be scattered abroad upon the face of the whole earth" (Genesis 11:4).

The most impressive biblical passages on unity in diversity are probably those New Testament (especially Pauline) texts that deal explicitly with the Christian church as the body of Christ, each member serving the others precisely by virtue of its particularity (Romans 12:4ff., 1 Corinthians 12:12ff., Ephesians 4:4 ff.). The two topics—unity of the world and unity of the church—should by no means be confused, but at the same time the way in which the apostle elaborates on unity in diversity immediately lends itself for analogy. Unity as community does not contradict diversity; rather it underscores the richness of variety. To be different is not necessarily to contradict; it can also mean to supplement, to stimulate exchange, to enrich.

However, it is inevitable that the following question will arise: How can creation faith stimulate unity in a world in which creation ideas differ and wide segments of humankind do not even profess a personal Creator? Within "the world of religions" the cosmogonic approaches in myths and tales vary to such an extent that, when taken more or less literally (as they generally are), they reinforce ancient controversies instead of introducing new approaches to understanding. It is also true that the image of the Creator and, linked with that image, the vision of the human place in creation are likely to foster more dispute than community.

These observations shall not be contested. If a fellowship of creation *ideas* were to constitute the basis for the unity of reflecting humankind, then these ideas would have to be completely vague and formal to serve as a common denominator even to the majority. The result would be something along the lines of: "We assert one human family by virtue of one source of common origin." The unifying effect of such a formalized "confession" would no doubt be rather meager. The drive toward unity is obviously much more efficiently upheld and reinforced through the various faiths and ideologies acting separately and in their own setting than through such a supercommunitarian "confession."

For Christianity, the real meaning of creation for human community is by and large indicated in the basic statement of the human species as being created "in the image of God" (Genesis 1:26-27). As is well-known, this formula has been a topic of controversy between the "Roman Catholic" and the "Protestant" tradition, the former being particularly keen to maintain the integrity of human personhood even after "the Fall," the latter asserting the total dependence of fallen humankind on saving grace. Both concerns seem to be justified in their respective perspectives, as do, correspondingly, conflicting interests in the traditional discussion on "general revelation." "For what can be known about God is plain to them, because God has shown it to them. Ever since the creation of the world his invincible nature, namely, his eternal power and deity, has been clearly perceived in the things that have been made." (Romans 1:19-20) In its Pauline setting, this famous passage contains no alternative doctrine of salvation that could eventually offend good Protestants. Nor, however, can it be interpreted as a nostalgic recollection of some "once upon a time." Seen in connection with the law "written in the hearts" of the Gentiles (Romans 2:14-15) and the emphasis on prebiblical revelation in two sequences in Acts (14:15ff., 17:22ff.), it obviously underlines a not unimportant reality: Even where people hold no coherent or biblically adequate idea of the Creator, intellectually unintegrated glimpses indicating that creation has some universal meaning demand control of human choice and activities.

This seems to be the truly unifying importance of creation. The Bible does not point to some common human idea of creation and its unifying consequences but to human createdness as an event with certain universal expressions. Open-minded human beings will inevitably pursue a series of common aims and values, even if the fellowship thus established cannot escape the Babylonic dimension of unity in the self-contradictory service of disunity: "For there is no distinction. Since all have sinned and fall short of the glory of God." (Romans 3:22-23) The unifying effects of the creation as well as of the Fall exist—regardless of whether or not these events are recognized. And on the practical level these effects always intermingle and make something radically ambiguous of actual human community. The immediate advantage of a conscious creation faith is that, through a reflective disclosure of unifying universal meaning, it tends to make conscious, and thereby reinforce, the Creator's will for his creation and thus even becomes an invitation to "logical worship" (λογικὴν λατρείαν, logikēn latreian, Romans 12:1). Correspondingly, the Christian view of a common Fall and a common togetherness "in Adam" serves to cut off any feeling of moral superiority and make those who truly share in it promoters of radical humility. That the encounter of Christians with their non-Christian environments so often does not follow this ideal description may be one more reason to reinforce that humility.

These observations lead us to the crucial question: Where do we find a common ground of human cooperation in a world that needs it as badly as our world of today? Here we seem to remain trapped in what could be called an "ecumenical impasse," which possibly has to do with the strong Barthian impact on ecumenical theology, an impact that undoubtedly persists to a higher degree than is generally observed. Briefly, the dilemma can be described as follows: If authentic discovery of the Creator's will for his creation is given only through the biblical history of salvation (*Heilsgeschichte*) and if authentic ethical criteria can be sought only in the Lordship of Jesus Christ, what basis exists for practical cooperation between Christians and non-Christians?

In principle, two affirmative answers can be imagined: that of "secular theology" and that of "cosmic Christology." The former sees Jesus Christ as the institutor of a "way of life" that expresses itself in certain social and political attitudes ("Christology from below"). Wherever this "way of life" is being lived, Christ is at work, whether the human agents identify it as Christian or not. The latter goes in the opposite direction ("Christology from above") and, starting with Christ as the eternal Logos of God, claims some universal—be it ever so "anonymous"—presence of his wherever authentic truth is discerned. The outcome of the two approaches is the same to an amazing extent: the exploration of a *Christus extra muros ecclesiae,* whose presence is not derived from preaching, nor from the sacramental practice of the church. The critical question arising from this is whether it does not automatically lead to a secularizing politicization of Christianity (in the first case) or to a spiritualizing generalization (in the second).

In both cases the problem is this: If Christians claim their practical cooperation *extra muros ecclesiae* (in issues of peace, justice, environmental protection, etc.) as principally legitimized only "in Christ," how can Christians establish a common platform with non-Christians without the integrity of either party being violated? In either case, would not such a platform have to reduce "Christ" to some universal principle, and the gospel to some aspect of general human insight? And would not this inevitably do injustice not only to the gospel but also to people who—either *on* or *against* their own will—would thus be nominally registered as "Christians"? Would not some idea of fellowship in the wider "room" of creation—as distinct from Christian unity "in Christ"—be a less problematic warrant of joint human initiatives than some wholesale immatriculation of humankind into the fold of Christianity?

A particularly interesting document in this setting is the 1984 "Theses de dignate necnon iuribus personae humanae" of the International Theological Commission of the Roman Catholic Church.[14] It starts by making a solid basis for Christian involvement on behalf of human dignity in the central Christian message of salvation:

> Missio Ecclesiae est annuntiatio kerygmatis de salute pro omnibus obtenta a Christo crucifixo et resuscitato. Talis salus primam originem habet in Patre qui Filium misit, et hominibus concretis communicatur, ut participatio vitae divinae, per infusionem Spiritus. Acceptatio kerygmatis christiani per fidem exigit atque nova vita collata per gratiam implicat conversionem quae plurimas habet consequentias in quolibet campo activitatum credentis.[15]

A compendium of a "Theologia dignitatis et iurium hominum" starts with "Perspectivae biblicae," the immediate orientation of which is (*not* creation, but) God's covenant with his chosen people, proceeding to the church as God's "novum et ultimum regnum" and as "novam creationem a Spiritu Sancto effectam."[16] Primordial creation enters the stage only in a later passage on "Dignitas et iura personae humanae sub lumine 'theologiae historiae salutis'," which deals with "Homo creatus," "Homo ut peccator," and "Homo redemptus a Christo."[17] Also the paragraph on created humankind starts by explicitly stating the importance of salvation history for human dignity, referring particularly to Christ "creating" (John 1:3), "incarnate" (John 1:14), and "given . . . for our sins" (Romans 4:25). The importance of human createdness is spelled out in three points: created "in the image of God" (Genesis 1:27), in a social dimension (Genesis 1:27, 2:24), and with a certain responsibility for overseeing the rest of creation (Genesis 1:26). But before this perspective is developed, there is a general remark of basic importance:

> Ratio tamen humana ab hac consideratione aliena non est (Romans 1:20). E contra, magnae convergentiae apparere possunt inter hanc doctrinam theologicam et philosophiam tam metaphysicam quam moralem, quando homo, saltem sub aliquibus aspectibus, consideratur ut creatio Dei.

---

[14]*Gregorianum* 66/1 (1985): 5-23.

[15]Ibid., 1.1:8.

[16]Ibid., 2.1.1:10-11.

[17]Ibid., 2.2.

Here, obviously, comes a certain opening for a conversation that transcends
the borders of Christianity, an opening that it is difficult to distinguish in the structuring of the document as a whole. If creation has such a comprehensive meaning
as is indicated in our last quotation, how meaningful is it to approach it only in
the third place and to include it in such an unrestricted way in a comprehensive
salvation paradigm that is literally established *"before* creation"?

Having reviewed the strikingly divergent conditions of human rights and dignity in different parts of the world, the document proceeds to a series of "Sug-
gestiones." First comes the development of a philosophical foundation, which is
designated as "personalistica" as opposed to "naturalismus materialisticus" and
"existentialismus atheisticus."[18] In the following practical deliberations, special
attention is drawn to the importance of searching for a common human base for
joint engagement:

> Ultrum iura haec fundamentalia sic institui poterunt, dependebit ex con-
> sensu obtinendo, qui transcendat conceptiones diversas (philosophicas et
> sociologicas) de homine. Qui consensus, si obtineatur, fundamentum in-
> terpretationis communis iurium hominis saltem in re politica et sociali
> erit.[19]

It is not clear on what level the indicated "consensus" is to be sought. Is it
really possible to imagine such a "meta" level, transcending the differences of
philosophical and sociological concepts? If such an agreement is to include also
the "naturalists" and the "existentialists," against whom the idea of human humanity has been so vigorously profiled, what could it look like in conceptual terms?
Do the "theses" leave us with any hope that the consensus—the vital importance
of which is so convincingly underscored—is at all possible? Does it indicate the
slightest concrete approach toward such a universal understanding?

Obviously the only means of seeking a solution to the dilemma is along the
lines already suggested: that the remaining imprints of divine creation still secure
elements of an essential fellowship in human ambition, even if this is not supported by joint subscription to a common creation doctrine. The fellowship of creation must be pursued as a socially operative reality—in spite of the present
controversy about interpretation. The essential thing is not what my partner *thinks*
about creation but that she or he *is* created and *has* a human identity, which in
some way always expresses aspiration toward universal integration. Obviously,
then, the sought for "consensus" should not primarily be in the direction of some

---

[18]Ibid., 3.2.1:20-22.

[19]Ibid., 3.2.2:23.

minimum common denominator—an ideological formula from which everything else could be derived—but rather from a consonant experience of humanhood (automatically reflecting the wider event of fellow creatureliness) as a joint resource to which a successful appeal could be made, not through structures of analytical argument but in concrete interhuman and intercreatural encounters. It is easier to agree with a Communist or a Hindu *that* particular rights of fellow creatures should be affirmed than it is to agree with them on a comprehensive theory as to *why* this should be so. As an underlying joint motivation, createdness transcends motivational reflection.

Why do the "Theses"—a representative Roman Catholic statement of the mid-1980s—so obviously end up in a sort of soteriological impasse with such a slight attempt to respond to what may be seen as its own most fundamental question? To what extent is this in harmony with Roman Catholic tradition, with its strong emphasis on "natural" right? The remarkable reorientation of Roman Catholic creation theology in the second half of the 20th century[20]—with its decisive turn from cosmology to soteriology and from a concept of "nature" as normative givenness to a more dynamic vision of "history" as eschatological fulfillment—has manifestly been inspired by Barthian "salvation history." The traditional approach had run into trouble in two directions: First, the established cosmological scheme of reflection had become sufficiently ossified to impede that responsible adjustment to new scientific disclosures demanded by its own Thomist axioms and threatened to entertain a never-ending series of apologetic disasters. Second, a static concept of nature had fostered a hierarchy of ethical prescriptions that hampered the adaptation of ethics to present societal realities and thus served to cut Christian moral orientation off from the contemporary world. This twofold tendency was by no means characteristic of Roman Catholic theology alone—exactly the same thing was prominent in much of official Protestant argumentation—but it is to be observed and analyzed most instructively in its Roman Catholic setting, where the mechanisms of authorization were more visible and tradition was inscribed and circumscribed in a less ambiguous way.

It is not difficult to observe that the recent Roman Catholic reorientation has had a great many constructive results. As a matter of fact, the far-reaching *aggiornamento* of the Roman Catholic Church during and after the Second Vatican Council could scarcely have taken place without an underlying reorientation of creation theology. Especially in view of the ethical aspects of the issue, there may

---

[20]Cf. Bishop Karl Lehmann's presentation at the October 1983 Strasbourg consultation ("Nature and Supernature—The Dimensions of Creation"), further reviewed here, pp. 178-79.

still be reason to ask whether the reorientation has been sufficiently consistent. But this question should not prevent one particular reflection in the opposite direction: Has this not resulted in certain insights connected with the old Thomist approach being pushed too forcefully into the background? This is a question to which we shall return in the confessional part of our deliberations. Here, we shall only indicate the dilemma: whether "creation" in modern theology—Roman Catholic as well as Protestant—has really been allowed to speak on culture to the extent that is demanded if creation is to be taken seriously in its capacity as creation. How can "culture"—the manifestation of diverse human conversation communities—be addressed, and a viable communication between different "cultures" be upheld, if not by virtue of the fact that "creation" is an underlying and unifying given? And how can the Christian church direct its endeavors toward preserving and reinforcing the unity of humankind (and the unity of the creature) if not by exploiting and promoting the vision of an all-embracing Creator?

That creation addresses and warrants cultural variety is an insight that must affect our endeavors to attain church unity, making us more sensitive to and more appreciative of differences that are brought about by geographical and historical factors, and seeing such "nontheological" givens as having essentially "equal dignity" in face of theological distinctions. Creation and the creation mandate given to humankind—and, incidentally, there seems to be widespread agreement today that this should not be interpreted as "subdue the earth" but rather along the lines of caring and sympathetic adaptation[21]—in a very basic way authorizes diversity in totality and totality in diversity. The "tower of Babel" expresses a monolithic unwillingness to accept this differentiation.[22] When language, the basic means of communication, is used to resist creation-based divergence, the Creator decides to maintain the differentiation mandate even at the cost of immediate communication. For the sake of authentic unity a manipulative pseudo-unity has to be shattered. In the blessing of Abraham "all the families of the earth" are again brought together in a unifying vision (Genesis 12:3).

But the question remains: If creation authorizes the differentiation of culture(s), what bearing does this have on the *variety of religion(s)*? Is religion not such a fundamental occurrence—with direct influence on all historically established cultures (at least in presecular societies and thus in most contemporary so-

---

[21]Klaus Koch at the Strasbourg Institute's October 1984 Klingenthal consultation (see also here, p. 45); and Gerhard Liedke, *Im Bauch des Fisches: Ökologische Theologie* (1979) 63-83.

[22]"Lest we be scattered abroad upon the face of the whole earth" (Genesis 11:4).

cieties that embrace religions of nature or are determined by world religions other than Christianity)—that authorizing a specific culture without including its religion would make next to no sense? So, then, to what extent *does* creation mandate religion—if not in all its factual appearances, at least in its basic right, including some right to historical diversity?

Wide segments of traditional theology will meet this question with a priori skepticism, perceiving a degree of exaltation of creation at the cost of redemption, and thus at the cost of the specific biblical history of salvation. Such a tension between creation and salvation concerns may have existed from the outset of the history of Christendom, and it has been particularly apparent since the Enlightenment.

Vigorous opposition to any self-sufficient "Deistic" model of creation in modern theology has partly served to suppress this sometimes somewhat sterile counterpoint. In any case, the idea of creature as an all-embracing, more or less self-redeeming organism should be destroyed once and for all. But the question of "created religion"[23] remains—not as a question about the possible legitimacy of some abstract "natural religion" in the old Deistic sense, but as the question about historically given religions as responses to some concern that cannot be removed from human "nature" in its createdness.

The idea of a "religious a priori," developed in continuity with the Kantian tradition, was already used by Friedrich Schleiermacher to legitimate the historical particularity of Christianity. A powerful attempt in this same direction was made by Anders Nygren with his method of "motif research": the "categorical question" of religion—that of "eternity"—is an assumption that makes it possible to compare the different, historically given answers and thus to extract their "basic motifs" (*agape, eros, nomos,* etc.) and review their basic differences within the actual world of religions. This model of one fundamental question with many different answers sees religion as both a fundamentally unifying and a possibly divisive factor in the history of humankind. The unifying effect lies not only in the universality of some fundamental "question," but also in the common scheme for classifying the "answers" and conquering an otherwise unsurveyable agglomeration of varieties. Paul Tillich's famous concept of "ultimate concern" also seems to belong in this a priori tradition and may assist religions in clarifying their proximity to and distance from each other. In a wider theological setting, a "religious a priori" can be understood only in terms of "creation," that is, of the Creator's design "that they should seek God in the hope that they might feel after him and find him" (Acts 17:27).

---

[23]Matthew Tindal, *Christianity as old as the Creation* (1730).

Since about 1970, a rather conspicuous trend in theology has been the rise in the interest for a theology of religion. In 1980 the *Christian Century* conducted a study on "How my mind has changed" (over the last 10 years)[24], and the most remarkable feature about the more than 20 contributions was the repeated emphasis on the rediscovery of religion. During this same period the World Council of Churches developed its program of interfaith dialogue, amid controversies that reached a spectacular peak during the WCC's 1975 Assembly in Nairobi, Kenya. The divisive line in the official ecumenical "dialogue on dialogue" has mainly been between the "mission" and "dialogue" centered approaches, expressed above all in different attitudes to "shared spirituality" (common acts of worship).

However, in the more purely academic debate, another divisive line has emerged that may be just as crucial to ecumenical reflection. Typical of the two competing points of view are John Hick's *God Has Many Names: Britain's New Religious Pluralism* (1980) and John B. Cobb's *Beyond Dialogue: Toward a Mutual Transformation of Christianity and Buddhism* (1982). Hick's pursuit of human unity takes him on a passionate quest for commonality: Only what is common to humans in their wide variety of cultural and religious expressions can be recognized as essential to their relationship with God. This leads to a radical depreciation of traditional Christian Christology/soteriology.[25] As a matter of fact, Hick's position is similar to that of 18th-century Deism. Even if he prophesies and accepts the continued existence of single religions, his prescription for a future world unity is to lay all stress on the universality of God as the common unifying ground. According to Hick, the future of ecumenism depends entirely on the development of such a minimum common denominator.[26]

---

[24]Published in book form as *Theologians in Transition,* ed. James M. Wall (New York: Crossroad Publishing Co., 1981).

[25]A view already strongly expressed by John Hick in his role as editor of *The Myth of God Incarnate* (London: SCM Press; Philadelphia: Westminster Press, 1977).

[26]In his *Problems of Religious Pluralism* (London/New York: Macmillan, 1985), Hick undertakes to develop "A Philosophy of Religious Pluralism" (28-45) in which he consistently rejects both "exclusivism" ("our religion is the only true one") and "inclusivism" ("other religions may in some way have a share in the benefit of ours") in favor of "pluralism" ("all the world religions are equally valid ways to salvation"). According to Hick, if the majority of theologians are still stuck in the halfheartedness of "inclusivism," this is due to traditional, absolutist "substance Christology." Among important contributions to overcoming this deadlock, he sees various modern attempts to formulate "degree Chri-

On the other hand, in a pronounced criticism of John Hick, John B. Cobb chooses to move in a different direction, even though he is also ready to renounce a good many traditional attitudes to promote new conquests of unity. His approach can be adequately assessed only against the background of his process orientation, according to which truth must be sought as an ever forward-moving development. Cobb consistently sees the task of reconciling different religions not in the curtailment of their visions (that is, retaining only what they may already have in common) but in the expansion of each of their visions and in accommodating the life-giving impulses of one tradition into another. This experimentation with mutual questioning and enrichment, which Cobb himself outlines in respect of Christianity and Buddhism, is not presented as an extraordinary case but as a paradigm of interreligious exchange in general. In spite of his unrestricted openness, Cobb thus comes closer to traditional Christian attitudes than Hick: First, he very much objects to abandoning Christocentrism for the benefit of some unspecified theocentrism; second, he is ready to accept personal conversions from one religion to another, not as an aim in itself but as one possible, minor contribution to the great aim—the mutual, transforming enrichment of religions through open communication with each other.[27]

The February 1986 issue of the international Roman Catholic review *Concilium* is dedicated to "Christianity Among World Religions." This issue gives

---

stologies," but, above all, Wilfred Cantwell Smith's energetic attempt to replace the concept of "religions" (as monolithic competing entities) with "faith" (as the expression of an underlying common human type of experience). Cf. esp. Wilfred Cantwell Smith, *The Meaning and End of Religion* (New York, 1962; London, 1978). In an entirely different perspective, the historically conditioned relativity of the concept of "religion" is approached by Ernst Feil in his *Religio: Die Geschichte eines neuzeitlichen Grundbegriffs vom Frühchristentum bis zur Reformation* (Göttingen: Vandenhoeck & Ruprecht, 1986).

[27]A quite different perspective on "dialogue" is that of Leslie G. Howard, *The Expansion of God* (London: SCM Press, 1981). While by no means shrinking back from maintaining a historical supremacy of Christianity over against other world religions, Howard claims that in order to fulfil its vocation Christianity has to adopt impulses from a self-critical encounter with them. "The Catholic and liberal experience has tended to become assimilated to the West and the fundamentalist experience to retain the Semitic element. . . . What Christianity has not adjusted to is the Spirit of the East, yet it is a mark of its universal . . . destiny that . . . it is intrinsically capable of doing so. . . . Such a capacity is more than could be claimed of Hinduism . . . or Buddhism . . . or Islam. . . . The question is, then, not whether Christianity . . . is capable of being a universal faith, but whether its adherents are willing to let it become that." (411-12)

concrete examples of exchanges between Christianity and Islam, Hinduism, Buddhism, and Chinese religion. In addition, it offers important evaluations by one Protestant and two Roman Catholic writers. In an assessment of a Protestant theology of religion, Leroy Rouner is harsh in his criticism of present-day interfaith dialogue, since it is being conducted entirely on Western Christian (including modern skeptic) premises and is obviously structured by the bad consciences of the old colonial powers. He advocates unconditional equality between the conversation partners, a position he finds best served by Cobb's Christocentric approach[28]. On the other hand, he sees John Hick's position[29] as being representative of a relativism whose basic orientation must be understood as unmistakably Western (and "Christian"). Of particular interest is the obvious conflict between the two main Roman Catholic contributors: Paul Knitter and Hans Küng. To a certain—but only to a certain—extent this seems to be the Hick/Cobb conflict all over again. Knitter reviews the historical encounter of Christianity with other religions as four alternative approaches, which reflect a more or less chronological process that has greatly accelerated in the years following the Second Vatican Council: first, Christianity *opposed to* other religions; second, Christ taken as being in some way *present in* other religions; third, Christ *standing above* other religions; and fourth, Christ seen *in* unprejudiced *community with* other religions. Knitter considers Karl Rahner to be the main representative of a crypto-Christological interpretation of the world of religion (followed, among others, by A. Dulles and Edward Schillebeeckx). And in Hans Küng (assisted by, e.g., H.R. Schlette, M. Hellwig, and Piet Schoonenberg) he sees the main advocates of the "Christ above" standpoint, which recognizes other religions as being independent ways of salvation in their own right, but at the same time insists on Christ as the supreme standard of religious value.[30]

---

[28]Leroy Rouner, "Theology of Religions in Recent Protestant Theology," *Christianity Among World Religions,* ed. Hans Küng and Jürgen Moltmann (English language editor: Marcus Lefébure), *Concilium* 183 (February 1986): 108-15. Rouner also identifies this with certain European approaches such as those of Jürgen Moltmann and Wolfhart Pannenberg.

[29]Comparable to those of Ninian Smart and Wilfred Cantwell Smith.

[30]Paul Knitter, "Catholic Theology at the Crossroads," *Concilium* (see n. 28): 99-107. In this classification Paul Knitter does not really pay attention to the dialectical line of approach taken by the Roman Catholic foundation Oratio Dominica in Freiburg im Breisgau (Federal Republic of Germany) in its *Schriftenreihe zur Grossen Ökumene* and by its leader Walter Strolz: All religions are seen as complementary, equally valid ways of salvation, but they should by no means be

In allying himself with the fourth alternative, Paul Knitter chooses such comrades-in-arms as R. Panikkar and I. Puthiadam, insisting on the necessity for consistent openness in dialogue even if this results in admitting that other saviors may turn out to be equally important as Christ. For his own part, Knitter champions a liberation theology of religions and indicates a "soteriocentric" hermeneutic that would eventually overcome the traditional Western narrowness not only of an "ecclesiocentric" and a "Christocentric" but even of a "theocentric" approach.

In his concluding presentation—and without making specific reference to Knitter—Hans Küng enters into a formidable counterattack. He starts by presenting four unsatisfactory basic positions—the atheistic (no religion is true), the absolutistic (only one religion is true), the relativistic (every religion is true), and the inclusivistic (all religions participate in the truth of one particular religion)—and demonstrates why he finds them all inappropriate. He then focuses on a more extensive polemic between a dialogue without faith commitments and a dialogue on the basis of faith commitments, which is very much in favor of the latter.

In pleading strongly for a unification of freedom and truth, Küng underscores the need for a set of criteria of religious truth, to be used not only in relationship between the different religions but also within each of them (including Christianity). In doing so, he endeavors to spell out a general ethical criterion, a general religious criterion, and a specific Christian criterion. On the latter he says: 1. Much of what is promoted today as brand new in theology is really only what was already expressed in old liberal Protestantism in its readiness to give up the normativity and finality of Christ—and against which the criticisms of Karl Barth (and even Rudolf Bultmann and Paul Tillich) have been decisive. 2. Whether we like it or not, in the whole of the New Testament Jesus is normative and definitive; he alone is the Christ of God. 3. In order to avoid both absolutism and relativism, a distinction must be made between the view of a particular religion from outside and from inside. 4. Seen from the outside, through the eyes of religious science,

---

comprised through syntheticizing experimentation: "Eine Theologie der Religionen als ein *diesen* übergeordnetes, die bleibende Vielfalt der Heilswege nicht respektierendes System, ist menschenunwürdig. . . . Was sich in der christlichen Begegnung mit Hinduismus, Buddhismus und Taoismus unter entschiedener Anerkennung des Lichtes, das durch Christus *jeden* Menschen erleuchtet . . . (Joh. 1:9) als tiefer, unüberbrückbaren Gegensatz erweist, ist nicht zu beseitigen, sondern in einem allerletzten Vertrauen auf Gottes unerforschliche Fügungen auszuhalten (Jes. 55:8-11). Die Vereinigung der Religionen ist für das endliche Blickfeld des Menschen kein irdisches Ereignis." (Walter Strolz, *Heilswege der Weltreligionen*, vol. 2, *Christliche Begegnung mit Hinduismus, Buddhismus und Taoismus*, [Freiburg: Herder, 1986] 222)

there are obviously several true religions, whereas: 5. Seen from the inside, through the eyes of a believing Christian, belief in the one true God as proclaimed by Christ is the true religion and all other religions are true with a reservation.

Against this background, Hans Küng launches a strong attack on Paul Knitter's position:

> Anybody who renounces the normativity of his or her own tradition and takes as his or her point of departure the equal validity of the different "Christs" (Jesus, Moses, Muhammad, Gautama): i) clearly presupposes as a result something that would not be unconditionally desirable even as the end product of a long process of understanding—such a method seems to be *a prioristic*; ii) it requires of the other non-Christian parties what most of them reject, namely, that they should from the outset give up their belief in the normativity of their own message . . . and take up the (typically Western and modern) standpoint of the basic equality of the various ways: Such a way seems to be *unrealistic*; iii) requires Christians themselves to demote Jesus Christ to the status of a provisional Messiah. . . . Such a stance would have to be characterized as *non-Christian*; iv) juxtaposes the various guiding figures as if they did not stand in a historical dependence on each other . . . and were not honoured in completely different ways within their own religions. . . . Such a way of looking at things seems to be *unhistorical*.

> The upshot of all this for practice is that anybody, whether as a Christian or not, who makes such a standpoint his or her own runs the risk of . . . distancing him- or herself from his or her own community of faith. . . . But the dialogue between the religions is not advanced by a few Western (or Eastern) intellectuals agreeing together. . . . Yet the Christian community of belief may allow itself to be persuaded to replace an ecclesiocentrism with a Christocentrism or theocentrism (which for Christians amounts to the same thing!) but they are hardly likely to be persuaded to take up some vague soteriocentrism. Practice should not be made the norm of theory undialectically and social questions should not be expounded as the basis and centre of the theology of religions.[31]

---

[31]Hans Küng, "Towards an Ecumenical Theology of Religions: Some Theses for Clarification," *Concilium* (see n. 28): 119-25, quotation from 123. In "Confessional Universalism and Inter-Religious Dialogue" (*Dialog* 25 [Spring 1986]: 149) Ted Peters voices a similar point of view: "In sum, the confessional universalist position . . . is more honest regarding the fundamental claims of the Christian faith; it is better able, on this account, to understand sympathetically the normative, if not exclusivist claims of other traditions such as Islam."

As a positive counterpart, Hans Küng describes his alternative as being a posteriori, patiently realistic, self-critically Christian, historical, and critically reflected.

We have paid rather lengthy attention to this issue of *Concilium* in order to illustrate how and in which way the contemporary debate on the theology of religions is moving. Particular attention has been paid to the concluding comments by Hans Küng, because in their impressive dialectical construction they endeavor to give credit to both of the contrasting tendencies in the present discussion. The intention is to reveal a maximum openness to the vast complexity of the world of religions and also to preserve a Christian (and, indirectly, a Muslim, Hindu, Buddhist, etc.) consciousness of unmodified, unique commitment to one's respective tradition. At first glance, the position of Paul Knitter may seem to go as far in the direction of intrareligious reconciliation as is at present possible. Hans Küng does not object that it goes too far; rather that it does not go far enough. In order to be able to respect the authenticity of other traditions, one has to respect one's own. What the extreme "liberators of religion" in fact do is impose the imperialism of modern Western relativism on their conversation partners, that is, they refuse to listen seriously to them.[32]

Even though Hans Küng's style of argument may sound convincing, certain questions can be directed to his dialectical combination of antiabsolutism and antirelativism. Is it really possible to admit the authenticity of other "saviors" and other "ways of salvation" at the same time as one insists on the historical Christian emphasis on the salutary uniqueness of Christ? It seems that Küng feels that the distinction between a "view from outside" and a "view from inside" takes care of the seeming contradiction. But is this sufficient?

Should a solution to the dilemma rather be sought in a distinction between Christ as God's unique integrative act in history and Christendom as the fallible—and, historically, in many cases even deceitful—attempt of humans to come to grips with this act? In this case: 1. *Either* Christians would have no superiority over other humans *or* their ostensibly self-appointed superiority would be immediately chastened by their inadequate stewardship of their apparently matchless vocation (cf. Romans 3:22-23). And: 2. The gospel would by no means challenge

---

[32]For a more comprehensive presentation of Hans Küng's position, see *Christianity and the World Religions: Paths of Dialogue with Islam, Hinduism, and Buddhism*, ed. Hans Küng, Josef van Ess, Heinrich von Stietencron, and Heinz Bechert (London: Collins, 1987). (Original: *Christentum und Weltreligionen: Islam, Hinduismus, Buddhismus* [Munich: R. Piper Verlag, 1985].) For that of Paul Knitter, see his *No Other Name? A Critical Survey of Christian Attitudes Toward the World Religions* (London: SCM Press; Maryknoll NY: Orbis Books, 1985).

non-Christian cultures to renounce their identity in favor of that of some traditionally Christian people; rather it would encourage a reception of Christ in critical conversation with traditional Christendom and in a conscious readaptation of their own cultural inheritance.

It is beyond the scope of our ecumenical creation study to solve the far-reaching problems of a theology of religions, even though it is today appearing with irresistible vigor in a variety of theological contexts and is in so many ways of basic importance for the self-understanding of Christianity. We have to conclude by noting the bearing of these questions on the issue of creation and cultural variety and observing that the option may be more complex than is immediately obvious from traditional (conservative and liberal) approaches—approaches that have reduced it either to a comprehensive cultural tolerance combined with an indifferent brand of theology or to a strong consciousness of historically established religious identity linked with an indispensable attachment to established cultural patterns.

However, once this is said, another set of problems arises. If the gospel (and religion in principle) is absolutely indiscriminative of cultural varieties, it would seem to follow that it neither affects culture in any significant way nor can its function in a society be stimulated or hampered by cultural factors per se. If such judgments are accepted, a consistent dualism arises, not only between Christianity and culture but also between God and world, religion and society, and spirituality and everyday life. And this brings us back to an orientation from which theology has been trying very hard to escape for at least the last 25 years.

Today, the challenge from the world of religions faces the churches not only in the general question about religious identity and human reconciliation but also and more specifically in the confrontation of different, mutually challenging visions of creation, world, and environment. From this confrontation there arises a question which, in turn, introduces still another avenue of reflection: If certain orientations of nonbiblical religions may reactivate—or at least recall—biblical visions that have been neglected by major segments of Christendom, how does this observation contribute to a theological reevaluation of these religions and, thus, of the phenomenon of religion in general?

Does this suggest the possibility of something more than a theoretical construction? Today probably very few informed observers would contest this. As a point of example, it suffices to return to the native American presentation at the Burlingame consultation. Even if many observers might be inclined to question the image of Christianity that is offered for comparison there, they will hardly be able to contest its value as a caricature which exposes tendencies that have been palpable during the history of Christianity and have been particularly conspicuous to people who have been exploited in the name of a politically manipulated Christianity. This being admitted, it is also clear that this confrontation model may serve the church as a useful looking glass, even if its value as a balanced historical assessment may be limited.

However, in our context, the following question is more important: How does this image of non-Christian (or in this case pre-Christian tribal) religion offer a vision of creation that is consistent with that of the Bible? And to what extent could it claim esprit de corps with the Bible against a traditional theological curtailing of creation? Even if the image of tribal religion offered here can be attacked as a rather romanticized description, and even if it could be accused of cherishing customs and patterns of a world that has "gone with the wind," a vision remains that may well speak eloquently in confrontation with Christian ambitions. More than pointing to particular elements, this vision points to an all-embracing mood of awe and to the motivating power offered by an underlying experience of some universal presence of the Creator. The tension between spiritual and secular—so well known in Western piety—seems to be overcome in an all-integrating religious approach. This feature is, of course, not unique to North American tribal religion; it could also be said to be characteristic of tribal religion of Africa and, to a certain extent, of the great religions of the East. Even if such world views should by no means be confused with biblical revelation, the question remains as to whether their particular creation emphasis—when compared with the Bible—cannot sharpen our biblical awareness, that is, to a certain extent they may well demand to be taken into account and adapted to our theological vision. Is it possible to detect a Christian "forgetfulness of Creation" and would it be possible to throw this back on its biblical testing ground in an encounter with "pagan" creation sensitivity? Unfortunately, the framework of our present research does not permit further investigation of this vital question.

What culture has to say about creation and what creation should be heard to say about culture are therefore reciprocal responses in one and the same exchange. In a conversation between Christian churches that are striving to express their given unity, the difference in cultural backgrounds serves to underline the richness of the variety of the Creator's work, including variety in patterns of human understanding (and this by no means omits theological understanding). As no other area of spiritual and theological diversity, creation—as constitutive of cultural variety—is at the same time constitutive of our different images of reality and thus of our whole way of seeing and sensing. Therefore, cultural diversity not only accentuates the richness of creation; it also indirectly legitimizes differences in theological styles of expression—not as dividing controversies of faith but as what could be superficially referred to as "spiritual geography." Subsequently, this observation may speak to the richness not only of creation thought but also of the orientation of Christian faith as a whole.

At the same time, this discovery endorses cultural variety as a historical given and warns us not only against seeing one cultural pattern as being authorized by Christianity (even though it is historically intertwined with it), but also and above all against making our own cultural preoccupations a prerequisite of theological reflection—or, worse still, of faith. The error of such an approach becomes particularly apparent when one observes how the world of the Genesis creation story may relate to the different ''worlds'' of cultural expression in our own day. In this perspective, it should be admitted not only that it is possible that Christians of different ''cultures'' may have something to learn from each other—and that those in the most ''advanced'' cultures may have the most to learn—but also that it is possible that cultures with a vision of reality founded in religions other than Christianity may be able to provide us with a fresh awareness of authentically biblical orientation. For the churches worldwide, this might strengthen critical self-awareness and ecumenical fellowship and lead to us meditating on this theme together in order to discover its bearing on mutual rapprochement as well as on joint witness vis-à-vis non-Christian environments.

3

Creation
and the integration of ethics

What is brought to the fore in this chapter relates principally to observations made in connection with the "inductive phase" of the Strasbourg study. The Institute plans to publish additional findings pertaining to a selection of the most controversial issues observed in the research as a separate volume and outside the framework of the creation project as such. What is offered here and now are brief comments on some basic aspects of these observations as they may relate to the ecumenical implications of creation theology.[1]

3.1 Fixing the position

The original concept of the Strasbourg creation project having two distinctly different phases—the one "inductive," the other "deductive"—to be dialecti-

---

[1]For additional information and observations, see Mark Ellingsen, "Observations on Creation and Ethics: A Summary" in "Creation—An Ecumenical Challenge? Documentation from a Study by the Institute for Ecumenical Research," ed. Per Lønning, *LWF Documentation* no. 27 (October 1989). Also issuing from the Strasbourg creation project, an observation of stands and motivations in different churches on a selected number of burning issues in contemporary social ethics, by Mark Ellingsen, is expected to be published by the World Council of Churches, Geneva, in 1990.

cally combined only toward the end of the total project had to be considerably modified in the course of the study.

First, although the *consultation program* was originally envisaged as a rather straightforward "deductive" procedure—to search for and examine the "practical" consequences of given theological principles—already the second major event (the consultation on "Tensions in a Contemporary Theology of Creation") began to rely heavily on an inductive method of operation. In order to make progress, this consultation had to make comprehensive observations about events and occurrences in contemporary church life and from there extrapolate more comprehensive patterns. The preconceived idea of "schools" and "trends" confronting one another was to a great extent complicated—and fruitfully so—by a joint endeavor to share and interpret common observations. Thus, to a not unimportant extent, this mutual confrontation was overshadowed by a shared confrontation with common problems. In this way, a constructive tension between deductive and inductive approaches already became palpable.

Later, a similar reorientation became apparent in the preparation of the consultation on "Creation and Culture," preparation in which there was close cooperation between the researchers responsible for each of the two envisaged "phases" of the project. In the "deductive" consultations, information lectures were included about progress in the "inductive" phase, and comments and advice were invited also on that part of the project. A cross-fertilization of the two "opposite" approaches was therefore more and more consistently sought and obtained at all the different stages of reflection.

A strong integrative factor was what could be referred to as the *Blochian challenge,* perhaps the most conspicuous expression of modern fear of and escape from creation.[2] Ernst Bloch's elaboration of the tension between creation and utopia—criticizing creation faith within a framework determined exclusively by social ethics of a neo-Marxist type—has gained a fairly universal role as a frame of reference for the contemporary theology of creation, positively as well as negatively. This even applies to proponents and opponents who are not too much aware of the particular historical source. A contemporary theology of creation is to a large extent determined by its affirmative or negative response to Bloch's main theses: that "creation" is basically a reactionary horizon of orientation, and "utopia" a progressive one. The extent to which the "deductive" and the "inductive" approach had to be concerned with this perspective—the one exploring how identical attitudes can *derive from* different premises and different attitudes to identical prem-

---

[2]See the presentation of Ernst Bloch's challenge to biblical creation faith, p. 15 in this volume, and Bloch in the name index.

ises; the other exploring how different premises can *lead to* identical attitudes and identical premises to different attitudes—is frequently seen in contemporary church life. Here, the reciprocal gravitation of the two problematics gradually became obvious. It thus would have been both artificial and sterile to adhere to some pattern of durable apartheid and postpone the reunification of these two "phases" to the conclusion of the project.

But even if of lesser methodological consequence than originally foreseen, the distinction remained useful, not least in order to establish some *heuristic points of departure* for the research. It remained practical to keep the comprehensive work of gathering and analyzing church statements and the main responsibilities for the consultation program as two procedurally separate tasks. It was also good for the two main working partners to be reminded of the interaction of these two basic aspects through this practical division of responsibilities. Against this background it may be stated with confidence that the input of the "inductive" operation is by no means to be found exclusively in the present chapter: It can be sought and perceived all the way through this study.

3.2 Creation and redemption in competition?

The following observation could have been made with little complex research: Contemporary stands by Christian churches on social issues are motivated *in some cases* by explicit or implicit *references to God the Creator* and to the universality of the Creator's design as obligatory to all; *in other cases*—by far the most numerous—they are motivated by *references to redemption* as a particular divine action within history, obligatory—at least at first glance—only to that selected portion of humankind who, individually or corporately, has become involved with that (salvation) history. The theological weakness of the first orientation is that it tends to see that Christians are no more concerned than the rest of humankind in general; the weakness of the second is that it tends to see that ethical imperatives are reserved exclusively for Christians, for it indicates no reason for concern on the part of people who are unfamiliar with the biblical *Heilsgeschichte*. Correspondingly, both have their merits: *the one* underlines the Creator's design as a pattern that is obligatory to all humankind (and all creation) and, to some extent, even operative in all, be they conscious of it or not; *the other* highlights the motivating force of the Christ event and thus reminds Christians that their focal commitment is faithfulness to Christ. The competitive as well as the constructive tension of these two orientations is bound to keep appearing in a study on the ecumenical implications of Christian creation faith today.

The first question relating to this observation must be to what extent the *alternation between creation and redemption motivations* follows some discernible pattern. Could they be said to relate to each other in some reflected way and thus serve different, complementary functions within one major, unified pattern of theological reflection? Could they eventually be observed as relating to different topics, perhaps to different kinds of clusters of topics? Or could they rather be understood as being characteristic of churches in different circumstances; confessionally, ideologically, politically, or otherwise?

It would seem that the material collected in the "inductive" study provides *no support for* embracing any one of these possibilities as *an overall explanation*—although none of the possibilities would be totally lacking in support. Here, therefore, there is no reason to discuss any one of them more thoroughly than any of the others. Obviously, the preference in any document for either creation or redemption arguments in general hardly reflects any ad hoc choice and still less any explicit reference to a reflected doctrine that assigns precise roles to "creation" and "redemption" as ethical motivations. The theological pattern to be discerned in an ethical proclamation frequently seems to be what, for more pragmatic reasons, has presented itself to the mind of the person or group involved. In cases where a plea is directed to some identifiable addressee, there may sometimes be indications that such an argument was chosen because it would most readily appeal to that person or constituency (*argumentum ad hominem*). In cases where there is minimal hope that a plea will be successful, arguments may be chosen to appeal to a wider audience, which, in the long run, could exercise pressure on the formal addressee. In theological and ecumenical terms, this somewhat diffuse picture supports the theory that the ecumenical movement and the individual churches have expended little effort in exploring the general significance of creation (versus redemption) theology for Christian ethics, and that the widespread unreflected appeal to redemption arguments somehow supports our general observations concerning the *Schöpfungsvergessenheit* in modern theology.

However, the fact remains that the overall picture reflects neither a general absence of creation arguments nor a totally arbitrary pattern concerning their use. Ecumenically, the two most interesting questions pertain, on the one hand, to confessional allegiance and, on the other, to "political" (sociocultural) orientation in the wider sense.

We will return to the question of *confessional trends and directions* in creation theology in greater detail in the final section of our research (§5. Creation and confessional divisions).

At this point, more comprehensive attention should be paid to the "political" dimension of our quest. The common assumption—strongly reinforced by Bloch and his successors in various "liberation" and "political" theologies—that there is a link between *creation* commitment and *conservative* social attitudes and between *redemption* commitment and *progressive* social attitudes can, of course, be interpreted in two ways: *either* that some people/churches tend to become conservative (or progressive) because they feel committed to creation theologies (or redemption theologies); *or* that some people/churches embrace creation theologies (or redemption theologies) because they are at heart conservative (or progressive). Even if it goes without saying that in the world of practical realities this choice can hardly be regarded as a simple either/or, it may be useful to keep the distinction in mind.

One major problem is that it is too easy for terms like ''conservative'' and ''progressive'' (or reactionary/radical, establishment/liberal, etc.) to become sloganized. This has to do not only with their adaptation to accustomed patterns of confrontation but also with the perplexing contradictions of our contemporary world. Developments that are characteristic of our highly technological society tend to reassert themselves in such a way that liberal (or rather liberalistic) trends may function as highly reactionary adaptations of fixed patterns, undergirding all hopes for a change of direction. And a conscious struggle for the preservation of inherited social structures can in many ways be seen as a ''utopian'' option for a ''new'' world that is in resolute opposition to ''established'' trends of development. A simplistic identification of conservatism and laissez-faire or progress and change becomes totally inadequate.

In theological ethics it has for some time been possible to discern *a certain polarization* between two lists of concerns, the one generally affiliated with ''conservative '' stands (theologically and often also politically), the other with ''progressive'' stands. On the first list we see such concerns as family life, ''old'' standards of sexual ethics, a rejection of induced abortion, an emphasis on accepted ideals for individual conduct, an affirmation of order and discipline in society at large, and charity as an appeal to individual conscience. On the second list we find the battle against such establishment-anchored evils as ''classism, racism, sexism,'' rearmament, ecological destruction, and economic exploitation. In the *oikumene* of today, it is clear that the two lists cannot be artificially separated, that there is a growing tendency for concerns from the two lists to meet and combine. But even if this historically conditioned clash of orientations has been diminished in some sections of Christendom, it still seems to persist in wide segments of Christendom and can hardly be overlooked. The material at hand does not indicate that one of these lists should be considered to be more creation-oriented or redemption-oriented than the other. And a quick reflection would suggest the inadequacy of seeing the ecological concern[3] as being less creation-related than, say,

---

[3]In the West, this is usually considered a ''leftist'' concern, but in the most literal sense of the word it is definitely ''conservative.''

sexual ethics, or seeing individual charity as being less redemption-oriented than, for example, the struggle against economic exploitation. Even though the material collected under the "inductive" phase does suggest a slight preponderance of creation arguments in favor of "conservative" positions, the bias is insufficient to support the general hypothesis of Bloch and his followers.

Later, in an excursus on "The theological foundation of 'human rights' " (§4.3), we shall pay attention to the striking fact that the concept of "human rights" emerged under the auspices of a dominant "creation theology." Even though the 18th-century founding of ethical obligation in a universal idea of a "Supreme Being" may be somewhat deficient when judged against the standards of a First Article faith in the Creator, its structural recourse to some vision of a perennial universal principle definitely falls on the side of creation faith over against any "liberation" reference to "merely" historically given impulses. In the Enlightenment vision of "human rights," creation definitely presides over liberation. And 18th-century creation thought questions historical data in the name of some timeless universal standard of righteousness that was once-and-for-all implanted in creation by its Maker. On the other hand, history, and particularly the "salvation history" of individual historical religions, is looked upon with suspicion in that it possibly (or most certainly) differs from that standard. This observation turns Bloch's vision upside down: Historical patterns of world formation—not universal creation—are attacked as legitimizations of present oppression, and their "utopian" promises are reduced to illusionary distractions; on the other hand, the unchangeable principles of creation become the revolutionary force, and its conviction of "natural rights" challenges all "positive" realizations in their given imperfection.

This observation by no means teaches us that Bloch's construction should be replaced by an opposing construction that proclaims creation as the "progressive" principle and redemption as the "reactionary" principle. But it does teach us that the whole question is a good deal more complex than is allowed for by such unilateral constructions. This corresponds with the complexity of our present observations and also with the dynamics of a relevant logic. It is obvious that in the concept of "creation," invoked as an ethical principle, there is an immediate ambiguity, as there is also in the concept of "salvation history."

This may most easily be demonstrated in connection with Bloch's counterpoint regarding the two biblical "beholds": the "behold, it was very good" of Genesis 1:31; and the "behold, I make all things new" of Revelation 21:5.[4] If the

---

[4]Ernst Bloch, *Atheism in Christianity: The Religion of the Exodus and the Kingdom,* trans. J.T. Swann (New York, 1972). Original: *Atheismus im Christentum* (Frankfurt: Suhrkamp, 1968) 59-64.

former speaks of our contemporary world as it presents itself, our basic ethical obligation must be to keep this world unchanged. So far, Bloch's criticism would be correct. But it is not even necessary to interpolate a doctrine of the Fall in order to make a different—and logically just as valid—statement: Since our world of today is obviously not "very good," it cannot be identical with the world of the Creator's making. Thus it does not deserve to be maintained as though it were the Creator's making but should be critically questioned on the basis of the image of the Creator and his purpose, as spelled out in the same Genesis text. Similarly, the Revelation statement has an ethically transformatory effect in as far as it is understood as "open," as historically unfilled, and thus calls into question any data that could possibly serve as protection against the all-embracing claims of God the Renewer. But the contrary is the case if it is taken to announce some divine action of yesterday—or some established idea of yesterday that announces some once-and-for-all stipulated act of tomorrow—which might grant the Christian community some guarantee of being once-and-for-all the only "chosen people" of God. When some "elect people" proceed in history as the authoritative agent of divine renewal, concepts like "redemption" or "liberation" can be changed into dreadful vehicles of oppression. Examples from the past (and maybe even from the present) are too notorious to require documentation. The historical dialectic of "liberation movements" ending up as triumphant oppressors applies not least to the history of religions and of the churches.

3.3 Ontological assumptions behind?

If, therefore, apparently similar patterns of theological reflection may lead to different ethical stances and if different theological patterns may lead to similar stances, what follows with regard to *theological reflection and ethical decision making*? A pragmatist, to whom ethical decision is everything, might conclude that theology is not of much importance since, according to our best observations, it is not what governs human actions. On the other hand, a strict theologian might conclude that ethics are only of relative importance: no ethical stance or lack of stance per se could be the object of a "status confessionis." Both might be easily convinced of the necessity for a different research: If theology does not decide on ethics, then what does? Could it, for example, be ontological assumptions that are more or less independent of theological control?

The fact that the ambiguity of unspecified creation or redemption references frequently occurs in everyday church argumentation suggests that the indicated relativization of theology as such is by no means the necessary conclusion. When people derive different ethical consequences from what they see as a Christian understanding of creation, it is not necessarily because they draw different conclusions from common principles; it could just as well be different principles under cover of a common language. And the same applies, of course, to discussion on redemption/liberation. In speaking of "creation," one may be referring to the contemporary world as it really is (or rather to what one sees as apparently constitutive strains of it); but one may just as well be referring to some normative, primordial state of affairs, prior to all observable actuality. In the first instance, the consequence would be a principle plea for preservation; in the second, a nonetheless eager plea for transformation. But this does not mean that different conclusions are drawn from similar premises; rather that different premises are present in the disguise of similar words. A familiar example of a corresponding confusion in redemption language is the frequently contradictory use in our world of today of terms like "liberation" and "freedom." Here, too, the basic differences in argumentation may be founded in philology rather than in ontology.

There is, however, good indication that in many cases some distinctive difference in *ontological orientation* may be "behind" and account for differences in philological preoccupations. In recent years, on their reflections on the *East/ West difference* in theological orientation, ecumenical observers have suggested that there is a deep-rooted confrontation in the style of Christian thinking. We shall return to this more comprehensively in our discussion on the various confessional contributions to creation theology, and particularly in the presentation on the Orthodox legacy (§5.1). What is being suggested here is not merely a different image of the world, but an entirely different way of looking at "reality": less analytical-objectifying, more synthetical-integrative. It may even be somewhat inadequate to review Orthodoxy within a framework of Western (and ecumenical) "competition" between creation and redemption, for Eastern theology invites us to see creation as the first event in—and the structural framework for—a successive series of salvation events.

Even if the old Eastern orientation can by no means be immediately identified with modern Western *process thought*—from which it neatly separates itself through its uncompromised distinction between uncreated and created being and, consequently, through its emphasis on divine being as unchangeable even in its relatedness to the ever-changing process of created life—one could say that it "goes in the same direction," in that it visualizes the created world as *becoming* rather than as *being* and sees single events and phenomena as basically revelatory manifestations of the underlying all-determining mystery. In this perspective, the basic Orthodox reluctance regarding definitions and precise formulae should not be seen as an expression of epistemological indifference but rather of a conscious ontological orientation. As far as ethical argument is concerned, this orientation is bound to lead away from a series of unchangeable "natural" directives and toward a more unifying and conceptually less rigid principle that—thanks to the mediating vision of the cosmic Christ—will favor an integrated creation/redemption approach. To what extent this observation may be useful ecumenically will be discussed in the last section of our research (§5. Creation and confessional divisions).

At the present stage of our reflection, it may be meaningful to add a few observations on the *ethical contribution of process thought,* since that is probably the most consistent contemporary expression of a "relational" orientation—not only as it may be sensed in the traditional (now also undeniably modern) legacy of Orthodoxy, but also as it has been identified by Mark Ellingsen in a good many contemporary church statements that consciously exercise ethical discernment as derived from some comprehensive model of social integration. As opposed to the deontologizing actualism of "situation ethics"—the younger partner of what was known one generation ago as "existential theology"—the ecologically inspired trend of today favors the *widest possible consideration of environmental integrity* as the basis for ethical decisions. More instructively than perhaps any other document of recent years, the joint work of the biologist Charles Birch and the theologian John B. Cobb, Jr. in its section "An Ethic of Life"[5] gives a clear example of what a consistently modeled relational ethic might look like. In a critical comment in *Dialog*[6] I tried to discern the merits (in terms of increased ecological sensitivity) as well as the weaknesses of such an approach, that is, how can a consistent relationally defined ethic avoid becoming relativ(e)istic?

Most relational-ethical approaches made by the churches in recent years seem to move within a framework of a social—and not, as in the case of Birch and Cobb, of an ecological—frame of reference (with the exception of statements dealing precisely with environmental issues). For good reasons, statements of a practical nature usually leave very little room for reflection on principles. Models of argument are being used, not being forged or questioned. But as to a *relational orientation* as such, there is little difference in principle between a *social* and an *ecological* frame of reference. As in the work of Birch and Cobb, social relations can easily be seen as one integral part of the global ecological issue of "life."[7] However, an ethical decision must be understood predominantly in terms of de-

---

[5]Charles Birch and John B. Cobb, Jr., *The Liberation of Life: From the Cell to the Community* (Cambridge: Cambridge University Press, 1981) 141-75.

[6]Per Lønning, "Process Theology and the Ethic of Life," *Dialog* 23 (Autumn 1984): 300-306.

[7]As is more explicitly elaborated in John B. Cobb's *Process Theology as Political Theology* (Manchester: Manchester University Press; Philadelphia: Westminster Press, 1982).

liberation, balance, and compromise. The ultimate value of "life," understood ecologically, is derived from factual observation of the interplay of live organisms and their environment in the widest sense. The result of such an observation claiming ethical normativity can only be a (somewhat modified) neo-Darwinian model of coinciding and conflicting interests, whereby no single concern is ever allowed to come through as being ultimately binding and any plea of obedience to an unapproachable "voice of God" has to be toned down.

What this means may be seen most concretely through reflections on the beginning and the end of life, and specifically on the themes of *abortion* and *euthanasia*. In both cases, similar solutions are offered: No single individual has the right to decide about life and death, whether it concerns an unborn child or a dying person in a situation of hopeless distress. Where such a right exists, it resides with the widest possible fellowship of concerned persons: family, doctor(s), close friends.[8] What this type of ethical reflection is ready to provide are not standards of ethical decision but a procedure for the ethical balancing of conflicting subjective interests. But are ethics not more comprehensive and profound than that?

This ecological model for the settling of ethical conflicts gives a rather instructive paradigm of the dilemma facing an ethic that makes a "relational" integration of concerns its fundamental concern. When standards of human conduct are defined as being predominantly relational and having no substantial weight of their own, what is at stake is above all the vision of individual human worth as being equal, incomparable, and correspondingly inviolable.

> If the locus of the intrinsic value of the human is in human experiences, and if these vary from persons to persons, then it seems clear that in fact there are differences of individual worth. . . . There is no substantial reason to believe that all persons have equal intrinsic value. . . .

> The rejection of anthropocentrism entails the rejection of absolutist arguments for human rights. Human beings, like all other living things, are both ends and means. . . . Human rights . . . should be worked out without the appeal to absolutes which have led to distortion and inconsistencies in the past.[9]

It is easy to see the correspondence between a relational view of ethics and a relational ontology in general (defining reality as basically being participation in some universal interrelatedness) but also between a relational view of ethics and

---

[8]*The Liberation of Life* (see n. 5) 167-68.

[9]Ibid., 164 and 175.

a *relational orientation of faith* (and thus of dogmatics) in general, understanding God as being essentially defined by his relationship with creature.[10]

An eloquent example of how an ethic and a dogmatic of ontological interrelatedness fit together is to be found in Dorothee Sölle's *To Work and to Love: A Theology of Creation*.[11] If the Creator is understood as being essentially delimited and qualified by some mutual interrelatedness with creature, it is only reasonable that a creature, like the Creator, should have its essence and dignity not as an "I" in face of a constitutive "thou" but as part of a global ecological interplay. In general, human value and normative ethical values have no essence in themselves; being and individual beings have no such essence; and there is essentially no author of being. Everything more or less takes its essence and its worth from its belonging-together-with-everything-else. In the long run, universal one-level relatedness cannot but turn into universal relativity, the overt inhumanity of which can be interrupted—and sometimes passionately so—only by emotionally motivated involvement. There is no vision of persistent values founded in a universal structure of once-and-for-all (creation) established meaning.

That patterns of reflection on creation and redemption can take us in seemingly opposite directions of ethical orientation must not lead us to jump to the conclusion that dogmatics is irrelevant to ethics, or vice versa; nor must it lead us to infer that one of the two is ecumenically relevant and the other ecumenically irrelevant. As we have seen, the impression that opposite consequences derive from one principle can be due to confusion in the use of language, not least in connection with a plurivocal use of the word "creation." It can also be due to a different ontological framework. Here, some correspondence can be observed between the basic distinction of process theology (*becoming* prior to *being*) and that of certain trends in contemporary theological ethics (judging some pattern of relational integration prior to concrete ethical obligations). However, this observation by no means authorizes the conclusion that, as ontologically founded, ethical disagreements cannot be "theological." *Ontology and theology interrelate in both directions*. The way we think about God as the author of reality necessarily involves an interpretation of, and thus some structural assumptions about, what "reality" is. And notions about God—as all other intellectual concepts—cannot but reflect the image of "reality" that makes up the foundation of our conceptuality in general.

---

[10]See the discussion in this volume on "What is creation?" (§4.1).

[11]1984. Discussed below, §4.1.

3.4 Can ethical disagreement be church dividing?

These observations bring us to the last—but certainly not least important—question in the present context: Can ethical disagreement be church dividing? The ties we have observed between dogmatics, ontology, and ethics should essentially imply that if dogmatics can be church dividing (not only de facto but also de jure), then so also can ethics. (It is probably not necessary to add "and so can ontology"; it would suffice to say "and so can ontologically related aspects of dogmatics and ethics.")

It is clear that there can be no clear border line dividing any one of these three "provinces" from any one of the others. We are not talking about a division of topic, but about a division of orientation. In any case, ontology is basically something that Christians share with all people. We live in the same perceptible world, and we observe and interpret it by means of common intellectual categories. The *interaction between ontology and theology* is certainly undeniable, but it should not be thought of as mechanical. In the vision of faith, any given supposition about world, reality, and being will be reexamined and reinterpreted in the light of divine self-disclosure, and any interpretation of that disclosure has to legitimize itself in critical confrontation with what is discerned by us as "reality" at large. Liberal theologies are sometimes negligent with regard to the former; and conservative theologies may be negligent with regard to the latter.

It is also obvious that in the Bible it would be meaningless to introduce a mechanical *separation between dogmatical and ethical insight.* Relationship with God and relationship with human beings (and with God's creation as a whole) are organically interrelated, and at the same time the distinction between Creator and creation remains uncompromised. Distinguishing between faith and works and between law and gospel does not mean that in Christian life one "pole" can function without the other "pole." We are not talking here about, say, living in Norway and having little concern about Sweden, the two countries being undeniably distinctive parts of the Scandinavian peninsula. There is a dynamic interaction that constitutes dogmatics and ethics as disciplines with no clear division of "matter," even though, in principle, the distinction in orientation should be clear enough. When ethics are taken as a common human responsibility, shared by non-Christians and Christians alike,[12] it is clear that the gospel of forgiveness in Christ makes no sense if seen in splendid isolation from its constitutive relationship with "the ethical demand." It is also clear that Christian faith confirms human encounter and integrates it in as comprehensive a vision as possible of conscienticized mo-

---

[12]As is most typically reflected in the Danish Løgstrup school, see below, §4.2.

tivation. The meaning behind the Grundtvigian "First be a human, a Christian next"[13] is not the isolation of common human identity from Christian faith but the proclamation of an intrinsic interrelatedness in dialectical distinction. Christians hold no monopoly over being authentically human or behaving genuinely ethically. But, on the other hand, one does not grasp the essential meaning of Christianity as long as the human challenge of ethical encounter is not taken seriously. And the universal meaning of true humanity is ultimately confirmed and transfigured in the gospel. This being so, it is obvious that a perverted understanding (and/or a perverted practice) of fellow humanity could be as destructive to Christian identity as any dogmatical heresy. Therefore: *Ethics can only be understood as ethics if we admit the possibility of church divisions as a searching challenge.* But in social ethics we are concerned with church divisions that are basically "more" than that, namely, that are disturbances of elementary human relationships, disturbances that are bound to cause division and confusion already on the level of fellow humanity. In this perspective it becomes clear that—and why—theological divisions eventually interrelate with political divisions. But, at the same time, this should teach us to exercise a certain amount of caution in "theologizing" social and political tensions, for it points a) to the general difficulty (as well as the eventual historical necessity) in identifying particular "political" stands[14] as an unambiguous expression of certain basic human or inhuman attitudes—and thereby unequivocally qualifying them as "evil" or "good"—and b) to the danger in authorizing particular programs in such as way as to proclaim "salvation by works."

However these considerations are not those that generally motivate the assertions so frequently expressed or implied in contemporary ecumenical debate about the church divisiveness of certain ethical stands. Where such assertions have been most frequently heard—even: where they emerged—has been in the debate on the racial issue: The official statement of the Dar es Salaam Assembly of the Lutheran World Federation (1977) on the situation in South Africa was the first to apply the classical notion of a *status confessionis* to this conflict, though its reflection on the theological implications of that stance was somewhat limited.[15]

Apparently the widespread ecumenical conviction—which has become more and more pronounced in recent years—that socioethical stands can be as critical

---

[13]See below, §4.2.

[14]The word "stand" is used in the widest possible sense, i.e., indicating allegiance to some programmatical pattern of joint human action.

[15]*In Christ—A New Community.* The Proceedings of the Sixth Assembly of the Lutheran World Federation, Dar es Salaam, Tanzania, June 13-25, 1977, ed. Arne Sovik (Geneva: The Lutheran World Federation, 1977) 179-80.

to church unity as traditional dogmatical questions, and that "confession" in an ecclesiological sense relates to praxis as much as to doctrine, is generally founded in an integrated vision of faith and faithfulness that is rooted not so much in a reflected dialectical interplay of creation and redemption (as sketched above) as in a unifying Christological vision that sees Christ simultaneously as our hope of salvation (by faith) and as the pattern for human solidarity (by imitation). If these two Christ-centered aspects have become so organically related that no practical split between them is possible, then it is obvious that the one dimension becomes as crucial to church unity as the other. "Orthopraxy" matters no less than "orthodoxy."

Again, the practical consequences of this Second Article approach will not necessarily be distinguishable from those of combined reflection on the First and Second Articles. In fact, on the contemporary scene, this seems to provide stronger support for the integration of confession and ethics, but—as is generally the case with Christocentric ethical models—it also seems to be lacking in universal appeal. That such an observation seems to have had little affect on the ecumenical discussion on racism might be related to the fact that in the geographical regions where the racist issue is most heated (South Africa, earlier also in the USA) the dominant influence of Christianity is taken to be so universal that appeal to purely Christian standards would have sufficient argumentative weight in the society as a whole. At the same time it is true that in the last generation arguments in favor of racial discrimination have been more inclined to seek their base in creation-related considerations about the role of distinctive cultural identities than in *heilsgeschichtlich* considerations about the rights of some "chosen people." Consequently, this style of argument calls for a thorough examination of such a creation presupposition. Even if a *status confessionis* in the domain of racial inequality should and could be proclaimed in the name of Christology as well as of creation theology, it should be obvious that such a claim lacks dimension if it is made without substantial reference to creation reflection.

As we shall see later in concluding our dealings with the creation commitments of the various denominations and confessional traditions, in today's world it is not possible to make a general declaration that creation theology is church divisive: Its bearing on innerchurch tensions seems far more critical than its bearing on interchurch confrontations. But at the same time it is impossible to imagine any deep-rooted doctrinal division in which divergences in creation theology do not play some sort of a role. And when social ethics are consciously drawn into the picture, this discovery may impose itself even more emphatically. With the possibly church-dividing implications of ethics, the ecumenical relevance of creation theology confirms itself in a particularly impressive manner.

At the same time, however, it should also be observed that the ethical patterns widely judged to be church dividing in today's world (predominantly that of racism) do not follow traditional confessional patterns in any strict sense; rather, they are founded in historicocultural patterns and seek their theological legitimation in arguments from various confessional traditions.

It is not the task of the present study to argue in favor of concrete ethical stances, nor to champion particular doctrinal positions. On the basis of the material collected during the "inductive phase" of the Strasbourg study, our task in considering the integration of ethics in an ecumenical creation perspective has been to observe the interaction of creation and redemption models in present Christian social thought. The bearing of these considerations will come more clearly to the fore in the following discussion on the general ecumenical importance of contemporary creation theology and, finally, on the historical and contemporary creation presentations of the main confessional families.

4

Creation—Actual
theological confrontations

The issues to be reviewed here are generally connected with the 1984 Klingenthal consultation, the main orientations of which have already been reported in the July 1985 issue of *The Ecumenical Review*. The questions emerging from that event were not explicitly formulated by the consultation itself but were the result of a subsequent analysis by the Institute for Ecumenical Research and were communicated to the participants for possible comments and corrections. The five clusters of issues that emerged will be dealt with in this section. For the sake of a somewhat systematically unified approach, it seems best to present the questions in a thematically structured order, even if this may to some extent obscure their indebtedness to that highly thought-provoking consultation.

4.1 What is "creation"?

A once-and-for-all given? A *telos* under realization? Or a unifying framework for ethical orientation? To what extent may differing answers to this question contribute to current theological and ecclesiological divisions?

The old theological distinction between "creation" and divine "governance" or "sustenance" is generally regarded as obsolete. And for several reasons a neat distinction between what God the Creator was doing "in the beginning" and what he is doing today seems to be more bewildering than illuminating. It was not first and foremost the encounter with contemporary evolutionary thinking that effected this reorientation in theology; it may be traced back at least as far as Friedrich Schleiermacher's dealing with creation and sustenance as complementary expressions of God's present relationship with the world, reflected by our religious self-consciousness.[1] In the Schleiermacher/Ritschl/Barth tradition, the rejection of a metaphysical approach to theology has its correlate in the rejection of "cosmogonic" and "cosmological" orientations in the doctrine of creation, and it finds positive expression as the proclamation of some holistic, integrative, Christocentric world-relatedness of faith *hic et nunc*. In the more politically oriented continuation of this tradition during the last 20 years (various brands of "liberation theology"), it has become increasingly clear that fear of creational givenness has deep (perhaps the deepest) roots in resistance to the idea of a "creation order" as a legitimization of given social, cultural, and political structures. If creation could or should be viewed as something (however relatively) created, the danger is that attention could be linked to a static pattern of *Schöpfungsordnungen* (orders of creation), which authorizes certain transmitted societal givens as being identical with "the Creator's will." Such a procedure is abundantly documented in the history of Christianity as well as of established religion in general. And it shows that a statically imagined order of creation can easily be used to support vested—feudal or capitalist—interests.

Such critical observations are commonplace today and should certainly not be questioned. However, what is far less observed is the historical role of an opposite trend in Western thought. What was the 18th-century discovery of "human rights" but an emphasis on creation-based principles over against the contingency of mere historical actuality? The history of the concepts of "natural right" and (derived from that) "human rights" demonstrates that the idea of creation as an inviolable, once-and-for-all givenness can be used for a radical questioning of existing social patterns in the name of a normative *principium* (in the basic meaning of "origin" as well as in the derived idea of "principle") just as readily as for a static defense of what is factually and actually there. It is also remarkable that the environmental awakening in contemporary theology has not dared to expose more directly the most elementary presupposition of its own argument, that is, that without some constants of creational identity, and thus of normative sustainability, it may be hard to argue consistently in favor of ecological responsibility.

---

[1]Friedrich Schleiermacher, *The Christian Faith,* ed. H. R. Mackintosh and J.S. Stewart (Edinburgh: T. & T. Clark, 1928) §§36-49. Original: *Der christliche Glaube* (Reutlingen, 1828).

It thus looks as if the notion (so widespread today) of an "ongoing" creation may at least need some dialectical clarification. The three answers[2] to the question suggested in the above heading ("What is creation?") can be interpreted in ways that make them mutually exclusive. But it is also possible to modify them in different ways and to imagine various patterns of coordination. Creation, as the event "before" and constitutive of all other events, can certainly also be seen as projecting itself into *all* events and/or as being reflected in a specific way in events that speak more explicitly to the wonder of "coming into being." Viewed as the Creator's ongoing approximation of his work toward its *telos,* creation does not say

---

[2]A much stricter designation of three distinctive types of creation theology is given in Wenzel Lohff, "Thesen zur Systematik einer Studie über die Schöpfung," *Schöpfungsglaube und Umweltverantwortung: Eine Studie des Theologischen Ausschusses der VELKD,* ed. Wenzel Lohff and Hans Christian Knuth (Hanover: Lutherisches Verlagshaus, 1985) 146-55: "Der *traditionelle (ontologische) Schöpfungsbegriff* . . . objektiviert Schöpfung zum Anfangsgeschehen der Erstellung des Weltheilraums. Schöpfung wird supranaturale Kosmologie. Die *existenz-analytische Schöpfungslehre* deutet Schöpfung als symbolischen Ausdruck für die Grundsituation menschlichen Daseins . . . verliert aber die Geschichtsbezogenheit des biblischen Schöpfungsbekenntnisses leicht aus dem Blick. Ausgehend von der traditionsgeschichtlichen Beobachtung, dass im Alten Testament der Schöpfungsglaube im Heilsglauben begründet ist, versteht *heilsgeschichtliche Schöpfungslehre* (Barth) Schöpfung als Ätiologie des Bundes. . . . Alle drei Schöpfungsbegriffe können anknüpfen an bestimmte *Voraussetzungen in biblischer Überlieferung.*" Although he does not explicitly say so, Lohff is clearly not ready to adopt one of the three in order to despatch the others; rather he seeks some dialectical synthesis.

His scheme may be useful as an observation of certain general lines of orientation but hardly as the global model that it pretends to be. The *existential-analytical* concept may today be discernible not as a particular school but as a particular emphasis within other, more comprehensive, orientations. It is therefore a good deal easier to identify the Barthian *Heilsgeschichte* approach at work as a determining direction. However, the major difficulty is to identify a "traditional (ontological) concept of creation" as "supernatural cosmogony." A powerful tradition—from medieval Scholasticism to contemporary "creationism"— probably deserves to be presented in similar terms. But would that include all brands of creation theologies that—taking distance from the narrowness of "existential" and *Heilsgeschichte* approaches—emphasize creation as a global givenness prior to both human self-understanding and ecclesial self-definition? Where does, for example, contemporary process theology fit into the scheme? And Pannenberg and the whole neo-Hegelian trend? And the Nordic Grundtvigian tradition (see here, §4.2)? In the context of a survey, is it perhaps better to stick to a looser classification and let single presentations speak for themselves?

everything that could be said about the bringing into existence of what formerly was not. In any case, there has to be some ontological distinction between primordial creation and continued creation.

Where do these observations take us with regard to ecumenism? As we shall soon see, the more or less explicit divergences on what we could call the "tense of creation" are deep-rooted and loaded with a great deal of consequence. However, it is difficult to see them as the immediate reflection of some traditional pattern of church division. Taken together, these two observations may make a more viable avenue for those who want to inspect the entanglement of theology and church division in our contemporary world.

Generally speaking, one could say that the traditional "cosmological" approach to creation—with an accent on creation as the basis of ethical "givens"— was more or less common ecumenical property up to the early 19th century. It existed in the Roman Catholic theology of nature, in the Lutheran idea of God's "kingdom to the left," and in the classical Calvinist predestinarian model of thinking as well as in the usually biblicist hermeneutic of the various Free church traditions. The general reorientation that Friedrich Schleiermacher started in Protestant theology began to reach the Roman Catholic Church at the start of the 20th century in the days of "modernism." Following an authoritarian suppression of this movement, a similar orientation succeeded in establishing a foothold in Roman Catholic theology around the middle of the present century.

In the present context, the most interesting question is as follows: To what extent has the idea of creation as an ongoing present event (and this may also imply a "timeless" process) succeeded in conquering the scene; to what extent is this leading to a rejection of traditional "metaphysical" approaches to creation; and to what extent is such an advance representative of present-day theology as a whole? It might be useful to take a quick look at two creation theologies of recent years, both of which—to different degrees and on somewhat differing premises— advocate the so-called "mainline" orientation, that is, that of Jürgen Moltmann and Dorothee Sölle. Afterwards, it may be meaningful to take a quick look at contemporary process theology's preoccupation with creation, because in the present ecumenical setup there is no doubt that this is the most consistent, the best coordinated, and the most extensive-expansive movement with regard to creation theology.

In order to understand the historical dynamics of Jürgen Moltmann's *God in Creation*,[3] it is particularly important to recall its location not only within the five-

---

[3]Jürgen Moltmann, *God in Creation: An Ecological Doctrine of Creation*, trans. Margaret Koch (London: SCM Press, 1985). (Original: *Gott in der Schöp-*

volume *Messianic Theology* that the author is in the process of publishing but also in all his work from his 1965 *Die Theologie der Hoffnung*[4] onward. Even if Moltmann has moved a long way from his starting point(s), there is also an undeniable continuity in his writing. His starting points—which from the outset gave his writings the fascinating dialectical tension between an unmistakable biblical *Heilsgeschichte* approach and a politically utopian-oriented concept of "hope"—implied a Barthian rejection of natural theology as well as a Bloch-inspired protest against creation as a possible legitimation of the present. The utopian idea of "future" transcends the classical Barthian concept of eschatology and gives historical concreteness to Christian "hope" through an organic integration of a penultimate orientation that is open to immediate political relevance. Conversely, Bloch's "Christian atheism"—with its unconditional "no" to the "Behold, it was very good" being seen as inseparable from the very idea of creation[5]—is modified by Moltmann through his observation that Bloch's criticism (justified as it may be with regard to the dominant tendency in traditional Christian creation thinking) fails to refute creation in its true biblical sense. Creation—understood as being integrated in a universal history of salvation—confirms rather than contradicts the perspective of political "liberation."

In the preface to his *God in Creation,* Moltmann explains that the concept "ecological" refers not only to the present "ecological crisis" but also to the Greek notion of *oikos,* a house, the etymological root of "ecology." In this context, it is taken to refer to the world as the "house of God," that is, the "indwelling of the Triune God in his creation."[6]

The preface also underscores the ecumenical orientation of the whole project: the importance of drawing on Roman Catholic as well as Protestant sources and particularly of listening to the "creation wisdom" of Orthodox theology, presumably less touched by the modern cult of science, technology, and industrial effi-

---

fung: Ökologische Schöpfungslehre [Munich: Christian Kaiser Verlag, 1985]). Cf. the more comprehensive evaluation by the present author, "Die Schöpfungslehre J. Moltmanns: Eine nordische Perspektive," *Kerygma und Dogma* 33 (1987): 207-33.

[4]Jürgen Moltmann, *Theology of Hope: On the Ground and the Implications of a Christian Eschatology,* trans. James W. Leitch (London: SCM Press; New York: Harper & Row, 1967). Original: *Die Theologie der Hoffnung* (Munich: Christian Kaiser Verlag, 1965).

[5]Ernst Bloch, *Atheism in Christianity: The Religion of the Exodus and the Kingdom,* trans. J.T. Swann (New York, 1972). Original: *Atheismus im Christentum* (Frankfurt: Suhrkamp, 1968) 59-64.

[6]Jürgen Moltmann, *God in Creation* (see n. 3) xii (German: 12).

ciency than the Western traditions. Particular attention is also given to the importance of Jewish orientation, especially the idea of the "Sabbath," the "Zimsum" (God's self-limitation), and the "Shekinah" (God's indwelling).[7] Thus the "ecumenical method" should be open for the "secular *oikumene,*" identified here as the sciences, technologies, and economics.[8]

Jürgen Moltmann develops eight "guiding ideas " for his creation theology:[9] 1. "Knowledge of nature as God's creation is participatory knowledge" and must get away from analytical thinking, with its distinctions between subject and object, in favor of a multidimensional "Messianic imagination." 2. "A Christian doctrine of creation is a view of the world in light of Jesus the Messiah," as a "home" directed toward the liberation of men and women, peace with nature, and the redemption of the community of human beings and nature from negative powers and from the forces of death. 3. "The sabbath is the true hallmark of every biblical doctrine of creation." The resting and celebrating God of the Sabbath should not be allowed to disappear behind his six days of creation, as has usually been the case in Christian theology. 4. The traditional dual schemes of "nature and supernature," "creation and redemption," etc., must be abandoned in favor of a plural dialectical and processual orientation: *Gratia . . . praeparat naturam ad gloriam aeternam.* 5. A Trinitarian understanding of creation will of necessity focus on the Spirit (the Hebrew *ruach,* as feminine) as the agent of divine action and thus as the constituent of a universal community of creation—a discovery that will restore a true ecological orientation to creation theology and effect the necessary epochal break with the age of subjectivity and mechanistic world dominion. 6. The distinction between God and world is bound to fade away and give place to the presence of God (his cosmic Spirit) *in* the world and of the world *in* God. This implies eliminating the causality approach in the theology of creation and introducing an immanent tension in God himself: his creating of the world immediately implies his entering into the world. 7. As is true of all relationships referring to God, God in the world and the world in God reflect the original reciprocal indwellings, including the mutual interpenetration of the Trinitarian *perichoresis.* 8. The word "Spirit" should be understood to designate the forms of organization and modes of communication in open systems: informed matter, living systems, different strata of living symbioses, human beings and human populations, the ecosystem "earth," the solar system, our Milky Way galaxy, and

---

[7]Ibid., xiii (13).

[8]Ibid., xiv (13).

[9]Ibid., 1-19 (16-33).

the whole complex of galaxies united in the universe. This instructs us to extend our human consciousness of "Spirit" to social, ecological, cosmic, and divine consciousness; and also to realize how the concepts of "God in creation" and "creation in the Spirit" help us to stop thinking of creation and evolution as opposing concepts, and instead to link them with one another as complements: "a creation of evolution, because evolution is not explicable simply in terms of itself" and "an evolution of creation, because the creation of the world has been so designed that it points in the direction of the kingdom of glory, and therefore transcends itself in time."

This design is certainly challenging and thought-provoking, but our immediate need is not for a critical assessment of Moltmann's model. What our project seeks first of all is the situation of the design in relation to traditional "ecumenical" theology. Such an observation will have to look for particularity as well as for trends that are recognizable in broader sections of contemporary orientation. This task cannot be solved by simply dividing up the eight "guiding ideas" into two categories: those that seem to be typical of a wider audience; and those that seem to be peculiar to Moltmann. All eight may to some extent be recognized as coming into both categories. The most rewarding approach may be to ask how Moltmann's theology of creation continues the "classical" Barthian *Heilsgeschichte* approach and how he eventually transcends or departs from it. Moltmann carries on the Barthian tradition in pursuing a Trinitarian "salvation history" approach to creation, with a definite emphasis on biblical orientation and with a definite rejection of any "natural theology" that is supported by some preconceived philosophical theory. At the same time and in several ways , "Messianic imagination" (his own expression!) makes possible a more open-ended and less exclusive orientation than that of his great predecessor. His emphatic Trinitarian orientation does not prevent him from arriving at a far-reaching identification of Jewish and Christian creation theology. But amazingly little attention is paid to the relationship with extrabiblical religions and their creation preoccupations. This latter observation may be all the more remarkable when one considers that he is at the same time concerned about establishing a wider "secular" ecumenism and about integrating dialogues with natural and social sciences. Judaism and science seem to be included in the extended perspective of *Heilsgeschichte*; philosophy and the "world of religion" are not. To what extent may this approach claim sufficient reflective coherence? In this regard, "classical" Barthianism may have had an easier task due to its more consistent programmatical "purity."

At the same time, the ecological integrative approach to creation/salvation, nature/grace, and future/glory seems to loosen up the transcendent orientation of original Barthian eschatology and to leave some open questions concerning the priority of penultimate vis-à-vis ultimate aims. This feature may be even more

conspicuous in Moltmann's preceding book *The Trinity and the Kingdom of God,*
in which the comprehensive use of the Holy Trinity as a model of social and political interrelatedness[10] may leave the reader in doubt as to the thematic priorities.
Does the Trinitarian vision shape politics, or do politics shape the Trinitarian
model?

With regard to our crucial question—to what extent "ongoing creation" may
have swallowed up creation as primordial event—Moltmann's position is unmistakably that of an "on-the-one-side-on-the-other." As he obviously intends to interrelate God the author of creation and God as visualized "in" creation, his
juxtaposition of "a creation of evolution" and "an evolution of creation" is clearly
more than an elegant play on words. And this can also be clearly distinguished
from his determined reservations about the undermining of the *creatio ex nihilo*
by Whitehead and process theology:

> If the idea of the *creatio ex nihilo* is excluded, or reduced to the forma-
> tion of a not-yet-actualized primordial matter, "no-thing," then the world
> process must be just as eternal and without any beginning as God him-
> self. But if it is eternal and without any beginning like God himself, the
> process must itself be one of God's natures. And in this case we have to
> talk about "the divinization of the world."[11]

In one and the same breath, a critical remark is directed toward Schleiermacher
allowing "God's creative relationship to the world to be . . . wholly absorbed by
. . . his relationship as its preserver":

> For if the creation of the world is reduced to God's general and present
> rule over that world, the world will once more cease to be a finite cre-
> ation, and will be turned into a world without a beginning, eternal as God
> is eternal.[12]

It is thus clear that Moltmann sees that creation is realized through evolution
as an ongoing event, at the same time as he resists having creation swallowed up
by that perspective. Through evolution, creation moves toward fulfillment, but at
the same time the *creatio ex nihilo* retains basic importance as the bringing into

---

[10]Jürgen Moltmann, *Trinity and the Kingdom of God: The Doctrine of God,*
trans. Margaret Kohl (London: SCM Press; New York: Harper & Row, 1981) ch.
6, "The Kingdom of Freedom." Original: *Trinität und Reich Gottes* (Munich:
Christian Kaiser Verlag, 1980).

[11]Jürgen Moltmann, *God in Creation* (see n. 3) 78 (German: 91).

[12]Ibid., 79 (92).

existence of the very potentialities of evolution. The coordination of these allegedly inseparable observations is expressed in an especially impressive manner in his doctrine of "heaven" as the created (Genesis 1:1) kingdom of God's creative potentialities.[13] This realm expresses "the openness of the world"[14] and assures us that "the continual making-possibilities-possible [*Ermöglichung von Möglichkeiten*] keeps the world in existence."[15]

In an Aristotelian-sounding vocabulary, Moltmann thus transcends the opposition to a static ("Platonic") concept of being and a universal philosophy of becoming ("process") by means of a—suggested but not developed—idea of existent "potentialities," theologically warranted through the concept of "heaven." This takes care of at least two urgent concerns: some preliminary integration of creation as a primordial event with creation/evolution as an ongoing development; and a meaningful integration of heaven (a concept so embarrassing to contemporary theology in general) into the vision of creation at large.[16]

Whether this courageous attempt at a coordination is successful or not will, above all, depend on two crucial terms (which, in this context, I take to be synonymous): the "making-possibilities-possible" (*Ermöglichung von Möglichkeiten*) and the "creation of evolution." In order to be assessed meaningfully, these terms may need some further clarification.

The *Ermöglichung von Möglichkeiten* may raise questions, in a purely semantic as well as in a theological context. In the first case, the idea of making possibilities possible is certainly intriguing. Is it also possible to make the possibilities of a possibility possible? It seems rather dubious whether the concept of possibility can be repeated as its own determinant without producing sheer tautologies. Besides, to talk of "making something possible" (something that up to now must have been "impossible") can hardly refer to some creation act *in abstracto*; it must envisage the concrete establishment of this or that condition (and, eventually, removal of this or that obstacle) as being essential to its implementation. In part, these observations apply also to "evolution" as a mere universal. It makes little sense to talk of the "creation of evolution"; one should rather talk of

---

[13]Ibid., 165 (172).

[14]Ibid., 163 (168).

[15]Ibid., 182 (190).

[16]A similar ontological (more than cosmological?) theory of "heaven" is developed by Moltmann's student Michael Welker in his *Universalität Gottes und Relativität der Welt: Theologische Kosmologie im Dialog mit dem amerikanischen Prozessdenken nach Whitehead* (Neukirchen-Vluyn: Neukirchener Verlag, 1986 [1981]).

producing such and such circumstances that open the way for evolution. Possibility never exists as an essence or entity per se: it is a relational term that signalizes the presence of circumstances, which under normal expectations would allow this or that foreseeable event to take place. "Possibility," thus, can only be "created" through some change of "actuality"! An *Ermöglichung von Möglichkeiten* can be imagined only as some effectuation of *Wirklichkeit* (reality). For logical reasons, what God produced from "nothing" through the primeval *creatio ex nihilo* could not be meaningfully designated by the concept of potentiality/possibility alone—nor by the abstract term "evolution."

The corresponding theological question would refer to the idea of God establishing "possibilities" prior to his effectuation of actuality. Is it theologically meaningful to understand the adage "with God nothing will be impossible" (Luke 1:37; cf. Genesis 18:14) through the filter of a "nothing will be impossible to make possible"? Obviously, it cannot be thought *a necessity* for the Creator to produce some intermediary, latent potentiality of creation before starting to create. And biblical or natural observations do not provide *actual* evidence for such a preestablished potentiality. On the contrary, divine omnipotence can be conceived only as belonging to the eternal majesty of God, and creation can only be understood as the Creator voluntarily delimiting his sovereignty—and, therefore, his possibilities—by giving (and, by his promise, assuring continued) reality to a world and to beings other than himself. After all, how can the production of actuality be conceived if not as a renouncing of potentiality (the freedom *not* to produce, or to produce differently)? What God did "in the beginning" (Genesis 1:1), then, could not have been to equip himself with possibilities that did not essentially belong to him from eternity. What he did was to start creation as a successive diminution of his divine possibilities in favor of an expanding, self-dependent creation.

To be sure, this observation should not be allowed to stand on its own. The aim of creation—adoration and praise to God by a self-conscious, self-dedicating creature—must, in the Creator's eyes (which is all that finally matters), be an infinitely greater thing than the divine possibilities "given away" in creation. Moltmann may also respond to our criticism by pointing to the particular character of his "ecological" vision: the indwelling of God in his creation. Here the actuality of the created universe is accentuated not as a diminution of the Creator's sovereignty but as a confirmation (if not, as in process theology, an *extension*) of the divine plenitude. For that reason, it would be hard to accommodate our pointing to creation as self-modifying "omnipotence" with Moltmann's vision. However, such a response would only overturn our point if divine "indwelling" is conceived as unconditional and as unaffected by the reality of creature. As soon as creature is conceived as more than an automaton that reflects at any moment the contingent volition of an inscrutable creator, and as soon as the Creator is conceived as having obliged himself to respect certain existent entities by holding on to certain rules and regularities established by himself, then the late Scholastic distinction between God's *potestas absoluta* (prior to all acts of creation) and his *potestas ordinata* (as limited by himself in and by his work of creation) becomes inevitable.[17] The only alternative would be the pantheistic identification of creator and created. As there is no reason to suspect Moltmann of being ready to draw that consequence, there is occasion to question his consistency.

Moltmann's concern to unite primeval and ongoing creation, and thus combine the historical Christian confession of a sovereign Creator with the modern concept of evolution, is in itself interesting, and it is carried out with remarkable imagination and determination. If he does not really succeed in establishing the link, this may, at least in part, be due to the fact that he is somewhat weighed down by Barthian and Blochian suspicion about creation as givenness and about any element of "natural theology" that is not organically structured by the global "Messianic" *Heilsgeschichte* vision. The consequences of such a vision for creation theology when maintained more or less consistently can be profitably studied in Dorothee Sölle's *To Work and to Love.*

But Sölle's creation theology can be understood only against the perspective of previous writings. The author was an influential spokesperson of the antitheistic wave of theology of the late 1960s and early 1970s, and also of a liberation orientation with a strong emphasis on the Second Article of the Creed (a "Christology from below") at the expense of the First. That she turns to a "theology of creation" may in several regards be typical of the time as well of the recent explosion of interest in ecology; but at the same time she does not hesitate to profess a certain shift in her own orientation:

> My theological overemphasis on Christ, which I shared with Dietrich Bonhoeffer and others, bypassed the question of God. Like the rest of the theological generation in Europe to which I belong, I was stripped of a naive trust in God the Father, Ruler and Sustainer after two world wars. We fixed our gaze on Christ, the sufferer, because an innocent trust in God was no more possible. . . . It may be that I am homesick for God and have been for a long time. . . . Today I find it necessary to ground my early, existentialist *solus Christus* position in a recognition of the source of life itself. Now that God is, for me, no longer imprisoned in

---

[17]Ockham, *Quodlibet VI,* qI. Biel, *Collectorium circa IV Sententiarum,* I, XVII, I a 3. The same point of view is confirmed from the Orthodox side by such a distinguished author as Georges Florovsky, *Creation and Redemption: Collected Works,* vol. 3 (Belmont MA: Nordland Publishing Co., 1976) 72.

images of ruler, king, and father, I want to reconcile my faith in Christ with my new understanding of God the Creator. As I move toward a spirituality centered not only in the imitation of Christ but also in creation, I want to spell out what creation means to me and how I participate in it.[18]

Sölle speaks of "a transformation in my own theological outlook" that consists in a new awareness of "the sacredness of the earth."[19] But in spite of this very solemnly declared change in orientation, she is by no means willing to make creation the structuring principle of her reflection. Characteristically enough, the first two chapters of her book are entitled: "Difficulties in Praising the God of Creation" and "In the Beginning was Liberation."[20]

This certainly gives a very clear line of orientation, although already here one might be inclined to question the consistency of the approach on two grounds. First, psychologically, the theological conversion so impressively depicted in Sölle's project seems unable to assert itself in face of her long-established liberation pattern of thought. As so often with thinkers in a process of transition, one can observe an unresolved tension between old and new, which the person concerned lacks the necessary distance and perspective to see. Second, semantically, the statement "in the beginning was liberation" could serve as a means of provocation to elicit critical reflection. But, in fact, Sölle intends much more than that. The sentence is used as a straightforward statement and is therefore open to our questioning: How can liberation be "in the beginning," that is, be imagined without presupposing the existence of 1. some liberator; 2. someone to be liberated; and 3. something to be liberated from? One could even add: 4. some given criterion for distinguishing liberty and absence of liberty?

---

[18]Dorothee Sölle, *To Work and to Love: A Theology of Creation* (Philadelphia: Fortress Press, 1984) 5.

[19]Ibid., 3.

[20]Ibid., 1-6, 7-21: "Biblical faith originated from a historical event of liberation, not from belief in creation. . . . The Exodus event is radical." (7) "If Genesis interprets Exodus, then the ontological project of our being serves the historical project of our becoming free. . . . If liberation precedes creation, then soteriology precedes cosmology." (8) "We need liberation before we can affirm creation. . . . Creation faith is susceptible to the danger of 'cheap reconciliation' . . . . The oppressed have an epistemological advantage: They wait for a greater God. . . . We need to achieve a synthesis of creation and liberation traditions that does not devalue the liberation tradition but rather apprehends the creation tradition from a liberation perspective." (10-11) "The question then becomes: Which elements in creation faith and creation thought are liberating and which are oppressive?" (13).

Sölle's use of biblical creation references is (as quoted) thoroughly directed by her search for liberating and/or "oppressive" elements. Even a first glance at the Genesis accounts makes her somewhat hesitant:

> There is the seed of separation between God and the world in Genesis and throughout the Pentateuch, because the stories were written in part to demonstrate Yaweh's superiority over Baal, Astarte, Marduk, and other nature gods.[21]

She starts with a frontal attack against "God's absolute otherness," a concept she sees as having harmful affects in three different regards. First, a sovereign God acting in absolute freedom can only be a God "beyond relatedness, beyond love, and beyond justice."[22] Only if we see God's "need for the other" as the beginning of creation is creation really apprehended as an act of love. Second, this "otherness of God" is seen to have consequences for the earth, making it into a completely "godless place."[23] Third, and consequently, human existence must be understood as a desolate, lonesome thing, bound to express itself in exclusively egocentric options.[24] "We need a critical awareness of the destructiveness of our faith. . . . A theology of creation must teach us how to love the earth better."[25]

It goes without saying that a *creatio ex nihilo* is bluntly rejected. At the October 1984 Klingenthal consultation, Sölle stated her point powerfully: "God did not create out of nothing; God created out of love." Whether this negation and affirmation can be taken to speak to the same question and thus to be mutually exclusive in the way they are presented is a minor issue in our present context. Her strong plea is for an ongoing creation—from which creation as some initial or primeval event cannot and should not be distinguished—and for human "co-creatorship with God" as a virtually irrestrictive vision.[26]

Sölle finally sums up her reflections on the creation theme by saying: "We cannot afford to have a naive trust in the first creation"—thereby referring once more to the prevalence of "liberation" by pointing to the "second" and "third" creations (the Exodus event in the Old Testament and the [symbolic?] conquest of

---

[21]Ibid., 13.

[22]Ibid., 14.

[23]Ibid., 16-17.

[24]Ibid., 19-20.

[25]Ibid., 20.

[26]"One premise underlying my concept of cocreation is that the first creation is unfinished; it is an ongoing process." (Ibid., 37)

death by Jesus Christ in the New Testament). Thus, in fact, the first and the last concrete expression in her "theology of creation" is a substantial reservation about the bearing of the recent creation orientation that is so emphatically proclaimed as the legacy of the book!

But Sölle's approach to creation theology deserves attention as more than simply an example—in many ways typical of the contemporary theological situation—of an orientation that purports to return to the First Article of the Creed after having long ago cut off its roots in the biblical proclamation of God the Creator. It deserves consideration also as a consistent and courageous demonstration of where an insistent liberation/*Heilsgeschichte* approach to creation will take us when no distracting veneration for the formulated Creed of the church intervenes and inapparently redirects the channel of thought (as in the case of Moltmann). It may sound rather strange to recommend Sölle for particular consistency immediately after having so bluntly accused her of inconsistency. But the conflicting judgments relate to different aspects. There is inconsistency with regard to the announced reorientation of the book (which certainly does not show through) and in a semantically unacceptable talk of "liberation" as "beginning" (and there may also be inconsistency with regard to other basic concepts, such as "creation" and "God"). But there is undeniable consistency in the unifying vision of "liberation" as the fundamental event that should not be obscured by any directive idea of a preexistent Creator. It would, of course, have served the purpose of clarification if Sölle had not undertaken to use "creation" and "theology of creation" as labels for a project that so openly and professedly departs not only from ecclesial orthodoxy but also—as bluntly admitted—even from the Genesis image of creation and Creator. Had she presented the book as "a theology of cocreatorship" or of "human creativity," the format would have been more understandable. However, in spite of this, the inner orientation of the book shows both coherence and systematical consequence.

One could immediately ask: Would Karl Barth not also have been bound to come out at this point if the *heilsgeschichtlich* covenant orientation of his creation approach had been carried through without the crossing modification of a different principle, that is, the ancient creeds in their historical and structural givenness? One might, of course, also add that, in terms of content, "liberation" to Sölle does not coincide with "salvation" to Barth, but this in itself has no bearing on the structural coordination of creation and historical actualization (redemption, in general, whether conceived in predominantly "spiritual" or predominantly "secular" categories). In any case, the genetic and structural connection between the Barthian *Heilsgeschichte* emphasis and the subsequent subordination of creation to salvation in the various shades of secular/political/liberation theologies seems apparent enough.

Of immediate relevance here is a comparison between Sölle's and Moltmann's approaches. An important difference between the two authors is established through Moltmann's emphasis on *creatio ex nihilo* as a primeval event and his clear aim to connect this conviction with creation as an ongoing process. But, as we have seen, it is not obvious that he has succeeded in uniting the two aspects, and it can hardly be doubted which of his two orientations sets the general agenda for his exposition. Structurally, his "Messianic" approach to creation is a "liberation" one, and his deep resistance to "nature" and any "order of creation" as a depot of possible "givens" plainly tends to reduce his *creatio ex nihilo* to some "creation of evolution." His insistence on the traditional term is, therefore, more readily understood as an expression of concern about contact with historical Christian belief than as a necessary foundation for, or consequence of, his creation theology as a whole. The "creation of evolution" may seem a confusing term, even to critics who do not favor the "creationist" opposition of creation and evolution as mutually exclusive alternatives. Conceptually, it is meaningful to "create" certain *conditions for* an evolution or else to "create" something *by means of* an evolution. In both cases, the object of the creative act is distinguishable from the evolutionary process (or from the creative act) itself. But there does not seem to be much meaning in delineating the word "create" through making its object an unobjectifiable abstract like "evolution." In biblical language, at least, there can hardly be any doubt that "creation" refers to the global realm of manifest givens: gifts presented by the universal Giver, the Creator.

Certainly Moltmann is not averse to using biblical creation language to relate concrete objects and events; nor is Sölle. But to both of them this direction of God's creative activity to the actual world and to our own situation as creatures in this world seems to speak of creation only as an ongoing process. Moltmann's assertion of a primeval *creatio ex nihilo* relates ongoing creation to an act prior to and constitutive of itself—or bases present reality in a transcendent origin of becoming—as much and as little as Sölle's rejection of the concept. At least, this becomes obvious as soon as we raise the question about the integration of that assertion into Moltmann's global understanding of creation. Obviously these observations refer just as much to the concept of God as to the concept of creation. Sölle explicitly defines God as "power-in-relation,"[27] which, of course, in itself *per definitionem* is sufficient to exclude any idea of a creator existing "before"

---

[27]Ibid., 40-41, 45. In concurrence with Isabel Carter Heyward, *The Redemption of God: A Theology of Mutual Relation* (Washington: University Press of America Inc., 1982) esp. 159.

his creation. Certainly, Moltmann presents a different vision, corresponding with his dialectical concept of creation:

> The Trinitarian concept of creation binds together God's transcendence and his immanence. The one-sided stress on God's transcendence in relation to the world led to deism, as with Newton. The one-sided stress on God's immanence in the world led to pantheism, as with Spinoza. The Trinitarian concept of creation integrates the elements of truth in monotheism and pantheism. In the panentheistic view, God, having created the world, also dwells in it, and conversely the world which he has created exists in him. This is a concept which can really only be thought and described in Trinitarian terms.[28]

Whether there exists such an essential correspondence between pan-en-theism and a viable adaptation of Trinitarian thought as here maintained may be a question to be contemplated on both historical and logical grounds. However, in our context, this is not the crucial point. Rather the question is whether pan-en-theistic orientations give a viable (and, as is really claimed here, the *only* viable) clue to a unified vision of a world-transcending and, at the same time, world-immanent Creator. Certainly the two formulae indicated—"God in the world" and "the world in God"—in themselves do not determine belief in a God who was when the world as yet was not, nor do they contain any claim about a *creatio ex nihilo*. In order to do so, the pan-en-theistic concept of the Creator's indwelling in the created world needs to be founded in, and informed by, a more comprehensive theory of God as existing when there was as yet no world to exist "in" and of God as the universal cause of that world in its existence. In order to be meaningfully integrated into Christian theology, pan-en-theism has to modify its ambitions and admit that it is not a valid theory of God the Creator but a description of his subsequent, self-ordained relationship with his creation! On this point, Moltmann's doctrine of creation seems to be lacking in basic clarity and coherence.

This gives some reason to stop and ponder, not only because of his strong—if ever so unintegrated—insistence upon a *creatio ex nihilo* but also against the background of his emphatically pronounced admiration for an Eastern Orthodox theology of creation.[29] The Orthodox insistence upon a fundamental distinction between "uncreated" and "created" reality, the consequences of which are drawn as far as to claim that created being (even) in eternity can communicate with God

---

[28]Jürgen Moltmann, *God in Creation* (see n. 3) 98 (German: 109).

[29]Ibid., xiii (13). Cf. Moltmann's preface to the German edition of Dumitru Staniloae, *Orthodoxe Dogmatik* (Cologne: Benziger Verlag, 1984/1985) 9-13.

only in his dynamics and not in his divine nature,[30] excludes any understanding of God based on his indwelling in the created as some determinant reference.[31] It must be clear that the dialectical understanding of creation that Moltmann wants to maintain—and to which he attributes so much importance in his critical riposte to process theology—can be upheld only in connection with a more open-ended dialectical concept of the Creator. It is not sufficient to speak of the Creator as being *in* his creation and the creation as being *in* him if this implies a virtual omission of God as being *outside* and *prior to* his creation.

Moltmann's loss of this distinction seems to be closely connected with his special kind of Trinitarian orientation, with its inherent rejection of a "monolithic," "monotheist" concept of Godhead:[32]

> The Christian church was therefore right to see monotheism as the severest inner danger, even though it tried on the other hand to take over the monarchical notion of the divine lordship. Strict monotheism obliges us to think of God without Christ, and consequently to think of Christ without God as well. The questions whether God exists and how one can be a Christian then become two unrelated questions. But if on the other hand Trinitarian dogma maintains the unity of essence between Christ and God, then not only is Christ understood in divine terms; God is also understood in Christian ones. The intention and consequence of the doctrine of the Trinity is . . . the Christianization of the concept of God. God cannot be comprehended without Christ.[33]

The predicament here seems apparent enough. Two alternatives are mentioned—but no attention is paid to an eventual third possibility. *Either* God is conceived as a monarchical entity ("monotheism") standing outside and above creation as the timeless, inflexible ruler. *Or* he has to be conceived from an "inside" perspective, comprehending not only creation but also the incarnation. God

---

[30]The *energeiai*. See Georges Florovsky, *Creation and Redemption* (see n. 17) 64-69; Staniloae, *Orthodoxe Dogmatik*, 139-41.

[31]A still more emphatic criticism about "an ambiguity regarding God and the world" is voiced against Jürgen Moltmann by Jószef Niewiadomski, *Die Zweideutigkeit von Gott und Welt in J. Moltmanns Theologie* (Innsbruck: Verlagsanstalt Tyrolia, 1982) see particularly 153. If that criticism may be too categorical, it is obviously because Niewiadomski sees that Moltmann's general orientation is more consistently unified than our observations seem to allow for.

[32]See Jürgen Moltmann, *The Trinity and the Kingdom of God* (see n. 10) esp. ch. 5, §1, "A Criticism of Christian Monotheism," 129-50.

[33]Ibid., 131-32.

the Creator, understood "in Christ," is a God who can be imagined exclusively from within the "salvation (encompassing also the creation) history." God can be spoken of only as manifest in his actual *oikonomía*. This could immediately be taken to have some similarity with the Orthodox doctrine of God's *kataphasía* (his pronounceability) as referring exclusively to his manifestations in the created world, but it fails to take account of what is in Orthodoxy the inextricable prerequisite of such an assumption, namely God's primordial *apophasía* (his unpronounceability) as the persistent point of departure for human speech about God. The uncreated source of creation as transcending human thought and imagination is the determinant reference of all God-language.[34]

The alternative overlooked in Moltmann's confrontation is the possibility/necessity of a duplex, *apophatic/kataphatic* approach: the restricted *potestas ordinata* of an "immanent" God—God present as he reveals himself in creation and in the incarnation—to be constantly understood as self-restricting manifestations founded in the ineffable *potestas absoluta*. God's "general revelation" in creation and his "special revelation" in the incarnation both contain a "backward" reference to his divine before-ness: God is, so to say, *per definitionem*, something infinitely more than all imaginable temporal manifestations of God. Only through such a dialectically restrictive qualification is the language of pan-en-theism brought into harmony with that of the Bible. Obviously Moltmann—in his special version of Trinitarian language attacking "monolithic monotheism" in the name of divine love, and in his pan-en-theistic language attacking creational givenness (as distinct from and, at the same time, as confirmative of the Giver) in the name of evolution—intends to give complementary expression to his basic vision of divine presence, clue to the mystery of ongoing creation,[35] as the exclusive term of reference for a Christian concept of Godhead. This, however, leaves his traditional proclamation of a *creatio ex nihilo* functionally inoperative, and it leaves his pan-en-theistic model of God without any virtual claim of transcendent reality. This is not to say that his talk about Creator and creation in toto boils down to this, but that—insofar as it transcends this limitation—his words can hardly be seen to be operatively integrated.

Does this mean that, in the end, Moltmann's energetic reservations in face of American process theology serve only to camouflage a deeper structural consen-

---

[34]See the chapter entitled "L'absolu" in Dumitru Staniloae, *Dieu est amour* (Geneva: Labor et Fides, 1980 [1968]) 40-48, with its explicit criticism of Karl Barth in this regard.

[35]"The Father creates through the Son in the Holy Spirit" (Jürgen Moltmann, *God in Creation* [see n. 3] 9 [German: 23]).

sus? The difference in actual background is obviously a little too manifest to allow for that kind of simplistic statement. After all, Moltmann (and Sölle, and the whole post-Barthian Continental tradition) has roots that can be traced back to Hegel and his strictly historically oriented ontology, whereas the process perspective of Whitehead and his followers is founded more in a nature-based model of thought. At the same time, it should not be overlooked that process theology has been able to develop a wide variety of advancements in dialogue with other contemporary trends (liberation theologies, theologies of religion, etc.). Of particular interest in our context may be John B. Cobb's comprehensive discussion with J. B. Metz, Jürgen Moltmann, and Dorothee Sölle in *Process Theology as Political Theology* and the discussion between Schubert Ogden and Sölle in the anthology *The Challenge of Liberation Theology*.[36] It may also be characteristic that at the 1984 Klingenthal consultation Dorothee Sölle spoke of process theology as "the finest fruit of the tree the Lord let grow on the other side of the Atlantic."[37]

In the main presentation of process theology at the 1984 consultation, David Griffin refuted the concept of *creatio ex nihilo* (to the extent that the *nihilo* might be understood as *absolute* nothingness) as being tied with the concept of "coercive" divine omnipotence. He felt that this latter concept was disastrous in several regards, not least when seeing God as a model for human imitation, a model that would inevitably endorse violence both to nature and to fellow human beings. Instead, he referred to the process concept of causal interaction as a transference of emotional incentives, creation being thoroughly a result of cooperation between Creator and creature. This, then, should rather reflect creation out of a "relative nothingness" through a "persuasive"—and not a "coercive"—divine influence.[38]

---

[36]John B. Cobb, Jr., *Process Theology as Political Theology* (Manchester: Manchester University Press; Philadelphia: Westminster Press, 1982). *The Challenge of Liberation Theology: A First World Response*, ed. Brian Mahan and L. Dale Richesin (New York: Orbis Books, 1981) 4-20, 127-40.

[37]Recorded by the author.

[38]A different angle for rejecting the *creatio ex nihilo* is represented by Grace M. Jantzen in her *God's World, God's Body* (London: Darton, Longman & Todd; Philadelphia: Westminster Press, 1984). From the idea of creation as the embodiment of the Creator, she declines any concept of timeless divine existence prior to the origin of matter. As is true also of process theology, her position is neatly distinguished from that of Sölle in that it rests on a purely ontological—and not a liberation—approach. And it is not looking to feminist or other political implications. At the same time, it also differs from Griffin and process theology, not only in principally retaining the priority of being over becoming, but also in offering a different interpretation of the alleged interdependence God/world (142).

In addition to the basic issue raised by process theology (reality = becoming, God being integral in the universal process of becoming), this presentation obviously raises the issue of God as the undialectically conceived-of model for human imitation. Does a concept of unrestricted divine sovereignty in itself favor attitudes of human domination? Such an assumption seems to be taken as given, and not only in process theology. The integral interrelatedness of "creation" and human conduct in Sölle's *To Work and to Love* is determined by the taken-for-grantedness of the same principle: God must be imagined in such a way as to provide the most acceptable model possible for human interaction. A similar pattern is obviously at work with Jürgen Moltmann, especially in his Trinity book, in which the final section, "The Kingdom of Freedom,"[39] draws a series of immediate references *from* the Trinitarian image of God *to* human interrelatedness in the field of contemporary political and social ethics. Indeed, it may seem here as though the obvious shortcomings of an autocratic political model constitute the decisive argument against "monarchical monotheism." Due to some obviously unquestioned character of such God-humanity correspondence, societal motives become just as important for our image of God as our image of God is for our ideas of society. Which of the two decides about which?

On the other hand, if the opposite orientation is being presented, the conclusion could just as well be that, because God is the unquestioned author of creation, sovereignty belongs to him and to him alone. Therefore: Since authority in the strict sense is a divine attribute, it should not be usurped by any earthly "ruler." Admittedly, the attitude that humans created in the "image" of their Creator should resemble their "Heavenly Father" (N.B.: in indiscriminate love of his creation) is not foreign to the Bible.[40] But the emphasis is equally on the dialectically complementary orientation: They should not be like God in self-supporting wisdom and unrestricted dominance.[41] When Sölle polemically attacks the biblical narrative of the Fall, it is in absolute consistency with her unquestioned idea of the divine as the unconditional model for the human being:

> The talk about the "disobedience" of Adam and Eve is misleading. . . .
> The story of the Fall is in many ways the story of a rise in human development rather than the story of our fall into guilt and sin. . . . There is only one moral choice: to disobey, to eat of the tree of knowledge, and

---

[39]See Jürgen Moltmann, *The Trinity and the Kingdom of God* (see n. 10) 191-222.

[40]Matthew 5:45-48; Ephesians 5:1.

[41]Genesis 3:5; Ecclesiastes 5:1; Matthew 20:1-6; 1 Timothy 6:15-16.

thereafter to live through the hardships of life. . . . Adam and Eve are now confronted with the consequences of being workers and lovers. And because they have changed through their courageous step, God the relational being also changes. God moves from parenthood to companionship. . . . They come in touch with a new God. . . . Here I draw on the excellent work by Erich Fromm, *You Shall Be as Gods* for my insights— we are called to choose freedom over a childlike obedience.[42]

Even if she pays no attention to the fact, Sölle can hardly be unaware that her interpretation of this account is diametrically opposed to that of the Jahvistic narrator, of later biblical contemplations, and of a practically unanimous Christian tradition—and not only to that of "Orthodoxy," the enemy she attacks in the same context for its alleged "dread of disobedience." But when the implicit understanding of the actual text is accepted—"You shall *not* be as God, for if you usurp the Creator's role the result will inevitably be social manipulation, competition, self-assertion, and devastating confrontations"— the determinant orientation becomes precisely the opposite. Neither Griffin nor Moltmann proceed to that kind of daring reversal of the old text, but the question remains whether this would not, in fact, have been demanded by their basic presupposition. Griffin's development of "persuasive power" and Moltmann's model of a Trinitarian ethic do in fact surmise that the true destiny of human beings is to "be like God" and—conversely—for God in his creative work to adhere to action that is immediately exemplary for his creature. But, according to the Bible, is that what Godhead or creation *ex nihilo* is really about?

In process theology the unilateral application of a pan-en-theistic model of Godhead—which seems to be more or less characteristic of the whole diversified school of process thought—may at first glance look somewhat surprising in view of the observation that process theology (already starting with Whitehead) is by no means adverse to the idea of a "primordial" and a "consequent" nature of God; in fact, it gives spectacular prominence precisely to such a distinction:

Thus, analogously to all actual entities, the nature of God is dipolar. He has a primordial nature and a consequent nature. The consequent nature of God is conscious; and it is the realization of the actual world in the unity of his nature, and through the transformation of his wisdom. . . . This [the primordial] side of his nature is free, complete, primordial, eternal, actually deficient, and unconscious. The other side originates with physical experience derived from the temporal world, and then acquires integration with the primordial side. It is determined, incomplete, con-

---

[42]Dorothee Sölle, *To Work and to Love* (see n. 18) 74-75.

sequent, "everlasting," fully actual, and conscious. His necessary goodness expresses the determination of his consequent nature.[43]

Such a distinction between God in his eternal, all-transcending freedom and God in his subsequent self-determined restrictedness in time and space may immediately recall the Eastern Orthodox distinction between the *apophasía* and the *kataphasía* of God—and, for that matter, between the "hidden" and the "revealed" God of Martin Luther. But process metaphysics makes a decisive difference in its uncompromised insistence on *becoming* as the determinant reference. In the Whiteheadian scheme, the God *"before* creation" (his "primordial nature") is understood as sheer potentiality, and will thus, at each moment of the evolving process, suffer from "actual deficiency": God is not yet what he is intended to be; he is en route with and in his creation at the same time as, in his primordial nature, he is the directive aim of that process and thus also the potential totality of a world to come. On the other hand, at every stage of the cosmic process, God *"in* creation" is the total of the process already realized, the God of actuality, perfectly conscious of the world as already developed—nothing more! It should be obvious why such a distinction does not provide for the distinction that we are seeking and see as ecumenically indispensable—that between a Creator existing, planning, and acting prior to his work, and his subsequent presence *in* (and voluntarily limited *by*) his work.

In this regard, to a not unimportant extent, the Continental authors Moltmann and Sölle may be seen as and criticized for following the process train. With Moltmann, this trend is formally contradicted (but not intrinsically overcome, neutralized, or integrated) by his profound commitment to a historically established theological tradition. With Sölle, the same trend is lacking explicit epistemological foundation and also more comprehensive theological reflection. But the main channel of orientation seems to be the same. The post-Barthian limitation of "God" to his manifestation—which can actually be seen as a further *heilsgeschichtlich* development of the Ritschlian/neo-Kantian struggle against "metaphysics" and "natural theology"—does in fact fit well with process neo-metaphysics in its denial of actuality in the "primordial" God and its affirmation of "conscious" divine concurrence as restricted to the present stage of processual actuality. This means: restricted to that of a purely pan-en-theistic model of God as "power-in-

---

[43]Concluding chapter of Alfred North Whitehead, *Process and Reality: An Essay in Cosmology* (London: Cambridge University Press, 1929) 488-89. Cf. *Process Theology: Basic Writings by the Key Thinkers of a Basic Western Movement,* ed. Ewert H. Cousins (New York: Paramus; Toronto: Newman Press, 1971) 89-90.

relation,'' excluding any idea of unconditioned, self-restricting power as the very ground of relation, and thus, finally, excluding the vital idea of relation (including creation) as *gift* in the deepest meaning of that word, as *grace*.

To state briefly the ecumenical consequences of our observations so far: It is immediately apparent that the advocates of what could in the widest sense be referred to as the "process view" of creation (encompassing a good deal more than the official process school in theology) come from a wide variety of confessional traditions. The process school itself represents an impressive confessional spread, Roman Catholic and Protestant.[44] At the 1984 Klingenthal consultation, Griffin (Disciples of Christ) had as his most immediate comrade-in-arms the Belgian Roman Catholic Professor Jan van der Veken. Moltmann has a Reformed and Sölle a Lutheran church background. Even if a Barthian impulse can be easily identified, at least in Continental difficulties with a prebiblical God-language, it is hardly unambiguous proof of a basically Reformed legacy. First, although (as Alasdair Heron showed in his analysis at the 1983 Strasbourg consultation) Barth's covenantal approach to creation has roots in a Reformed tradition of "federal" theology, this tradition has over the centuries coexisted with Calvinist predestinarianism, albeit in a sometimes rather frustrating tension. Second, if Barth can be accused of promoting a Ritschlian tradition,[45] Ritschl himself was a solidly established Hanoverian Lutheran of his day. Up to now our findings have shown little immediately relevant "ecumenical" substance. But, in the process of our research, this is a fairly provisional conclusion, one that needs to be further explored not only in confrontation with other aspects of contemporary theology of creation but— still more—in view of our enquiry about the protecting and neglecting of creation faith in the various confessional traditions (§5).

4.2 Can the modern *Heilsgeschichte* approach to creation survive the contemporary quest for an operative, viable theology of creation?

The reflections here will start from the historical observations recorded under §1.2. However, some additional comments on contemporary developments and

---

[44]Cf. *Religious Experience and Process Theology,* ed. James Cargas and Bernard Lee (1976).

[45]Wolfhart Pannenberg, *Basic Questions in Theology,* vol. 3, trans. R.A. Wilson (London: SCM Press; Philadelphia: Westminster Press, 1973) 99ff. (Original: *Gottesgedanke und menschliche Freiheit* [Göttingen: Vandenhoeck & Ruprecht, 1972] 29ff.) Cf. Carl-Heinz Ratschow, *Gott existiert: Eine dogmatische Studie* (Berlin: Walter de Gruyter & Co., 1966) 61ff.

on readjustments of the Barthian approach may be appropriate before we observe some actual thrusts that might suggest other directions.

As far as we can determine, the most clear-cut evidence of a pure, classical *Heilsgeschichte* approach to creation from recent years is one that in many ways could be seen as being "more Barthian than Barth," namely that of Hans-Joachim Kraus.[46] But this work will be more meaningfully reviewed in the chapter on the confession-oriented section of our report when we look at "the Reformed contribution" (§5.4). Here and now, various adaptations and modifications of the Barthian approach are more interesting than unmodified repetitions.

To date, Moltmann's creation theology is in many ways the most noteworthy attempt to pursue a consistently "Messianic" interpretation of creation. Even as biblical revelation remains the only genuine source of creation faith, and conscious participation in a covenantal event is seen as the only authentic response to creation, *Heilsgeschichte* is reinterpreted "ecologically" in a way that also involves observations of the natural and social sciences. But this does not mean that science is invited to speak on creation, as for example, on the Creator's design or the global meaning of the universe; nor is any other religion invited to participate in a rather indiscriminate *entente cordiale* between Judaism and Christianity. Moltmann is not in search of a universal platform common to biblical and other brands of creation faith or reflection; nor does he search creation faith for meanings behind or beyond a "Messianic" vision of salvation. His "ecological" approach implies an emphatic plea for Christian involvement in the protection of the environment today, but the motivation for this is none other than for Christian involvement in general, involvement that will serve the Messianic liberation of the world and prepare for the coming of the kingdom.

Pleas for a new "natural theology"—as it has been voiced by neo-Barthians like Eberhard Jüngel[47] and Christian Link—should be seen in a similar perspective. Even if Jüngel does not deal explicitly with creation theology, his reflections do have an immediate bearing on it. His aim is to endorse what he sees as the legitimate concern behind the tradition of a "natural theology," namely to observe God as "generally and unconditionally interesting—for his own sake,"[48] that is, irrespective of the profit we ourselves or our world may draw from dealing or not

---

[46]Hans-Joachim Kraus, *Systematische Theologie im Kontext biblischer Geschichte und Eschatologie* (Neukirchen-Vluyn: Neukirchener Verlag, 1983).

[47]Three of the contributions in Eberhard Jüngel's collection of essays, *Entsprechungen* (Munich: Christian Kaiser Verlag, 1980), focus precisely on this question (158-77, 193-97, 198-201).

[48]Ibid., 196.

dealing with him. At the same time, he considers it vital to reject definitions and stipulations that claim validity prior to God's revelatory self-presentation.[49] This double aim can be fulfilled only by integrating the theology of nature into, and subordinating it to, the theology of revelation. "In the face of so-called 'natural theology,' theology of the word of God is always and incomparably the more natural theology."[50]

Christian Link finds a key to the same issue in Jesus' parables of the kingdom. "One cannot maintain the existence of God and at the same time accept a world model that subsists without God."[51] What he wants to avoid is the presumable inheritance from "the age of metaphysics,"[52] namely "the retroactive inference from positively given 'ordinances,' in which humankind as cognizant or acting 'stands' to their assumed superhistorical ground."[53]

Summed up in plain words, this seems to say: With regard to "nature," theology has a genuine task. This task does not consist of observing nature in order to discover the Creator or his scheme of creation, but rather in searching the Bible for whatever light it may shed on nature as God's creation. The new "natural theology" that is being sought then comes to mean no more and no less than a biblical theology on nature, a theology that opens the way for a meaningful conversation between those who believe in the Bible but has no immediate address to humankind as a whole. Humankind remains a not unimportant part of the subject, but it is neither a responsible conversation partner nor a reliable informant of genuine creation discourse. And, correspondingly, creation (that is, "nature") becomes a

---

[49]Ibid., 177.

[50]Ibid., 177.

[51]Christian Link, *Die Welt als Gleichnis: Studien zum Problem der natürlichen Theologie* (Munich: Christian Kaiser Verlag, 1982 [1976]) 71.

[52]Ibid., 170.

[53]"Damit verlässt die Gotteserkenntnis den Boden der Metaphysik: sie erhebt weder die Natur in ihrer puren Vorhandenheit noch die Geschichte in ihrem historisch ermittelten Ablauf in den Rang einer theologischen Erkenntnisquelle. Vielmehr geht es ihr—wie den Gleichnissen Jesus—darum, dass der Glaube Wirklichkeit *ergreift*, statt sich nur auf sie 'einzulassen' . . . : *Credo, ut intelligam.* Wenn der hier zu beschreibende Weg . . . noch einmal als der Weg einer 'natürlichen' Theologie beschrieben wird, so zunächst deshalb, weil der Widerspruch gegen die Tradition gerade nicht die Entlassung der Natur aus dem Umkreis des theologischen Denkens bedeutet." (Ibid., 72) A similar stand is defended by Hermann Dembowski ("Natürliche Theologie: Theologie der Natur," *Evangelische Theologie* 45/5 [1983]: 224-28), but, as indicated by the title, with the proposal of a change of name.

topic of genuine theological concern only *when* and *where* salvation is already
known and accepted as the all-determining event. In its theological validity, ''nature'' is understood as a strictly Christian concern.[54]

The immediate question to this Barthian and post-Barthian position—which
is more or less common to the authors we have quoted so far—should not address
itself to their stated positions as such but to the way in which they are directly and
indirectly legitimized, that is, through a supposition of some alternative that is only
half clarified. As so often happens, a standpoint is supported by the negative assumption of some exclusive alternative to be avoided and not primarily by positive
confirmation. [A] is justified as the only possibility for escaping (the terrible) [B].
In this case we are left with the following option: *either* the 18th-century ''metaphysical'' idea of a providential Deity, which is derived from empirically observable ''nature''; *or* a 20th-century vision of a Creator who is traceable exclusively
through his liberating, ''Messianic'' operation in history—be this ''liberation''
understood in predominantly theological or largely political terms. Over against
this rather simple option we have to ask: Is there not some possibility of *combining*
a theology of creation that is firmly based on biblical revelation *with* an understanding of creaturely interrelatedness, thus in some way admitting the voice of
the Creator to come through also where it is not recognized in the liberating context of a salvation history? Does creation not enable some kind of intercreational
exchange that may be of importance in the Creator's dealing with his creation,
even if it is not apt to restore the height and depth of the relationship between the
Creator and that same creation?

Among contemporary impulses toward such a mediation the most eminent may
be that of Wolfhart Pannenberg. It is also characteristic that in developing his new
sketch for a ''natural theology'' Eberhard Jüngel unhesitatingly turns to Pannen-

---

[54]An interesting mediating standpoint on ''natural theology'' is taken by the
Dominican Christian Duquoc in ''La théologie naturelle: Son enjeu dans le débat
ouvert par la réforme,'' *Lumière et Vie* 32/161 (1983): 75-88. In this article, he
sharply criticizes Barth and his followers for the reductionist presupposition: ''Dieu
est le moyen de sa révélation'' (80)—and at the same time commends Luther for
having clearly seen in his own day the disastrous role of ''natural theology,'' that
is, in manipulating the freedom of God by pretending to make final statements on
his essence: ''La théologie naturelle est la forme du respect que le christianisme
même reconnaît à la pensée venue d'ailleurs, mais elle cesse d'être acceptable dès
lors que cette pensée prend le pouvoir.'' (84). Duquoc thus sees the vision of the
Reformation as superior to both Roman Catholic traditional natural theology *and*
a modern Protestant ''theology of the Word'' (82).

berg as his natural adversary and discussion partner.[55] Among Pannenberg's writings, a comparatively small collection of essays from 1972 may give the most direct access to his discursive orientation. Like the neo-Barthians, Pannenberg takes for granted the post-Kantian presupposition ''that there is no assured way leading from nature to God.'' But contrary to them he goes on to say: ''Therefore the whole burden of proof of the truth of faith in God falls upon . . . anthropology.''[56] Like his discussion partners, he sees the Creator at work not in some *past* event distinguishable *behind* the realm of present-day phenomena but in a confrontative coming of God as the Lord of the *future*, exposing freedom as the very meaning of our existence.

However, at the same time there is a deep-rooted difference between the Pannenbergian idea of God/future/freedom and the neo-Barthian concepts of God/future/liberation. Whereas to the latter this vision is qualified Christologically from the very outset, and thus enclosed in a frame of reference of biblical ''Messianic'' salvation history, Pannenberg endeavors to demonstrate the universality of human God-relatedness and voices severe criticism against the Barthian enterprise for establishing Christianity on the intended ruins of human religiosity.

> If it cannot be shown that the issues with which religion is concerned . . . are an essential of man's being . . . then every other viewpoint . . . is an empty intellectual game, and what is said about God loses every claim to intellectual veracity.[57]

> The present-day tendency to argue away and exclude the idea of God in Protestant theology must be understood as a consequence of the movement which began with the rejection of ''natural'' knowledge of God, and with it of all philosophical theology. . . . Herbert Braun's demythologization of the idea of God, Robinson's *Honest to God* and the American ''Death of God'' theologians are the heirs of Barth and Bultmann. For if all philosophical theology is to be dismissed, what justification is there for continuing to maintain and believe what Jesus says about God?[58]

> If personality can be distinguished from the modes of existence of what exists here and now, it is perhaps not so completely hopeless to look for

---

[55] Eberhard Jüngel, *Entsprechungen* (see n. 47) 158ff.

[56] Wolfhart Pannenberg, *Basic Questions in Theology*, vol. 3 (see n. 45) 82 (German: 11).

[57] Ibid., 89 (18).

[58] Ibid., 101-102 (31-32).

God as the origin of freedom, in the fact that freedom refers to the future.[59]

Over against the Barthian trend—to orient theology, including the doctrine of creation, from a liberation concept based on a history of covenantal relationship between God and his chosen people—Pannenberg and his "school" see freedom as a universal human orientation that is inseparably linked to an anthropologically founded concept of Godhead. More recently, this vision has been confirmed in his *Anthropology in Theological Perspective*. Having observed the right of Karl Barth to warn against a theological anthropocentricity that allows that "human beings doing theology may be concerned only with themselves and not with God," he argues that precisely through his unwillingness to face the anthropological challenge, Barth ends up in a "form of dependence on anthropological suppositions."[60]

But even if Pannenberg's work deals with creation a good deal more implicitly than explicitly, his endeavors may be characterized as being predominantly *schöpfungstheologisch* in that he pays such comprehensive attention to the universality of human God-orientation, the meaning of historical revelation depending entirely on prestructured references common to humankind as a whole. Compared to the creation theology of, say, Moltmann, this gives a basically different perspective, namely a universal platform of conversation. At the same time, the anthropological orientation is being carried through with such energy that a new narrowness threatens with regard to nature and nonhuman environment. Even allowing for the fact that in 1983 Pannenberg published an anthropology and not a study pretending to be a global theology of creation, it could still be maintained that the human being is presented here in a quasi-isolation which (especially bearing in mind the new ecological challenge) screens out perspectives that are essential to human humanity. Like his philosophical hero Hegel, Pannenberg takes the Kantian revolution and its surrender of phenomenal reality to interpretation by the human mind for granted; but, at the same time, both Pannenberg and Hegel challenge Kantian (Schleiermacherian, Ritschlian, and Barthian) "agnosticism," and see the reality of God as constitutive for human freedom (that is, rationality) and, thus, for the existence of a rational world (history). In this perspective, creation seems to be confirmed: Christianity being legitimized as unrestricted acceptance

---

[59]Ibid., 111 (42).

[60]Wolfhart Pannenberg, *Anthropology in Theological Perspective*, trans. Matthew J. O'Connell (Edinburgh: T. & T. Clark; Philadelphia: Westminster Press, 1985) 15-16. Original: *Anthropologie in theologischer Perspektive* (Göttingen: Vandenhoeck & Ruprecht, 1983) 15-16.

of the world as the Creator's gift at the same time as the vision of creation seems substantially reduced through the superimposed anthropocentricity of the vision. As a matter of fact, there is a good deal more "nature" in Moltmann's "Messianic" theology than in Pannenberg's "natural" theology.

In the somewhat complex and contradictory situation in which contemporary German creation theology thus finds itself, it might be appropriate to take a quick glance at the somewhat independent attempts to renew and reemphasize creation theology that have taken place in Scandinavia (and especially in Sweden and Denmark) during the last generation.[61]

In Sweden these endeavors have, above all, been connected with the name of Gustaf Wingren. In order to gain a proper understand of his major work in this field,[62] one should bear in mind that Wingren had started out with major studies on Luther's doctrine of vocation[63] and Irenaeus' theology of recapitulation,[64] both of which vigorously underline the importance of creation not only to Christian ethics but also to a global vision of the incarnation. In continuation of this he launched a heavy attack on the Kantian inheritance in theology, particularly as it has been championed in our century by Anders Nygren and the Lundensian school. Wingren challenged the tendency to dilute theological thinking into historical observation and structural analysis, insisting that, as determined by the vision of creation and redemption, it is the task of theology to speak on reality, on everyday life and work.

Wingren's creation study is somewhat impetuous in its attack on Barthian Christocentricity:

> If we put the second article before the first . . . we thereby deny the faith which the Church has held for two thousand years in God's work in Creation, and which has now become altered in the twentieth century of the

---

[61]A good introduction to these endeavors is *Creation and Method: Critical Essays on Christocentric Theology,* ed. Henry van der Goot (New York: University Press of America, 1981).

[62]Gustaf Wingren, *Creation and Law,* trans. Ross Mackenzie (Edinburgh: Oliver & Boyd, 1961). Original: *Skapelsen och lagen* (Lund: C.W.K. Gleerup, 1958); German: *Schöpfung und Gesetz* (1960).

[63]Gustaf Wingren, *The Christian's Calling: Luther on Vocation,* trans. Carl C. Rasmussen (Edinburgh, 1952). German: *Luthers Lehre vom Beruf* (Munich, 1952).

[64]Gustaf Wingren, *Man and the Incarnation: A Study in the Biblical Theology of Irenaeus* (Edinburgh/London: Oliver & Boyd, 1959). Original: *Människan och inkarnationen enligt Irenaeus* (Lund: C.W.K. Gleerup, 1947).

Church's life. To those who accept the view of Barth, the word "neighbour" presents some difficulties.[65]

One thing is certain. If we thus put the preaching of the Gospel before
the Law, and put the second article before the first, we inevitably obscure
the sovereignty of God.[66]

Certain reservations about well-known traditional trends and a too simplistic confusion of creation and creation faith are, however, necessary in order to avoid misunderstanding the first-things-first principle:

To allow the first article of the Creed to stand first simply means that Creation took place first, and not that we gained a full and clear knowledge
of God when we were created.[67]

Life has not been established in Creation once and for all, to be maintained and preserved subsequently under certain orders defined by God.
This is a false consequence of the belief in Creation, or rather, if the concept of Creation itself is false, this doctrine of order will follow. In this
misinterpretation of Creation, which has generally arisen through con-
fining God's work of Creation to a particular point in the past, there is
no real understanding of God as continuing to create in the present, or of
life itself as God's continuing Creation.[68]

When the word "Creation" is used, one is inclined to think of a *result*
of the creative act. . . . We find this way of thinking in an institutional
form in the theology of order, which thinks in terms of result. . . . If we
are determined to look for results in this way, we shall cut the nerve of
the belief in Creation, viz., the assurance that God is actively creating
now, and that life itself is the other side of God's continuing creative activity. . . . To consider first a single result and move backwards from the
result to its cause may be the typical method of the later proofs of God,
but it is not characteristic of the Bible.[69]

In this perspective, Wingren reacts strongly to every attempt (as he sees it) to make
out of the Christian church an instrument of political power—be it as in the *Theologie der Schöpfungsordnungen* of the 1930s through an "institutionalizing of the

---

[65]Gustaf Wingren, *Creation and Law* (see n. 62) 156 (German: 157).

[66]Ibid., 66-67 (73), cf. 53 (59).

[67]Ibid., 157 (158).

[68]Ibid., 30 (36).

[69]Ibid., 46-47 (52-53).

concept of order as a relatively permanent and self-preserving form of community,''[70] or as in the Barthian use of the Second Article as a political factor.[71] To be an instrument for the Creator's ongoing creation is the adequate horizon not only for a Christian but also for any human being in her/his social responsibilities. Referring to the traditional Lutheran doctrine of the law, where the first usage (*usus civilis*) is that of instructing all people (irrespective of creed) about the will of the Creator for his creation, Wingren says: ''The first article of faith and the first use of the Law belong together.''[72]

A similar polemical orientation to that of Wingren lies at the root of another Swedish contribution (from David Löfgren) of approximately the same time:

> Dass in der modernen Theologie—für die ja eine gewisse Beziehungslosigkeit zum gewöhnlichen Erleben des Menschen ebenso charakteristisch ist wie ein manchmal nicht zu verbergender Mangel an Konkretion—der erste Glaubensartikel in verhängnisvoller Weise der Stellung beraubt wurde, die er bei dem Reformator innehatte.[73]

Some critical comments from Danish authors to the Barthian creation approach are no more vague. Here it is useful to bear in mind the continuing influence of the 19th-century Danish church father N.F.S. Grundtvig. At the same time ''folkly'' (with a strong sense for national culture as historically given) and ''churchly'' (with a passionate Lutheran emphasis on the sacraments and on the live confession of the historic faith as vital to the church), Grundtvig developed a remarkable vision of the goodness of creation, stressing human life in community as essential to the discovery of grace and forgiveness in Christ: ''First be a human, a Christian next!''[74]

This famous quotation reflects no ranking of priorities and certainly does not contest Matthew 6:33. It simply states that salvation is not an escape from but a confirmation of what is entrusted to us all by the Creator. Grace does not suspend

---

[70]Ibid., 43 (50).

[71]Ibid., 93 (98).

[72]Ibid., 161 (162).

[73]David Löfgren, *Die Theologie der Schöpfung bei Luther* (Göttingen: Vandenhoeck & Ruprecht, 1960) 7.

[74]''Menneske først og Christen saa!'' Cf. the contribution of Kaj Thaning, ''Das Menschliche und das Christliche bei N.F.S. Grundtvig'' in *Kontroverse um Kierkegaard und Grundtvig*, ed. Knud E. Løgstrup and Götz Harbsmeier (Munich: Christian Kaiser Verlag, 1966) 50-80.

daily life in its complexities and perplexities, but it makes clear that precisely this is the Creator's gift to us for the fulfillment of his creation plan.

Two Danish theologians of the last generation have contributed most to carrying on this particular legacy, Regin Prenter being oriented more by the "churchly," Knud E. Løgstrup by the "folkly" (folkelige), Grundtvig. In "Creation and Redemption,"[75] Prenter's reflections on creation focus on a quadruple biblical observation: 1. creation is seen against a dualistic background as "God's fight against death in favor of life"; 2. it is present-day (*jetztzeitlich*); 3. it unites nature and culture; and 4. it is thus history.[76] In contrast to "the philosophical idea of creation . . . the biblical witness of creation explains neither the origin of the world nor the rise of evil.'"[77] Prenter interconnects creation and redemption, but on premises somewhat different to those of Barthianism:

> Die Schöpfung ist der Beginn der Erlösung, und die Erlösung ist die Vollendung der Schöpfung. So ist es, weil wir Gottes vollkommene Schöpfung nicht kennen. Wir kennen nur Gottes Schöpferwerk, wie es sich in der Welt entfaltet, wo die Auflehnung des Sündenfalls gegen Gottes Schöpfung dauernd vor sich geht. . . . Daher ist in der Verkündigung von der Erlösung stets ein mächtiges Ja zur Schöpfung vernehmbar.[78]

This interaction of creation and redemption does after all have some similarity with the Barthian approach. However, redemption is not mainly thought of as "covenant" but as triumph over the forces of evil and destruction. In a "covenant" perspective, creation seems more or less restricted to an interpretative reference. But in the "dualistic" perspective creation is omnipresent as a constitutive event—only it cannot be unambiguously identified in history since history is an ever unfathomable infiltration of life and death.

Prenter's position is demonstrated in the following polemical sketch:

> Vergleichen wir nun die hier geschilderten Typen von Schöpfungstheologie . . . finden wir als gemeinsamen Zug bei ihnen allen eine Gegenüberstellung von Natur and Übernatur. . . . Bei Thomas und den Orthodoxen [the 17th-century Lutherans] ist es Gott als Welturcache und

---

[75]Regin Prenter, *Skabelse og Genløsing* (1955). German: *Schöpfung und Erlösung* (Göttingen, 1960).

[76]*Schöpfung und Erlösung,* 181-82.

[77]Ibid., 186.

[78]Ibid., 187.

Gott als Heilsziel, bei Schleiermacher ist es der Naturzusammenhang und das Gottesbewusstsein, bei Ritschl das ursachenbestimmte Reich der Natur und das zweckbestimmte Reich der Ethik, bei Barth die analogische Profangeschichte (*Kirchliche Dogmatik,* III/1) und die eigentliche *Heilsgeschichte.* . . . Die offenbarte Theologie wird dann in sämtlichen Fällen—von Thomas bis Barth—eine von der Schöpfung isolierte Soteriologie. Das Heil . . . wird als etwas Höheres über das gewöhnliche erschaffene Dasein hinausgehoben.[79]

In fact, this recalls the traditional Eastern Orthodox accusation of the total Western theology being one, Scholastically imprisoned attempt to apply distinctions where no such distinctions are biblically or patristically legitimated. Prenter's own vision, however, has an "existential" Lutheran twist, which can hardly be adapted to the Eastern tradition. According to him, creation faith expresses "a dynamic image of God . . . which can only be observed during the movement of faith away from wrath and into grace."[80]

Wir haben von einem Weltbild der Schöpfung gesprochen, das in seinem Dualismus einen scharfen Kontrast zu allen philosophischen, monistischen Welterklärungen älteren und neueren Datums bildet. Das biblische Weltbild wird durch seine Polaritäten charakterisiert, die keinen rationalen Brückenbau zulassen.[81]

Das biblische Verständnis der Schöpfung ist anthropozentrisch . . . in dem Sinne, dass Gottes Schöpferwerk in seiner Ganzheit von seiner Schöpfung des Menschen her verstanden wird . . . und zwar verschieden, je nachdem ob der Mensch in der Gnade oder im Zorn steht. Und das Bild der Welt der Schöpfung ist das Bild der Welt als Heimstätte des Menschen, wo der Mensch Gott und seinem Nächsten begegnet.[82]

Thus Prenter's purpose is to overcome (ontological) dualism in the theology of creation by means of an entirely different but even more accentuated (soteriological) dualism. The all-decisive distinction is not that between nature and supernature—negatively authorized also by the "antimetaphysical" Schleiermacher/Ritschl/Barth tradition—but that between wrath and grace, the basic orientation of faith being that of human relation with God, the Creator and life-giver.

---

[79]Ibid., 190.

[80]Ibid., 216.

[81]Ibid., 224.

[82]Ibid., 231.

Against the background of recent environmental theology, it is easy to question Prenter's anthropocentric emphasis (which he shares fully with his Barthian counterpart and even with Pannenberg) and also his rather "existentialist" statement that creation faith does not "explain" the origin of the world. Certainly, in spite of Prenter's "start-with-creation" theology, his writing shows a lack of environmental perspective that is not unlike the corresponding deficit in the "start-with-covenant" theologies of his day. His existential preoccupation with creation as a present, ongoing event does not encourage sensitivity to creation as an ecosystem of givens calling for preservation and nurture. But in that day did anyone really think differently? At the same time, however, Prenter's emphasis on creation as the basic presupposition of redemption—the Creator's good gift deserving of and being ready for redemption—involves a conscious anti-Gnostic orientation that points a good deal beyond the limits of an anthropocentric-existentialist vision.

Løgstrup's approach is different. In form and method it to a great extent deviates from the lines of conventional theology, and many would see it as a more philosophical project. His most influential book, *The Ethical Demand*,[83] is an "attempt to formulate the attitude of the neighbour implicit in the content of Jesus' proclamation."[84] Although it is intended as a purely ethical presentation, held within strict philosophical limits, and the word "creation" does not stand in the foreground, this is one of the most exciting contributions to a theology of creation produced in postwar Europe. It starts with "the radical demand" that is silently present in any human encounter and is by no means to be confused with existing "social norms" in their relativity. The relationship between these entities is seen as ambiguous, the "norms" reflecting and at the same time threatening to usurp the authority of the "demand." Any idea of a particular "Christian" ethic tends to ossify Christianity into an ideology,[85] and that is precisely what our resistance to the "radical demand" is looking for. Modern "antimetaphysical" thinking is particularly subservient, its program being to leave behind those objects already recognized.[86] The basic contradiction of our ethical existence is illuminated by the mystery of creation as an opposite approach to reality:

---

[83]Knud E. Løgstrup, *The Ethical Demand*, trans. Theodor I. Jensen (Philadelphia: Fortress Press, 1971). German: *Die ethische Forderung* (1959).

[84]Ibid., 3 n. 1 (German: 1).

[85]Ibid., 119 (124).

[86]Ibid., 134 (German).

> Inherent in the insight that trust and love are not of our making is the understanding that life as a whole, our very existence, is a gift which we have received . . . that [humankind] was created and has been placed in an ongoing relationship with his creator.[87]

> The conflict with the nonmetaphysical philosophy is and remains unavoidable. The demand . . . cannot subsist in the place to which it is assigned by nonmetaphysical philosophy. Its one-sidedness presupposes a power which has given a person . . . life and . . . world and which at the same time presents itself as the authority of the demand.[88]

> If we believe that it is God himself whom we meet in the life of Jesus, then the demand, the guilt, and the forgiveness, which are the central content of his proclamation, become realities.[89]

Later, the author returns to creation in the fourth volume of his *Metafysik,* "Creation and Destruction."[90] In this work Løgstrup also underscores the role of metaphysics, this time with the existentialist and Barthian concepts of salvation as the main enemies. Creation as proclaimed by Judaism and resurrection as proclaimed by Christianity give a new emphasis to the indissoluble entanglement of life/creation and death/destruction, which historically marks also the contemporary post-Christian orientation, even if the emphasis there is narrowed to the perspective of destruction.[91] Luther and his age represented a more straightforward and authentic ontology than does modernity. For the Reformer it was natural to speak of the world in "creation philosophical" terms at the same time as he denounced any tendency to adapt or probabilize the unique event of the gospel by means of philosophy (the latter then understood as a general reflection on "possibilities").

> Even if one cannot have communion with God, it is not given that God could not be the one people think and speak of. . . . Contrary to the way of existential theology, Luther did not exploit the difference between faith and ontology . . . to deny that faith involves an ontology.[92]

> Luther's creation philosophical deliberations . . . are not about revelation; they do not apply to the unforeseen element in Christianity. They

---

[87]Ibid., 148 (157).

[88]Ibid., 181 (193).

[89]Ibid., 224 (236).

[90]K.E. Løgstrup, *Metafysik: Skabelse og tilintet-gørelse* (1978).

[91]Ibid., 58-59.

[92]Ibid., 62, translation PL.

are a religious interpretation of the universe and of the being and the world of humans; they envisage the universal in Christianity, the experiences and insights by means of which we understand the Christian message. . . . What Luther really turns against is putting knowledge as knowledge above God and his work in its uniqueness.[93]

Since contemporary ontology has turned against faith in a way completely unfamiliar to the 16th century, a philosophical preoccupation with creation is more important today than at the time of the Reformation.[94] We must refute the two "basic illusions" of our day: that "resistance to destruction conquers destruction" and that "we ourselves represent the power of existing."[95] Even though Kant deserves thanks for doing away with the "cosmological religious philosophy" of his day, he did overlook the immediacy of comprehension and thus the possible foundation of a new and more genuine metaphysics.[96]

The metaphysics we foresee is of a different kind. It breaks forth from within, so to speak. . . . It relates to our immediate experience. . . . It is through the phenomena and problems that are open to religious interpretation that we understand the message of Christianity. Apart from them faith threatens to become void of understanding and to lose spontaneity.[97]

It is important to see how creation and destruction relate to each other, the latter being an inevitable condition of the former, as ordered by the Creator.

Certainly creation is full of glories . . . but we possess them only on the conditions of destruction. . . . The Creator has tied deployment and corruption together in his creation. . . . The Creator's work is dreadful in its glory and destruction; it surpasses both our intellectual and our emotional capacity for comprehending.[98]

Existentialist theology takes the shortest cut and sees the language of biblical creation only as symbolic of the unconditional character of demand and forgiveness. That "God by the power with which he sustains the universe should effectuate

---

[93]Ibid., 63.

[94]Ibid., 65.

[95]Ibid., 78.

[96]Ibid., 94.

[97]Ibid., 224.

[98]Ibid., 229.

that kingdom of which Jesus speaks'' is thus rejected as a mere dream. This twist, however, makes the whole preaching of Jesus "ethically untenable.''[99]

Whereas Grundtvig takes the cohabitation of life and death seriously, according to Løgstrup another Danish hero, Søren Kierkegaard, equates Christianity with eternal life in such a way as to deprive life temporal of its intrinsic value.[100] He thus masterfully anticipates our modern day by "preaching Christianity on the conditions of irreligiosity.''[101]

> If Kierkegaard does not touch on the idea of God in creation, it is because this idea in the shape of rationalist theology is void of contradiction and thus irrelevant to the Christian message, the truth of which is hiding in the highest contradiction imaginable.[102]

In his "polemical epilogue''[103] Løgstrup, in the main, settles his account with dialectical theology:

> Barthian theology is correct that the coming of the kingdom lies outside philosophy, and . . . a historical event is not a theme of philosophy because of its unpredictability. . . . But I do not follow Barthian theology in maintaining that the universal contexts (supposed by the kingdom) . . . cannot originate in the heart or brain of any person without the Christian message. Nor can I follow it in its view of philosophy . . . as a-religious. . . . When universal contexts are seen as being specifically theological . . . can it then be avoided that they overwhelm the Christian message, threaten its event character, and make it the vehicle of some universal knowledge?[104]

Karl Barth and Eberhard Jüngel are accused of maintaining that "the world and we were created for the sake of revelation." Obviously, this must be a "narrowing of both creation and atonement—as if creation were not created for its own sake, and as if atonement did not take place for the sake of created being.''[105]

---

[99]Ibid., 239.

[100]Ibid., 249.

[101]Ibid., 259.

[102]Ibid., 260.

[103]Ibid., 264-84.

[104]Ibid., 267-68.

[105]Ibid., 269.

There is a difference between God's self-presentation in revelation and in creation. In revelation, the content of the word consists in its being of God. If it is not believed to be God's word, it becomes meaningless. In creation, expressions of life . . . do not lose meaning even if it is contested that God's power may be in them. God has not made it a condition for keeping us alive that we recognize his doing it. God . . . works in expressions of life and in phenomena independent of our interpretation.[106]

Rudolf Bultmann is commended for having "segregated the Christian message from the framework of the worldview in which it was promoted," but he is criticized for maintaining that one can separate it from any other worldview.[107] Having completed Luther's vision of creation and law with his own emphasis on destruction as embedded in creation[108] and having underscored the importance of Grundtvig's discovery of "life temporal and secular as having significance already in itself,"[109] Løgstrup finally concludes his criticism of "Christianity without creation faith."[110] If modern theology is correct in accepting "irreligious ontology in its contestation of transcendence as intrinsic to the existence of the human individual,"[111] then we have "made the difference between Greek and biblical orientation so unambiguous that creation faith is turned down."[112]

Nevertheless, the theologian faces the task of reconsidering what it means that life and world are created and of entering into the altercation that is forced upon him/her by irreligious ontology with its challenge to the creation idea, even if this means running the risk that the distinction between Greek and biblical becomes diffuse.[113]

The recent accusation that Christianity is the root of the lack of environmental awareness in the West cannot be denied if the Barthian-existentialist exclusion of creation theology is a correct interpretation of Christianity.[114]

---

[106]Ibid., 271.

[107]Ibid., 275.

[108]Ibid., 278.

[109]Ibid., 280.

[110]Ibid., 281-84.

[111]Ibid., 281.

[112]Ibid., 282.

[113]Ibid., 283.

[114]Knud E. Løgstrup gives a concise summing up of his creation theology in explicit theological terms in his essay "Schöpfung und Ethik," *Neue Zeitschrift für systematische Theologie* 8 (1966): 52-66.

As we have observed, Løgstrup sees an integral tie between creation faith and a philosophical approach to reality, which is most paradigmatically demonstrated in his own program of a "descriptive metaphysics." Revelation and, with it, Christian faith relate to historical events, contingent and perfectly unpredictable, and are per se definitely ametaphysical. However, as such, these events relate to creation as a realm of universal structures, accessible to experience by all humans. Therefore, "metaphysics," in the meaning of a unifying vision of life, becomes the necessary prerequisite even for an authentic reception of the gospel. To deny that this is not, as the Barthians insist, to safeguard the purity of divine revelation but, on the contrary, to refashion the gospel itself into an equally timeless vision of the world implies attributing to it the role of its own (and exclusive) epistemological presupposition. The gospel understood as a "no" to metaphysics has taken over the role of metaphysics and is thereby turned into metaphysics itself.

One may be surprised that Løgstrup so vigorously opposes the main stream theology of his day yet rather uncritically follows the existentialist line: 1. in relating his creation concept to humanity and human encounters and paying little attention to nonhuman nature; 2. in deriving his "metaphysics" so exclusively from individual immediacy, and paying little attention to social structures and dynamics. Can metaphysics, understood as a global reference system, really work on such limited, purely anthropological premises? Therefore, in spite of their obvious differences, our questions to Løgstrup are very much the same as those to Pannenberg.

An attempt to make Løgstrup's approach constructive for a wider ecological orientation is most emphatically made by his student Ole Jensen in his *I vaekstens vold* (1976).[115] Jensen describes the tragic genealogy of Western Christian thought as an ideology of domination and exploitation of nonhuman nature. Descartes, Kant, Herrmann, Bultmann, and Cox are names he uses as examples to demonstrate the historical right of Lynn White's thesis[116] about the responsibility of theology for the present global threats to survival.[117] This tradition denies any sacred element in nature, hails the human species as the only elect creature, and proclaims it the sovereign lord of the future.[118] Basically, ideological liberalism, es-

---

[115]German version: Ole Jensen, *Unter dem Zwang des Wachstums: Ökologie und Religion* (1977).

[116]Lynn White, Jr., "The Historical Roots of Our Ecological Crisis," *Science* 155 (10 March 1967). Cf. *The Environmental Handbook* (1970).

[117]Ole Jensen, *Unter dem Zwang des Wachstums* (see n. 115) 49-80.

[118]Ibid., 60.

tablished Marxism, and existential and secular theologies all share the same destructive vision.

Against this, Jensen intends to establish a totally different human attitude toward creation as the authentically Christian attitude, one that is based on free, cooperative involvement with the whole of our given world.

> Christian thought has engendered a contradiction in our consciousness: Creation means that this life is of extreme importance. But, simultaneously, creation means that . . . everything must perish. . . . Post-Christian existence is harnessed up by this insufferable contradiction. . . . Christian existence can live with it. . . . Christianity as gospel provides the answer to the problem that it has evoked with the idea of creation. . . . God is at the same time Creator and Liberator.[119]

Jensen understands Christianity "as an interpretation of creation, as utopia and gospel in one."[120] Whereas the gospel is the preaching of faith, creation reflection—with its particular image of humankind in nature—interprets "reality as it is when people look sufficiently clearly and deeply into it, and it can therefore be accepted independent of faith."[121] Agreeing with Løgstrup, Jensen says that life in its immediacy should be interpreted as "sovereign expressions of being."[122] And against this background, his analysis of Genesis 1 provides the final blow to Harvey Cox (as an exponent of secular theology) and to all attempts to base a confrontation between humankind and the rest of creation on that narrative. Irenaeus, Francis of Assisi, Luther, and Grundtvig, together with the hymnic tradition of the church, are presented as heroes of the "historical-poetical materialism" reflected in an authentic creation theology,[123] and guidelines are suggested for the protection of nature through a new and consciously reflected setting of taboos.[124]

As a criticism of the post-Cartesian tradition and as a practical apropos to the environmental crisis, Jensen's book says little to distinguish it from a dozen other pleas of the past decade for an ecological theology. What makes it especially interesting is its combination of these concerns with a creation "philosophical" approach, along with its plea for people of goodwill to become engaged in ecology

---

[119]Ibid., 130, translation PL.

[120]Ibid., 132.

[121]Ibid., 132-33.

[122]Ibid., 134-38.

[123]Ibid., 144-51.

[124]Ibid., 157ff.

based on a given common insight: creation thought (not creation belief!) as essential also to Christianity, not as a part of revelation but as a common human presupposition from which the gospel can no more abstract than it can absorb or monopolize it.

It is profitable to interrupt our Nordic excursion here. These glimpses from an area where theology has been very much a German province—but within which there has grown a strong resistance to the main anti-"metaphysical" road with its purely soteriological approach to creation—does accentuate the question as to whether the return of creation (so extensively called for in theology today) is really possible within the framework of a universalized *heilsgeschichtlich* theological project. If creation is not basically or exclusively understood in the light of a Christian redemption experience but is seen as a dimension that is basic to and presented by the entire created universe—including human beings in their involvement with each other and with nature, irrespective of credal commitments—will a Second Article approach to creation then serve its purpose? How broad a platform for interhuman communication follows from our *Credo in Deum patrem omnipotentem, creatorem caeli et terrae*? And how broad a platform of interhuman communication has to be brought about in order to assess adequately the meaning of creation? In their inescapable interaction, these two questions may delineate the basic conflict not *in* but *about* creation theology today. And their vast ecumenical repercussions are immediately visible.

It would, however, be wrong to finish our sketch of the *status questionis* without taking another glance at process theology, not only as the obviously most powerful but also as the most characteristic and most characteristically consistent trend in the present-day discussion. Even if in recent years this school has done much to overcome a certain tension with liberation theology and thus modify its traditional, somewhat apolitical image,[125] and even if much attention has been given to the historical specificity of Christianity,[126] the dominant orientation of process thought as introduced by Whitehead and Charles Hartshorne is unmistakably the philosophical theory of becoming as the determinant structure of reality. In a way,

---

[125]Cf. John B. Cobb, Jr., *Process Theology as Political Theology* (see n. 36); Schubert M. Ogden, *Faith and Freedom: Toward a Theology of Liberation* (Nashville: Abingdon Press; Belfast: Christian Journals, 1979); and Ogden's contributions in *The Challenge of Liberation Theology,* ed. Mahan and Richesin (see n. 36) 17-20, 127-40.

[126]John B. Cobb, Jr., *Beyond Dialogue: Toward a Mutual Transformation of Christianity and Buddhism* (Philadelphia: Fortress Press, 1982); Schubert M. Ogden, *The Point of Christology* (London: SCM Press; New York: Harper & Row, 1982).

the whole progress of theological argument in process theology is solidly rooted in creation—this concept being taken not as a traditional theological *locus* but as a general vision of the universe in its relationship with God. The theory referred to by Hartshorne and his students as "neoclassical theism" or "neoclassical metaphysics" is based on the assumption that becoming is prior to being, and that God—seen in relation to becoming—must not be understood as some causal principle *behind* the all-embracing process. He is *in* it; he is *part of* it. Finite creature contributes to the essence of God through a universal exchange in mutual freedom. God the Creator must be understood as both the potentiality of perfection and a yet-incomplete actuality in its constant moving forward toward perfection.

At the 1984 Klingenthal consultation, it was interesting to observe how the reflections of Dorothee Sölle and the representatives of the process orientation (Griffin, van der Veken) converged on certain important points: rejection of a *creatio ex nihilo* and of "coercive" divine power; insistence on active human participation in creation; emphasis on God being *in*, not *above*, the world; and insistence on an image of God corresponding with what can meaningfully be taken as a model for interhuman relation partners. On several occasions, Sölle explicitly underscored her comradeship-in-arms with process theology. But at the same time it was obvious that the point of departure for the two orientations is about as different as it could possibly be. From the assumption that "in the beginning was liberation,"[127] there is no line whatsoever that takes us to the "metaphysical" approach of process thought, or vice versa. In the one case, a distinctive historical commitment is the all-determining point of reference; in the other, reflection starts with the structure of being as such. How is it possible for the two lines of thought to meet—or at least to draw together in some rather challenging demarcations vis-à-vis traditional theology? Obviously because: in the one case, salvation history as a frame of reference is not being taken as strictly unique (*einmalig*) but as a— however illustrative and inspiring—model of "liberation" as a global pattern, the ontological priority of which it is there to safeguard; in the other case, creation (that is, becoming) as the basic characteristic of reality is not conceived as the "bringing into being" of something that did not so far exist, but as a transition from a metaphysically conceived potentiality to empirical actuality through a free and self-affirming evolution of what is already there. Therefore, an ontology of "liberation" and an ontology of "becoming" need not come out very far from each other. And certainly Sölle's "in the beginning" applied to "liberation" is not to be understood temporally, but ontologically! In both cases, the general trend of thought gravitates in the direction of an ontology not of *creation* but of *crea-*

---

[127]Dorothee Sölle, *To Work and to Love* (see n. 18) 7.

tivity, the Creator being seen not as the author or the cause of evolution, but as its ultimate qualifier, God himself/herself/itself being brought to a fuller, richer, and more authentic self-congruence through the contributory participation of creature in its free self-deployment. The interpretations of creation and of salvation history thus fuse into one, albeit in such a way that each of these loci loses the distinctive characteristics of its traditional ecumene-wide meaning. Creation is no longer understood as the all-constitutive act of a sovereign creator, and salvation is no longer regarded as a strictly unique act that cannot be explained by general historical laws and structures. The most basic theological question that may arise here is if this does not, in both camps and in both cases, suspend divine initiative as gift and as grace. Can creation—when essentially linked to human creativity— really be understood as the work of God in a generosity that is infinitely beyond all human accomplishments? And is salvation—when seen as essentially effectuated in and through the human struggle for liberation—really conceived as divine grace in a biblical meaning?

In this perspective, process theology's rehabilitation of creation (that is, becoming, seen as a universal event related to and qualified by faith in God) may, after all, be less theologically helpful than it appeared at first glance. To see how this really works out it may be useful to look at a contribution that makes the involvement of process thought with creation particularly explicit, *The Liberation of Life* (1981). This is the joint project of a well-known Australian biologist, Charles Birch (for years one of the driving forces in the World Council of Churches' Working Committee on Church and Society) and a leading American theologian, John B. Cobb, Jr., both of whom profess deep allegiance to the process school of thought.[128] By means of an empirical analysis, "life" is explained here in an "ecological" model, as the global interaction of living organisms with each other in their natural environment. Seeing a "metaphysical framework" as being implicit in any model of reality, the authors plead the superiority of their ecological model over against earlier attempts such as the "mechanistic model," the "vitalistic model," and the "emergent evolution model." They also plead that it is necessary to move away from "substance thinking" to "event thinking" lodged in a concept of "life without boundaries."[129] "A blow is struck" against "the idea of a gulf between human beings and the remainder of the universe . . . encouraged by both humanists and scientists."[130] Following this, "an ethic of life"

---

[128]Charles Birch and John B. Cobb, Jr., *The Liberation of Life: From the Cell to the Community* (Cambridge: Cambridge University Press, 1981) 7, 195ff.

[129]Ibid., 67-95.

[130]Ibid., 138.

is developed, not as in Albert Schweitzer's "reverence for life" (*Ehrfurcht vor dem Leben*; an unrestricted protection of all living entities) but as an adjustment to the vast ecological interplay, with death as the necessary handmaid of life. In fact, this strikes a balance between Schweitzer's "reverence for life" and Charles Darwin's "struggle for life," and includes a careful "yes" to contemporary sociobiology.[131]

The religious apex of the book is the chapter on "Faith in Life,"[132] in which God and life are identified, with certain modifications.

> Life is the creator of the world. Life creates by bringing order out of chaos. It does not create the chaos, for the chaos is uncreated.[133]

> Life as the central religious symbol is God. The Whiteheadian idea of God is appropriately called Life not only because the immanence of God in the world is the life-giving principle but also because the life-giving principle is alive. A lifeless principle could not ground or explain the urge to aliveness that permeates the universe. Indeed, God is the supreme and perfect exemplification of the ecological model of life.[134]

> God is not the world, and the world is not God. But God includes the world, and the world includes God. God perfects the world, and the world perfects God. There is no world apart from God, and there is no God apart from some world. . . . God's life depends on there being some world to include.[135]

In our setting, the important thing is how this strikingly modern and consistent attempt toward a "natural theology" reinstalls the universality of creation as the base of theological reflection—albeit a concept of creation that is somewhat remote from the distinctive connotations traditionally associated with the word. If one compares the process insistence on "metaphysics" as a necessary clue to creation with that of the Løgstrup school of thought, there is, of course, a remarkable formal similarity. However, the material incongruity becomes clear when we try to see where, for example, Ole Jensen would fit into the alternative brands of metaphysics compared in *The Liberation of Life*. He would, no doubt, be closest to the "ecological" alternative, the one favored also by the authors. But at the

---

[131]Ibid., 141-75.

[132]Ibid., 176-202.

[133]Ibid., 192.

[134]Ibid., 195.

[135]Ibid., 196.

same time their vision is radically different from Jensen's, because he stresses life as a given, as a gift, in a way that assigns a much more humble, "receiver" role to creature than in process theology. The idea of God as "the supreme and perfect exemplification of the ecological model of life" seems somewhat foreign to the Løgstrup school. To Løgstrup, God's self-manifestation in creation, which is emphatically distinguished from his self-revelation in the historical event of Jesus Christ, consists in demonstrating that "the power to exist" is an unconditional gift which, in turn, puts an unconditional demand on us. Here, the idea of creatures contributing to some perfection of God would be intolerable, as would the idea of God's dependence on the world. Process theology abolishes the notion of "gift," in the strict sense, for there is no basic distinction between giver and given, nor between giver, given, and receiver.

This deep-rooted difference no doubt reflects the very characteristic of process metaphysics: the ontological priority of becoming over being. Creation is to be thought of exclusively as the process of becoming, as an open-ended event, and not as a hierarchy of gifts given and received or as a pattern of meaning established with indisputable validity. *Given* in the strict sense is simply the process of an all-comprehensive, qualifying event, the self-transformation of timeless potentiality into actuality. The created world as a constantly growing accumulation of actuality is not to be seen as essentially given in its givenness. It would make no sense to step out of the process event and review the world (or some part of it) as it *is*. This abstraction would simply screen out the all-constitutive character of reality (that is, becoming). No statement on reality is admissible if it does not take into account the prevalence of becoming over being. This has consequences also for the image of the Creator, who cannot be imagined as being, or as acting from, outside the process event (and thus acting as a giver of givens); the Creator can only be imagined as being intrinsic to the process, as that qualifying aspect of process that gives unity, meaning, and unsurpassable dignity to the whole.

In this perspective, process theology does not really side with contemporary efforts to reinstall creation in its seemingly self-evident role as the point of departure for the whole theological enterprise; it rather conforms to the post-Kantian appraisal of the creative role of the human mind. Creation is not there as a gift from the Creator's hand, but as an uninterrupted common enterprise of self-production, projected most intelligibly in the human realization of personal freedom as becoming. The coincidence of Sölle's extreme variant of a Messianic *heilsgeschichtlich* theology of creation and the integral process motif may be less incidental than seemed apparent at first glance.

The general question we have raised is whether the modern *Heilsgeschichte* approach to creation can survive the contemporary quest for an operative and viable theology of creation. This question does not refer exclusively, nor predom-

inantly, to the pragmatical short-term challenge: Can it meet the demands of the
contemporary environmental "revival" by providing theological impetus for a
successful ecological ethic? Certainly, this evidently pragmatic question should
not be underestimated; "the proof of the pudding is in the eating." And a theology
that gives no guidance to actual Christian world involvement disqualifies itself (or,
at least, disqualifies the actual presentation of itself) on the grounds of being inadequate. But, on the other hand, a theology gives no proof of general applica-
bility—of "truth"—simply because it offers useful ad hoc guidance in a concrete
situation. If unlimited confidence is placed in it, the theory promoted could turn
out to be a trap for the church of tomorrow. It may therefore be shortsighted to
limit a discussion of creation theology to the observation of actual ecological in-
spirations. Rather we have to ask what can motivate a stable, long-term responsibility for the earth (and the universe) of God's creation, not only among Christians
but among all caretakers of God's creation, in steadfast cooperation.

But this orientation does not authorize ecological efficiency—however long-
term the perspective—as *the* overarching theological goal. It would obviously be
unjustifiable to state concrete practical aims and then to enquire which theological
approach would best serve them—if the purpose of this exercise is to determine
the key theological issue. In a process of theological self-reflection, considerations concerning ecological efficiency could and should play a role as incentives,
but in themselves they can prescribe no conclusion. They should serve as excla-
mation and interrogation marks, not as full stops. For theology, the order of procedure is to derive patterns of action from faith, not to distill faith from programs
of action.

In many cases it can be observed that the link between theological premise
and ethical application is not one of logical necessity; inferences from doctrine to
practical implications presuppose a high awareness of distinctions. As became clear
in the "inductive" phase of the Strasbourg study project, apparent identity in
theological presuppositions does not prevent opposing ethical conclusions; and
fairly identical ethical conclusions can be obtained from procedurally different
dogmatical approaches. "Creation" models of thought can lead to a radical questioning of historical structures in the name of timeless "human rights" (as was
most manifest in the 18th-century Enlightenment) or else to a defense of the same
structures through some unquestioned identification with the Creator's work (the
theology of *Schöpfungsordnungen* in the 19th and 20th centuries). It is thus possible to make "creation" as a socioethical principle either emphatically radical or
emphatically conservative. A historical *Heilsgeschichte* approach can be used in
a similar duplex way: the concepts of "covenant" and of "God's chosen people"
can be applied to some ruling group and thus serve to defend established privi-
leges (e.g., Pilgrim Fathers vis-à-vis native Americans, Boers vis-à-vis Bantus,

Israeli Jews vis-à-vis Palestinian Arabs) or it can be applied to some oppressed group yearning for liberation (the poor, the "people," one or another disinherited nationality). History, or some idea of a formative history within history (salvation history, liberation history, "progress," etc.) seems to be at least as ambiguous an ethical warrant as "creation." It all depends which of the conflicting interests in contemporary society is seen to represent the "real" (that is, normative) trend of that history. In their positivism, historicist approaches to ethics (and, reviewed structurally, *Heilsgeschichte* is certainly one of them!) tend to abolish all para-historical standards to the benefit of some ideologizing conflict partner—be it some established authority or some chosen "people." "Messianic" thinking can be advocated in favor of "law and order" and of uprising, and the same is true for "creation." Generally speaking, the two principles seem equally ambiguous, and ethical conclusions cannot be deduced from either without intervenient mediating terms, which will have decisive influence on the further direction of the argument. Neither creation/nature nor redemption/liberation are sufficiently unambiguous terms to set a direction of ethical argument by themselves. Further distinctions are needed, and these could easily lead to a shift of roles between one formal orientation and the other.

These observations by no means argue the ethical indifference of (Christian) doctrine; rather they indicate the necessity of self-critical awareness and semantical preciseness in both the formulation and the application of doctrinal stances. They also remind us that doctrine does not primarily exist as a resource for ethical decision making but for the sake of faith as response to divine revelation. That such a response will inevitably involve also a reexamination of our premises for that decision making is another matter, though the importance of it should not be underestimated.

Our main question, then, is not whether the Christocentric orientation in and/or of "modern" creation theology will be able to survive and, possibly, contribute to the overcoming of the present-day ecological crisis. Rather the issue is whether, in order to assert itself (and thus, indirectly, safeguard the historical authenticity of revelation) the universal orientation of creation faith does not demand that creation be understood in a setting of its own, prior to reflection on salvation history. Such a conclusion could be argued not only from a strictly dogmatical, but also from a practical-ethical, point of view. In the long run, will the submission of ecological ethics to some theology of redemption not force the following choice upon us: either to reinterpret salvation into a general program of ecological renewal/preservation; or to let theology withdraw from the orbit of ecological involvement and concentrate on the "pure" gospel of personal salvation? In the long run, will it therefore not be necessary to reinstall creation in its traditional right not only as the basis of theological reflection but also as the orientation of our Christian commitment to the universal human exchange that is so badly needed today? How else can Christian faith uphold its dialectical combination of unconditional universality and irrevocable historicity?

This question has such comprehensive repercussions in the present theological situation and has for so long been so widely neglected that it would be meaningless to extrapolate a definite answer from one limited study project such as ''Creation—An Ecumenical Challenge?'' An answer has, however, been suggested in as provocative a manner as possible in order to elicit a future—and indispensable—discussion.

4.3 The role of contemporary ''liberation'' theologies

Reasons could no doubt be given for raising this question already in the context of ethical issues (§3) in immediate light of our ''inductive operation.'' This might also have adapted our reflection to a pattern commonly favored by liberation theologies themselves, that is, to explore theological principles from the starting point of actual praxis instead of from statements of principle. However, this could easily have: 1. confined our observations of movements (that see themselves as integral theological approaches) to an assessment of ethical priorities; and 2. established different standards for dealing with these theologies than for dealing with other theological movements.

However, in approaching liberation theologies in the present setting we should be aware that important (they would maintain the most important) aspects will not come to the fore. In our project a line of reflection developed that is momentous in its own right: the search for balance and interaction between creation and redemption and between nature and (salvation) history. But, basically, we do not intend to make a comparison of different soteriologies as such. Our immediate question to liberation theologies will therefore be whether—as their unmistakable historical dependence on Blochian liberation dialectics[136] may suggest—they are to be seen as manifestations of a modern anthropocentric approach to reality, their main innovating thrust being some politico-utopian model for a human self-realization with no reference to a created universe as the normative bearer of some ecological order. In this perspective, liberation theologies will be of interest primarily as models for relating creation and redemption theology, and only secondarily as patterns of redemption to be compared with other soteriologically centered theologies. Therefore, the way in which they do or do not reflect the Barthian cov-

---

[136]See here, pp. 15, 74-79.

enantal approach to creation is of no more concern than the way in which they transform or preserve the core of the Barthian doctrine of salvation. Only if this perspective is borne in mind can we meaningfully include liberation theologies in our research. Against this background, too, it is clear that we do not pretend to say everything (or maybe even the most important thing) there is to say about these theologies.

In speaking of liberation theologies in the plural, we are adopting a terminology that has become more and more common in view of 1. the increasing variety of endeavors in Latin America that originally gave the name to that whole orientation; and 2. the understanding a) that a profound fellowship exists between a wide variety of contemporary demands for a basic change in patterns of theological reflection in the name of population groups hitherto virtually excluded from the theological enterprise, and b) that no better "umbrella" term exists for this multiplex reorientation.[137] If one compares such culturally diverse phenomena as, inter alia, the Latin American family of liberation theologies, black theology (USA), African theology, Minjung theology (Korea), feminist theology,[138] and various brands of political theology,[139] it is and always has been obvious that to some extent they can also be seen as agents of competing priorities. There is an

---

[137]Reinhard Frieling in his *Befreiungstheologien: Studien zur Theologie in Lateinamerika* (Göttingen: Vandenhoeck & Ruprecht, 1986) consistently uses the plural term for the whole Latin American movement and specifically points out that his project does not include "other emancipatory systems from 'black theology' to 'feminist theology' " (6).

[138]A particularly emphatic expression of how feminist theologians feel themselves to be neglected by the Roman Catholic Church—and of how the struggle against racism, colonialism, classism, sexism, and monopolized heterosexuality must be understood as one and the same fight against a patriarchical system of universal oppression—is *Women—Invisible in Theology and Church* (German: *Das Schweigen brechen—sichtbar werden*), ed. Elisabeth Schüssler Fiorenza and Mary Collins in *Concilium* 182 (December 1985), *Concilium*'s first issue on feminist theology.

[139]On how the relationship between Latin American "liberation" and European "political" theologies has gradually developed into increasing understanding and solidarity, see Gustavo Gutiérrez, *The Power of the Poor in History,* trans. Robert R. Barr (London: SCM Press; Maryknoll NY: Orbis Books, 1983). (Original: *La fuerza historica de los pobres* [Lima: Centro de Estudios y Publicaciones, 1979]; German: *Die historische Macht der Armen* [1984].) On the discovery of a wider liberation solidarity by a leading "black theologian," see the contribution by James H. Cone in *Theologians in Transition,* ed. James M. Wall (New York: Crossroad Publishing Co., 1981) 185-93.

overt rivalry about the relative importance of particular social changes. However, at the same time it is obvious—and this has been increasingly underscored by the various movements themselves—that there is not only a basic dialectical identity; to a large extent, the practical goals of each may depend on, or at least relate to, each other.

The basic structure of a liberation theology—be it one of the movements listed above or any other conceivable version—is as follows: Consciously or unconsciously, any brand of theology has it sociopolitical function, which is geared toward either the transformation of present society and its inbuilt structures of oppression or the justification of the same. An authentic Christian theology must serve the holistic liberation of humankind (against the dualistic separation between "spiritual" and "corporal," "celestial" and "terrestrial" that implies the exploitation of religion by inverted power interests!) and will therefore reflect on theological issues only in light of its liberation legacy. Reflection belongs in the setting of praxis. Whether it is classism, racism, or sexism that is being accentuated as the main evil from which the others follow—or, at least, in the light of which they finally have to be assessed and overcome—the common quest for a reorientation of theology in identification with the socially underprivileged is essentially the same, as is also the angle of attack against traditional theology, that is, against the alleged academical aloofness of theological modernism no less than against the diehard conventionalism of theological fundamentalism.[140]

Obviously, one should not to be too quick in assuming a common historical source for this wide-ranging communion. Even if in all cases some roots can be traced back to Marxist social analysis, the "liberation" impulse has obviously gone through different stages and processes of readaptation and entered into relationship with a variety of others. Seen in this perspective, there is a great distance between the internationalism of a classical orientation of a class struggle and the ethnic self-consciousness of oppressed racial groups, and also between the almost myth-

---

[140]A completely different political approach to creation theology can be found in Socialist countries on the part of theologians who are strongly concerned about reconciliation with dominant trends in their own society. An instructive example may be Hans-Hinrich Jenssen, *Naturerkenntnis: Sünde oder Gottesauftrag? Die Erkennbarkeit der Natur als Bestätigung des Schöpfungsglaubens* (Berlin GDR: Union Verlag, 1985). In this book all skepticistic and "neo-positivistic gnoseological assumptions" are declined—also with reference to the author's "political" objective (17; cf. 14); the creation orientation arises harmoniously from the inspection of scientific facts; and the rootedness of the author in his established type of (Marxist) society hinders any "liberation" perspective from emerging and disturbing the harmonious integration in the existing society!

ical veneration of "the poor" in many of the Latin American liberation endeavors and the conscious academic self-assertion by much of contemporary feminist theology. But even these conspicuous differences should not distract our attention from the commonality in dialectical orientation.

The Klingenthal consultation on "Contemporary Tensions in Creation Theology" (1984) discussed various aspects of liberation theologies in several different settings. One of the four umbrella themes of this consultation was "Creation Faith and Responsibility for the World." Three main presenters advocated very different perspectives relating to liberation and creation theology: Severino Croatto (a Roman Catholic from Argentina) was invited as professed spokesperson of Latin American liberation theology; Elisabeth Bettenhausen (an American Lutheran) was chosen as an interpreter of feminist concerns; and John Pobee (an Anglican from Ghana) was selected to speak on behalf of a contemporary African setting. Bettenhausen was the most critical of conventional church doctrine in that she saw the "masculinist notion of God creating out of nothingness" as an expression of a "dualistic, patriarchal worldview" and termed it the deepest source of sexist oppression in the contemporary world. Describing three different lines in present feminist theology, she said the first tended to "minimize creation faith" by using Christology to attack "fixed ontic structures"; the second reinterpreted creation in terms of process in the light of Logos Christology; and the third rejected creation and redemption altogether in the name of unrestricted human responsibility for the world. No clear choice emerged from her presentation of these options, but the trend was clearly in the direction of reinterpreting creation faith to serve as the vehicle for a more active understanding of human world responsibility and for allowing women their full share in that responsibility.

Before returning to the other two main "liberation" contributions at Klingenthal, it should be noted that two women with more or less the same orientation as Bettenhausen contributed to the opening brainstorming session, which covered a wide range of contemporary creation concerns. Kari Børresen (Roman Catholic, Norway) focused mainly on the *imago Dei* as proclaimed in the biblical creation account and pleaded for adopting that generically inclusive concept to an extent hitherto prevented by traditional sexist God-language. In her warning about what she called "exterminism," Dorothee Sölle (Lutheran, Federal Republic of Germany) was more immediately occupied with ecology, economic justice, and nuclear disarmament. In contemporary threats to "undo creation" she saw the call for a new creation theology going beyond the post-Bonhoefferian Christological concentration. For a new creation theology "in the light of liberation theology," she said it would be essential to turn one's back on the "trivial idea of a Deistic Maker" as well as on any concept of divine transcendence, a concept that ultimately makes this world void of God and hinders creative human participation.

In the meantime, Sölle's argumentation and her attempt to rehabilitate creation theology based on a global vision of liberation have been worked out in greater detail in her book *To Work and to Love*[141] and are more extensively dealt with in another section of the present study (§4.1). What should be observed here and now is the common critical approach in, at least, the orientations of Bettenhausen and Sölle to the idea of creation as involving some normative givenness; Børresen in principle accepts such a givenness but advocates a reinterpretation of its implications. What Bettenhausen proposes in the name of feminism, Sölle champions in the wider liberation context, but there is obviously a basic consistency between the two approaches. The real obstacle to true liberation/redemption is the image of a transcendent Creator creating the world out of nothing, an idea that is not only taken (in its pretended masculinism) to deliver the women to male oppression; by and large it also empties the created world of divine presence and deprives the human species of its assumed cocreative dignity.

And how was the theme "Creation Faith and Responsibility for the World" approached by Bettenhausen's two fellow presenters? In stating the practical orientation of liberation theology and demonstrating the necessity of dealing with God as "liberator" from the point of view of the Latin American situation, Croatto was concerned to establish a biblical framework whereby creation is by no means seen as secondary to redemption. As a matter of fact, it may have surprised the audience that one of the main polemical orientations of his paper was against the Barthian (*in casu*: H. Berkhof) subordination of creation to redemption. An Old Testament scholar, Croatto resisted the common temptation (the school of von Rad) to draw consequences in terms of theological priorities from the undeniable chronological priority of redemption in the history of Israel. In a biblical juxtaposition of creation and redemption, where the two are integrated with equal value, Croatto discerned the importance of both universality (creation) and particularity (salvation history). Creation leads up to the creation of humankind as God's image— henceforth God's partner and the one responsible for carrying on the Creator's work—in such a way that eschatology confirms creation as a "universal *historia salutis*." This orientation does not eschew the *creatio ex nihilo* nor the transcendence of the Creator, but it avoids consequences in the direction of dualism and divine alienation by stressing the human *imago Dei*. Is it more than merely accidental that on that point the Roman Catholic Croatto agreed with the Roman Catholic Børresen?

During the brainstorming session, Pobee had already profiled his plea for an African creation theology as liberation from "North Atlantic captivity." Now, his main contribution concentrated on a positive elaboration of the interaction be-

---

[141]See n. 18.

tween basic New Testament insights and African experience. That "creation must be Africanized and made to engage the African context" did not mean an open-ended theological authorization of traditional African cosmology but rather a cleansing of the latter through the Bible. His reflections on contemporary responsibility for the world as seen from an African setting took the general shape of a creation perspective: humankind as created in God's image sharing responsibility for "impressing God's image of order on the world," an idea of particular pertinence to human rights. In Pobee's presentation, these rights were unambiguously founded in creation faith. Christology came into the picture only through the observation that Christ restored "the goodness of creation" through his "not my will, but thine." Thus, Pobee's plea for an African adaptation of creation theology did not so much pay tribute to a Messianic *heilsgeschichtlich* model of history as to a creation-based vision of human rights. He also pointed to the necessity for each culture to have its religious presuppositions questioned, purified, and confirmed by biblical creation faith, with equal right and obligation to safeguard a spiritual identity of its own, contributing precisely through its specificity to our common exploration of the universality of creation.

What will now emerge if we assess the similarities and the differences between these contributions, not in terms of different soteriologies or divergent political attitudes but simply with regard to the dialectical interplay creation/liberation? The Bettenhausen/Sölle model definitely posits a certain view of human self-realization and asks what creation faith must be like in order to meet the demands of this view. The result is a somewhat overwhelming rejection of what has traditionally been understood as "creation theology" and a proposal for a new model structured by the actual idea of liberation: creation is not normative, creation becomes normalized. In its practical consequences, the Pobee model may be no less critical of a given societal status quo, but it challenges (historical) givenness with (creational) givenness. It does not echo the diastatic constellation of Ernst Bloch; rather it echoes the classical confrontation between natural law (conceived as timelessly valid) and institutional law (as historically conditioned). For the sake of simplification, Croatto's approach could be seen as a dialectical in-between: Creation as expressing divine universality is the ultimate normative principle. But in history this comes to expression only through human involvement as "cocreator," in a particular setting where the concrete, immediate aim will actually present itself as "liberation." However, it is remarkable that this attempt at a balanced assessment of creation/liberation comes precisely from the heart of Latin American liberation theology.[142]

---

[142]José Miguez-Bonino, *Towards a Christian Political Ethics* (London: SCM Press, 1983) also makes a conscious effort to base liberation theology on a bal-

It might be tempting to follow the basic aspects of this discussion into the other "umbrella" themes of the Klingenthal consultation. Under "Theological Discourse on Creation—Christian or Pre-Christian," the traditional Barthian resistance to "natural theology" was voiced by Christian Link—though his redemption perspective was directly opposed to that of Bettenhausen and Sölle through his emphasis on *creatio ex nihilo* to express the eschatological orientation of creation faith. At the same time, contemporary versions of Roman Catholic and Lutheran creation-centeredness were defended by, respectively, Christian Duquoc and Jörg Bauer. Further, in the section on "Being—Becoming— Actuality," a process orientation integrating the divine in the universal event of becoming and, consequently, presenting an unconditional resistance to *creatio ex nihilo* (David Griffin) was in opposition to a more Thomist plea for a "complementarity" faith/science (Alexandre Ganoczy) and to a universal experience of creation awe to be both distinguished from and confirmed by Christianity (Ole Jensen). However, to elaborate on this would lead us too far back to perspectives already dealt with (§§4.1 and 4.2) and thus draw attention away from our search for the specific contribution of liberation theologies.

The (July) 1986 annual International Ecumenical Seminar of the Strasbourg Institute, on the topic "Liberation in Theology as an Ecumenical Challenge," received introductory presentations from Latin America (two), North America, Africa, and Asia by reflectors who were in general in sympathy with the main currents of liberation theology observed in their geographical area. Additional presentations included an Evangelical critique (North American) and an exhibit on "Liberation Theology and the Vatican" (European). In the final panel, a Latin American and an Asian participant conversed with a member of the Institute staff. The assignment given to the two Latin American reflectors differed from that given to the other three continental representatives in that in addition to giving a regional

---

anced assessment of First and Second Article concerns, but less in terms of reflections on creation motifs than through a balanced evaluation of the two kingdoms doctrine (22-25; cf. also 25ff.) and a Trinitarian vision: "Protestantism is sometimes prone to a Christological reductionism in which creation and the dynamism of history are almost deprived of . . . meaning. In Catholic natural theology, on the other hand, the autonomy of creation as perceived by reason becomes a foundation for apologetics and ethics in which the specificity of the Christian revelation is almost lost to sight. A fully Trinitarian approach, by contrast, not only strengthens the positive aspects of the "two kingdoms" idea—God's distinct presence as Father and Son—but also precludes the danger which has beset it, namely an emancipation of the secular kingdom from the influence of the gospel." (124 n. 5)

panorama they were each assigned a specific topic: "Latin American Liberation Theology with Special Reference to Christology" and "The Primacy of Praxis: Theological and Biblical Hermeneutics."

Unlike the 1984 Strasbourg seminar with its creation-related theme, the liberation seminar was not particularly geared toward creation theology, and the choice of topic was not motivated by the long-term creation study. However, its impact on this study may be described in terms of a growing awareness of the interrelatedness among the various contemporary brands of theological liberation emphases through discovering how the existing varieties were geographically conditioned. The active participation of women—encouraged also by the "feminist" orientation of the 1985 seminar (on Mariology and the role of the woman in the church)—and the North American presentation by Dr. Constance Parvey combined to set a useful paradigm for spelling out the liberation perspective in contemporary feminist theology and also greatly helped to explore the unity of liberation theologies in their wider complexity.

Not only in our description of the Klingenthal event but also in the previous presentation on *To Work and to Love*,[143] we have seen that Dorothee Sölle's liberation approach to creation is a faithful theological follow-up of Ernst Bloch's idea of an irreconcilable tension between liberation and creation. It may be of vital importance to ask how constitutive such an emphasis may be of liberation theologies as a whole. We have already seen that Croatto expressed serious reservations about this. But to what extent does that reservation apply to the present-day complexity of theological liberation orientations?[144]

---

[143]See n. 18 and §4.1.

[144]In his much observed challenge of the alleged creation-destructive consequences of historical Christendom, *Das Ende der Vorsehung: Die gnadenlosen Folgen des Christentums* (Reinbek: Rowohlt TB, 1974), Carl Amery sees Marxism as a continuation and aggravation of this tragedy. In consequence, the scheme of Ernst Bloch and its echoes in liberation and God-is-dead theologies leads to an increased threat to the future of creation. The antinomy of creation and utopian promise is seen as being common to Christianity and Socialism (1984 ed., 137). "Das dunkle Prinzip ist der Schöpfer des Himmels und der Erde selbst. Ihm gegenüber befinden sich die progressiven Theologen . . . in Verlegenheit. . . . Entweder wird er als Nichts behandelt . . . oder er wird, wie bei Altizer, Sölle und Bloch, manichäisch aufgewertet zu einem Heerfürsten der Nacht, gegen den uns das Licht der Menschlichkeit in Pflicht nimmt. In beiden Fällen muss *gegen* ihn gesiegt werden; muss der Mensch seine eigene Schöpfung bauen . . . mit der Hoffnung, dass die Geschichte des Menschen auf eben diesen hominisierten Kosmos angelegt ist." (Ibid., 138)

It was probably no mere accident that at the Klingenthal consultation the most emphatic reservations about a traditional theology of creation came from conscious champions of feminist theology. As may be remembered, Bettenhausen saw three different trends in contemporary theological feminism: the minimizing of the importance of creation by reference to Christology; the transmuting of it into a process concept of creation; and the rejection of the conceptual framework of traditional theology altogether. Parvey's approach at the 1986 seminar was less confrontational, probably partly due to the fact that she was less concerned about the self-understanding of feminist theologians than about the integration of theological feminism into a global survey of liberation impulses.[145]

In the literary self-presentations of various geographically rooted liberation theologies, a basic reflection on creation/redemption—and thus a critical examination of other than political elements in one's own presuppositions—is generally lacking. The role of creation faith has to be studied mainly through negative observations: how a global theological horizon can be constituted with little or no creation references. A characteristic example is to be found in James H. Cone's presentation on black theology in *God of the Oppressed:*

> The hermeneutical principle for an exegesis of the Scriptures is the revelation of God in Christ as the Liberator of the oppressed from social oppression and to political struggle, wherein the poor recognize that their

---

[145]In our context, it may be particularly instructive to consult the study by Rosemary Radford Ruether, *Sexism and God-Talk: Toward a Feminist Theology* (London: SCM Press, 1983). This book is particularly representative, not only because of the leading position of this author within contemporary theological feminism but also because of the comprehensive orientation of the study. Wherever the term "creation" appears, it is with positive connotations. But it is never the subject of a comprehensive reflection, and ultimately it remains unclarified. On the one side, it is completely clear to Ruether that feminism claims "the prophetic-liberating tradition of biblical faith as a norm through which to criticize the Bible" (23-24; the unconditional priority of liberation!), and it is from this principle that the theological reflection is consistently conducted. On the other side, creation is confirmed in terms of "goodness of nature and bodily existence" (36). This leads to the exposure of an amazing "paradox" in the ancient church: on the one hand, there is Gnosticism, representing the genuine prophetic liberation line but rejecting the unity of the spiritual and the physical universe; on the other, the Roman Catholic Church struggles passionately to preserve that unity but definitely opposes liberation (36-37). To this, one may ask: Does history really contain "paradoxes," or do such "paradoxes" merely signalize the incongruence of the parameters we are using?

fight against poverty and injustice is not only consistent with the gospel but is the gospel of Jesus Christ.[146]

Still more significant may be the collection of papers edited by Jürgen Moltmann, *Minjung: Theologie des Volkes Gottes in Südkorea,* and particularly the 1973 "Manifesto of Korean Christians" with its three-part statement of faith, which is intended as a contemporary reinterpretation of the Creed. Here the "First Article" reads:

Wir glauben, dass wir von Gott, dem Richter und Herrn der Geschichte, zu Vertretern des ganzen Volkes bestimmt sind, für die Freilassung der Unterdrückten und unschuldig Leidenden zu beten.[147]

In our context, the question is not whether this is a true observation of a practical consequence (and maybe a most important one) of actual faith in God, but whether it can in fact be taken as a valid expression of this faith in its global orientation. Obviously, God is seen here as the sovereign agent of historical change, with no explicit reference to creation and no reflection whatsoever on nature and universe. And history starts with the particularity of election, "the people" being already essentially identified as "oppressed." Natural right and universal creation standards could hardly be more remote than they are in this perspective!

In the Roman *Congregatio de doctrina fidei*'s "Instruction" on (Latin American) liberation theology (September 1984), it is interesting that among the heretical tendencies attributed to certain types of this theology particular attention is focused on a political distortion of Christology, soteriology, and ecclesiology, together with a hermeneutical relativization of truth as such.[148] In the listing of errors to beware of (§17), no single word refers to the First Article or to topics particularly pertaining to it. That this dimension has generally been absent in the official liberation controversy in the Roman Catholic Church is clearly documented in recent publications.[149] The most representative self-presentation we have

---

[146]James H. Cone, *God of the Oppressed* (London: SPCK; New York: Seabury Press, 1975) 81-82. German: *Gott der Befreier* (1982) 58.

[147]"Manifesto of Korean Christians" (1973), *Minjung: Theologie des Volkes Gottes in Südkorea,* ed. Jürgen Moltmann (Neukirchen-Vluyn: Neukirchener Verlag, 1984) 172.

[148]*Herder Korrespondenz* 38/10 (October 1984): 464-75.

[149]E.g., *Konflikt um die Theologie der Befreiung: Diskussion und Dokumentation,* ed. Norbert Greinacher (1985); *Théologies de la libération: Documents et Débats,* ed. Bruno Chenu and Bernard Lauret (Paris: Les Editions du Cerf/Edition le Centurion, 1985).

to hand is Leonardo and Clodovis Boff's *Introducing Liberation Theology,* which intends to be a total review. The authors are very much aware of the development of an international network of liberation theologies with different contextual references,[150] and while the book contains no explicit reflection on creation theology, it moves entirely within a Christological-salvation-historical perspective, in which the God of the Bible, "fundamentally a living God, the author and sustainer of all life," enters the stage only as the partisan Lord of history, the liberator of the poor.[151] Creation theology in a more specific sense is neither confirmed nor critically reviewed; it simply is not there. There is certainly no reason to suspect the Boff brothers of consciously concealing a critical perspective on creation theology in order not to aggravate their conflict with the official magisterium. A rather obvious explanation for the omission is that their praxis-oriented approach activates those elements in the classical theological inheritance that immediately offer themselves in support of the unifying liberation vision, without eliciting fundamental reflection on the intrinsic coherence of that inheritance as such. Thus even elements that are traditionally seen as constitutive can remain at the same time unquestioned and unactivated, an attitude which, from a logical point of view, may be seen as less satisfactory than the traditional Bloch/Sölle approach with its heavy invocation of liberation as a challenge to creation faith.[152]

---

[150]Leonardo and Clodovis Boff, *Introducing Liberation Theology,* trans. Paul Burns (Tunbridge Wells: Burns & Oates/Search Press Ltd.; Maryknoll NY: Orbis Books, 1987) 78-95. German: *Wie treibt man Theologie der Befreiung?* (1986) 95-108.

[151]Ibid., 44 (German: 57).

[152]One exception to the general rule of creation simply being absent in the presentations of Latin American authors associated with liberation theology is a 1969 essay in Gustavo Gutiérrez, *The Power of the Poor in History* (see n. 139) 25-35 (German: 29-42). Here, the explanation in traditional catechisms of creation being "the explanation for the existing world" (*das Bestehenden*) is mildly rebuked as "incomplete," while in the Bible creation is "not a stage prior to the work of salvation; it is the first salvific activity. . . . Creation is inserted in the salvation process, in God's self-communication. . . . When we say that women and men fulfill themselves by carrying on the work of creation through their own labors, we are asserting that they are operating within the framework of God's salvific work from the very first. Subduing the earth . . . is a salvific work. To work in the world and transform it is to save it. Inasmuch as it is a humanizing factor that transforms nature, work tends to build a society that is more just and more worthy of humankind—as Marx clearly saw. . . . Building the earthly city actually immerses human beings in the salvation process that touches all human-

That that radical line of thought has by no means been absent within Latin American liberation theology is amply documented in the collection *The Idols of Death and the God of Life: A Theology,*[153] issued in the name of the staff of the Departemento Ecumenico de Investigaciones in Costa Rica. Even if this intentionally unified work focuses on the concept of God and not on that of creation, certain basic assumptions with regard to creation theology are immediately apparent, and the resonance of Bloch is deafening:

> The central question in Latin America today is not atheism—the ontological question whether God exists or not. . . . All systems of oppression are characterized by the creation of gods and of idols that sanction oppression and antilife forces.[154]

Particularly characteristic may be the contribution by Joan Casañas, "The Task of Making God Exist," in which the author passionately rejects:

> . . . God as someone known now, who is here, who is like this or that, who does and undoes, who speaks to us, and to whom we speak in return

ity." (31-32; German: 38) What is the real role of "creation" here? Is it simply to secure a universal qualification of work = human self-liberation = salvation = creation as the comprehensive horizon for our historical realization of what is supposed to be the Creator's total purpose for humankind? The text stems from the infancy of liberation theology, but I have found no later clarification, and it was republished as late as 1984.

Similar questions could be raised about another integrative approach, namely that of Rosemary Radford Ruether in the chapter entitled "Toward an Ecological-Feminist Theology of Nature" in her *Sexism and God-Talk* (see n. 145) 85-92: "There can be no ecological ethic simply as a new relation of "man" and "nature." Any ecological ethic must always take into account the structures of social . . . exploitation . . . in favor of . . . the dominant class, race, and sex. An ecological ethic must always be an ethic of eco-justice that recognizes the interconnection of social domination and domination of nature." (91) The issue here is not so much the general statement of principle as the question as to how it functions and what it warrants in the actual setting. It looks very much as if to Ruether concepts like "ecology" and "nature" carry no weight on their own, but are brought in to support the claims of a feminist liberation theology with the contemporary appeal of ecology: If you want to save the world around you—as people generally do these days—then do opt for the appropriate model of liberation theology!

[153]*The Idols of Death and the God of Life: A Theology,* ed. Pablo Richard (1983).

[154]Ibid., introduction.

> . . . a "deductive theology," making the faith . . . into the schemata, affirmations, and language of the Bible. . . . A personalistic view of the matter of God, as a unique individual to whom all human beings could be related on their own account . . . could, insidiously, lead to highly individualistic, closed, and anticollective attitudes.[155]

In stark opposition to this, Casañas wants to focus on:

> . . . the historical futurity of God's existence. . . . We know nothing about God, except that God will be, because our freedom is bent on constructing that kingdom. And if God is not, but will be, we still know nothing; whether God is someone, something, or what mode of reality God is. . . .
>
> If many of those fighting and dying selflessly for the people's liberation . . . have not discovered that "God exists" and is "Father," is it not possible that this "message" that "God exists" and is "Father" may not be as profound . . . as it has generally seemed to us?[156]

This is, of course, an extreme position, and not one for which liberation theology as a whole should be taken to account. But, on the other hand, it does occur in a rather official symposium with a pronounced common trend—a trend that this particular contribution presses to the maximum—and there is no counterbalance in the anthology as a whole. Even if the vast majority of liberation theologians are far from reaching consequences like those of Casañas, one would not find many criteria in their works that would restrict this kind of theological destruction. To some extent, however, exceptions can be made for the already cited contributions from Croatto and Miguez-Bonino!

A fascinating introduction to theological liberation thought is to be found in Harvey Cox, *Religion in the Secular City: Toward a Post-Modern Theology* (1984), a book that in certain regards confirms and in other—no less important—regards corrects his famous *Secular City* of 19 years earlier. Although he does not see himself as an immediate associate of liberation theology, Cox has considerable experience of Latin American theological communities and combines sympathetic insight with a rather careful critical perspective. He reflects on the marvellous "comeback" of religion in the modern "secular city," a development that neither he nor many other observers foresaw in the mid-1960s. In that perspective, two strong contemporary movements—at the same time marvellously consonant and marvellously contradictory—are analyzed: fundamentalist conservatism and

---

[155]Ibid., 118, 141.

[156]Ibid., 118, 142, 121.

liberation radicalism. Both mass movements oppose "modernity" in its academic-individualistic exclusivism as well as its belief in a more or less automatic progress. Cox sees major strengths and weakness in both movements, but his major hope for a viable "postmodern theology" lies in the liberation emphasis.

Particularly interesting are Cox's observations on the lost "universality of God," even if, finally, he attributes the death of modernity not to a changed vision of God as such but to a reversed paradigm of theological communication.

> Modern theology's God pole also began to teeter. Previous theologians disagreed mainly about the details. . . . But they all agreed that God was universal. . . . There was little room in modern theology either for a partisan God who takes sides in historical struggles or for a God who has to be sought in radically dissimilar ways by different peoples. Now, however, this assumption of universality was questioned too. . . . Blacks and women, poor people and non-Westerners all insisted that these allegedly all-inclusive theologies were narrow and provincial—white, male, Western, "bourgeois."[157]

> Unitive systems of thought usually become ideologies of domination. The effort of modern theology to be all things to all people everywhere may itself be one of the qualities of its modernity that should not survive into a postmodern world in which particularity will flourish.[158]

Cox thus sees that the basic theological tension to which liberation theology addresses itself is not that between creation and redemption, or theocentricity versus Christocentricity, but between (inoperative) theoretical universalism and (praxis-determined) theological partisanship. In the Latin American concept of the *Dios pobre* (the poor God) theology and Christology combine and form a new center of gravitation that is historically equally important as, and biblically even more focal than, the Reformation's *sola fide*.[159] The concepts of Creator and creation do not play a constitutive part in this new vision, but thematically it is clear that the poverty and partisanship of God as hermeneutical code, along with the pronounced suspicion of divine universality as a bourgeois pretext for stripping historical involvement of religious relevance, result in a very pronounced subordination of creation ideas to and into the global vision of liberation. Even if in seeing religion as a "return to the secular city" Cox is radically correcting his

---

[157]Harvey Cox, *Religion in the Secular City: Toward a Post-Modern Theology* (New York: Macmillan, 1984) 178-79.

[158]Ibid., 213.

[159]Ibid., 263ff.

mid-1960s popularization of the Bonhoefferian vision of a secular age, he basically remains consistent with his previous orientation in declining religion as some universal, creation-based dimension as well as in giving priority to the particularity of historical responses. In several ways he endeavors to overcome what he sees as the narrowness of theological "modernity": Its "fascination with the mind" should be superseded by a "concentration on the body, on the nature of human community, on the question of life and death."[160]

Modernity's feeling of religious superiority, says Cox, should yield to a new awareness of "the world faiths" and "people's religion."[161] Throughout, the motivation is one and the same: "Interfaith dialogue becomes . . . a step in anticipation of God's justice. It becomes practice. . . . Popular religion persists as a source of inspiration for the poor."[162] Particularly enlightening is the duplex judgment about feminist theology:

> Perhaps the most promising resource for a postmodern theology is the religious imagination of . . . women. . . . Feminist theology . . . has already made an enormous impact in nearly every field of theology. . . . But . . . it still bears the marks of its critical, academic milieu, and has not yet been nourished by the liberating potential of people's religion.[163]

Cox sums up his hopes for a coming postmodern theology—based basically on the insights of Latin American liberation theology—in the multiple role he has observed of a religious symbol: Our Lady of Guadalupe. As a cultic expression, highly beloved by her vast constituency today, she becomes a comprehensive synthesis of liberation motifs:

> A dark-skinned mestiza, she personifies the anger and persistent dignity of people of color everywhere. A woman, she embodies the never-completely-dominated jouissance of the second sex. A poor person, she inspires the hopes of all those who believe that God is preferentially present in the lives of the disinherited. An echo of a pre-Christian goddess, she

---

[160]Ibid., 209. How Latin American liberation theology itself views its opposition to "progressive theology" is developed by Gustavo Gutiérrez in his *The Power of the Poor in History* (see n. 139). "The breach of liberation theology with other theological perspectives is not simply theological. It transcends the world of theology strictly so called—the realm of ideas—and enters real history where persons and social groups live in confrontation." (93; German: 63)

[161]Harvey Cox, *Religion in the Secular City* (see n. 157) 222-39, 240-61.

[162]Ibid., 238, 248.

[163]Ibid., 254-55.

reminds us of the larger and older family of faiths of which ours is a part. A victim of clerical manipulation, she recalls the destructive role churches often have played in perpetuating injustice and in robbing the dispossessed of their most valuable symbols of identity and hope.[164]

As a global program, this clearly testifies to a theological vision whereby creation is not only conceptually anonymized but also intrinsically repressed. Without consciously echoing Ernst Bloch's criticism of creation as a "reactionary" principle, it gives a rather representative demonstration of how one may—and wide segments of liberation theology certainly do—give finality to an orientation whereby creation faith is virtually defunctionalized and God the Creator seems to be reduced to certain (however authentic and relevant) aspects of historical manifestation.

One final observation should be added to our reflections on liberation theology and creation faith, namely recent attempts at a synthesis, as has been undertaken mainly by process theology. As will be borne in mind, this theology has a strong creation orientation in the sense of giving prominence to the universal presence of God the Creator as well as to the religious dignity of the phenomenal world as a whole. For several years many criticized this theology for its lack of political awareness, but more recently this objection has been met with conscious attempts at a more inclusive self-presentation. Two representative works that indicate this turn are Schubert M. Ogden, *Faith and Freedom: Toward a Theology of Liberation* (1979) and John B. Cobb, Jr., *Process Theology as Political Theology* (1982). The somewhat theoretical rapprochement toward liberation theology represented by Ogden's book—and clearly illustrated in the confrontation between Dorothee Sölle and Ogden at a 1979 consultation in Chicago[165]—continues to take rather vigorous exception to what is seen as a confusion of the religious (redemptive) and the liberating (emancipatory) functions of Christianity. The endeavor toward a synthesis is a good deal more emphatic in Cobb's contribution. Regretting the fact that in their dealing with liberation theology process theologians have so far mainly confined themselves to a principal discussion about "freedom," Cobb finds it necessary to expand the horizon and take a more comprehensive note of European "political theology" (as represented by J. B. Metz, Jürgen Moltmann, and Dorothee Sölle),[166] a term that to him seems still more important than "liberation

---

[164]Ibid., 260.

[165]See *The Challenge of Liberation Theology,* ed. Mahan and Richesin (see n. 36) 12-14, 17-20.

[166]John B. Cobb, Jr., *Process Theology as Political Theology* (see n. 36) ix-xii.

theology.'' Cobb calls for a global integration of the concern of political liberation into a wider ecological model, a model that allegedly has its best support in a process understanding of reality. Using a formula of Sölle's, he wants "the indivisible salvation of the world" in an even more indivisible sense than the author of the slogan intended.[167]

> For process theologians the ecological horizon is even more important than to Moltmann, and the question arises whether this excludes us from political theology.[168]

> Political theology in Metz's form is based on Kantian anthropocentrism. In that context there can be no interest in plants and animals except as they are given being in human experience. . . . Process theology, on the other hand . . . has been deeply informed by the quite different philosophy of Whitehead. . . . Theology which aims to be truly inclusive will be "ecological theology."[169]

And here is the final synthesis of process and liberation theologies:

> Much in the experience of blacks, of Latin Americans, of Africans, of Hindus, and of Buddhists, as well as of women, favors this ecological view of nature against the mechanistic one. There is, therefore, some prospect that others seeking their own liberation may join the more farsighted women in the recognition of the need to challenge the fundamental ideas on which our scientific-technological society has been built.[170]

It is striking to compare the vision of John Cobb with that of Harvey Cox: the one trying to overcome the limitations of "modern theology" by extending the scope of universality in view of the ecological wholeness of God's creation; the other stressing the political partisanship of divine involvement by particularizing the scope of historical involvement. In a certain sense, Cobb could be said to offer a new possibility of organically relating creation and liberation theology through integrating the latter into the former. At the same time, as became clear at the Klingenthal consultation, there is a far-reaching concord between process theol-

---

[167]Ibid., 15, 111.

[168]Ibid., 111-12.

[169]Ibid., 125.

[170]Ibid., 155. It should be borne in mind that this book appeared at almost the same time as Cobb's (and Charles Birch's) *The Liberation of Life* (see n. 128) and Cobb's *Beyond Dialogue* (see n. 126).

ogy and political theology (as represented, above all, by Dorothee Sölle) in that the concept of God as sovereign Maker and Creator *ex nihilo* is rejected to the benefit of human participation in a mystery of universal creativeness. The process stress on universal interrelatedness is on ecological rather than on creational incorporation.[171]

The emergence and expansion of a geographically and sociologically wide spread of liberation theologies contribute to accentuate and illustrate the issue of creation-based versus Christologically-based social ethics, even though, in itself, this differentiation process basically adds no new orientation to the question of principles.[172]

As declared global approaches to the adventure of theology, these theologies also serve indirectly to actualize the question of *Schöpfungsvergessenheit*. Attempts to construct "ecological" bridges between creation and liberation approaches by such different and influential theological thinkers as John Cobb and Jürgen Moltmann[173] may signalize that the established confrontation is historically conditioned and by no means insurmountable—even if, each in their own way, Cobb's "process" reluctance to accept the *creatio ex nihilo* and Moltmann's Barthian-Blochian attempt to give precedence to a Messianic, *heilsgeschichtlich* perspective may serve, rather conspicuously, to curtail a traditional creation theology.

---

[171]A somewhat different attempt to integrate creation and liberation is that of Gibson Winter, *Liberating Creation: Foundations of Religious Social Ethics* (New York: Crossroad Publishing Co., 1981). Winter is also concerned with the vital importance of liberating culture from the "mechanistic paradigm" of the age of "industrial capitalism" for the benefit of "a good creation" (99, 103-104), but he blames liberation theology for not seeing the basic importance of an "artistic vision of creation" and an "organistic paradigm" as ontological "dwelling"— and, thus, for being imprisoned by the metaphysical presuppositions of modern "mechanism" (113). In his opinion, only a true rediscovery of creation can effect sociocultural liberation.

[172]A parallel—but definitely different—critical approach is that of Dennis McCann, *Christian Realism and Liberation Theology: Practical Theologies in Creative Conflict* (Maryknoll NY: Orbis Books, 1981), whereby the critical issue is not that of creation but that of "the Hidden God's relationship to human history" (4)—this referring to Reinhold Niebuhr's concept of "Christian realism." However, this is also a question about how the Second Article of the Creed (the particularity of historical Christian revelation) relates to the First (the universality of divine presence).

[173]See here, §4.1, pp. 92-99, 103-10.

So far, the ecumenical importance of liberation theologies with regard to creation faith seems to be more to *expose* problems than to *shape* problems (on the one side) or to *solve* problems (on the other). What if, as background for the reflection, Bloch's equalizing of the "Behold, it was very good" in Genesis with an uncritical support of given status quos were challenged by the human rights' thinking of the 18th century, a thinking whereby the term " . . . it *was* good," referring to a primordial design of meaning, was taken as a critical stand over against what it all actually *is* and *has become*? Is there a better logical justification for making the assumed goodness of creation a legitimation of actual societal givens rather than making it a challenging critical principle? For one reason or another, this simple, basic question has been left unobserved in post-Blochian theology—and, as a matter of fact, in unilaterally *heilsgeschichtlich*-oriented theologies long before that.[174]

Excursus on the theological foundation of "human rights"

"Human rights" and the contemporary ecological challenge are probably the two issues that serve most to highlight the relation between creation and redemption. While, for obvious political reasons, ecumenical discussions on human rights have had a tendency to focus on the mutual priorities of the different "rights" (a

---

[174]In the framework of a practical vision—with no explicit reflection on unifying principles—an impressive synoptic presentation of creation and liberation concerns is offered in the report from the Protestant Kirchentag in Düsseldorf, *Die Erde bewahren: Versöhnung von Arbeit und Leben. Impulse von Düsseldorfer Kirchentag,* ed. Ingrid Überschär (Stuttgart: Kreuz Verlag, 1985), perhaps particularly in the rich variety of biblical studies by various authors with remarkably different approaches to Leviticus 25:1-13 (114-44). Here, it looks as if the biblical concepts of "work" and of "rest," in the life of humans as of the total creation, could provide a unifying approach to creation and redemption, nature and history, liberation and preservation.

A rather moving—seen in its historical perspective—plea for an organic interrelatedness of creation and redemption could already be seen in Rudolf Bultmann's sermon "Der Glaube an Gott den Schöpfer" (Marburg, 1 July 1936): "So steht der zweite Artikel neben dem ersten. Der erste führt zum zweiten, und der zweite führt zum ersten zurück." (See Rudolf Bultmann, *Das verkündigte Wort* [Tübingen: J.C.B. Mohr (Paul Siebeck), 1984] 272.) If the inner strain of the sermon is on the Second Article as a clue to the First, the reason is stated clearly enough: to avoid a mixing of human claims based on nature or history with the loyalty claimed by the Creator alone (264-65, 273).

discussion that was particularly spectacular in the 1970s), the "liberation" emphasis has increasingly become *the* theological avenue of approach, thus favoring a Christocentric-historical approach over a "natural" creation one. In the course of this development little, if any, attention has been paid to the significance of the obvious theological foundations of the concept of human rights as manifested by the great liberation events of the late 18th century, the American and French revolutions.[175]

The reason for this neglect may be the secularizing orientation of the ideological leadership of that day, which can too easily be interpreted in a way that, theologically, invalidates their argument. Without making the slightest concession to Enlightenment Deism as such, it is possible—and even necessary—to observe that faith in a common universal origin (whether "the Creator" or "Nature" is said to be the supreme principle) here warrants universal human participation in inviolable "rights," rights that function as critical principles in face of any historically maintained order. This is precisely the opposite of the assumption of Ernst Bloch and Bloch-inspired theology that creation-based ethics are univocally "reactionary."[176] As opposed to all—essentially positivistic—"historical" approaches, which are determined by the particular social self-identification of the agent,[177] the concept of creation-based human rights offers a critical principle that

---

[175]A creation foundation is most visible in the American Declaration of Independence (1776): "We hold these truths to be self-evident, that all men are created equal, that they are endowed by their Creator with certain inalienable Rights." The United Nations Universal Declaration of Human Rights (1948) may be symptomatic of the majority of subsequent national and international statements in that it leaves out any explicit religious reference and concentrates on "all human beings" being "born free and equal in dignity and rights" (Article 1). Among modern constitutions, the West German (1949) may be of particular interest, not only because it starts by proclaiming human dignity as inviolable (thus motivating the German people to confess invulnerable and inalienable "human rights" to be the ground of human community) but also because, in the official preamble, it gives voice to the consciousness of the German people of their "responsibility before God and humanity" (*Verantwortung vor Gott und den Menschen*). In our century, this comes rather close to echoing the American profession of creation as the basis of human rights!

[176]See Jürgen Moltmann, *Im Gespräch mit Ernst Bloch* (1976) and H. Deuser and P. Steinacker, *Ernst Blochs Vermittlungen zur Theologie* (Munich: Christian Kaiser Verlag, 1983).

[177]In Christian *Offenbarungspositivismus,* founded in the historical legacy of the Christ.

is equally valid in face of all patterns of established order as it denies allegiance
to any one of them.

Important monuments to confessionally based reflection are *Christian Faith
and Human Rights*[178] and *How Christian are Human Rights?*[179] The study project
of the World Alliance of Reformed Churches (1970–1976), reflected in the first
publication, leads up to a statement of principles (adopted by a February 1976
consultation in London) whose first four theses, each with a brief paragraph of
comments, contain "Theological Guidelines."[180] The first of these may sound as
though it refers to the First rather than the Second Article:

> We understand the basic theological contribution of the Christian faith,
> in these matters, to be the grounding of fundamental human rights in God's
> right, that is, his claim on human beings.

However, the explanation moves in a different direction:

> That is to say that human rights . . . reflect the covenant of God's faith-
> fulness to his people and the glory of his love for the church and the world.
> . . . It is in the light of this covenant as fulfilled in . . . Jesus Christ and
> . . . the Holy Spirit . . . that Christians express solidarity with all those
> who bear a human countenance.

Here, it is clear that the "covenant" of God and "his people" is expressed
as the guiding orientation and, consequently, the *church* is brought in as prior to
the *world*. The motivating force of human rights is laid in the Trinitarian vision
of Christian faith—a motivation, therefore, speaking immediately only to believing Christians. "All those who bear a human countenance" are explicitly included in the vision, but not basically as fellow agents who are able to confirm or
promote the same rights; more as fellow objects.

---

[178]*Christian Faith and Human Rights: A Declaration on Human Rights,* ed.
Allen O. Miller (Grand Rapids MI: Wm. B. Eerdmans, 1977). German: *Gottes
Recht und Menschrechte,* ed. Jan Milič Lochman and Jürgen Moltmann (Neu-
kirchen-Vluyn: Neukirchener Verlag, 1977).

[179]*How Christian are Human Rights: An Interconfessional Study on the Theological Bases of Human Rights: Report on an Interconfessional Consultation, Geneva, April 30-May 3, 1980,* ed. Eckehart Lorenz (Geneva: Lutheran World
Federation, 1981). German: *" . . . erkämpft das Menschenrecht." Wie christlich
sind die Menschenrechte?,* ed. Eckehart Lorenz (Hamburg: Lutherisches Verlagshaus, 1981).

[180]*Christian Faith and Human Rights* (see n. 178) 144-46.

The parallel process in the Lutheran churches, reflected in the second publication, did not lead to a basic statement with a similar bearing on principles to the Reformed declaration. *How Christian are Human Rights?* is the report of a multiconfessional symposium held in Geneva (May 1980) with Lutheran, Orthodox, and Reformed participation, and it tries to wind up the conclusions of a more comprehensive study process. The discussions focused around Jürgen Moltmann's main presentation on "Christian Faith and Human Rights."[181] The ecumenical merit of this paper is that it overtly states the confessional differences and suggests some challenging points of view on them. With special reference to these two confessional human rights studies (of which it gives a condensed description), the differences in theological emphases are also observed by Eckehart Lorenz in his preface. The conference report ends with a series of conclusions and recommendations, a section of them being dedicated to "Theological Approaches to Human Rights."[182]

This section's concluding statement spells out the "likeness of God," to which humans were created, as the common ground for a Christian approach to human rights, but sees "several approaches":

> One approach proceeds from the creation of the human being and considers the sources for recognizing human dignity and fundamental human rights to be implicit in the natural law of humanity. Recognition in Christ is the criterion for dealing with the historically developed natural and human rights.

> Another approach is based on the experience of God's covenant with his people. Here it is deemed that the story of the biblical covenant is an exemplary representation of human dignity and fundamental human rights. The new covenant in Christ conclusively manifests God's righteousness and the justification of the human being.

> A further approach takes the event of justification of sinners through God's grace to be the basis of their freedom and from there proceeds to people's responsibility for their neighbors in the world.[183]

The trichotomy of this "ecumenical" statement may cause some misunderstanding. A closer look makes it clear that the third "approach" does not imme-

---

[181]*How Christian are Human Rights?* (see n. 179) 11-24. Published also in the report of a 1978 consultation of the Irish School of Ecumenics in Dublin, *Understanding Human Rights,* ed. Alan D. Falconer (1980) 182-95.

[182]*How Christian are Human Rights?,* 84-86.

[183]Ibid., 84-85.

diately relate to the other two in the way that they relate to each other. The first and second—universal creation and particular redemption emphases, respectively—are immediately seen to be competitive and need some fairly substantial readaptations in order to fit in with each other; while the third could obviously be seen in continuity with either of the first two without special readjustment—even if interpretations would necessarily vary in the two cases. "Justification" here offers itself more as an expansion and precision than as a separate alternative.

In his reflections on "Christian Faith and Human Rights," Jürgen Moltmann first surveys recent ecumenical human rights studies, not only the parallel Lutheran and Reformed projects but also two Roman Catholic documents—the Roman Synod of Bishops' 1974 "Message Concerning Human Rights and Reconciliation"[184] and The Church and Human Rights of the Pontifical Commission "Justitia et Pax"[185]—and certain initiatives within the World Council of Churches. He then deals more explicitly with "Work on the Theological Basis of Human Rights" as reflected in these events[186] and, in the following section, comes to "Theological Differences and Open Questions."[187] As far as confessional confrontations are concerned, he sees mainly two: "Reformed-Lutheran" and "Roman Catholic-Reformed."

Concerning the Reformed-Lutheran issue, Moltmann finds that in recent documents "it is not easy for an outsider to grasp the real difference." This statement is based on his comparison of two formulae: "reason enlightened through faith" (Heinz-Eduard Tödt and Wolfgang Huber, in the Lutheran study process) and "human rights based on God's right to man" in the Reformed 1976 statement. But before saying this, he has already pointed out that the latter document, as we have already observed, sees humankind's

> . . . being an image of God in the federal-theological context of the covenant of God. This mode of substantiation has certainly the disadvantage that it is only acceptable for Christians. But it has the advantage that it motivates and activates Christians for human rights . . . as Christians and not just by the way. The Lutheran critique of Tödt and Huber gets under

---

[184]In The Gospel of Peace and Justice: Catholic Social Teaching since Pope John (Maryknoll NY: Orbis Books, 1976) 513-629.

[185]The Church and Human Rights, Working Paper No. 1 (Vatican City, 1976).

[186]How Christian are Human Rights? (see n. 179) 15-19; Understanding Human Rights (see n. 181) 186-90.

[187]Ibid., 19-21 and 190-92, respectively.

way with the two kingdoms teaching. . . . A "Christian foundation" of human rights is rejected.[188]

Moltmann concludes his assessment of this confrontation:

> However, the question remains open as to how the particularity of the Christian faith is to be referred and applied to the universalism of human rights.[189]

From this, it is not easy to see how he can reduce the difference between the two approaches to a mere trifle that can be explained through "the different historical characteristics" of the two traditions. On the one hand, ever since the Puritan revolution the Reformed have been involved in political planning; on the other, Lutherans have for centuries been confined by outward circumstances to react to already completed political events. But however important the differences in sociopolitical genealogy of Lutheranism and Calvinism may be, this does not reduce the weight of the dilemma: Is the task of a theology of human rights (exclusively) to design a motivation that is valid for Christians as Christians? Or should it indicate a platform that is common to everybody created "in the image of God"?

Moltmann's conclusions with regard to the Roman Catholic-Reformed difference follow much the same direction:

> Both perspectives, properly understood, do not exclude each other. The grace, which nature presupposes, establishes a universal horizon. The grace, which justifies sinners, makes it possible to experience concretely God's justice.[190]

It would seem that this observation is beyond objection. The only question is whether the two historical positions are adequately taken care of in the formulae presented for comparison. What if the Roman Catholic principle were put this way: "The grace, which establishes a universal horizon, presupposes and subsequently confirms an authentic relationship with nature?" And the Reformed phrased thus: "The grace, which justifies sinners and makes it possible to experience concretely God's justice, is the only opening to a viable knowledge of nature as an ethically obliging given?" Is the reconciliation that Moltmann suggests not gained through formulae so vague that they rather tend to hide the issue?

---

[188]Ibid., 19 and 190.

[189]Ibid., 20 and 191.

[190]Ibid., 20 and 191.

The question of basic principle implicit in any discussion on human rights may make this discussion more immediately suited to suggest an answer in the direction of history, anthropology, liberation, or covenant than the discussion on ecology, or creatural rights, in which concepts such as creation, nature, and universe present themselves more readily as vehicles of interpretation. On a practical level, there is undoubtedly the possibility of a certain amount of competition between "human rights" issues and "ecological" concerns, and it is even possible that the contemporary ecology-oriented criticism of the anthropocentricity of post-Cartesian/post-Kantian thought may promote a certain relativization of human rights questions. It is not unlikely that we may be able to take a step toward overcoming such a threatening polarization if we were to undertake a thorough reconsideration of the historical roots of "human rights" in the 17th- and 18th-century contemplation of "natural" principles/laws and of the then noted relatedness of these principles to a meaningful universe of creation. Indeed, this would also mean a step toward a substantial revision of the post-Blochian accentuation of the split between creation and liberation orientations in theology.

4.4 Are contemporary tensions in creation theology ecumenically relevant?

This question was made the global topic of the October 1984 Klingenthal consultation, and several observations on that event have been considered earlier in this chapter. In the overall context of the ecumenical creation study, the investigations and findings of that consultation are dialectically related to and combined with those of the 1983 Strasbourg consultation on the confessional aspects of creation theology. It therefore goes without saying that conclusions from the Klingenthal consultation can only be fully harvested when considered in connection with the previous event, that is, in §5 of this study. However, some preliminary observations should be noted already here.

The present review of "actual theological confrontations" has consciously been limited to two sets of dominant concerns, which are rather obviously interrelated but which have little apparent bearing on institutional church divisions: 1. what could, rather simplistically, be labelled "the tense of creation"; and 2. the interrelatedness of creation and redemption. Our reflections are related to—but have not been strictly guided by—the three questions that crystallized toward the end of the preliminary report from Klingenthal:

   1. If creation is understood as an ongoing process (evolution) and its dynamics as persuasive rather than coercive divine power, does this ex-

clude a *creatio ex nihilo* and/or a final triumph of the Creator over every will which resists persuasive influence?

2. Does an understanding of human beings as "cocreators" . . . imply a basic coeternity of Creator and creation? And would that be an opening for some idea of the human individual (or species) as its own creator and redeemer?

3. How might the idea of a "sacramental universe" have a retroactive impact on the doctrine of the sacraments? And how might this influence the crucial ecumenical conversation on that issue (as reflected in the references of the WCC's Sixth Assembly to the "eucharistic vision")?[191]

In the foregoing presentation we have tried to show *how* these questions arise and *how* they become installed in the context of ecumenical reflection rather than to elaborate answers. A previous part of this study (§4.1) takes up and pays a good deal of attention to the dialectical interaction of the first two questions, and another (§4.2) returns to an issue already stated in the previous consultation report,[192] that is, the relative independence of creation faith, an issue which again came up strongly in Klingenthal under the umbrella theme "Theological Discourse on Creation—Christian or Pre-Christian?" The reason for taking up this issue under "creation and theology" and not simply transferring it to the final section on "creation and confession" (where it is bound to crop up again) is that— in spite of persistent references in modern ecumenical conversation to a confrontation between the "*Lutheran* two kingdoms approach" and the "*Reformed* kingship of Christ orientation"—our research has found that the alternative is less confessionally grounded than is traditionally assumed. It is most important to review and to test also this polarization in the context of the general dynamics of contemporary creation theology as a complex area of cross-denominational tensions; or, as stated so convincingly by Professor Reinhard Slenczka at the 1983 Strasbourg consultation: an area in which not "confessional" but "confessory" tensions are today seen to be by far the most dominant ones.[193]

---

[191]*The Ecumenical Review* 37/3 (July 1985): 370.

[192]*The Ecumenical Review* 36/2 (April 1984): 213.

[193]A recent attempt to push this confessional confrontation to the foreground is to be found in Jürgen Moltmann, *On Human Dignity: Political Theology and Ethics*, trans. M. Douglas Meeks (London: SCM Press; Philadelphia: Fortress Press, 1984). (Original: *Politische Theologie—politische Ethik* [Mainz: Matthias-Grünewald; Munich: Christian Kaiser Verlag, 1984]). Even if Moltmann sees definite strengths and definite weaknesses in both concepts, it is clear that he pre-

The third question noted after Klingenthal, that is, the one on the implications of a "sacramental universe," is a fascinating and highly actual issue, but its historical roots and ecumenical ties are so clearly discernible that there are good reasons for making it the subject of substantial review in the context of confessional contributions, and more specifically in the section on Anglicanism (§5.5).

Although we are well aware that contemporary tensions in creation theology will have to be included and reassessed in the section on confessional divisions (§5), we should now make some comments on the immediate ecumenical importance of our observations to date.

Participants at the Klingenthal consultation were chosen primarily with a view to their overall theological orientation and to a representative selection of their probable areas of concern. Confessional representation was therefore of only secondary importance. And as may be observed from the outline of the discussions in *The Ecumenical Review,* it did indeed become more and more evident that confrontations were by no means determined by denominational allegiance.

This was but one (even if an unusually spectacular) manifestation of something that is revealed again and again in theological confrontations: nonconfessional divergences (and even contradictions) in the interpretation of the common Christian faith may be much more visible and loaded with considerably more consequences than the more immediately confession-related controversies on the same issues. But if this is the case, what constitutes and what breaks Christian communion? Is membership in a church (usually decided by circumstances beyond one's control) that officially adheres to some unacceptable doctrine more destructive to fellowship than personal support of some noninstitutionalized doctrine that may be considerably further away from our common ecumenical creeds?

---

fers the Reformed orientation, and the development of his own "Messianic" approach to social ethics is unambiguously in the tradition of Zwingli and Calvin (as he understands them) and Barth. His attempt at a theological foundation of human rights (3-17; German: 166-79) starts with a solemn statement of a Trinitarian orientation, but concludes with a clear subordination of creation to *Heilsgeschichte*: "The biblical witness of liberation, covenant, and the right of God leads to a corresponding praxis of the Christian world. The universal presupposition of the special history of God with Israel and Christendom lies in the faith that the God freeing and saving them is the Creator of all human beings and things." (17; German: 168) Here, creation belief basically comes in as a predicative qualifier to liberation, ascribing universal validity to biblical revelation as a historical event. Probably, nobody would object to this as a (highly!) partial perspective; but does it keep up the vision of creation as the one constitutive event, and does it really warrant "human rights" as a reality valid to and recognizable by the whole of humankind as God's creation?

These considerations certainly do not apply exclusively to creation theology; in principle, they apply to any area of theological argument. However, creation constitutes a particularly striking example of that general observation, and could therefore be a useful testing ground for the general interaction of denominational and cross-denominational factors in church divisions.

Ecumenical relevance does not simply bear upon the established pattern of institutional church division, although this is its final location since it is the puzzle that all ecumenical endeavors aim at resolving. But taking note of theological polarities en route may be useful, both with regard to 1. the possibilities of a relativization of confessional discords by means of comparison (why stick to the divisive effects of traditional disagreements when much more momentous disagreements are not seen as obstacles to eucharistic fellowship; the issue per se is not one of conviction but simply one of institutional allegiance?) and 2. the necessity of reviewing new and transinstitutional controversies at the cost of institutional confrontations, thus moving the momentum from institutionalized to noninstitutionalized polarizations. Again, creation may be a highly illustrative example, since the contemporary tensions with regard to its ontological status and implications obviously bear on the most fundamental of theological fundamentals, namely: What do we ultimately understand by "God the Creator"? Does the Creator possess ontological reality and validity prior to that which is created and of which he is, at least traditionally, claimed to be the author, or is he/she/it simply to be viewed as "power in relation"?[194] Is it not obvious that as long as even an issue of this character is not treated as church divisive in any conventional sense, there is little meaning in attributing a church-dividing character to dogmatical questions of considerably lesser consequence for the structuring of faith as a whole?

As we have seen, the contemporary tensions with regard to the First Article have very little immediate denominational orientation. A reinterpretation of the fundamental concept of Creator/creation—no less remote from a traditional ecumenical understanding of the First Article than the one advocated at Klingenthal by the Disciple Griffin and the Lutheran Sölle—has been championed by the Anglican Don Cupitt, the Roman Catholic Gotthold Hasenhüttl, and the Methodist John B. Cobb, Jr.,[195] to name but a few who reflect the confessional variety discernible in and behind the issue. This being so, what can be the real meaning of

---

[194]As Isabel Carter Heyward, *The Redemption of God* (see n. 27) 159; supported by Dorothee Sölle, *To Work and to Love* (see n. 18) 40.

[195]Don Cupitt, *Taking Leave of God* (London: SCM Press, 1982); Gotthold Hasenhüttl, *Einführung in die Gotteslehre* (Darmstadt: Wissenschaftliche Buchgesellschaft, 1980); John B. Cobb, Jr., *The Liberation of Life* (see n. 128).

declaring dogmatical issues to be church divisive, that is, of seeing dogmatical unity as a constitutive of church communion? This by no means suggests that dogmatical differences should not be proclaimed as church divisive; but simply that our observations of the ecumenical *Sitz im Leben* of contemporary creation theology make a reexamination of the rationale of theological (versus nontheological) factors in church division rather urgent.

Immediate observations from contemporary creation theology, then, do not speak so directly on particular confessionally embedded issues as they do on the role of confessional vis-à-vis other theological polarizations as well as on the role of such polarizations with regard to church unity/disunity. Single observations may result as, from here onward, we start to interrelate already suggested observations with those of the confessionally structured part of the Strasbourg approach. By and large, observation of contemporary creation theology suggests that the occurrence of ''confessory'' polarizations are far more of a problem than the ''confessional.'' And if we want to hold to the assumption of an intrinsic unity of reflected theologies, we should surmise that this observation has a certain bearing on our ecumenical vision as a whole—even if we are not yet equipped to pursue that suggestion by means of systematical evidence.

5

Creation
and confessional divisions

In the present analysis the first major event within the project "Creation—An Ecumenical Challenge?" is treated last. The consultation on "The Theology of Creation: Contributions and Deficiencies of our Confessional Traditions" took place already in October 1983. Much could have been said in favor of lodging this exchange at the end of the whole study procedure or—even better, if resources had permitted—to repeat it in a different setting as a summing up of the study. In fact, there were good reasons for the strategy adopted, even though this gave the exchange on the crucial ecumenical aspect of the study a more preliminary and exploratory character than might otherwise have been the case.

It was not unimportant to start the study with reflection on the crowning theme, especially in light of what is, after all, the main legacy of ecumenical theology: to clarify the actual meaning of institutionalized church division as well as the immediate possibilities for overcoming such division. How do creation faith and creation theology relate to confessionality as the basic determinant of Christian disunity? At the same time, however, it was important that final conclusions from that exchange not be drawn during or immediately after the consultation; it was necessary to reexamine these preliminary conclusions at the end of the whole study in light of all other findings and integrate them into what could then be seen to be the burden of the project. In this way, the first/last setting of the confessional orientation would contribute to giving profile and coherence to the whole of the ecumenical creation study.

We are now at the point in our deliberations when the final, integrative approach to the study can begin and can be meaningfully undertaken with, of course, constant reference to that rather exploratory beginning.

5.1 The Orthodox contribution

The overriding issue at the initial Strasbourg conversation in 1983 concerned the East-West encounter, the main difficulty being to reach a viable synchronization of language and style of thought between the Orthodox participants and their Roman Catholic and Protestant conversation partners. As the dominant trend in ecumenical theology had so far been to overlook a possible East-West confrontation in creation theology—or, more recently, to echo Eastern accusations against Western environmental shortcomings without premising a serious critical comparison of the two main theological traditions[1]—a more open and straightforward East-West exchange on creation theology may be the ecumenical assignment of top priority today.

In part, Eastern Christianity has difficulty in relating to the traditional Western distinction between creation and redemption, and this already from a formal point of view. Even the underlying dialectical distinction was questioned: On what premises is it meaningful to distinguish between a first and a second activity of God the Creator and Redeemer? Did creation take place as a fixed event, distinctive from its implementation in incarnation? Is creation even conceivable without salvation as its primeval content and its final realization? Orthodox participants several times suggested that the word "redemption" be replaced by, for example, "adoption": the integration of human life into full, conscious, and organic fellowship with God. The gospel of Jesus Christ is not primarily intended to restore a destroyed creation but to promote the integration of an as yet incomplete creation into the all-transfiguring glory for which it was and is being created.

At the same time, the basic ontological distinction between life *created* and *uncreated* makes "creation" a much more distinctive category than, say, "becoming," "making," "formation," "production," etc. It was maintained that the following presupposition should remain extremely clear: Creation is the work

---

[1]Cf. *Faith and Science in an Unjust World.* Report of the WCC Conference on Faith, Science, and the Future, Massachusetts Institute of Technology, Cambridge, USA, 12-24 July, 1979, vol. 2, *Reports and Recommendations,* ed. Paul Abrecht (Geneva: World Council of Churches, 1980) 28-38.

of the uncreated alone and consists in bringing into being that which hitherto was not. On the one hand, this precluded any straight equation of "creation" and, say, "evolution"; but it does not preclude any possible interaction, since "evolution" is eventually seen as a wider empirical framework and "creation" as the very coming-into-existence in its radical newness.[2] On the other hand, any "cocreatorship" by created beings that is likely to relativize the uncreated in his inviolable sovereignty should be unconditionally dismissed. Continuing creation becomes subject to initial creation, not in the sense of a distinction in time but in the sense of ontological priority.

In questioning the traditional Western creation-and-redemption (or "creation-and-new-creation") dialectic, the Orthodox approach more or less challenges basic presuppositions of Western theology—Roman Catholic as well as Protestant. But its emphatic distinction between uncreated and created—even if often clothed in a different conceptuality (especially: immortal/mortal; less characteristically: celestial/terrestrial, eternal/temporal, infinite/finite)—seems to take in established presuppositions of the classical Western tradition(s). At the same time, however, it totally rejects modern Western trends whereby the term "creation" is broadened in such a way that the semantic claims of the word seem to be reduced to conferring some ultimate dignity on human participation in the drama of universal cosmic development.

However, the discussion about such modern trends reflects tensions within contemporary creation theology in general and, as we have seen, has little to do with established confessional divisions.

---

[2]This does not preclude that an official Orthodox statement—the presentation of Metropolitan Emilianos Timiados at the 1981 Orthodox-Reformed bilateral dialogue in Geneva—can use creation and evolution as absolutely contradictory terms. See *The Theological Dialogue Between Orthodox and Reformed Churches,* ed. Thomas F. Torrance (Edinburgh: Scottish Academic Press, 1985) 39-40: "Evolution moves toward a mechanistic interpretation of the universe." Such a formulation may indicate that, in spite of the frequently repeated claims to the contrary, brands of Orthodox theology today may be even more stuck in the aftermath of a static Aristotelian terminology than the main trends of Western theology. A couple of rather different approaches to the issue of evolution can be found in *La théologie dans l'eglise et dans le monde,* ed. Damaskinos Papandreou (1984): "On the question of evolution, theology and the church can formulate no doctrine or dogma." (Stanley S. Harkas, 246) And: "No official Orthodox pronouncement exists on these topics. . . . A response that is more characteristic of the Orthodox approach . . . may be characterized as theistic evolution." (Statement by Holy Cross Greek Orthodox School of Theology, 1982, 242-43)

An emphatic Western challenge to Eastern theology in the domain of the First Article is nothing new, and the Strasbourg consultation was by no means the first occasion that this was brought to light. In view of the number of strong expressions of this concern in theological literature (also in the postwar era), it is amazing how seldom it has been taken up in official ecumenical exchange and dialogues.[3] The East-West discussion has had a tendency to become fixed on the level of institutionalized ecclesiology without the Western conversation partner paying much attention to the concern that has been repeatedly raised from the Orthodox side, that is, the basic difference in theological style of thought, which is visible on all levels but is particularly apparent in the fundamental vision of God and world.

Even if the following examples may be more immediately related to the understanding of *God* than to the idea of *creation,* it is clear that these visions are basically interrelated and that reference to the one contains an immediate assessment of the other:

According to Paul Evdokimov, the understanding of God is one of the questions most apt to "make us grasp a certain difference of theological perspective in East and West and thus serve the ecumenical dialogue."[4] He then goes on to describe the difference as follows:

> Pour l'Occident, le monde est réel et Dieu est douteux, hypothétique, ce qui excite à forger des arguments en faveur de son existence. Pour l'Orient, c'est le monde qui est douteux et illusoire; le seul argument en faveur de sa réalité est l'existence autoévidente de Dieu.[5]

---

[3]In "Creation in the History of Orthodox Theology" (*St. Vladimir's Theological Quarterly* 27 [1983]: 27-37), John Meyendorff deviates from the common Orthodox trend by consciously minimizing the East-West confrontation: "The categories of East and West in terms of Christian theology are largely transcended by the realities of our world today . . . the very authority and merits of the fathers lies in that they responded to the concrete challenges of their day." (37) This conclusion follows an analysis of the two historical occasions when "creation was formally on the agenda of theological debates . . . in the East": the discussion caused by Origen in the ancient church and that about the Russian sophiologists (the school of Vladimir Soloviev) in the early 20th century. While siding with official Orthodoxy in criticizing both of these for violating the Athanasian distinction between uncreated and created with their philosophical speculations about an eternal creation, Meyendorff at the same time commends these challengers for their readiness to approach creation theology by way of questions raised by their own time.

[4]Paul Evdokimov, *La connaissance de Dieu selon la tradition orientale* (1967) 7.

[5]Ibid., 86.

It may be interesting to observe the similarity between what is presented here as the Eastern position and 17th-century Western Cartesianism, whose imprints on subsequent Western thought have certainly not been minimal. This raises the question whether certain Eastern structures of thought may not have a considerably greater affinity with modern Western idealistic orientation than with Scholastic Aristotelian realism.

The Palamite controversy focused on the human ''vision of God'' and, in the 14th century, seriously aggravated the ecumenical climate between East and West. With St. Gregory Palamas, an Eastern tradition reached its most consistent expression through stating the absolute inaptitude of created beings to see God, the uncreated Light. God can be seen by his creatures only in his *energeiai,* his voluntary manifestations in the created world—a distinction that is supposed to be maintained even in the future state of eternal glory. The progressive divinization (*theosis*) of the created human is a permeation that communicates a basically illimitable participation in divine love and purity but does not touch on the basic distinction between Creator and created.[6] In a somewhat heated attack on ''modern Occidental theology,'' Dumitru Staniloae undertakes to show how the Orthodox theology of creation transcends an alleged Western oscillation between an absolute immutability and a total changeability of God, and how the Eastern vision safeguards the mystery of an unalterable divine essence manifesting itself only in its voluntary self-expressions through historical revelation.[7] In ''Occidental theology'' he sees an obstacle to the true progress of humankind, conditioned by a ''lack of confidence'' in creation and an overemphasis on divine omnipotence at the cost of God's will to authentic communion with the created world.[8] It may be interesting to ask how this accusation fits in with the above-mentioned statement by Evdokimov, about the West having too much confidence in the existence of the world compared with an Eastern confidence geared exclusively to the reality of God.

In *The Human Presence: An Orthodox View of Nature* (1978) and *Cosmic Man: The Divine Presence* (1980), Paul Gregorios defends the distinction be-

---

[6]Georges Florovsky, *Creation and Redemption: Collected Works,* vol. 3 (Belmont MA: Nordland Publishing Co., 1976) 43-78. The concept of creation is particularly clarified on 43-62; that of the *energeiai* on 62-71; and *theosis* on 71-78.

[7]Dumitru Staniloae, *Dieu est amour* (Geneva: Labor et Fides, 1980 [1968]) 28ff.

[8]Dumitru Staniloae, *Orthodoxe Dogmatik* (Cologne: Benziger Verlag, 1984/1985) 204.

tween a Western (mainly Augustinian) tradition that is allegedly inclined to identify "nature" with evil[9] and a more balanced Eastern assessment as shaped, in
particular, by Gregory of Nyssa. Even as Gregorios consciously wants to safeguard a basic distinction between the Creator and the created,[10] he also tries to
establish an alliance with process theology, an alliance that obviously tends to
modify the Orthodox orientation:

> Process theologians . . . face squarely the question of transcendence.
> They claim that it is naive to conceive of God's transcendence in spatial
> terms since this, by making the cosmos other than God, makes God less
> than the whole package God-world. The transcendence of God is tem-
> poral, that is, in terms of the future. . . . The future of the universe . . .
> is in fact the future of God.[11]

In a modern attempt to champion the Orthodox tradition against what to him
is "Occidental Scholasticism," Gregorios here seems to destabilize the very cornerstone of the traditional Orthodox argument, that is, the unabridgeable distinction between uncreated and created reality, between the Creator and his creation.
For if it is maintained that God is "no less" than some "package God-world,"
then creation is equipped with no reality of its own; it simply exists as part of a
comprehensive joint "package" Creator-creation. That in Orthodox (and ecumenical!) tradition God is to be seen as distinct from his created world—and thus
(if one insists on such a model of thought) as, in *our* perspective, "less than" reality as a whole—can only be seen as a reflection of God's sovereign deed of creation: God "limits" himself in order to give "room" to a world distinct from
himself. As Creator he does not comprise "creation" as some expansion of his
own essence. Even if process theology, like the Orthodox theology of creation,
places itself in basic opposition to a classical Western approach to creation-God-
and-world, its attack comes from too different an angle to make possible an authentic comradeship-in-arms—an observation that seems surprisingly foreign to
Gregorios.

The most appropriate key to an Orthodox theology of creation seems to be in
the central concept of *theosis* (divinization, deification), a concept lacking in the

---

[9]Paul Gregorios, *Cosmic Man: The Divine Presence* (1980) 184, 210ff.

[10]"Gregory of Nyssa, faithful to the Judeo-Christian tradition, rejects the Indo-
Hellenic theory of continuity between the One and the Many and adopts the Jewish solution of discontinuity." (Ibid., 74)

[11]Paul Gregorios, *The Human Presence: An Orthodox View of Nature* (Geneva: World Council of Churches, 1978) 48.

Western tradition, Roman Catholic as well as Protestant. Some uncertainty or even disagreement seems to prevail about whether divinization applies to the human person alone or to creation in its fullness. At the 1983 Strasbourg consultation, John S. Romanides, who gave the main presentation on "Theosis: The Aim of Creation," described *theosis* as "a cure of the malfunctioning noetic faculty of the human heart" enabling people to experience "the uncreated glory of God in Christ," to see "all of creation in the uncreated glory of God and thus to know that creation is very good." *Theosis,* then, is a process of transformation that essentially applies to human consciousness in its existential, prayerful relationship with God; creation in its fullness is only subsequently affected, namely as comprehended in the new theotic vision of reality by human persons. This anthropological orientation was strongly emphasized by Romanides, also in the ensuing discussion.

A different and remarkably wider perspective has been developed by Timothy Ware:

> Deification is something that involves the body. Since man is a unity of body and soul, and since the Incarnate Christ has saved and redeemed the whole man, it follows that "man's body is deified at the same time as his soul" (Maximus Confessor, P.G. XC, 1168A). . . . Not only man's body but the whole of the material creation will eventually be transfigured. . . . Creation is to be saved and glorified along with him. . . . This talk of deification and union, of the transfiguration of the body and of cosmic redemption, may sound very remote from the experience of ordinary Christians; but anyone who draws such a conclusion has entirely misunderstood the Orthodox conception of *theosis.*[12]

This even seems to transcend Gregorios' presentation of the "human presence" as a mediator between God and his creation and of "cosmic man" as the active expression of "divine presence":

> Even as God has no other source of being, it is given to man, as a gift from the Creator, the freedom to create himself, to be a coworker with God in perfecting His creation . . . the free cooperation (*synergeia*) of man as a necessary element in God's plan for the creation. . . . Man is capable of being the highest evolved recapitulative center of the universe . . . the participant mediator between Creator and Creation.[13]

---

[12]Timothy Ware, *The Orthodox Church* (Hammondsworth: Penguin Books, 1973 [1963]) 237, 239-40.

[13]Paul Gregorios, *Cosmic Man* (see n. 9) 154, 224-25.

In such observations the self-transcendent character of a basically anthropo-logically-conceived idea of *theosis* has found an explanation that seems suffi-ciently clear and consistent. But is this not taking place at the sacrifice of the immitigable Orthodox distinction between created and uncreated? The human being as executor of the divine creative activity is here placed more or less inbe-tween, as created fellow-creator. Certainly, this is consistent with process theol-ogy, as with some other influential trends in contemporary Western theology, but it becomes more problematic in face of the Oriental tradition, even if Gregory of Nyssa is claimed as a sort of main reference. Of course, such a synergetic vision provides a concrete explanation of how *theosis*—the dynamic element in a human relationship with God—may expand into an event that has comprehensive con-sequences for the whole of creation.[14] If the event of *theosis* is to take on cosmic proportion—or, even, to be seen as *the* fundamental cosmic event—this syner-getic perspective obviously has to be considerably restricted, and the vision of a cosmic redemption (Romans 8:18-25) at the base of Gregorios' interpretation can hardly be understood to be basically determined by some active humano-techno-logical contribution to the final outcome. In the Pauline vision, humankind is not changing the universe but is being changed together with the universe through a joint experience of divine transfiguration!

Orthodox writers generally insist that *theosis* should be seen in the perspec-tive of the dialectic (although this word does not come from the Orthodox theo-logical language) of an "apophatic" and "kataphatic" understanding of God, that is, of divine ineffability and predicability. In his uncreated (precreational) being, God is as inaccessible to the human mind as he is to the human eye, and no ade-quate statement can pronounce his divine *proprium*. But in the manifestation of his creative activities—in the divine *energeiai*—God makes himself known and predicable to and by humans. However, this knowledge of God always remains lodged in a global awareness of the unspeakable mystery of divine transcen-dence.[15]

---

[14]But hardly as a universal key to the implementation of creation? That would be to overestimate even the future possibilities of technology. Cf. Paul Gregorios: "Technology is the way of humanizing the world of matter in time-space, and thereby of extending the human body to envelope the whole universe." (*The Hu-man Presence* [see n. 11] 89) Here something may be lacking in the basic medi-tation of cosmic proportionality!

[15]"Die apophatische Gotteserfahrung . . . kann . . . als etwas für die Ortho-doxie Spezifisches und Charakteristisches bezeichnet werden. Sie . . . ist anders als die abendländische Gotteserkenntnis, die ihrerseits entweder rationaler oder

How such a vision relates to creation is made clear in a striking way by Stephanos Charalambidis. Having observed that "cosmology" as such is not taught as a separate theme in theological schools, be it in the East or in the West, the General Vicar of the Greek Orthodox Archbishop in France proceeds to detect the different reasons for this. In the Eastern Church he sees the major occurrence in the fact that neither the Fathers nor the great teachers of spirituality up to our day made a distinction between "natural life" and the "supernatural gifts of the Holy Spirit." Spiritual life was never seen as a quality added to natural existence. The contemplation of nature is fundamental to the understanding of God: As all things created are an image of him, it is possible for spiritual reality to reveal itself also in matter.[16]

On the other hand, Charalambidis sees the Western theology of creation as a historical deviation from the pattern of the Fathers, and this in a twofold way. First, the established interpretation of Genesis 1:28, combined with a simplified concept of progress, has made of humankind a manipulator rather than a mediator, and thus engendered the present environmental crisis. Second, the West has misunderstood asceticism, that is, seeing it as a submission of the body to the demands of the (individual) soul instead of as an expression of communion between body and soul and between all people (and the whole of creation).[17] In response, Charalambidis demands a new "ecumenical start," that is:

> L'élaboration d'une éthique eucharistique nouvelle, capable de donner une orientation réellement paschale à la puissance technique de notre siècle afin que l'humanité ne défigure pas la terre mais la transfigure."[18]

To a large extent, Charalambidis shares in Gregorios' vision of the "human presence." He speaks of the human person as "microcosme" and "hypostase du

---

gefühlsmässiger Art oder beides zugleich ist. Apophatische Erfahrung bedeutet ein ahnendes Gespür für das Mysterium, sie eröffnet die Möglichkeit für ein Leben im abgrundstiefen Geheimnis. . . . Inhaltlich erfahren wir über Gott nichts als seine vielfältigen Wirkungen, die auf die Welt bezogen sind. . . . Darüber hinaus wissen wir nur, dass diese ihren Grund in einem Sein haben, das in personaler Art da ist; wie dieses Sein aber näher beschaffen ist, wissen wir nicht. Alles, was wir von Gott erkennen, ist sein Dynamismus, der in seinen Beziehungen zur Welt erfahren wird." (Dumitru Staniloae, *Orthodoxe Dogmatik* [see n. 8] 131, 138)

[16]Stephanos Charalambidis, "Cosmologie chrétienne," *Initiation à la pratique de la théologie*, ed. Bernard Lauret and François Refoule (Paris: Les Editions du Cerf, 1982/1983) 3:16.

[17]Ibid., 16ff.

[18]Ibid., 18.

monde,'' and even as ''créateur'' and ''Seigneur et . . . Roi qui domine l'univers.''[19] But with him these expressions seem more explicitly balanced through a strong emphasis on ''the original Fall'' as a ''cosmic catastrophe'' having ''veiled the original sacramentality of the world'';[20] thus on history as an intersection of the two opposite processes of progress and regress;[21] and, correspondingly, on true cosmology as ''a *gnosis* given to us by Christ through the Holy Spirit in the mysteries (sacraments) of the church.''[22]

The plea for a Christological and sacramental understanding of the universe, which is so movingly expressed here, may be more comprehensively developed in recent Anglican theology. And as, in the form indicated by Charalambidis, we seem to have an elaboration on traditional Orthodox motifs more than an immediate echo of them, it may be meaningful to return to this theme in our conversation with contemporary Anglicanism. In the attention given to the Fall and to the constitutive importance of redemption, Charalambidis may come closer to the Western tradition than several Orthodox writers—whose polemic against ''Augustinian'' anthropological ''pessimism'' may, to put it mildly, be somewhat biased. At the same time, however, this observation gives increased weight to Charalambidis' critical remarks on Western theology, particularly, perhaps, about its alleged ''objectivizing,'' ''manipulative'' pattern of reflection over against contemplative Eastern reflection on nature as the element of divine presence.

But even if a Western observer might be willing—today, perhaps, even *more* than willing—to grant the author and Orthodox criticism in general this capital point, there would obviously still be many questions to clarify vis-à-vis Charalambidis' wide-ranging comments (and this even before we proceed to the important issue of a sacramental incarnation-oriented universe): 1. How does the talk about the human being as ''microcosm'' and as ''mediator'' fit in with the growing contemporary conviction of creation having intrinsic value and validity? Are

---

[19]Ibid., 22-23, 25.

[20]Ibid., 28.

[21]Ibid., 27.

[22]Ibid., 28. ''La contemplation de la nature . . . constitue un aspect entre autres majeur de la mystique de l'Eglise Orthodoxe d'Orient: l'homme ici cesse d'objectifier l'univers par sa convoitise et son aveuglement pour l'identifier au 'Corps du Christ'. . . . Le fait que le Christ, en récapitulant l'histoire humaine, donne en même temps aux cycles cosmiques la plénitude de leur sens. . . . La cosmologie est subordonnée à l'anthropologie ou plutôt à l'histoire de la divino-humanité. . . . La cosmologie est christocentrique. . . . Les galaxies les plus lointaines sont en fait des poussières qui gravitent autour de la Croix.'' (Ibid., 32-33, 46-47)

the dangers of an anthropocentric world orientation thereby overcome or not? 2. In their rather unmodified absoluteness, can the expressions about human sovereignty and creatorship be distinguished from a similar language in radical trends of contemporary Western theology? If so, how? That there is here a difference in meaning and emphasis—and one that has fairly comprehensive consequences—should follow from the difference in approach as a whole, even without specific clarification at crucial terminological junctures. But this question certainly needs a more explicit study. 3. How can the idea of a cosmology, as given exclusively in Christ, fit in with the unrestricted identification of natural and spiritual life? Can people who are unfamiliar with the proclamation of Christ have any adequate cosmological insights? If they can, would this not mean that Christ, as historical event, inscribed in time and space, is essentially swallowed up by Christ the universal pre-, post-, and extra-incarnate Logos? 4. Therefore, in view of the foregoing: How can it be avoided that a *theosis* vision of nature and reality is trapped in an idea of general transfiguration that may ultimately involve an unmistakable perspective of denaturation?

If one considers the principle importance given to the icon in Orthodox theology,[23] and the obvious denaturalizing trend of the Eastern iconographic tradition, what bearing may this have on the very vision of creation? With the strong Eastern challenges to Western creation theology in recent years, it should not be taken as an expression of unecumenical arrogance if some questions are directed also in the opposite direction—although, of course, not in such a way as to escape those questions that have already been on the table for several years!

All these questions may have some affinity to the Orthodox approach in general, particularly as it itself claims a distinctively different profile from that of Western theology. But the problems seem to be particularly apparent in the challenging cosmological sketch by Charalambidis. We have seen that in its ecumenical self-presentation Orthodoxy in general attributes high importance to its specific approach(es) to creation. Recently, leading Western theologians have also called attention to the fact that an Eastern corrective might be useful on this very point, and listening to this challenge might have particularly stimulating consequences for ecumenical progress.

Probably more than with anyone else, this has come to the fore in recent works of Jürgen Moltmann. For an example, one need only consult his preface to the

---

[23]Cf. the chapter on "La connaissance de Dieu dans la tradition inconographique," Paul Evdokimov, *La connaissance de Dieu selon la tradition orientale* (see n. 4) 107-25: "L'iconographie . . . s'épanouit aisément dans le platonisme de la patristique orientale." (Ibid., 107)

German edition of Staniloae's *Orthodoxe Dogmatik,* in which he greets the Orthodox participation in ecumenical exchange as *the* major ecumenical event of our time and indicates several reasons for this. In his *Trinity and the Kingdom of God,* Moltmann strongly recommends the operative functionality of Orthodox Trinitology and expresses great sympathy with the Orthodox stand on the famous *filioque* controversy.[24] The Greek concept of a *perichoresis,* an interpenetration of the three divine persons,[25] is taken as the perfect expression of freedom in communion and thus extolled as the great model also of human fellowship in church and society.[26] In the same context he also advocates the concept of *theosis.*[27] In a later work, Moltmann elaborates on the concept of *perichoresis* as a doctrine of universal validity:

> Our starting point here is that all relationships which are analogous to God reflect the primal, reciprocal indwelling and mutual interpenetration of the Trinitarian *perichoresis*: God *in* the world and the world *in* God; heaven and earth *in* the kingdom of God, pervaded by his glory; soul and body united *in* the life-giving Spirit to a human whole; women and men *in* the kingdom of unconditional and unconditioned love, freed to be true and complete human beings. There is no such thing as solitary life. . . .
> It is this Trinitarian concept of life as interpenetration or *perichoresis* which will therefore determine this ecological doctrine of creation.[28]

To what extent the concept of *perichoresis,* as paraphrased in Moltmann's theology of creation and with the extensive range of consequences there claimed, may really be in conformity with the Orthodox tradition is not a question to be discussed here. The word *perichoresis* was introduced by the Greek Fathers and indisputably advocates an idea of dynamic and organic unity that reflects a style of thought incompatible with the Scholastic principle of distinction. The question may be to what extent one can do justice to Orthodox tradition by extending its

---

[24]Jürgen Moltmann, *The Trinity and the Kingdom of God: The Doctrine of God,* trans. Margaret Kohl (London: SCM Press; New York: Harper & Row, 1981) esp. 178-87. Original: *Trinität und Reich Gottes* (Munich: Christian Kaiser Verlag, 1980).

[25]Ibid., 148-50, 174-76.

[26]Ibid., 212-22.

[27]Ibid., 213.

[28]Jürgen Moltmann, *God in Creation: An Ecological Doctrine of Creation,* trans. Margaret Kohl (London: SCM Press, 1985) 17. Original: *Gott in der Schöpfung: Ökologische Schöpfungslehre* (Munich: Christian Kaiser Verlag, 1985) 30.

scope to include intramundane as well as, eventually, divino-mundane relations. If an intrapersonal *perichoresis* on the human level may still be defended in light of the concept of a mirror—the world reflecting the image of its Creator—the alleged *perichoresis* between God and the world may be more difficult to uphold, because it relativizes the distinction between Creator and creature in order to make this relationship suit a preconceived analogy of Trinitarian interaction. Such a consequence would probably be in contradiction to basic Orthodox insights. In any case, the question as to whether Moltmann's creation theology really does serve as an ecumenical bridge between East and West should be answered in the affirmative. It has to be admitted that his use of Greek conceptuality and patterns of reflection channels a considerable number of impulses to his own creation meditations and may—together with his searching openness toward Eastern theology—serve a real ecumenical rapprochement. A further question is whether, in the long run, he will be able to convince the East that on this point its concerns have been genuinely received by and integrated into Western theology.

By and large, much has still to happen before there will be genuine East-West encounter, exchange, and sharing in the field of creation theology. And, after what we have seen, it should be more than clear that creation does have a central place in the East-West theological stalemate. In the traditional controversy—a controversy that has so often been repressed (particularly in the West) and never really been the subject of an open exchange—it is in itself futile to discuss what is "prior," the doctrine of God or the doctrine of creation, because, in our understanding, the two are linked together in a way that makes a neat separation meaningless. It could, of course, be argued that the communication gap is caused by different—implicit and explicit—assumptions on the access to divine reality on the part of the human mind. In this setting, the Orthodox distinction between an "apophatic" and a "kataphatic" understanding of God is just as important a landmark as that between the *ousía* (essence) of God and his *energeiai* (dynamic manifestations) and the understanding of *theosis* as an unconditional refusal and unconditional confirmation of human participation in divine life.

That these profound issues—with their determining influence on theological orientation as a whole—have not yet emerged on the contemporary ecumenical agenda is as remarkable as it is regrettable, especially because allusions to them are not lacking in contemporary, particularly Orthodox, ecology-related theology. Much seems to indicate that the concentration on ecclesiological questions in the ecumenical East-West dialogues to date has served to distract attention from the essential and complex East-West theological issues, issues that are not primarily about ecclesiology but about fundamental theology and the First Article of the Creed (in interaction with and, partly, as a key to the two others).

When, in its section report on "Humanity, Nature and God," the 1979 WCC conference on "Faith, Science and the Future" somewhat vaguely criticizes "modern Western Christian theology," "Western theology," and "the Occident" for a lack of ecological awareness,[29] this is obviously not as a result of some conscienticized East-West dialogue or of any profound analysis of the ecumenical implications of different theological directions; it is much more a reflex response to unchallenged individual voices, perhaps not least to the booklet prepared ahead of and for the conference by its moderator.[30]

Especially against the background of the current environmental crisis, it is to be expected that the choir of Eastern voices accusing (and one-sidedly accusing) Western church and theology of having prepared the way for the crisis—and arguing that a basic theological reorientation is the only way for Christendom to deal constructively with the challenges of the day—would be heard within the *oikumene* and provoke a real exchange. So far, this has not happened. But why? It is crucial that this area of concern now receive paramount attention in the East-West dialogues, and this for two reasons: 1. the urgency of the environmental issue as such (thus, perhaps, giving credence to the old proverb, *Ex Oriente Lux*, Light from the East?); 2. the obviously decisive bearing of the First Article of the Creed on the mutual understanding of the churches of the East and the West, and thus on ecumenical identity as a whole. East and West are not separated by disunity in the confession of God the Creator as such. But there is no doubt that the remaining obstacles to a comprehensive mutual understanding are to a large extent connected with—and can profitably be approached through an assessment of—differences in ontological adaptation and in the practical application of creation theology.

5.2 The Roman Catholic contribution

At the 1983 consultation the contribution of the main Roman Catholic representative, Bishop Karl Lehmann, received particular attention because of its ecumenical perspective. Since the topics had been selected in order to deal with as characteristic—and ecumenically touchy—perspectives as possible, Lehmann had been given the theme "Nature and Supernature: Dimensions of Creation." His presentation strongly underscored the radical reorientation that has been taking place in Roman Catholic creation theology since the 1950s, the main impulses of which he identified in a renewal of biblical studies and the influence of the Barthian *Heilsgeschichte* orientation.

---

[29]*Faith and Science in an Unjust World* (see n. 1) 29, 30, 35.

[30]Paul Gregorios, *The Human Presence* (see n. 11).

His criticism of earlier theology for its rigid cosmological and ontological approach—prevalent for centuries but particularly triumphant in the late 19th and early 20th centuries—was sharp, even though he did commend the tradition for having managed at an early stage to refuse monistic as well as dualistic one-sidedness and for conceiving of grace as neither a denial nor a mere extension of "nature" per se. However, the old predilection to frame a doctrine of "nature" as something given apart from the history of salvation did tend to pull apart what theologically belongs together and also to turn attention away from theology's genuine concern and to provoke futile conflicts with emerging science. One of the most influential spokespersons of contemporary middle-of-the-road Roman Catholic theology, Lehmann nevertheless also saw a certain danger in the tendency of several modern theologians, including Roman Catholics, to overlook the relative independence of creation[31] and to view creation and salvation as being so harmoniously unified that the reality of evil may be unduly modified. Even if the traditional designation of "nature" may not be the most fortunate term for the further reflection of the church, it is essential to keep up the classical concern of continuity—as well as distinctiveness—between creation and redemption.

As a general description, the observation concerning a comprehensive turn in Roman Catholic creation thought in the second half of our century seems very appropriate.[32] To a great extent this must be seen in connection with a reorientation of Roman Catholic theology as a whole, effected above all by the Second Vatican Council—a quest for *aggiornamento,* a new emphasis on biblical studies, a more relaxed attitude to established tradition, a new desire for ecumenical rapprochement, etc. It would, however, be highly unsatisfactory to see the shift of emphasis in creation theology exclusively as the fruit of some general overall reorientation.

---

[31]Cf. the judgment of another Roman Catholic author of recent years, Alfons Auer in *Umweltethik: Ein theologischer Beitrag zur ökologischen Diskussion* (Düsseldorf: Patmos Verlag, 1985 [1984]) 239: "So sicher aber die Heilsgeschichte ihre Ausgipfelung in Christus findet, so darf doch die Christologie die Schöpfungswirklichkeit nicht veruneigentlichen."

[32]A captivating example of how a synthetic (and, in that regard, traditional) contemporary Roman Catholic approach to faith and science may look is: Stefan Niklaus Bosshard, *Erschafft die Welt sich selbst? Die Selbstorganisierung von Natur und Mensch aus naturwissenschaftlicher, philosophischer und theologischer Sicht* (1985). The author sees no principal difficulty in reconciling an evolutionary image of the world with the all-comprehensive assurance that "God has created world, nature, and man" (148) and in interpreting creation as "implizite Heilsgeschichte" open to the appearance of a verbal revelation that transcends the realm of the created (ibid.).

For several reasons it may be just as adequate to see it as a cause more than a result. This becomes obvious when we confront the apologetical aspects of the reorientation, but perhaps even more when we view the ontological implications.[33]

In an apologetical setting, the Galilei controversy in the early 17th century may be as enlightening as the Darwinian clash in the second half of the 19th. In both cases, the forceful reactions of the official Roman Catholic Church (which were by no means unparalleled in the Protestant world) were not dictated by opposition to scientific exploration as such; rather they were dictated by a determined will to defend what seemed to be the privilege of empirical observation and "natural" reflection over against what seemed to be a violation of the basic principles of sound understanding. Traditional Roman Catholic apologetics was never hostile to—or even basically suspicious of—natural science as such. What it did object to was what it saw as the perversion of science. In general, its first goal was not to defend Scripture but to defend science as a natural and reliable access to the truth. This orientation is solidly embedded in the Scholastic tradition, particularly

---

[33]It may be appropriate to supplement the attention given to the influence of Barth and the impact of revitalized biblical studies in Karl Lehmann's presentation with the following observations of Jürgen Hübner: "Von besonders grosser Brisanz und Reichweite ist der Paradigmenwechsel in der katholischen Theologie gewesen. Die Natur-philosophie und -theologie Pierre Teilhard de Chardins hat die Weise theologischen Denkens in der katholischen Kirche nachhaltig beeinflusst. . . . Die Schöpfung ist danach angelegt auf ihre evolutive Vergeistigung . . . die liebende Vereinigung der Menschheit untereinander und mit Gott. Freilich ist die Auseinandersetzung . . . noch nicht abgeschlossen. . . . Es ist noch nicht ausgemacht, ob Teilhard als Ketzer oder Heiliger in die Geschichte eingehen wird." (Jürgen Hübner, *Die neue Verantwortung für das Leben: Ethik im Zeitalter von Gentechnologie und Umweltkrise* [1986] 171-72)

Teilhard's dialectical relationship with Protestant theology in terms of a give-and-take was already comprehensively documented by Sigurd M. Daecke in *Teilhard de Chardin und die evangelische Theologie* (1967). Presenting themselves as a more or less unified group, "Teilhardians" played an important role at a top theological consultation in New York City (October 1971) on "Hope and the Future of Man" (see *Hope and the Future of Man*, ed. Ewert H. Cousins [London, 1973]). Since then, Protestant theology's interest in Teilhard seems to have established itself as a given and important fact.

How close contemporary Roman Catholic and Protestant environmental theology are to each other may be seen from a representative Roman Catholic collection of essays, *Macht euch die Erde untertan? Schöpfungsglaube und Umwelt*, ed. Philipp Schmitz S.J. (Würzburg: Echter, 1981), not least the bibliography, 213-23.

in its Thomist version, and has deep not only epistemological but also ontological roots. The study of nature is recommended not only by the "natural" goodness of the phenomenal world as such but also by the goodness of observation, reflection, and knowledge, activities prescribed by "nature" itself. The tragedy of the 17th and 19th centuries was that this brave principle of (essentially Aristotelian) *epistemology* was obscured and to a large extent compromised by the remainders of outdated Aristotelian (and Ptolemaic) *science*. Observations once made, and later supported through everyday experience by everybody, refused the test of new observations, allegedly in order to prevent the confusion and uncertainty that would arise from abandoning long-established observations. In this situation, the concern for biblical infallibility came as a most impressive support. Whereas in Roman Catholic reflection biblical considerations seemed to enter the arena in the second place in support of natural insight, in Protestant countries the priorities were generally the other way round.

In contemporary Eastern Orthodoxy we have noted a rather clear-cut tendency to criticize the Western theology of creation, Roman Catholic as well as Protestant. Is there a Roman Catholic answer to this accusation in terms of polemical demarcation? Or—ever so interesting from an ecumenical point of view—is there an unambiguous dividing line vis-à-vis the churches of the Reformation, whether it be intentional or unintentional? As we have seen, in the case of Eastern Orthodoxy the tendency here is to observe and criticize Western theology as a whole, with no essential distinction between Roman Catholic and Protestant trends—except that the latter is frequently viewed as a further development of tendencies inherent in the former, and thus as a more explicit revelation of where the common Western trend is leading.[34] The really divisive line is therefore seen as running between East and West. But how does this statement look from "the other side of the fence"?

It must again be observed that there has been an amazing lack of response to this Oriental challenge on the part of the Western churches, including Rome. In official dialogues as well as in general theological discussions East-West issues have tended to be limited to ecclesiological and canonical discrepancies (with perhaps some side glances to soteriological implications); creation has been conspicuous only by its absence. One reason for this may be that the historically established East-West controversy in the realm of the First Article was never creation theology as such; rather it was the vision of God and the nature of divine presence in the created world (especially the Palamite controversy in the 14th century): Does

---

[34]As a typical example, see Dumitru Staniloae, *Dieu est amour* (see n. 7) 40-48, esp. 45, 47.

the Creator make himself available to human experience in his divine essence, or is he discernible only through his created *energeiai*? However, it is clear that—indirectly—this distinction has tremendous bearing on the doctrine of creation as such; or rather, on the given relationship between the Creator and the created. Even up to the Second Vatican Council, this controversy still tended to pop up from time to time on the Roman Catholic side.

The last—critically biased—Roman Catholic contribution we have found in this field is by Bernhard Schultze, S.J., *Das Gottesproblem in der Osttheologie* (1967). According to Schultze theological Palamism was historically almost dead when certain Russian theologians started to revive it in the 1930s; and their attempt remains successful only for as long as the Palamitic "no" to an understanding of God in his divinity meets with and receives support from the modern Kantian agnosticism that is channeled into Orthodoxy through Protestant modernism. The author thus reverses the popular Orthodox "*we* against the rest" into an equally emphatic "the rest against *us*," whereby the two-headed enemy of the solid Roman Catholic Scholastic tradition is Orthodox Palamism coupled with Protestant Kantianism. As can be seen, this construction is diametrically opposed to that prevalent in contemporary Orthodox neo-Palamism, which views Kantianism and critical Western thought as the aftermath of Augustinian pessimism combined with Scholastic conceptualism.

In the realm of the First Article there has also been a traditional Rome-Wittenberg controversy: on the one side, there has been the accusation of an agnostic fideism tending toward unintended atheism; on the other, there has been the accusation of some speculative metaphysics that forgoes the unobjectifiable Godhead of God in favor of some harmonious philosophical system.[35] However, this is an official polemical setup, and by and large it may be seen to have been bypassed. In general, the contemporary approach to the question of God in Roman Catholic theology may be characterized as soteriological rather than ontological, anthropological rather than cosmological—a point of view held by a wide spectrum of authors, from the fairly conservative Walter Kasper, to Heinrich Fries, Karl Rahner, Hans Küng, and J. B. Metz and on to Gotthold Hasenhüttl on the extreme left.[36]

---

[35]Cf. Per Lønning, *Der begreifliche Unergreifbare: "Sein Gottes" und modern-theologische Denkstrukturen* (Göttingen: Vandenhoeck & Ruprecht, 1986) 96-103.

[36]A typical "Barthian" approach to creation—with a formal imprimatur from the Jesuit superior of the author, is Piet Schoonenberg, *Covenant and Creation* (London/Sydney: Sheed and Ward, 1968): "In both testaments . . . God is first

However, echoes of the old tensions could still be heard up to the last generation. The statement of the First Vatican Council that "God as the beginning and end of all things can be known with certainty from the things created, by the light of natural human reason"[37] is echoed in the *New Catholic Encyclopedia*:

> The Reformation, although essentially a religious movement, served as an introduction to rationalism and fideism. Properly speaking, Luther did not have a philosophy. However, the topics he discussed . . . were further developed by his successors. . . . The implied breach between faith and reason eventually led to rationalism.[38]

A similar judgment from about the same time can be found in the work of a progressive spokesperson, Edward Schillebeeckx:

> It was particularly by its denial of the traditional conviction that it was possible to speak about God in a meaningful way within the rational sphere of understanding that the Reformation really encouraged the advance of the process of secularization that had already begun. This interpretation, which the Catholics labeled "fideism," left the world, as world, in its full secularity. . . . Sooner or later, this was bound to produce Bultmannism and post-Bultmannism, notwithstanding the protests of Karl Barth.[39]

A recent statement by the Jesuit André Manaranche is more extreme and far more typical of the pre-Vatican II era than of the present day:

> Une influence typiquement luthérienne . . . une théorie bien connue de Luther ou de Melanchthon: à savoir qu'il ne sert à rien de connaître Dieu en lui-même. . . . La foi, pour ces réformés [!], c'est d'acquiescer à ce que Dieu est pour nous . . . c'est d'utiliser sans contempler. J'ai montré . . . où a mené cette théorie funeste: à Feuerbach et à son humanisme

---

recognized as Yahweh . . . as God of the covenant and God of history. Only in reflection upon this fact does God reveal himself as Creator, so that it is only in a second chapter that Creator and creation are discussed." (ix) German: *Bund und Schöpfung* (1970) 8. As one immediately sees, this is not an observation of a chronological fact but of a dogmatic principle.

[37]Vaticanum I, cap. 2.

[38]*New Catholic Encyclopedia,* vol. 6 (1967) article on "God."

[39]Edward Schillebeeckx, *God the Future of Man,* trans. N.D. Smith (London/Sydney: Sheed and Ward, 1969) 59-60. Original: *Gott die Zukunft des Menschen* (1969) 54.

athée. Car, si l'homme est le pôle de Dieu et si Dieu est pure fonction de l'homme, c'est l'homme qui est Dieu.[40]

It is obvious that ecumenical accusations such as these have a tremendous bearing also on the theology of creation, especially on its general orientation and its *Sitz im Leben* within theology as a whole. Even if they do not touch on cosmogony as some particular delimited "area" of faith, they certainly relate to the vision God/reality, Creator/creation and, thus, to the entire orientation of faith.

There is no reason for us to respond by referring to Protestant counterattacks in Fundamentalist literature that has remained largely unimpressed by the ecumenical rapprochements of recent years. Let us rather listen to a voice representing mainline Continental theology: Eberhard Jüngel! To him, the main challenge in a traditional Roman Catholic *Gotteslehre* is not the one with which the Barthian school was occupied—a *theologia naturalis*—but a tendency that seems to run in the opposite direction, that is, that of conceptually overemphasizing the transcendence of God:

> Ökumenische Verständigung mit der besagten katholischen Lehre von der in aller Bestimmbarkeit Gottes immer noch grösseren Unbestimmbarkeit Gottes . . . kann es aber vor allem deswegen nicht geben . . . weil damit unser Heil . . . theologisch zur Disposition gestellt wird.[41]

This statement occurs within a critical analysis of the old adage *Deus semper major*, God is always greater. One could easily imagine this formula to be a weapon directed against natural theology and any attempt to fashion philosophical assertions about God—and thus as a rather useful tool for the traditional Protestant polemic against Rome. However, Jüngel intends to show that its historical function has been different. In stressing its unconquerable "more," it has, above all, served to abolish the ultimacy of biblical revelation and invited speculation to go beyond God's self-presentation in Jesus Christ. In this perspective, even Jüngel's accusation is an attack on natural theology, though he is less upset by the possibility of making philosophical speculation the foundation of biblical theology than by that of launching it as an invitation to "go beyond." The consequences of his polemic seem to be to emphasize salvation history as the only authentic clue to "nature" and "reality." However, it should be borne in mind that recent efforts in

---

[40]André Manaranche, *Le monothéisme chrétien* (Paris: Les Editions du Cerf, 1985) 37; cf. 220-21.

[41]Eberhard Jüngel, *Entsprechungen* (Munich: Christian Kaiser Verlag, 1986 [1980]) 248.

favor of a new "natural theology" (here understood as a strictly biblical exploration of the human relationship with nature), as advanced by Jüngel[42] and developed more comprehensively by his comrade-in-arms Christian Link,[43] indicates
a remarkable increase in interest for nature and transanthropological reality in neo-
Barthian Protestant theology. The strong biblical emphasis in German ecotheo-
logical literature in recent years should also be seen in the same context (among
others: Gerhard Liedke, Odil Hannes Steck, Günther Altner).

The Barthian trend in contemporary Roman Catholic theology—so impressively highlighted in Karl Lehmann's presentation to the 1983 consultation—has,
of course, greatly contributed to reducing the distance between the average Roman Catholic and the average Protestant approach to this issue—in spite of (or
perhaps because of) Karl Barth's defiance vis-à-vis traditional Roman Catholic
creation theology. This rapprochement is due mainly to the general triumph of soteriology over cosmology in the contemporary Roman Catholic interpretation of
creation, but also to the corresponding victory of anthropology over ontology in
Roman Catholic fundamental theology. If this is mainly to be seen as a shifting of
old Roman Catholic positions in an unmistakably "Protestant" direction, then it
is just as true to maintain that the growing ecological awareness and the emerging
interest in "nature" as a theological concern in the Protestant camp implies a reorientation in a traditionally Roman Catholic direction. The two positions have
definitely come closer to each other.[44]

---

[42]Ibid., 158-77, 193-97, 198-201.

[43]Christian Link, *Die Welt als Gleichnis: Studien zum Problem der natürlichen Theologie* (Munich: Christian Kaiser Verlag, 1976).

[44]An adequate testimony to this may be the general fixing of positions in the
introduction to Leo Scheffczyk, *Einführung in die Schöpfungslehre* (Darmstadt:
Wissenschaftliche Buchgesellschaft, 1987 [1975]). Having stated how the legitimate criticism of the earlier cosmological orientation in recent Roman Catholic
theology may have gone too far and how a certain reestablishment of balance may
be required (vii), the author provides an equally balanced criticism of Protestant
theology in its admitted influence on Roman Catholic thought: "Nachhaltiger und
bestimmender wirkten wohl auf die Schöpfungsauffassung der Reformatoren, die
in ihrer biblischen Grundeinstellung, in ihrer Kritik an der einseitig metaphys-
ischen Ausrichtung wie in der Hervorkehrung des "pro me" der Heilswahrheiten
durchaus positive Ansätze zeigten, die Überbetonung der Souveränität Gottes
(Calvin), die Hervorkehrung der Nichtigkeit der Geschöpfe (Luther, "Kreaturen
Gottes [als] Larven und Mummereien," WA 30/1,136) und der aus der Gnaden-
und Rechtfertigungslehre stammende Monergismus im göttlichen Handeln. Diese
Momente liessen die (relative) geschöpfliche Selbständigkeit nicht zur vollen Gel-

For better or for worse, the Institute for Ecumenical Research had linked the Roman Catholic presentation at the 1983 consultation to the concepts of *nature* and *supernature*. Even if, to a large extent, contemporary Roman Catholic authors seem to avoid these words and seek alternatives that are less marked by the terminological rigidity of Scholasticism, it is hard to assess the specific Roman Catholic contribution to the ecumenical exchange on creation without focusing attention on the history of the term ''nature'' as it is used in theology. The Aristotelian concept of nature (*physis*) received theological profile through Thomas Aquinas, not only as an integrated element in a more comprehensive theological framework but also as an active, formative factor with decisive effect upon the whole architecture of theology. ''Natura nihil est aliud, quam ratio . . . indita rebus, qua ipsa res moventur ad finem determinatum.''[45] *Natura* is not simply identical with creation or with the realm of created beings as a whole; and the Creator is spoken of in terms of nature—''natura divina,'' ''natura increata.''[46] A simple substitution of ''nature'' by ''creation'' would, therefore, not be sufficient to overcome our contemporary terminological predicament. Traditional use of the term ''nature'' reveals an amazing complexity in its rigidity as well as rigidity in its complexity. This may be illustrated by the fact that supernature does not occur as a noun, but only as an adjective: ''super-naturalis,'' ''that which is absolutely beyond the unaided powers of any creature.''[47] Every realm of being is in full conformity with its own ''nature,'' but it transcends the natural potential of any being to share in the ''nature'' of a higher level of existence than its own: ''et ideo oportet fieri superadditionem habitus supernaturalis.''[48] ''Supernatural,'' then, is used to qualify any gift of grace presented by God to human beings that makes it possible for them to transcend the limits of human ''nature'' and to communicate with ''nature'' divine. The focal expression of supernatural participation is the all-transforming vision of God in his divine essence (*visio Dei per essentiam*); pure gift by divine grace distinct from the common human (that is, natural) vision of

---

tung kommen.'' (3) Even if the author has put aside half of the distance that traditionally separates the churches, the directions in the landscape are left essentially unchanged.

[45]Thomas Aquinas, *Expositio in 8 libros physicorum,* 2:14-15.

[46]Deferrari, Barry, McGuiness, *A Lexicon of St. Thomas Aquinas* (Baltimore: Catholic University of America Press, 1948) 722.

[47]Ibid., 1076.

[48]Thomas Aquinas, *Exposition in Psalmis,* Q. 62, art. 3 ad 1.

God in created being.[49] But in this, as in every, regard the principle remains firm: "Gratia non tollit naturam, sed perficit."[50]

Throughout the 19th and most of the 20th century the crucial question for a Roman Catholic theology of nature has been about the ethical implications of "natura." This issue has been as embarrassing to Roman Catholic theology as the issue of creation ordinances (*Schöpfungsordnungen*) has been to Lutheran theology. To a certain extent these are parallel issues, but *only* to a certain extent. Both controversial terms postulate a specific concept of creational givenness as a basic ethical principle, and this apparently makes some identifiable ideal of stability and preservation essential to both the church and society at large. But, in the one case, this givenness is basically conceived as a system of rules empirically derived from an observation of facts (nature); in the other, they are conceived as constitutive structures derived from general biblical directions that are only subsequently supported and concretized by such empirical exploration (creation ordinances). The difficulties caused *by* and *to* the "nature" approach in the contemporary world have to a large extent been located in the area of sexual ethics and family life. The predicaments caused by and to the "creation ordinances" were (and are?) mainly to be found in political ethics—as was particularly eloquently illustrated by the confrontations in the "Third Reich."[51]

Where does a basic appeal to "nature" take us in the realm of ethics? The most instructive case we could refer to is probably that of the most debated papal encyclical of the last generation, *Humanae Vitae* (1968), which spells out and reinforces the Roman Catholic doctrine on birth control. In this fairly short document, the words "nature" or "natural" occur 22 times. But a reading of the full

---

[49]See Thomas Aquinas, *Summa Theologiae*, I.12,7,1, III Supplement 92,1.

[50]Thomas Aquinas, *Summa Theologiae*, I.1,8,2. A sober attempt to combine a modern ecologically oriented theology of creation with a Thomist reflection on nature is Alexandre Ganoczy, *Theologie der Natur* (1982).

[51]Striking expressions of a convergence between traditional Roman Catholic and Lutheran reflections on social ethics are the strong "two kingdoms" oriented statements by Joseph Cardinal Ratzinger in his comments "Liberation Theology" in *Herder Korrespondenz* (1984) 4:365: "Es werden da die Ebenen verschoben, die christliche und die sozial-ethische. . . . Aber das geht nicht, indem ich einen Mischmasch aus den beiden mache; dann wird aus Schwärmerei eine Ideologie entwickelt. . . . Es wird dann mit Hilfe der Theologie ein Grad von Gewissheit, sogar von theokratischem Anspruch erhoben, der den sozialen Ordnungen, die immer kontigent sind, ihrem Wesen nach nicht zukommt." From this, one could almost suggest that the good Bavarian cardinal had done his theological studies with the old Erlangen Lutherans Paul Althaus, Werner Elert, and Hermann Sasse!

text immediately shows that this fact alone does not prove the basic importance of "nature" and "natural law" as ethical constitutives. On the one hand, "the blind evolution of *natural* forces" is denounced (§8), the control of "*natural* drives" is urged (§21), and "rational organization of the forces of *nature*" as the chief characteristic of modern culture is critically, but by no means negatively, assessed (§2); on the other hand, "nature" in terms of "laws of *nature*" (§11), "*natural* moral law" (§4), the "*nature*" of marriage (§§4, 10) or of "married love" (§8), and the "*nature* of man and of woman" (§§12, 13) and of "specifically sexual faculties" (§13) are taken as being ethically normative.

> No member of the faithful could possibly deny that the Church is competent in her Magisterium to interpret the *natural moral law*. . . . Jesus Christ . . . constituted [Peter and the other disciples] . . . as the authentic guardians and interpreters of the whole moral law . . . also of the *natural law*, the reason being that the *natural law* declares the will of God, and its faithful observance is necessary for men's eternal salvation. . . .

> God has wisely ordered the *laws of nature* and the incidence of fertility in such a way that successive births are already *naturally* spaced through the inherent operation of these laws. The Church, nevertheless, in urging men to the observance of the precepts of the *natural law* . . . teaches as absolutely required that any use whatever of marriage must retain its *natural* potential to procreate human life. . . .

> Neither the Church nor her doctrine is inconsistent when she considers it lawful for married people to take advantage of the infertile period but condemns as always unlawful the use of means which directly exclude conception. . . . In the former [case] the married couple rightly use a facility provided them by *nature*. In the latter they obstruct the *natural* development of the generative process.[52]

From these quotations it should be clear how the ethical case is being decided: the *Roma locuta*, so far, is unconditionally equalized with a *Natura locuta, definit causam.* Even if this part of the perspective is not strongly emphasized, it is clear that the underlying presupposition is that of nature being identical with God's creation, or rather of nature being understood as the inherent determinant principle of that creation. Seen as a unified whole, to be rationally explored and discovered also in the operation of single "natural" processes, but definitely opposed to "natural drives" experienced as more or less isolated events, "nature" proclaims the Creator's will and is a constitutive part of the church's legacy to the world.

---

[52]*Humanae Vitae*, §§4, 11, 17. Emphasis added by the author.

It is interesting to compare this 1968 encyclical of Paul VI with John Paul II's approaches to the same question in his public speeches of 1984. That summer a series of papal allocutions at the weekly general audiences in the Piazza San Pietro in Rome were dedicated to the theme of marriage and responsible parenthood. Of particular interest, too, is the papal address given in Rome on June 8, 1984 to the participants of two congresses on "Marriage, Family and Fertility," which included the following statement of great consequence:

> The ultimate reason for any *natural method* [of family planning] is not simply its biological effectiveness or reliability, but its consistence with a Christian view of sexuality as expressive of conjugal love. For sexuality reflects the innermost being of the *human person* as such, and is realized in a truly human way only if it is an integral part of the love by which a man and woman commit themselves totally to one another until death. . . . At the heart of this work in *natural family planning* must be a Christian view of *the human person* and the conviction that married couples can really attain, through God's grace and commitment to the *natural methods,* a deeper and stronger conjugal unity. Their unity, mutual respect, and self-control are achieved in their practice of *natural family planning.*[53]

In his series of discourses at the public audiences, John Paul II starts with a number of biblical reflections on what he refers to as the "theology of the body," and from there he comments on *Humanae Vitae.* The following may be seen as a distillation of these comments:

> The norm of the Encyclical *Humanae Vitae* concerns all men, in so far as it is a norm of the *natural law* and is based on conformity with human reason. . . . All the more does it concern all believers . . . since the reasonable character of this norm indirectly finds confirmation and solid support in *the sum total of the "theology of the body."* . . . The norm of the *natural law,* based on this "ethos" [of the redemption of the body], finds not only a new expression, but also a fuller anthropological and ethical foundation in the word of the Gospel and in the purifying and corroborating action of the Holy Spirit. These are all reasons why every believer and especially every theologian should reread and ever more deeply understand the moral doctrine of the encyclical in this complete context.[54]

---

[53]John Paul II, 8 June 1984. *L'Osservatore Romano,* 18 June 1984. Emphasis added by the author.

[54]John Paul II, 18 July 1984. *L'Osservatore Romano,* 23 July 1984.

In the section immediately preceding our quotation John Paul II has made it very clear that what the encyclical promotes as being consistent with "natural" reason could and should be emphasized as being in harmony with "tradition stemming from biblical sources," and especially with "biblical anthropology," in the knowledge of "the significance that anthropology has for ethics." His strong support of the conclusions of the encyclical is thus coupled with a catalogue of argumentation that rather overtly constrains the *argumentum e natura* (so prevalent in the encyclical) in favor of an anthropological approach with strong claims on biblical support. While sharing the conclusions of Paul VI, John Paul II nonetheless depreciates his predecessor's argumentation in a rather ostensive manner. In John Paul II's comprehensive analysis of the encyclical there is—for good reason—not the slightest formal indication of a critical rethinking, but it is evident that he tries to pull the interpretation in a more personalistic direction:

> And it is precisely this that the Encyclical . . . stresses in a particular way: the virtuous character of . . . the "natural" regulation of fertility is determined not so much by fidelity to an impersonal "*natural law*" as to the Creator-person, the source and the Lord of the order which is manifested in such a law. . . . The document certainly presupposes that biological regularity . . . but it always understands this regularity as the expression of the "*order of nature,*" that is, of *the providential plan of the Creator,* in the faithful execution of which the true good of the human person consists.[55]

In this 1984 series of addresses the most impressive attempt to found a personalistic ethic in, at the same time, a depreciation and confirmation of traditional "naturalism" was that of August 22. Here, the problem is said to be that of combining "domination . . . of the forces of nature" with the "mastery of the self," both expressions found in *Humanae Vitae* (§§2, 21):

> Extension of the sphere of the means of "domination of the forces of nature" menaces the *human person* for whom the method of "self-mastery" is and remains specific. The mastery of self, in fact, corresponds to the fundamental constitution of *the person*: it is indeed a "*natural*" method. On the contrary, the resort to artificial means destroys the constitutive dimension *of the person*; it deprives man of the *subjectivity* proper to him and makes him an object of manipulation.[56]

---

[55]John Paul II, 28 August 1984. *L'Osservatore Romano,* 3 September 1984.

[56]John Paul II, 22 August 1984. *L'Osservatore Romano,* 3 September 1984.

However tempting it may be, it is not our task here to discuss this extremely interesting and provocative argument. Arguments for sexual continence as a means of strengthening human self-control have a comprehensive history, also within branches of conservative Protestantism. But to plead in favor of a "natural" family planning prescribed by the integrity of human personhood is a different thing. How can it be argued convincingly? The attempt is made through resorting to the foregoing biblical reflections on a "theology" or "language" of "the body":

> The human body is . . . the means of expressing *the entire man, the person,* which reveals itself by means of *the "language of the body."* This "language" has *an important interpersonal meaning,* especially in reciprocal relationships between man and woman. . . . In this case the "language of the body" should express, at a determinate level, the truth of the sacrament. . . . Man and woman express themselves in the measure of the whole truth of *the human person.* . . . The interior order of conjugal union is rooted in the very *order of the person.*[57]

The least one can say about the difference between the original encyclical and the papal reinterpretation of 16 years later is that an unmistakable extension of scope corresponds with an unmistakable shift in emphasis. A predominantly biological consideration of human "nature," founded on an essentially rational exploration, is replaced by a comprehensive anthropological development of human personhood that is supported by extensive biblical observations. Ecclesiologically, this relocation of emphasis can probably be understood and defended as the fruit of an ongoing historical development within the church, supplementing and clarifying former reflection—especially as the final practical conclusion remains unchanged. But in terms of the underlying creation theology the change is rather striking. To a certain extent this change seems to reflect the (already observed) general reorientation of Roman Catholic creation theology. The concept of nature—and the use made of it in *Humanae Vitae*—may still be seen to be fairly representative of a traditional Roman Catholic creation theology: an objective ontological and cosmological vision whereby the essential thing is the established cosmic order as such. In this regard, the encyclical seems far more conventional than, for example, *Gaudium et Spes* of three years earlier.

The move from an essentialistic to a personalistic interpretation of "natural law," especially as reflected in the speeches of the present pope, may be influenced less by Protestant theology (Barthianism) than by philosophical trends (Kantianism, existentialism, personalism), trends that nevertheless indicate vig-

---

[57]Ibid.

orous—though somewhat complex and diffuse—ties to 19th- and 20th-century Protestant thought. If not identical with, the effect is at least parallel to the reorientation of Roman Catholic creation theology in light of the Barthian *Heilsgeschichte* emphasis.[58]

Seen in a wider perspective, this may today be interpreted as a sort of ecumenical rearguard action. At the same time as it will generally be seen as an argumentative "progress" vis-à-vis the apparently essentialistic understanding of "nature" in *Humanae Vitae* (more flexible, more empirical-functional, more immediately catering to observable human needs), it may also be seen as reflecting the anthropocentric approach to reality that is so characteristic of modern (first Protestant, but in recent decades also more and more Roman Catholic) theology. "Nature"—and implicitly "creation"—is not primarily understood as the functional totality of entities created; rather human personality is the overarching principle of phenomenal integration. In a way, the essentialistic, Thomist approach could be seen as being more "ecological," locating the value of phenomena and events not predominantly in human personhood but rather in the universality of the created world and its response to the uncreated, eternal ground of its being. Thus the new approach could rather be taken for a diminution of what today, throughout the *oikumene,* is gradually being seen as an indisputable Roman Catholic contribution to ecumenical creation theology: the vision of the universe, reality as a whole, relevant to our faith in God the Lord Universal. For this vision, the concept of "nature" may serve a comprehensive structure of meaning, whereby the human being is helped to understand her/his existence in terms of her/his essential relatedness to everything there is. And this also means seeing science as an appropriate and necessary instrument of the intelligent human being in exploring and affirming her/his relatedness to being in its totality.

---

[58]At the same time, the personalistic philosophical orientation of Cardinal Wojtyla (see Ignacy Dec, "Person als Subject: Zum Personbegriff bei Karol Wojtyla," *Theologie und Glaube* [1986] 3:294-307) may have to be borne in mind for a balanced assessment of the ecumenical importance of this observation. To what extent are we hearing the voice of the Roman Catholic Church as such, and to what extent are we hearing the voice of one particular theologian, the spokesperson of one particular (though certainly influential) current *within* that church? On the other hand, in Walter Schöpsdau's "Die Kompetenz des Lehramts in Fragen der Moral," *Materialdienst des Konfessionskundlichen Instituts, Bensheim* (1986) 5:91-96, we find observations that very much indicate that the switch from a "naturalist" to a "personalist" type of argument involves no deep-rooted reorientation; it is rather to be seen as a kind of cosmetic makeup. Such a judgment is understandable if one focuses on conclusions rather than on premises, but in our present perspective that orientation definitely seems to be too narrow.

Such observations take our attention back to the basic dilemma of an orientative theology of creation: On the one hand, how can this theology avoid sacralizing structures (and established theories linked with structures) and thus banning activities in favor of a new and better world? On the other hand, how can it protect creation from peremptory human exploitation and disintegrative officiousness? If "the world as it is" is basically to be interpreted as creational givenness, established structures will be solidified and ethical obligation will generally be thought of in terms of steadfastly keeping things steadfast. But if, on the other hand, this world is seen exclusively as raw material for human enterprise (in terms of Jean-Paul Sartre's "l'existence précède l'essence"), then creation as a whole contains no regulative principle to keep the bustle of human inventiveness in check.

Especially in the Thomist tradition, the apparent rigidity of Scholastic essentialism has always been moderated by a concept of nature that is consciously geared to organic growth, that is, to the teleology of an as yet unattained aim, and thus to a functional understanding of identity: Things are not what they "are"—disjointed entities—but what they are intended to be in an—as yet unattained—universal harmony. However, over the centuries the main problem has been that this harmony has been so well defined that the same theory could become repugnant to itself and thus (highly) vulnerable to the onset of new discoveries and reflections. The concept of a universal, creation-given openness tended to become consolidated into patterns of cosmological givens in such a way as to eliminate any growth in observation from the historical process. A similar undialectical distortion is, however, a possibility inherent in every theological (and ideological) position; one should therefore not leap toward a seemingly opposite line of thought without careful reflection.

But could it even be maintained that, to some extent, such an "unreflected" leap is taking place in contemporary Roman Catholic theology? And that the common needs of the *oikumene* would have been better served if Roman Catholic theology had remained more consciously Roman Catholic? The obvious integration of modern Protestant impulses into Roman Catholic creation thought has been necessary in order for the Roman Catholic Church to overcome a long-standing stalemate. The aftermath of this stalemate may still be felt, albeit more in practical attitudes and established customs than in governing thought patterns. Does the recent personalistic reinterpretation of *Humanae Vitae* not testify to this? At the same time, however, today's ecological challenge may be an indication that recent anthropocentricity may render a lesser service to creation than a somewhat revised edition of an established cosmological orientation. At any rate, the question should be raised.

5.3 The Lutheran contribution

Within the Lutheran "world" it would appear that there is a certain amount of tension with regard to creation theology. This first came to expression at the 1984 Strasbourg consultation: on the one hand, the Swedish theologian Kjell Ove Nilsson strongly underlined that a Lutheran (vis-à-vis Reformed) profile was represented by a particular emphasis on the First Article; on the other, the main Lutheran spokesperson, Professor Reinhard Slenczka underscored that creation theology was denominationally uncontroversial, and that the real confrontation was of a *confessory* rather than *confessional* nature and related to an extremely urgent concern about the common Christian confession rather than to a confrontation between specific versions of it. He referred to some of the contemporary cross-denominational tensions that we have already touched in §4.

It may be slightly more than accidental that the opposing voices come from Scandinavia and Germany. As we have already seen, especially in the last century there has been a very conscious creation emphasis in Scandinavian theology (Knud E. Løgstrup, Regin Prenter, Gustaf Wingren, et al.); whereas German theology has been more concerned to overcome the trauma of the 1930s, that is, the conscious and unconscious exploitation of creation theology to authorize obedience to the state. The whole doctrine of the "two kingdoms"—so emphatically focused upon from the time of mid-19th-century neo-Lutheranism onward—seems to have encouraged an attitude of civil subservience in both the Bismarck and the Hitler eras.[59] Seen in a wider systematical setting, this issue is closely related to creation theology, since the structures of sociopolitical life derive their legitimacy directly from a projected realm of creation, understood as existing prior to biblical revelation.

One should not overlook the relationship between this doctrine and Roman Catholic tradition (the Augustinian *Civitas Dei* and also the medieval distinction between natural being [creation] and supernatural [redemption]). The dialectical interplay of givenness (creation) versus renewal (salvation)—the tension between

---

[59]Cf. Ulrich Duchrow, *Christenheit und Weltverantwortung: Traditionsgeschichte und systematische Struktur der Zweireichelehre* (1970); *Umdeutungen der Zweireichelehre Luthers im 19. Jahrhundert,* ed. Ulrich Duchrow, Wolfgang Huber, Louis Reith (1975); *Die Vorstellung von zwei Reichen und Regimenten bis Luther,* ed. Ulrich Duchrow, Heiner Hoffmann ([2]1975). See also Wilfried Joest, "Die Lehre von den Zwei Reichen Gottes und der Gedanke der Schöpfungsordnungen," *Schöpfungsglaube und Umweltverantwortung: Eine Studie des Theologischen Ausschusses der VELKD,* ed. Wenzel Lohff and Hans Christian Knuth (Hanover: Lutherisches Verlagshaus, 1985) 239-63.

the "Behold, it was very good" and the "Behold, I make all things new"—is very much the same, irrespective of certain differences in accent. In both cases, the danger of uncritically authorizing some status quo seems rather apparent, but at the same time the possibility of using "nature" (or "orders of creation") as a standard for judging historically conditioned givens should also be sufficiently clear. In the history of Roman Catholicism it has not been unusual to confront actual political powers and criticize what is taken to be notorious injustices in the name of natural principles. A similar thing may be said to happen in a good deal of contemporary Lutheran world involvement, and it even happened during the Hitler period, when the "two kingdoms" doctrine was used in two opposing ways. During the Norwegian church struggle, the church made particularly spectacular use of this doctrine for criticizing the state authorities through the rather epochal proclamation "Kirkens Grunn" (1942).[60] Thus far, the structural similarities between these two confessional traditions are obvious.

To what extent, than, can emphasis on a pre-Christological theology of creation be seen to be characteristic of the Lutheran theological inheritance? Luther's own theology of creation has been explored by David Löfgren, who concludes:

_{l}_

---

[60]"The Foundation of the Church." This is thoroughly analyzed in Torleiv Austad, *Kirkens Grunn* (Oslo, 1974); cf. particularly §5: "On the right relationship with public authority for the Christian and for the church" (30-31). See also: Carsten Nicolaisen, " 'Anwendung' der Zweireichelehre im Kirchenkampf," *Gottes Wirken in seiner Welt*, vol. 2, *Reaktionen,* ed. Niels Hasselmann (Hanover: Lutherisches Verlagshaus, 1980) 15-26, which, using the examples of Dietrich Bonhoeffer and Emanuel Hirsch, shows the possibility for polarization that opens up when making the doctrine of the "two kingdoms" the ethical foundation of practical decision making.

A good deal more simplistic is the interpretation by Jürgen Moltmann: "Der Lutheraner ist der 'ewige Positivist,' sagt ein Scherzwort. . . . Er folgt leichter dem positivistischen Grundsatz 'auctoritas facit legem' als dem naturrechtlichen Grundsatz 'veritas facit legem'. . . . Die Zweireichelehre [gibt] keine Kriterien für eine christliche Ethik her." (Jürgen Moltmann, *Politische Theologie—politische Ethik* [Mainz: Matthias-Grünewald; Munich: Christian Kaiser Verlag, 1984] 136). (English: *On Human Dignity: Political Theology and Ethics,* trans. M. Douglas Meeks [London: SCM Press; Philadelphia: Fortress Press, 1984].) May this simplification have to do with an unquestioned elimination of "natural theology," which immediately excludes everything but a formal, positivistic interpretation of "the kingdom to the Left"?

Dass in der modernen Theologie . . . der erste Glaubensartikel in ver-
hängnisvoller Weise der Stellung beraubt wurde, die er bei dem Refor-
mator innehatte.[61]

The confrontation between Luther and modern (Barthian) theology in the realm
of creation is seen in a comprehensive theological perspective by Gustaf Wingren.[62] As a whole, since around 1950 the Aarhus/Lundensian "school" of creation theology[63] has strongly advocated Luther as its immediate precursor, its
interpretation of Luther and its own understanding of creation becoming close to
identical. Polemic occurs in two directions: against Barthian "Christo-monism"
(the main contemporary challenge), and against the conceptual rigidity of Scholastic natural theology, including its aftermath in 17th- and 19th-century Lutheran
orthodoxy, and even against the more recent idea of "orders of creation." Thus,
the main concern of this "school" is not a simple transmission of perennial Lutheran "two kingdoms" doctrine; far from it! Rather than providing an avenue to
a global realm of "nature" or to some authoritative structure of sociopolitical interdependence, the emphasis is on creatureliness as immediacy, a conscious or
unconscious response of created being to its Creator.[64]

---

[61]David Löfgren, *Die Theologie der Schöpfung bei Luther* (Göttingen: Vandenhoeck & Ruprecht, 1960) 7.

[62]In, esp., Gustaf Wingren, *The Christian's Calling: Luther on Vocation*,
trans. Carl C. Rasmussen (Edinburgh: T. & T. Clark, 1952; German: *Luthers Lehre
vom Beruf* [1952]) and *Creation and Law*, trans. Ross Mackenzie (Edinburgh:
Oliver & Boyd, 1961; Original: *Skapelsen och lagen* [Lund: CWK Gleerup, 1958];
German: *Schöpfung und Gesetz* [1960]). The latter is reviewed here, pp. 117-19.

[63]See here, §4.2, pp. 117-29.

[64]"We also see more clearly how the phrase 'earthly government' in the 16th
century came to have reference to the obtaining of food, protection to life and limb,
etc. Only when pietism has turned its back upon Creation . . . do we begin to ask
questions about this natural ethic. . . . We therefore analyse it for the purpose of
letting the second article alone provide us with knowledge even about the law,
order, and justice." (Gustaf Wingren, *Creation and Law* [see n. 62] 42, cf. 46-
47; German: 48; cf. 52-53)

"That a natural knowledge of God exists is clear to Luther. The existence of
God is self-evident. A certain knowledge of God on the level of creation must be
there, or God could not have assigned man to be the ruler of creation with his reason and his will. . . . Only this knowledge and this experience do not suffice for
a personal God-relationship." (Knud E. Løgstrup, *Skabelse og Tilintetgørelse*,

There is no doubt that Løgstrup is one of the authors who, in his emphatic plea for understanding human encounter (and thus ethical structures) as an immediacy principally prior to biblical revelation, places himself at the furthest distance from modern theological Christocentrism and accords the most comprehensive importance to a "metaphysical" founding of theology, that is, in a consistent (not specifically Christian) ontology of creation. He claims Luther as a supporter of this approach, but at the same time admits that it is necessary today to reinterpret and establish ontological presuppositions, which to the Reformer and his day were too evident to need clarification. Without pleading a Lutheran confessional identity as some specific concern, he very consciously refers to Luther as a precursor and ally. Regin Prenter and Gustaf Wingren are less inclined to make human immediacy a topic of specific reflection, but hasten to interpret it in light of the Bible. Both of them, however, emphasize creatureliness as an experience common to all people, regardless of what their conscious relationship with the Creator may be. Of the two, Prenter places strongest emphasis on an integration of creation and redemption. But at the same time as he clearly adheres to the "classical" sequence of events (outlined by the old creeds) as an access to understanding, he underscores that creation in its full sense can be understood only when fulfilled in redemption: the two are complementary aspects of one and the same event.

> Indem Gott erschafft und die Mächte der Vernichtung bekämpft, streitet er also gleichzeitig gegen das Heer der Bosheit, den Teufel und alle Mächte der Vernichtung. . . . Daher vollzieht sich das Werk der Erlösung Hand in Hand mit der Schöpfung. Aber das Werk der Schöpfung ist in seiner Einheit mit dem der Erlösung doch von diesem verschieden. Die Schöpfung vollzieht Gott durch Sein Gesetz, die Erlösung durch Sein Evangelium.[65]

If this "school" sees law and creation as being closely related, it is obvious that law here is not predominantly seen in the historical perspective of covenant (Sinai as revelation event), but rather in the universal perspective of our very createdness. Contrary to the law, the gospel is an event that cannot be derived from

---

Metafysik 4 [Copenhagen, 1978] 64)

"Hier wird kein 'natürliches Gottesbewusstsein' ausgeschlossen, sondern eine 'natürliche Theologie' . . . [als] Versuch, um die Offenbarung herum zu einer vorläufigen Erkenntnis Gottes zu gelangen, die später mit der Erkenntnis Gottes vereint werden kann, die die Offenbarung gibt." (Regin Prenter, *Schöpfung und Erlösung* [1960] 32. Original: *Skabelse og Genløsing* [1955].)

[65]Regin Prenter, *Schöpfung und Erlösung*, 194.

or supported through an observation of "natural" events. It can be articulated only in interaction with the law, its aim being the renovating confirmation of creation and not the replacement of it. The sequence "law and gospel" can therefore not be reversed; this would inevitably invalidate creation and naturalize redemption.

Here, it will suffice to observe that this far-ranging Nordic consensus may constitute a fairly important challenge to contemporary Lutheran self-understanding. Is it really essential to Lutheran identity, as historically given, to emphasize the thematic priority of creation theology in such a manner? Do the "two kingdoms" and the "orders of creation"—even if terminologically debatable and in need of practical readaptation—express some concern that is really fundamental to the Lutheran Reformation? How is this seen today outside Scandinavia?

In this context, one rather important American work is by Carl E. Braaten (*Principles of Lutheran Theology*). In this book "creation" has no chapter heading of its own, but the topic is dealt with in the context of "The Sacramental Principle" and "The Two Kingdoms Principle." Even though, from an ecumenical point of view, it may be just as helpful to deal with the first of these issues in the following section on Anglican theology, the second issue fits into the present stage of our research. Braaten states the question in a truly ecumenical way:

> Is there another way of understanding the source and function of law which both overcomes the most serious limitations in the Catholic natural law theory, in the Lutheran doctrine of orders of creation, or in the Barthian Christological ethics, and yet hopes to retain the deepest elements of truth and relevance in each? We would not wish to accomplish less than a comprehensive synthesis in an ecumenical theology of human rights. A complete repudiation of any one of the three approaches seems impossible to me. First of all, they are not mutually exclusive alternatives in every response; second, each has developed in its own way in response to a particular historical situation; and third, each one calls attention to some deficiency in the others.[66]

In his review of "Principles of Lutheran Theology," Braaten places importance on "The Ecumenical Principle,"[67] and in cases of seeming contradiction this makes his immediate aim the search for some reconciliation of legitimate interests "behind." In the case before us, he sees that all three emphases are worthy of being reconciled. Braaten sees the consonance of Roman Catholic and Lutheran tradition in maintaining the priority of law as a universally given structure

---

[66]Carl E. Braaten, *Principles of Lutheran Theology* (Philadelphia: Fortress Press, 1983) 128.

[67]Ibid., 27-62.

of common human experience, a guarantee of clear and unambiguous moral principles rooted in a common human nature. At the same time, the Barthian accusation that natural theology expresses a nonbiblical view of a static world—holding against it an emphatic concern for the kingship of Christ—seems to be justified. This concern is only partly answered by the Lutheran switch from (Roman Catholic) natural law to "orders of creation," as long as these are understood "as an autonomous locus of theology completely separate from the revelation of God in Christ." It is this lack of Christological center and criterion that, according to Braaten, is rightly opposed by Barth. On the other hand, in deriving political community from the Christian communion, Barth tends to bar effective exchange on ethical concerns between Christians and other people. And here Braaten sees that a Lutheran objection is equally justified. Thus, the ecumenical synthesis called for goes as follows:

> The Lutheran concern has been for a clear differentiation between law and gospel as two modes of divine activity in the world. . . . This means that human rights can be defined and realized in common among Christians and non-Christians without reference to the gospel as the condition of this possibility. The Barthian concern is for the ultimate unity of gospel and law under the one Lord so that no sphere of existence can remain outside his dominion. . . . These two dimensions of concern are not incompatible. In the light of the revelation of God in Jesus Christ, Christians possess a new basis for *understanding* the realities of government and law. However, these realities are established by God prior to the incarnation of Jesus Christ and can at least be partially understood and administered by those who do not acknowledge the lordship of Christ. . . . In the New Testament there is a "cosmic Christology" which expresses that the Christ who is Jesus in the flesh is also the medium of creation and the fulfillment of the law. Therefore, also, the meaning of the law must be interpreted from a Christological perspective, but not in such a way that Christians would claim to be able to derive specific social principles from Christology. There is no specifically Christian "bill of rights."[68]

We have reviewed Braaten's line of thought so extensively because his statement on the Lutheran contribution to an ecumenical theology of creation speaks so immediately to the scope of our project. Braaten sets himself apart from the above-quoted Scandinavian authors, and this not only from a formal perspective. Whereas the Scandinavians tend to speak from within the Lutheran tradition and try to draw a clear dividing line, Braaten basically represents an ecumenical out-

---

[68]Ibid., 130-31.

look, trying to combine what he sees as the vital concerns in as many camps as possible. Also, his "solution" seems to be convincing—as far as it goes. Can any contemporary theologian do anything but reject such one-sided accents as an independent creation theology that is exempt from the lordship of Christ, or a political Christocracy that threatens to deprive non-Christians of civil rights? The critical question is whether the historical confrontation between a "two kingdoms" and a "kingship of Christ" approach to social ethics—and thereby between a creation and a redemption oriented approach to phenomenal reality—really boils down to the fact that reconciliation is as readily at hand as in Braaten's sketch. What an ecumenical blessing it would be if it were! The seemingly simplistic question of "what comes first—creation or salvation?" could and should be answered either way. But—as J. Robert Nelson so convincingly spelled out at the 1983 Strasbourg consultation—certainly not at the same time! Which comes first depends on the meaning of the question. If we are asking about the prime experience of nascent faith, then it is certainly salvation. But if we are reviewing faith in terms of reflective contents, then the answer will inevitably be creation. But this certainly does not mean that in any given situation we are left with a free choice!

It can scarcely be denied that the conclusions in Braaten's exposition tend to accommodate traditional Lutheran principles in a way that can hardly be reconciled with the theological focus of Barth and his school.

> The living God was at work among the nations . . . prior to the election of Israel, and God acts in the realm of international relations today without any direct contact with the preaching of his Word. The instrument of his activity is the law, and this law confronts every person, community, and nation in his, her, or its empirical existence, creating a degree of order in spite of the destructive consequences of sin. . . .

> The Christian message in its totality . . . speaks of two things that God is doing in the world. God is pressing for the historical liberation of human beings through a host of secular media, and for Christ's sake he promises eternal salvation through the preaching of the Word and the administration of the sacraments. Historical liberation and eternal salvation are not one and the same thing. They should not be equated.[69]

Consequences such as those suggested and protested here were hardly intended by Barth. But the question is whether the way in which they are challenged by Braaten may be reconciled with Barthian theology. Braaten seems to presuppose that the Barthian sequence (gospel *before* law) is of no—or at least need not

_____

[69]Ibid., 131, 134.

be of any—material consequence to the function of law (and creation) as a common human ground of ethical orientation.[70] It may, however, be asked whether the order between law and gospel—which in effect reflects the principal succession between the First and the Second Article of the Creed—is not basic to the whole vision of theology. Where does theology start? This is not only a question of procedure; above all, it regards creational givenness as a referential partner for faith and reflection. Does the Word as message of salvation refer to creational responsibility as a reality given to and already present for all human beings—or is it oriented throughout by the ''new creation'' that it intends to serve?

It is easy to see how the conflict between a full-blooded natural theology (which draws final ethical conclusions with no regard to the incarnation) and a Christocratic submission of social and political ethics to purely biblical assumptions could and should be alleviated through reciprocal modification. Thus far, Braaten's peacemaking attempt should be welcomed. But making the allowances he calls for is hardly a solution to the issue as such. If gospel basically comes before law, as with Barth, is it possible to justify Braaten's own claims concerning the function of the law in the fallen world and concerning God's two activities? It is not easy to see how this could be so. On a practical ethical level, the reconciliation called for may be easier to achieve than in the domain of fundamental theology. It involves no break with a classical Lutheran (or, for that matter, Roman Catholic) tradition to admit that, for a Christian facing practical decisions, intuitive knowledge of natural law is subject to scrutiny and purification by the revealed Word. Nor is it un-Barthian to admit that in issues of peace and survival Christians are requested to talk with people irrespective of faith and to hope that biblically authorized concerns will find an echo. But this practical agreement will not suffice for a common ground of theological reflection! Here, it is obvious that an either/or must be posited between a creation and a redemption starting point, and this will have to be settled before a common theological line can be sought.

On the present German scene, attempts to outline a particular Lutheran contribution in the realm of creation are not commonplace. This is, of course, partly due to the experience of the 1930s and the mediocre success of creation-oriented theologies to resist the Nazi onset—not least compared with the impressive record of the Barthian kingship of Christ orientation.[71]

---

[70]Ibid., 131.

[71]Concerning semiofficial attempts to reinterpret and revitalize the historical concerns behind the ''two kingdoms'' doctrine, reference should be made to our observations about study projects carried out by the Lutheran World Federation (LWF) and the United Evangelical Lutheran Church of Germany (VELKD), here pp. 157-60, 204ff.

So far, a general rehabilitation of informed arguments about the order of creation and the two kingdoms has not been fully convincing to theological opinion in general. At the same time, there seems to be growing resistance, especially among Lutheran theologians, to what is sometimes referred to as the "Christomonistic" model of Barthian theology. Above all, this resistance has been voiced by Wolfhart Pannenberg as well as by other theologians influenced by him. However, since its epistemological horizon has to a large extent been informed by Hegel and contemporary German neo-Hegelianism, this thought does not so much refer to nature, orders of creation, or law as to history, anthropology, and the concern for human freedom. By viewing the simul-simul of Hegelian dialectic as an echo of Luther's challenge to the simple rationality of Aristotelian conceptual discipline, such a reorientation has been defended as being particularly "Lutheran."[72] Obviously, the interesting questions in our context would then be: 1. To what extent can Hegelianism be seen as a particular Lutheran contribution to posterity? 2. To what extent may it serve an ecumenical clarification of creation belief?

In a certain sense, the general theological interest of Pannenberg is not so easily synchronized with the traditional confessional confrontation as is that of the Nordic authors quoted, since Pannenberg's anthropological orientation to a certain degree limits his exchange with the more "ecological" trends in contemporary creation theology. His *Wissenschaftstheorie und Theologie* (1973) is no less determined by a dialogue with social philosophy than is his *Anthropologie in theologischer Perspektive* (1983), references to natural science and to an emerging ecological awareness being by no means commonplace. His theology is certainly not creation oriented in the sense of being geared toward the whole breadth of the realm of creation. But it is creation oriented in that it pays decisive attention to conditions of human personhood as reflected in the dynamics of history, which is, according to him, also a prerequisite for an authentic approach to historical revelation. In the Pannenberg "school," the First Article of the Creed is certainly rehabilitated, but not in terms of some traditional "theology of creation."[73]

---

[72]E.g., Ulrich Asendorf, *Luther und Hegel: Untersuchungen zur Grundlegung einer neuen systematischen Theologie* (Wiesbaden: Franz Steiner Verlag, 1982).

[73]Cf. Wolfhart Pannenberg, *Wissenschaftstheorie und Theologie* (Frankfurt: Suhrkamp Verlag, 1987 [1973]) and *Anthropology in Theological Perspective*, trans. Matthew J. O'Connell (Edinburgh: T. & T. Clark; Philadelphia: Westminster Press, 1985) 15-16. (Original: *Anthropologie in theologischer Perspektive*

A document with a rather distinctive theological profile is the 1985 report *Schöpfungsglaube und Umweltverantwortung*[74] issued by the Theological Commission of the United Evangelical Lutheran Church of Germany (VELKD). According to this document it is not coincidental that creation occurs in the first place in the Bible as well as in the Creed; it should also be at the base of our response to the ecological crisis.[75] Neither a purely *heilsgeschichtlich* nor an existential-anthropological view of creation takes care of the unifying vision of heaven and earth so bitterly needed today.[76] A "step into a new territory of ethics" is required in order to "break through and transcend the anthropocentric limitation of former ethics."[77] But this demands the realism to recognize that humans are and remain creatures, not creators, and also to opt for reason and readiness to compromise.[78] "The big step into the future can only be made through the small steps of people living today."[79] It is maintained that "Lutheran ethics is permeated by this priority of political ethics in the widest sense."[80] Even if it is maintained that "a focal point of this study" is "the close belonging together of creation and redemption"—as opposed to not only Christocentric one-sidedness but also any theology of "creation orders"[81]—the general impression may be a certain bias in the direction of a (politically more than ecologically) visualized realm of creation with a distinctive anti-utopian emphasis.

As already indicated, at the 1983 Strasbourg consultation it was observed that there was a clear distance between the standpoints of the two official Lutheran

---

[Göttingen: Vandenhoeck & Ruprecht, 1983].)

The most consistent spokeperson for this Lutheran anti-Barthianism is probably Pannenberg's faculty colleague in Munich, Trutz Rendtorff, whose focal concern is what he himself defines as "the systematically necessary idea of a societal function at large as specific to religion" (Trutz Rendtorff, *Gesellschaft ohne Religion* [1975] 21), with a strong emphasis on church as *Volkskirche*. See also Rendtorff's contribution in *Volkskirche: Kirche der Zukunft?*, ed. Wenzel Lohff and Lutz Mohaupt (Hanover: Lutherisches Verlagshaus, 1977) 104-31.

[74]*Schöpfungsglaube und Umweltverantwortung* (see n. 59).

[75]Ibid., 10.

[76]Ibid., 15-16.

[77]Ibid., 30.

[78]Ibid., 32-33.

[79]Ibid., 42.

[80]Ibid., 38.

[81]Ibid., 18.

spokespersons. Whereas Kjell Ove Nilsson from Sweden took up the ideas of, especially, Gustaf Wingren and advocated a decisively Lutheran profile in the domain of creation, Reinhard Slenczka (Erlangen, FRG) was not prepared to admit
any confessionally relevant confrontation in this area. He noted that the church-
dividing confrontations with regard to creation (the Gnostic and Manichean rejection of God, the Father of Jesus Christ, as Creator of the actual world) had already been overcome in the ancient church and that similar doctrines had never
staged a comeback in mainline church life. He saw the real challenges to creation
faith today in a threatening revolution of priorities, which may subject creation as
well as redemption to the demands of an imperialistic political theology. In this
light, he was particularly concerned to overcome any suggestion of a basic split
between Lutheran and Reformed ambitions.

It is interesting to compare this inner-Lutheran disagreement with the discussion that took place in the 1970s between, in particular, the former leadership of
the Lutheran World Federation Department of Studies and the Theological Commission of the United Evangelical Lutheran Church of Germany (VELKD). The
controversy reached its peak at a confrontative consultation in Pullach in 1979 and
resulted in two volumes on *Gottes Wirken in seiner Welt* (1980).[82] This discussion
did not focus on Lutheranism in a wider ecumenical setting but on internal tensions within the Lutheran tradition as such. But, in spite of this, the one discussion
obviously has a bearing on the other. There was a sharp polarization between a
more unified salvation-liberation approach (as championed most sharply by Ulrich Duchrow) and a dialectical "two kingdoms" approach (advocated by the
VELKD Theological Commission in a series of theses). However, the presuppositions in creation theology were barely touched upon by either party, even
though the implicit interrelatedness of creation and redemption was palpable.

More striking, in the present setting, is an earlier study project of the Lutheran World Federation on "The Quest for True Humanity and the Lordship of
Christ."[83] Ivar Asheim's introduction to the study includes a presentation on its
prehistory, beginning with Lund 1947, when Luther's explanation of the Second
Article of the Creed ("in order that I might be his, live under him in his kingdom,
and serve him") was accentuated as a corrective to any false autonomy of the secular realm.[84] In a study on the history of the *regnum Christi* concept in Protestantism, Wolfgang Trillhaas shows that:

---

[82]*Gottes Wirken in seiner Welt: Zur Diskussion um die Zweireichelehre,* ed.
Niels Hasselmann (Hamburg: Lutherisches Verlagshaus, 1980).

[83]Ivar Asheim, "The Quest for True Humanity and the Lordship of Christ,"
Lutheran World 14/1 (1967) esp. the working paper, 79-88.

[84]Ibid., 1-14.

The concept of the lordship of Christ, which must be understood as the basis of contemporary social ethics, developed outside the Lutheran ecclesiastical and theological tradition. Part of the reason lies in the fact that Lutheranism was more interested in the spiritual character of the gospel and in the scrupulous distinction between law and gospel.

For the Lutheran church and its theology, the significance of the contemporary concept of the lordship of Christ lies in its clarion call to revise our, frequently very conservative, traditions. . . . It will be necessary to seek to make the structures of love known also in law.[85]

The working paper prepared at that time (1967) by the LWF Commission on Theology is highly elucidating and includes the heading "The 'Two Kingdoms' and the Lordship of Christ."[86] Of particular interest are, on the one hand, the clear and repeated references to creation and, on the other, the distinctive outlining of a Lutheran profile combined with a conscious self-criticism. Having shown that "the twofold lordship of God" was founded already in the Old Testament distinction between the universal acts of God the Creator and the specific acts of God, the Lord of covenant, and then further elaborated in the New Testament, a profile of "the so-called doctrine of the two kingdoms" is drawn up:

God . . . is the creator of all things and has all things in his hands. . . . Men are in God's service whether they know it or not, whether they believe in him or not. This lordship of God is a *hidden lordship*. . . . Christians and non-Christians can therefore act in common ethical understanding. . . . In the very worldliness of the world we are therefore under God who has created and continues to create this world. . . . But it is the same God and Father of Jesus Christ, who—revealed and hidden, in the Word of the gospel and in the law—provides for his creation and preserves it for the future.[87]

Speaking of God's government in two realms has often been understood as separating a private Christian sphere from a public sphere in which Christian norms had no validity. . . . Such misinterpretations took a deep root in the history of Lutheranism. The root is the pessimism of the understanding of man, the consequence of which was the idea that sinful man was to be coerced under the severity of the law. . . . The idea of the possibility of a moral life and . . . mistrust of reason . . . fostered an authoritarian patriarchalism. Lutheranism was thus paralyzed and . . . was

---

[85]Ibid., 58.

[86]Ibid., 79-88.

[87]Ibid., 81-82.

not to comprehend the democratic system of government. Here a future revision of the presuppositions of ethics must begin.[88]

The concept of the lordship of Christ is explored in a similar way, through its breakthrough in postwar theology, its New Testament foundations, its possible and actual distortions, and the ways to adapt its vital concerns without yielding to the delusions.

> Understanding the lordship of Jesus Christ as an ontocratic or trium-phalistic rule . . . overlooks the fact that the rule of God in Christ is hidden in the structures of creation. . . . This misunderstanding has expressed itself in history as theocracy or ecclesiocracy. . . .
>
> Another misunderstanding sees Christ as the lawgiver for the world, either by changing the gospel from God's merciful gift to a new demand for obedience, or by understanding Christian obedience as an anachronistic and literalistic imitation of Christ. . . . Either conception loses the liberating power of the gospel. . . .
>
> A third misunderstanding gives divine sanction either to an existing order or to secular programs of improvement or revolution. This position . . . forgets the ambivalence of all human activity as well as the difference between human aspirations and the divine purpose.
>
> The derivation of all social ethics from the lordship of Jesus Christ . . . may transform the gospel into law, thus changing Christian obedience from a free response to the grace of God into an anxious preoccupation with deserving God's gifts. . . .
>
> In order that the doctrine of the lordship of Christ may do justice to the significance of the realm of creation, the church must work both rationally and with realism.[89]

At first glance, this elaboration may seem to anticipate Carl Braaten's plea, 16 years later, for a dialectical combination of the two kingdoms and the lordship of Christ theology. But when one takes a closer look there is an obvious difference. Whereas Braaten basically calls for a coordination of the two doctrinal approaches on equal terms, the LWF paper clearly uses the two kingdoms concept as a basic model and introduces the lordship model mainly to specify and prevent obvious misunderstandings of the former. The lordship orientation gains full weight *within* a vision whereby the organizational frame is that of a critically revised and

---

[88]Ibid., 83.

[89]Ibid., 86-87.

refined two kingdoms doctrine. In effect, what the paper is saying is that the historical alliance between this doctrine and an unreflected acceptance of societal givens should be abandoned, not only for political but also for theological reasons; however, the doctrine itself needs to be maintained, for the sake of soteriology as much as of creation theology. Neither creation nor redemption can be adequately understood in isolation from one another, but at the same time the event of redemption has to be integrated into the more comprehensive framework of creation. Salvation, however, is no isolated accidental event; and creation is seen as an act of God's grace and as foreshadowing the final victory of this grace:

> The unique gift which the church owes to all men . . . is the gospel of the love of God, the good news of the justification of sinners. Man is created in the image of God and cannot achieve true humanity without being reconciled to his Creator.[90]

Referring to the participation of Christ in creation (Colossians 1:16ff.), it is underscored that this by no means weakens the Old Testament understanding of creation as God's omnipresence in history, since this participation "is a hidden mystery within the reality of our world and not a manifest activity of Christ after his incarnation."[91] This conclusion might have been very much strengthened if it had been noted that the whole passage in Colossians qualifies not creation theology but incarnation: the Savior who brought about salvation in history receives legitimacy through representing God the Creator in a unique and mysterious way. Creation as a "known" is used to make incarnation known; not the other way round. What is offered here is not a Christological approach to creation but a creation approach to Christology!

In the course of the consultation process between the Lutheran and Reformed churches in Europe following the Leuenberg Agreement (1973), the relationship between the two doctrines was discussed by two different study groups.[92] The Leuenberg Agreement (§39) lists the relationship between these doctrines as being among the doctrinal differences that still exist between the two confessions but that have no church-dividing character. In view of confessional implications, the first of the two reports is more explicit, presenting "die Lehre von den zwei Re-

---

[90]Ibid., 87.

[91]Ibid., 82.

[92]*Konkordie und Kirchengemeinschaft: Texte der Konferenz von Driebergen/Niederlande (18. bis 24. Februar 1981)*, ed. André Birmelé, Ökumenische Perspektiven 10 (Frankfurt-am-Main: Verlag Otto Lembeck/Verlag Josef Knecht, 1982) 39-43, 43-51.

gierweisen Gottes'' as ''sachgemässer Ausdruck des grundlegenden Verständnisses lutherischer Reformation, dass Gottes Herrschaft sich auf zweierlei Weise vollzieht,'' and ''das Reden von der Königsherrschaft Jesu Christi'' as it is ''von reformierter Seite . . . entfaltet.'' Both doctrines are developed in the way intended by their proponents, and in both cases ''selbstkritische Rückfragen'' are proposed. The two concepts have taken shape in different situations and as answers to divergent questions. But the fact that in the contemporary world they are used to provide solutions to the same questions urges a clarification of their mutual relationship, and not least the manner in which the main orientation of the one may be historically integrated into the other. The possible—and, in the course of history, sometimes real—abuses of each of the two doctrines are approximately the same as those listed in the 1967 LWF working paper.

The second of the two Leuenberg groups starts by clarifying the role of reason in Christian ethical discourse and arrives at a balanced statement, although with no reference to possible ecumenical implications. This is followed by ''Gemeinsamkeiten und Unterschiede zwischen der Zwei-Reiche-Lehre und der Lehre von der Königsherrschaft Jesu Christi,'' which includes at least one explicit ecumenical statement:

> Beide Lehrkonzeptionen enthalten in sich keinen Grund zur Kirchentrennung. Sie haben im Laufe der Überlieferung konfessionelle Akzente erhalten, sind aber von ihrem Ursprung und ihrem Inhalt her nicht konfessionsspezifisch. . . . Die Konsultationen haben die Erfahrung gebracht, dass das Gespräch zwischen den Vertretern dieser beiden Konzeptionen wesentlich ist, um den Weg des Gehorsams für Christen und Kirchen heute klarer zu erkennen.[93]

Without in any way challenging the conclusion of these two reports, it may be appropriate to note a certain limitation in their theological horizon: that the ethical (and ethicoepistemological) aspects of the dialectic dominate the field of orientation, and there is no reference to creation theology or to the bearing of recent exchange on the notorious eclipse of creation in ecumenical theology. Is it possible to arrive at an integral reconciliation of the two doctrines without deciding where theological reflection has its basis, that is, with the First or the Second Article of the Creed? And can the dialectic of law and gospel—so constitutive of the Lutheran doctrine of justification—be upheld without a solid ontological foundation in creation faith? Even if a polarization of the two doctrines should by no means be advocated—and especially not in order to characterize the Lutheran/Re-

---

[93]Ibid., 49.

formed encounter in general—it is hard to see how a Lutheranism conscious of its Reformation legacy could adapt to the modern trend of reducing creation to some subtheme of redemption. How this trend may relate to the Reformed tradition will be examined in the following section.

During the 1983 Strasbourg consultation, the exchange on the possibility of a Lutheran/Reformed polarization attracted a good deal more attention than another (originally much more passionate) confrontation between Roman Catholic "optimism" and Lutheran "pessimism" in evaluating human nature. The latter was mainly referred to in, and in connection with, the introductory challenge to the main Lutheran presentation, a task assigned to the Roman Catholic Professor Raymond Mengus of Strasbourg. Mengus noted a certain paradoxality in the fact that contemporary ecological involvement of theology was particularly strong in German Lutheranism.[94] This stands in overt opposition to what people might have expected from a traditional Lutheran concentration on the question of salvation. In the following discussion, Mengus' question was elaborated on in an anthropological direction: To what extent is creation damaged by the Fall? And to what extent is "new creation" a confirmation, restoration, and/or replacement of original creation? Whereas the Thomist tradition sees "nature" as the very expression of the Creator's design, as something to be perfected but by no means corrected by "grace," Lutheranism has preferred to speak of "law" as the Creator's initiative to discipline sinful humankind and to keep evil within limits.

In what sense and to what extent has fallen humankind deviated from the Creator's design? As one immediately discovers, this basic ecumenical issue is indissolubly linked with the theology of creation. How does the created world as we know it in its empirical, "fallen" state (the only "creation" accessible to human observation)—relate to the world as intended by its Maker? The discrepancy between the two traditions' reply to this question is, at least, a significant difference

---

[94]As a matter of fact, Alfons Auer, who might be seen as being rather representative of contemporary Roman Catholic creation theology, criticizes an almost equally representative German Lutheran, Jürgen Hübner, for understanding "theology of nature" as a "genitivus subiectivus" and thus of "venturing to proceed on the road of analogy with a determination that would have been astonishing even to Catholics." (Alfons Auer, *Umweltethik* [see n. 31] 193-94)

It could also be added that one of the most remarkable official church initiatives in the area of creation defense was the consultation arranged in the early 1970s by the Board of Social Ministry of the Lutheran Church in America. *The Human Crisis in Ecology,* ed. Franklin L. Jensen and Cedric W. Tilberg (1972) represents a strong invitation to ecclesial self-criticism and to a new type of active involvement with ecology.

in emphasis. But can it be said to signalize irreconcilable contradiction? Although paying broad attention to "justification" where a "far-reaching consensus" is seen to be developing,[95] it is remarkable that the international Roman Catholic/Lutheran bilateral dialogue did not pay particular attention to the question: justification from what; what precisely is the damage from which redemption is meant to redeem?

To be sure, there is concord between the Tridentine formula "aversio a Deo" and the lack of fear and confidence in God described by the Confessio Augustana,[96] but the 16th century also demonstrated disagreement concerning the loss of human integrity affected by the Fall and the compelling power of sin over the will of fallen man. In other words: The two churches disagree about how and how far the Creator's will is reflected in the actual thoughts and deeds of human beings. The observable world is a less ambiguous reflection of the Creator's work in the Roman Catholic vision than it is in the Lutheran understanding, a controversy that was most spectacularly reflected in the discussion between Erasmus and Luther on the freedom of the will. This issue became the focus of a deep-rooted anthropological confrontation.[97] In its consequences, this conflict concerns also our faculty to discern the Creator's design and draw valid ethical criteria from "nature."

The main clash—the formulations concerning original sin in Article II of the Augsburg Confession, the ensuing criticism in the Refutations, and the riposte in the Apology—leads to a more or less officially agreed disagreement, which, in practice, has remained unchallenged over the centuries and has been left aside in recent dialogues. The Roman Catholic position is most concisely formulated by the Council of Trent in Canon 5 on justification:

> Si quis liberum hominis arbitrium post Adae peccatum amissum et extinctum esse dixerit, aut rem esse de solo titulo, immo titulum sine re, figmentum denique a satana invectum in Ecclesiam: anathema sit.[98]

---

[95]"Malta Report," 1972, §26. In *Growth in Agreement: Reports and Agreed Statements of Ecumenical Conversations on a World Level,* ed. Lukas Vischer and Harding Meyer (Ramsey NY: Paulist Press; Geneva: World Council of Churches, 1984) 174.

[96]Council of Trent, Decr. de justificatione, Canon 5, *Enchiridon symbolorum,* ed. H. Denzinger and A. Schönmetzer (Freiburg: 1963), 1525. Cf. Article II of the Augsburg Confession.

[97]Denzinger and Schönmetzer, 1521, 1555.

[98]Ibid., 1555.

On the Lutheran side, the challenging position is finally worked out in the Formula of Concord:

> Scriptura igitur hominis naturalis intellectui, cordi et voluntati omnem aptitudinem, capacitatem et facultatem in rebus spiritualibus aliquid boni et recti (ex semetipso) cogitandi, intelligendi, inchoandi, volendi, proponendi, agendi, operandi adimit.[99]

At the same time, the following "Manichean error" is also rejected:

> Peccatum originale per Satanam in naturam infusum et cum ea permixtum sit, quemadmodum venenum vino admiscitur.[100]

The main question is whether this apparently rather far-reaching contradiction between the two churches may implicitly be overcome through the recent common formulations on justification. Logically, reconciliation would be possible if one or both of the discussion partners retracted their former position; but it would also be possible if the questions at stake could be reformulated in a way that bypasses the old stalemate without abandoning the real concerns "behind." In the latter case, there would be no need for a formal proclamation of reconciliation; in itself, the new concord would be sufficiently convincing to make old controversies irrelevant. It would, however, be doubtful if such a concord would survive if its premises were not explicitly spelled out—not only in order to comply with the demands of conservative believers who were particularly concerned about historical authenticity, but also in order to reassure and confirm that a legitimate demand for clarification had been met. In order to overcome historical contradiction, either some old answer has to be retracted or some old question has to be seen to be no longer adequate.

As things stand, neither the ecumenical exchange process at large nor the Strasbourg creation project in particular allow us to go much further in commenting on this issue. We must limit ourselves to noting an ecumenical issue that is of importance for soteriology as much as for the doctrine of creation. In a creation perspective, the questions would be: How and to what extent does humankind as we may observe it today (society as well as individuals) deviate from the role ascribed to it by the Creator? To what extent may the old polarization between

---

[99]Formula of Concord, Solid Declaration II,12, *Die Bekenntnisschriften der evangelisch-lutherischen Kirche* (Göttingen: Vandenhoeck & Ruprecht, 1959) 876. Cf. *The Book of Concord,* trans. and ed. Theodore G. Tappert (Philadelphia: Muhlenberg Press, 1959).

[100]Formula of Concord, Solid Declaration, I,26, *Bekenntnisschriften,* 852.

Rome and Wittenberg concerning this question be a hindrance to further ecumenical rapprochement? The progress of the dialogue between the two churches may provide some rather promising suggestions of a growing mutual understanding. But this understanding will certainly presuppose a more explicit dealing with the old polarization on the original state of humanity (*Urstand*) and with the possibilities for overcoming or dealing with that polarization in light of the common insights that have been established in the meantime.

Common to the Roman Catholic and the Lutheran tradition is a particularly emphatic rejection of any Gnostic tendency to identify evil with created matter, a rejection that is linked not only to a common emphasis on the "real presence" in the sacraments but also with an understanding of the dignity of creation as given prior to any restorative act of redemption (or any revolutionary event of liberation). A certain Roman Catholic "surprise" about the recent Lutheran involvement in ecological theology *may* thus be due to a historically simplified idea of Lutheranism as a rather unambiguous construction of existentialist anthropology—an image that can be explained from certain modern positions as much as from a possible evaluation of highly contextual 16th-century slogans as though they were intended as formulations of timeless principles. Likewise, a certain self-portrayal of Lutheranism as the tradition of theological preoccupation and reflection sometimes tends to distract awareness from the historical complexity of Lutheran spirituality—among Lutherans themselves as well as among their conversation partners.

A 1979 collection of essays, *Frieden mit der Natur* pays particular interest to historical trends and currents influencing the contemporary vision—and lack of vision—of nature in Christendom. In an introductory survey, Klaus M. Meyer-Abich observes:

> Die Naturfrömmigkeit, die zu finden es hier gilt, hat u.a. im frühen Luthertum schon einmal bestanden. Auch ohne den Rückgang in die damalige Zeit zu suchen, liegt es doch nahe, uns das sogar in die Neuzeit immerhin schon einmal Erreichte daraufhin zu vergegenwärtigen, wie weit es Vorbild für unsere eigene Bemühungen sein kann.[101]

This remark relates in particular to Jürgen Hübner's contribution in this collection.[102] Hübner begins with a selection of quotations from Luther's own writ-

---

[101]*Frieden mit der Natur: Ansätze einer "grünen" Wertordnung*, ed. Klaus M. Meyer-Abich (Freiburg, 1979) 36.

[102]Jürgen Hübner, "Die Sprache evangelischer Naturfrömmigkeit als praktische Theologie der Natur," ibid., 75-90. Cf. also Hübner, *Die Welt als Gottes Schöpfung ehren* (1982).

ings in which he praises the Creator for his faithfulness as reflected in the world of his making. Although this joyful veneration of the Creator is to a large extent compromised by the Aristotelization in subsequent Lutheran orthodoxy, it nevertheless remains alive in the devotional literature of the age,[103] and still more so in the hymnody of Paul Gerhardt.[104]

One chapter of history that deserves particular attention, because of its greatness as well as its deficiencies, is the "physicotheology" of the 18th century. This phenomenon is fairly characteristic of that age in general, but in those days it flowered within Continental Protestantism (Lutheran and Reformed) as much as in British apologetics. The Luther/Gerhardt devotional emphasis on the actuality of creation (in dialectical symbiosis with an emphatic *theologia crucis*) and the Wolff/Klopstock meditative emphasis on the practicality of nature (within the framework of an optimistic theological vision of the world[105]) are both elements in the history of one and the same denominational tradition—elements that strongly protest an image of Lutheranism that is confined to a unilaterally anthropocentric-existential approach or to a simplistic lamentation of creatureliness as ethical deficiency and corruption.

Even if some normative identity of Lutheranism can hardly be meaningfully defined by the historical complexity of theological manifestations within churches calling themselves "Lutheran," it is obvious that the ecumenical contribution of a denomination is not limited by the way in which it defines its own particularity—whether that be by reference to historical origin, to some founding father, to some particular synod, or to a certain written confession. Its ecumenical endowment is the complexity of its history and its past and present contributions to inter- and cross-denominational discussion, to ecumenical contacts, to devotional literature, to worship practices, to hymnody, to styles of piety, and to artistic expression. The inner tensions of intended dialectical balance and unintended undialectical imbalances and contradictions—both types of tension possibly more conspicuous within the history of Lutheranism than within the history of any other confessional family—may make of Lutheranism a particularly eloquent paradigm to answer such questions as: What in effect is confessional identity (if it is anything at all)? What do we mean when we talk of confessional contributions serving

---

[103]*Instar omnium*: the fourth of Johann Arndt's books on *True Christianity*, trans. and introduced Peter Erb (London: SPCK, 1979).

[104]Jürgen Hübner, "Die Sprache evangelischer Naturfrömmigkeit als praktische Theologie der Natur" (see n. 102) 81ff., 86ff.

[105]See Wolfgang Philipp, *Das Werden der Auferklärung in theologie-geschichtlicher Sicht* (Göttingen, 1957).

a universal ecumenical fellowship? Such principle implications may come to the fore in, not least, an ecumenical creation theology.

5.4 The Reformed contribution

The presentation on "Creation in Light of Covenant" by Alasdair Heron, professor of Reformed Theology at Erlangen, the traditional Lutheran stronghold, aroused particular interest at the 1983 Strasbourg consultation, because it very much challenged the widespread image that the Reformed tradition unilaterally favored a Barthian salvation history approach and derived creation theology from Christology. According to Heron, the history of Reformed theology has more or less been shaped by a centuries-old tension between a predestinarian tradition (focusing on the sovereignty of God the Creator and placing the main accent on the First Article of the Creed, as with John Calvin, Theodore Beza, Gisbert Voetius, and Abraham Kuyper) and a federal *Heilsgeschichte* approach (favoring biblical history as Christological fulfillment and, thus, the Second Article as the clue to theology, as Heinrich Bullinger, Johannes Cocceius, and Karl Barth). The fact that our century has seen a most spectacular triumph of the federal tradition over the predestinarian should not turn our attention away from the fact that the Calvinistic "line" is also there and may contribute to balancing what many have feared as an undue devaluation of creation in the Barthian school. Although speaking in preference of the federal tradition, Heron himself was not unwilling to go further than the proclaimed Barthians in accepting correctives from a creation-centered orientation.[106]

Heron's distinction may no doubt be helpful, not only as an introduction to history but also as a key to the present ecumenical stalemate. The Barthian impulse seems to be prevalent in a good deal of contemporary (particularly Continental) Reformed theology. A lucid example is the dogmatic of Hans-Joachim

---

[106]It is, however, clear that the later Reformed and Barthian concept of the "kingdom of Christ," with its implicit demarcation against Lutheranism, was already prefigured in Calvin: "Der Unterschied gegenüber Luther kann an vielen Punkten festgestellt werden, aber an keinem so grundsätzlich wie in Calvins Verständnis Gottes als 'legislateur et roy.' Demgegenüber hat einer der tiefblickendsten Gegenreformatoren, Ambrosius Catharinus Politus OP, es als den Kern des 'lutherischen Irrtums' bezeichnet zu leugnen, dass Christus zugleich redemptor *et* legislator sei. Calvins durchgängiges Thema ist die Weltregierung Gottes, der Christus zum König, zu seinem vice-roy eingesetzt hat." (Heiko A. Oberman, *Die Reformation: Von Wittenberg nach Genf* [Tübingen: J. C. B. Mohr (Paul Siebeck), 1986] 256-66)

Kraus, professor of Reformed theology in Göttingen and for several years moderator of the Reformed Alliance (Reformierter Bund) and thus, presumably, one of the most representative spokespersons of Reformed Germany. By and large, Kraus does not only continue but considerably sharpens the Barthian emphasis. Programmatically, he advocates "die im dogmatischen Christozentrismus sich isolierende Theologie und Kirche,"[107] and the whole complex "God the Creator"[108] is incorporated into "The God of Israel in the Testimony of his Coming."[109] According to Kraus, speech on God must "refer exclusively to the God witnessed in the Old Testament,"[110] and "faith in God the Creator is finally and confidently founded in the knowledge of Jesus the Christ."[111] It is probably legitimate to see the work of Kraus as a testimony of how strong the "federal" approach is in Continental Reformed theology of today, not only toward creation but also toward the doctrine of God.[112]

Another testimony in the same direction may be Jürgen Moltmann's theology of creation, which is simultaneously "ecological" and "Messianic." We had ample opportunity to explore Moltmann's remarkable book, *God in Creation*, in

---

[107]Hans-Joachim Kraus, *Systematische Theologie im Kontext biblischer Geschichte und Eschatologie* (Neukirchen-Vluyn: Neukirchener Verlag, 1983) 103.

[108]"Gott der Schöpfer," ibid., §§80-88.

[109]"Der Gott Israels in der Bezeugung seines Kommens," ibid., §§52-137.

[110]Ibid., 133.

[111]Ibid., 212.

[112]An impressive collection of sermons by Kurt Marti, *Schöpfungsglaube: Die Ökologie Gottes* (Stuttgart: Radius Verlag, 1983), may however give the opposite impression. He represents an integrative Reformed approach to creation/redemption that emphatically puts creation in the first place, and whereby Christology appears on the stage only in the premise of an already established ecological vision: "Allein, das Geheimnis der Schöpfung besteht darin, dass hier alles mit allem zusammenhängt. . . . So hat es der Schöpfer gewollt. Und darum bleibt das Schicksal der irdischen Schöpfung mit dem Verhalten des Menschen verknüpft und Gott selber bildet durch Christus und durch seinen Heiligen Geist mit uns Menschen und mit der Schöpfung so etwas wie ein Biotop höherer Ordnung." (97) This seemingly complete reversal of the Barthian perspective is, however, no surprise if one bears in mind how easily a dialectically unrestricted integration of two concepts is turned from a definition of A in terms of B to a definition of B in terms of A. Since creation is first understood as salvation, there is nothing, at the next stage, to protect salvation from being logically derived from creation, thus making out of the Creator a Savior *per definitionem*. "Esse est salvari"—see our review of George S. Hendry's criticism of Barth, here pp. 218-19.

the more general setting of contemporary creation theology[113] and therefore shall not deal too comprehensively with its confessional orientation here. But even if Moltmann openly identifies himself as Reformed, he is not an official Reformed spokesperson in the same way as Kraus. His creation theology is programmatically "ecumenical" and not intentionally oriented by particular confessional trends—apart from his rather spectacular renewal of the old Lutheran/Reformed controversy over the ontological status of heaven.[114] In that context, he sees a major point in keeping up the old Reformed emphasis on the "duality of creation" over against the old Lutheran explanation model of "heaven" as a spatially unidentifiable divine presence. Whether a return to that issue may be fruitful for contemporary ecumenical progress, it is not immediately easy to assess. As remote as the issue may seem to the modern mind, Moltmann may after all be right when he warns us against minimizing its consequences. But can the dualistic cosmological aspect be championed as per Moltmann without again provoking the Lutheran accusation against Reformed theology (so often turned down with contempt by the Reformed themselves) concerning some abstract *finitum non capax infiniti*?[115]

However, we have a different reason for returning to Moltmann in this connection, namely his "Messianic" approach as such. His ecological doctrine of creation is by no means "ecological" in the sense of, say, process theology, in which ecological dynamics as such become a major source of theological insight.[116] Moltmann's doctrine of creation is "Messianic" in the sense that it takes a global vision of salvation economy as a frame of reference. In the historical appearance of Jesus Christ, we are faced with an ecological model of universal interaction, as prefigured by the Triune God in his historical self-manifestation. Irrespective of considerable observations from natural and social sciences, this

---

[113]See here, pp. 92-99, 103-107.

[114]Jürgen Moltmann, *God in Creation* (see n. 28) 158-84 (German: 167-92), particularly 173-75 (181-83). Cf. Per Lønning, "Himmel—Schöpfung—Umwelt: Aspekte der Schöpfungslehre Jürgen Moltmanns," *Lutherische Monatshefte* (March 1986): 126-28.

[115]For the nonidentifiable background of this sentence, see J. Weerda, "Reformierte Kirche I," in *Die Religion in Geschichte und Gegenwart*[3], col. 887. According to Heiko A. Oberman—*Die Reformation* (see n. 106) 276ff.—it is by no means characteristic of the Swiss Reformers, but it certainly is characteristic of many Reformed writers throughout the centuries.

[116]Cf. Charles Birch and John B. Cobb, Jr., *The Liberation of Life: From the Cell to the Community* (Cambridge: Cambridge University Press, 1981).

makes Moltmann a typical exponent of the covenantal-historical tradition. The "Messianic" orientation definitely determines the "ecological." This is perhaps a more powerful confirmation of particular Reformed trends in contemporary theology than Moltmann's more spectacular but certainly less typical observations on the nature of "heaven."

For the sake of balance, however, let us also take a look at some not uninfluential Reformed theologians of this century who speak a completely different language. This will be done not only to exemplify the historical duplicity claimed in Heron's paper but also in order to complete the picture of the possible confession-relatedness of distinctive creation trends today.

It may be meaningful to start with a look at Karl Barth's contemporary, his comrade-in-arms and later favorite antagonist, Emil Brunner. Over the years Brunner developed a comprehensive and challenging table of creation concerns. His critics have pointed out how characteristic the and (*und*) is in the titles of his books (Die Mystik *und* das Wort, Gott *und* Mensch, Das Gebot *und* die Ordnungen, Natur *und* Gnade, Offenbarung *und* Vernunft, etc.) and that this indicates a general trend toward a synthesis between creation and salvation. The historical importance of Brunner's creation theology has been assessed by Ivar H. Pöhl:

> Es war ohne Zweifel eine grosse Tat Brunners, trotz des grossen Sogs der Barthschen Theologie die Frage der Schöpfung und der Anthropologie . . . in die Diskussion miteinzubeziehen. Hier nahm Brunner biblische und lutherische Gedanken auf. Kritisch ist aber zu bemerken, dass er trotz klarer Ansätze im biblisch-geschichtlichen Denken oft zu sehr im Einflussbereich idealistischer und aristotelisch-scholastischer Fragestellungen befangen blieb.[117]

Even if, more than anything else, this judgment puts the observer somewhere halfway between Barth and Brunner, it does certainly show that in this regard Brunner is closer to a Lutheran than a Barthian position. But, recalling the classification of Alasdair Heron, this does not mean that Brunner advocates a predestinarian way of thinking. In his relatively late dogmatic, Brunner is somewhat reticent in his criticism of Barth's creation theology:

> Gegen die falsche Verquickung von Kosmologie und Schöpfungslehre hat die Theologie Schleiermachers und Ritschls im umgekehrten Sinne falsch reagiert, insofern als beide die Auffassung vertreten, dass der christliche Glaube an einer Lehre von der Schöpfung nicht interessiert

---

[117]Ivar H. Pöhl, *Das Problem des Naturrechtes bei Emil Brunner* (Zurich/Stuttgart: Zwingli Verlag, 1963) 195-96.

sei. . . . Karl Barths Schöpfungslehre bedeutet einen grossen Fortschritt
durch ihre konsequent christologische Orientierung, die aber infolge der
Rückkehr zur Auslegung des Sechstagewerks und der dadurch bedingten
allegorischen Methode nicht völlig zur Auswirkung kommt.[118]

This remark is somewhat surprising because the recommended Christological
orientation has not, to any large extent, affected Brunner's own presentation, in
which the traditional disposition of a dogmatic is carefully followed.[119] As it is
placed and developed in the whole dogmatical context, Brunner's doctrine of creation acquires a different—and, ontologically, a more fundamental—importance
than Barth's. In *Das Gebot und die Ordnungen* (1932), Brunner took up—and essentially supported—the controversial neo-Lutheran concept of orders of creation. At that time, his position was not very remote from that of his Lutheran
Erlangen colleagues Paul Althaus and Werner Elert. And his fear of static cosmogonic and metaphysical concepts was no more emphatic than theirs. If a simple
two-kingdoms versus kingship-of-Christ model in social ethics should be seen as
the line of demarcation between Lutheran and Reformed, then Brunner would definitely be found on the Lutheran side. However, this affinity seems to have caused
no problem to his own Swiss Reformed identity, and in his understanding of the
church and the sacraments there is hardly anything that would indicate a Lutheran
rather than a Reformed orientation. The case of Brunner could thus be used as a
noteworthy argument against a rigid confessional understanding of the "kingdoms" controversy. Notwithstanding the dominant influence of the Barthian position in contemporary Reformed thought (and considerable influence also in
Roman Catholic and Lutheran constituencies) and also its historical connection
with impressive trends in Reformed theology of the past, it is true to say that Reformed creation theology today is a good deal more than the Barthian position. If
the Reformed tradition were to be so simplistically defined, Emil Brunner was no
Reformed theologian—but then neither were Zwingli or Calvin!

One modern Reformed position in a polemically more accentuated opposition
to Barth is that of the Scottish-born Princeton theologian George S. Hendry. In

---

[118]Emil Brunner, *Dogmatik 2: Die christliche Lehre von Schöpfung und Erlösung* (Zurich: TVZ, ³1972 [1950]) 50. English version: *The Christian Doctrine
of Creation and Redemption* (Philadelphia: Westminster Press, 1952).

[119]Volume 1: *The Christian Doctrine of God* (1950; original: *Die christliche
Lehre von Gott* [1946]); volume 2: *The Christian Doctrine of Creation and Redemption* (1952; *Die christliche Lehre von Schöpfung und Erlösung* [1950]); volume 3: *The Christian Doctrine of the Church, Faith, and the Consummation* (1962;
Die christliche Lehre von der Kirche, vom Glauben und von der Vollendung
[1960]).

his *Theology of Nature* (1978 Warfield Lectures), Hendry launches a massive attack on dominant tendencies in post-Reformation, and especially 20th-century, creation theology. His target is an alleged anthropocentric contraction of the entire vision of reality, which was already prepared by the energetic "pro me" in Luther's explanation of the Creed[120] and—for the sake of confessional fairness—also in the Heidelberg Catechism (1562).[121] However, he finds that the climax is reached with Kant and Schleiermacher as well as in ensuing developments. What finally happens with Barth is merely a transfer of accent *within* the anthropocentric framework:

> The theological revolution that was led by Karl Barth may be simply described as a shift of focus from the psychological to the political parameter of theology, or from the third to the second article of the Creed. . . . It is a similar position, in a more extreme form, which we have in Bonhoeffer. When Bonhoeffer asked what Christ can mean in a religion-less world, he was, in effect, asking for a unitarianism of the second article.[122]

> It is interesting—and ironical—to observe that Barth, despite his difference from Schleiermacher, gave the doctrine of creation a similar place in his theology. . . . The heart of faith is Jesus Christ, and faith in God as creator is more precisely an "insight" which is derived from faith in Christ (*KD* III/I, §40).[123]

During the 1983 Strasbourg consultation, one of Hendry's earlier books was quoted by Alasdair Heron as having criticized Barth of having a sort of neo-Gnosticism—*esse est salvari,* a more emphatic version of the criticism we have already observed.[124] Hendry himself advocates a comprehensive vision of nature as a whole to be embraced as the Creator's work, an advocacy by no means without parallels in recent theology, albeit usually not, as in this case, linked with a rather profiled

---

[120]See my discussion of this statement in "Schöpfung—Mensch—Umwelt: Ist Luther für die Umweltkrise mitverantwortlich?," *Lutherische Monatshefte* (1983): 208-10.

[121]George S. Hendry, *Theology of Nature* (Philadelphia: Westminster Press; Edinburgh: T. & T. Clark, 1980) 17, 20-21.

[122]Ibid., 25-26.

[123]Ibid., 180.

[124]George S. Hendry, *The Holy Spirit in Christian Theology* (London/Philadelphia, 1965) 109.

Presbyterian approach to theology. This is how Hendry interprets creation, seeing nature as reflecting the universality of the Creator:

> When the creed asserts that all created being, in its duality and diversity, is to be referred to the unity of God as creator, it makes the unity of God equivalent to his universality . . . a faithful transcript of the biblical understanding of God. . . . The Old Testament clearly reflects this advance; the faith of the people of God is construed first in particular . . . terms, and only slowly did it grow universal. The universality of God becomes articulate in the prophetic literature, and it received monumental documentation when the final collection of the literature . . . was prefaced with an account of God as universal creator and ruler over all.[125]

It is interesting to see here how Hendry uses the stages of biblical formation not to degrade creation by virtue of its relatively late emergence (as is common in modern theology) but rather to see creation as the crowning, all-embracing vision.

A particularly interesting contemporary Reformed contribution to creation theology is that of the prominent professor and church leader Thomas F. Torrance, who—according to Heron at the Strasbourg symposium—together with Moltmann may have made the most visible contributions in this generation toward a fruitful synthesis of the creation-centered and covenant-oriented approaches. Torrance's most interesting contribution in this regard is probably *The Ground and Grammar of Theology* (1980),[126] the title of which, according to the preface, should really read: "The Ground and Grammar of a Realist Theology in the Perspective of a Unitary Understanding of the Creation." It is particularly interesting to compare the positions of Torrance and Hendry, especially as they both come from the same branch of the Reformed tradition. They share very much the same view in their vision of nature and their readiness to accept creation in its fullness in an open exchange with natural science, but the polemical lines of demarcation run rather differently. Whereas Hendry sees the threat to creation in a century-old anthropological contraction, which contemporary Barthianism has transformed and cosmeticized but by no means overcome, Torrance sees the enemy in an abstract and outdated "Scholastic" approach to reality, in theology as well as science, and in the clash between the two different—and equally abstract—cosmologies that resulted from it. The contemporary revolution in the style of scientific thinking, introduced above all by modern physics, should really challenge theology to develop

---

[125]George S. Hendry, *Theology of Nature* (see n. 121) 117-18.

[126]Cf. also Thomas F. Torrance, *Reality and Scientific Theology* (Edinburgh: Scottish Academic Press, 1985).

a new style of reflection, a style that would not only do better justice to its own concerns but also throw the doors open to a new and promising dialogue with science. In this context, Torrance sees as the great renewer none other than Karl Barth, who, more than anyone else, contributes to preparing the coming exchange.

The differences between Torrance and Hendry concern not only strikingly different Barth interpretations, with Torrance very much opposing the conventional image of Barth (an image that no doubt at least hits an undeniable trend of decade-long "Barthian" influence), whereas Hendry may be said to embrace and squeeze this image to the utmost. The difference is already there in the choice of enemy: which is worse, traditional anthropocentricity or old-fashioned "natural theology"? A few texts from Torrance:

> It is more and more clear to me that, under the providence of God . . . the damaging cultural splits between the sciences and the humanities, and between both of these and theology, are in process of being overcome . . . and that a massive new synthesis will emerge in which man, humbled and awed by the mysterious intelligibility of the universe . . . will learn to fulfill his destined role as the servant of divine love and the priest of creation.[127]

> Our modern world is one in which dualist modes of thought have already been destroyed in the advance of scientific knowledge. . . . The old epistemological, cosmological, and religious dualisms . . . are shown to be without any force. The same applies to the epistemological, phenomenological, and deistic dualisms that evidently underpin the revival of nineteenth-century theologies, notably those of Schleiermacher and Ritschl.[128]

> Today we live in a world being changed by science, which is far more congenial to Christian theology than any period in the history of Western civilization. Here the task of Christian theology must be the recovery of the doctrines of creation and incarnation in such a way that we think through their interrelations more rigorously than ever before, and on that ground engage in constant dialogue with the new science, which can only be to the benefit of both.[129]

> Karl Barth's objections to natural theology . . . certainly have nothing at all to do with some kind of deistic dualism between God and the world

---

[127]Thomas F. Torrance, *The Ground and Grammar of Theology* (Belfast: Christian Journals, 1980) 14.

[128]Ibid., 42.

[129]Ibid., 73-74.

. . . or with some form of Marcionite dualism between redemption and creation implying a depreciation of the creature, as so many of Barth's critics have averred. . . . On the contrary, Barth's position rests upon an immense stress on the concrete activity of God in space and time. . . . The failure to understand Barth at this point is highly revealing, for it indicates that his critics themselves still think within the dualist modes of thought that Barth had himself long left behind.[130]

Barth's opposition to the traditional type of natural theology . . . rests upon a radical rejection of its dualist basis and constitutes a return to the kind of unitary thinking we find in classical Christian thinking . . . in which . . . we are unable to make any separation between a natural and a supernatural knowledge of God. . . . But if Barth's position is to be accepted, as I believe it is, then I also believe that there must be a deeper connection between the basic concepts of theological science and natural science than he seemed to allow. . . . If that is the case, then a proper natural theology should be *natural* both to theological science and to natural science.[131]

It may be important to look at these reflections from Torrance's book at some length. They are clear, unconventional, and (if generally accepted) rather rich in consequences. Advocating increased and deepened dialogue between theology and the natural sciences, they may be fairly typical of recent theology in general, a fact demonstrated not least at the First European Consultation on Science and Religion in Loccum, Federal Republic of Germany, in March 1986.[132] However, they are also unconventional in the way in which they relate the main force in ecumenical theology in the last generation—Karl Barth—to this recent orientation.

Interpretation of Barth per se is not the task of ecumenical theology. But in the present case certain ecumenical implications are palpable, and some questions should be noted even though we cannot pursue them here. If this is an authentic representation of Barth, why has it taken such a long time to discover the adequate perspective? So far, why has the outcome of the Barthian "No" been just about the exact opposite in the history of theology? How does the unrestricted epistemological openness in Torrance's book fit in with Barth's emphasis on the exclusiveness of biblical revelation? Does the Barthian *Heilsgeschichte* approach really open the way to a multilateral exchange on creation as suggested by Torrance?

---

[130]Ibid., 87.

[131]Ibid., 93-94.

[132]The papers of this conferences have been published in *Creation and Evolution,* ed. Svend Andersen and A. Peacocke (Aarhus: Aarhus University Press, 1988).

Can one simply overlook the accusations so frequently voiced against modern philosophy and theology—and often Barth—regarding their unecological anthropocentricity? Do they not require at least some attention?

In addition to these questions about Barth interpretation, one could of course add others with regard to the position of Torrance himself. Is his image of modern science unconditionally converging with biblical creation and incarnation faith not too indiscriminate? Is his opposition to abstract dualism not so abstract that any clarifying distinction between faith and common observation seems to fade? When other neo-Barthians (Jüngel, Link) are advocating a new "natural theology" as a biblical theology of nature, it may well be asked whether the terminology as such is helpful—but at least they are advocating a distinct theological alternative. However, in recommending his version of trans-Barthian "natural theology," Torrance is obviously envisaging something more comprehensive, and—fascinating as it may sound—it would probably be necessary to see his suggestion developed in a much more concrete way before one could decide on its worth.

In the present context the salient point is the possible ecumenical importance of Torrance's position. He himself does not immediately reflect on confessional implications, nor does he express indebtedness to Henry Drummond or other predecessors within the Scottish Presbyterian tradition who championed a "natural law in the spiritual world."[133] But Torrance's renown within the contemporary Reformed world, his radical reinterpretation of the Barthian creation controversy, and his profiled position in relation to the other Reformed theologians we have quoted do make his contribution a fascinating a propos to the very plurality of the Reformed tradition that was suggested in Heron's paper and is so frequently overlooked, not least by Lutherans. Even if Torrance does bypass the basic tension between predestinarian creation theology and *Heilsgeschichte* covenant theology (the frame of reference of Heron's paper) he does add new—though not specifically defined—aspects to the general image of diversity without himself losing contact with the Reformed tradition in a more comprehensive sense.

After these fascinating glimpses at the spectrum of Reformed creation theology, there may be reason to ask if there is not a common denominator that gives some really distinctive profile to this theology. Even if the Barthian *Heilsgeschichte*/kingdom of Christ approach is the most impressive influence ever exercised by a Reformed theologian on ecumenical creation theology, and even if this impulse is often regarded as *the* Reformed contribution, our observations warn against such an oversimplification. There may be some solid truth in the above-mentioned post-Leuenberg study's reference to doctrines which "in the course of

---

[133]Cf. Henry Drummond, *Natural Law in the Spiritual World* (1883).

tradition have acquired confessional accents'' without in themselves being church divisive, and also in its description of the two kingdoms and kingdom of Christ approaches as, respectively, expressing "the basic understanding of the Lutheran Reformation" and being "developed from the Reformed side." [134] But what, then, can be said to be common between the creation theology of Barth and Brunner, Kraus and Moltmann, Hendry and Torrance? Even if it is true that not all theologians belonging to a specific church (usually for reasons beyond their control) can be said to speak for that church, we are talking about theologians who, programmatically speaking, identify with the church to which they belong and enjoy a representative position within their respective constituencies.

In spite of the historically proven danger of ending up with somewhat artificial polarizations, the search for a common Reformed profile in creation theology could probably be most meaningfully carried out by observing the similarities they share with and the distinctions that separate them from their closest neighbors— the Lutherans. But this should be done with the utmost care, always bearing in mind that we are comparing not two distinctive camps but two complex streams of tradition with slightly differing gravitational pulls, and also remembering that the present conflict was not so much informed by different doctrines of creation as by different understandings of the created world as the vehicle of divine presence. What can be meaningfully compared are, first, officially proclaimed confessional bases and, second, the past and present complexities in the theologies which lead to the distinct gravitational pull in each of the two churches. The conclusion would then be not that Lutheran theologians say one thing and Reformed another; rather that among Lutherans there is a tendency to move in one direction and maintain this, among Reformed there is a tendency to move in another direction and maintain that. It may well be impossible to observe a distinction in confessional formulations that speak immediately to creation. Differences may have to be sought in the broader context of theological approach.

Certain 16th-century Reformed statements do not underline creation, simply because they are condensed presentations of issues in the ongoing confrontation with Rome, and creation was not seen to be one of these issues. [135] However, the confessions that do give a full survey of the faith generally proclaim creation as it is located within the framework of the Creed, the sole exception being the Heidelberg Catechism (1562), which, for pedagogical reasons, adopts an analytical

---

[134]Here, pp. 207-209.

[135]Zwingli's Sixty-Seven Theses of 1523; The Ten Theses of Berne, 1528; The Lausanne Articles, 1536. Cf., on the Lutheran side, The Smalkald Articles, 1537.

method, stating what it means to belong to Christ the Savior and the three things it is necessary to know in order to communicate with him—sin, liberation, and gratitude. In all other main Reformed confessions we find the conventional synthetical scheme: an exposition of the three articles. Typical deviations from the corresponding Lutheran statements are: 1. the tendency to elaborate on the canonical authority of the Scriptures; and 2. the emphasis on divine glory as a defiance to the idolatrous veneration of creature(s), in some cases combined with the idea of predestination. The approach to Scripture may be of ecumenical significance, mainly due to its critical attitude toward tradition in worship and church order. But in the context of creation the second feature is more important. A few characteristic formulations follow:

> Following, then, the lines laid down in the Holy Scriptures, we acknowledge that there is one only God. . . . And since he is spirit, he is to be served in spirit and in truth. Therefore we think it an abomination to put our confidence or hope in any created thing, to worship anything else than him, whether angels or any other creatures . . . and likewise to offer the service, which ought to be rendered to him, in external ceremonies or carnal observations, as if he took pleasure in such things.[136]

> We know him [God] by two means: first, by the creation, preservation and government of the universe; which is before our eyes as a most elegant book, wherein all creatures, great and small, are as so many characters leading us to contemplate *the invisible things of God,* namely, *his eternal power and Godhead,* as the Apostle Paul says (Romans 1:20). All which things are sufficient to convince men, and leave them without excuse. Secondly, he makes himself more clearly and fully known to us by his holy and divine Word.[137]

> Since God as Spirit is in essence invisible and immense, he cannot really be expressed by any art or image. . . . Therefore we reject not only the idols of the Gentiles, but also the images of Christians.[138]

> We also believe that God has created all things by His Spirit, that is, by His power; and therefore, God sustains and governs all things as He created them. Hence we confess that before He created the world God elected all those upon whom He willed to bestow inheritance of eternal salvation.[139]

---

[136]Geneva Confession, 1536, Article 2. *Reformed Confessions of the 16th Century,* ed. Arthur C. Cochrane (London: SCM Press, 1966) 120.

[137]Belgic Confession, 1561, Article 2. Ibid., 189-90.

[138]Second Helvetic Confession, 1566, Article 4. Ibid., 229.

[139]First Confession of Basel, 1534, Article 1. Ibid., 91.

A particularly interesting composition of orientative motifs is found in the Westminster Confession (1647), in which "the distance between God and the creature" serves as the point of departure for the development of "covenant" by "some voluntary condescension on God's part." As the only way to establish communion between Creator and creature, then, covenant is understood in the double terms of: a "first covenant . . . a covenant of works, wherein life was promised . . . upon condition of perfect and personal obedience" of which "man by his Fall . . . made himself incapable"; and "a second . . . covenant of grace . . . in reference to the death of Jesus Christ . . . differently administered in the time of the law and in the time of the Gospel," the Old Testament in its proleptic way having an equally authentic orientation toward the salvation in Christ as the New. The basic distinction between the two covenants—that of work and that of grace—is thus emphatically distinguished from that of the two Testaments. The Bible in its entirety is interpreted as gospel and grace; creation is understood, on the one hand, in terms of disproportion and lack of personal relatedness between creature and Creator, and, on the other, as a universal "Adamite" covenant of "works," existentially relevant only in a prelapsaristic age (that is, before the Fall). The distinction between law and gospel seems to be as sharp as in the Lutheran tradition, but it is accommodated entirely *outside* the biblical history of revelation.[140]

It should also be noted that already in his *Commentarius de vera et falsa religione* (1525), Zwingli followed the traditional order of the Creeds. In a comparatively extensive presentation of God as "the object of religious veneration," he distinguishes neatly between a universal knowledge of the existence of God (which he strongly confirms) and a knowledge of the nature of God (only to be attained through revelation).

> Was Gott ist, geht vielleicht über Menschenverstand hinaus, aber dass er ist, übersteigt den Verstand des Menschen nicht. . . . Was aber Gott sei, das wissen wir aus uns ebensowenig, wie ein Käfer weiss, was der Mensch ist. . . . Es steht fest, dass man von Gott selber lernen muss, was Gott sei . . . so weiss auch niemand um das Wesen Gottes, denn allein der Geist Gottes.[141]

A general concept of religion and the understanding of the quest for God— the object of ultimate veneration—as a universal given is, obviously, of consti-

---

[140]Westminster Confession, ch. VII, 1-6. S. W. Carruthers, *The Westminster Confession of Faith* (Manchester: R. Aikman & Son, 1937). Müller, *Die Bekenntnisschriften der reformierten Kirche* (Leipzig, 1903) 559-60.

[141]"Von Gott," *Zwingli: Hauptschriften. Der Theologe 1* (1941) 20, 23-24.

tutive importance to Zwingli's understanding of Christianity. But the concept of creation—somewhat sparsely discussed—does not serve to undergird the general theory of religion but rather to expose the heterogeneity between Creator and creature. The divine initiative to overcome human ignorance is not so much seen as being projected in a *Heilsgeschichte* succession of events; rather it is seen in the divine Word conceived as a superhistorical occurrence. Thus, in a certain way, the Third Article of the Creed overshadows the Second. Zwingli is quite far away from Karl Barth!

As has already been suggested, this last observation applies no less to Calvin. The first book in his *Institutio religionis christianæ* is wholly dedicated to the knowledge of God and the doctrine of creation. Great importance is attributed to a universal knowledge of the Creator, and several Greek and Roman philosophers are quoted to testify to this. "That there exists in the human mind, and indeed by natural instinct, some sense of Deity, we hold to be beyond dispute."[142] It is strongly underscored that the meaning of creation, which focuses in that of human self-realization,[143] is knowledge of God; creation serves to make the Creator's glory known.

> Since the perfection of blessedness consists in the knowledge of God, he has been pleased, in order that none might be excluded from the means of obtaining felicity, not only to deposit in our minds that seed of religion of which we have already spoken, but so to manifest his perfections in the whole structure of the universe, and daily place himself in our view, that we cannot open our eyes without being compelled to behold him. His essence, indeed, is incomprehensible, utterly transcending all human thought; but on each of his works his glory is engraven in characters so bright, so distinct, and so illustrious, that none, however dull and illiterate can plead ignorance as their excuse.[144]

In the first book, the whole of chapter XI is devoted to refuting the foolishness of idolatry, with many quotations from the Old Testament. It is stated as a general doctrine "that everything respecting God which is learned from images is futile and false."[145] And just because "the human mind is, so to speak, a perpetual forge

---

[142]*Institutes of the Christian Religion,* trans. Henry Beveridge (Edinburgh: T. & T. Clark, 1879). (French: *Institution de la religion chrétienne* [Geneva: Labor et Fides, ²1967]) I.III.1, 43 (French: 9).

[143]I.XIV.22, ibid., 157-58 (130-31).

[144]I.V.1, ibid., 51 (17).

[145]I.XI.5.3, ibid., 94 (65).

of idols,''[146] contemplation of creation does not help us to authentic knowledge of God; it only serves to deprive us of an excuse. People do not ''conceive of God in the character in which he is manifested, but imagine him to be whatever their own rashness has devised. . . . It is not him they worship, but, instead of him, the dream and figment of their own heart.''[147]

The dominance of the Old Testament orientation should be noted. This is, of course, to some extent due to the fact that most biblical distinctions with regard to God and creation are to be found there. But at the same time it is a characteristic trend of the Reformed tradition (not least when compared to the Lutheran) that there is little principal distinction between the Old and the New Testament. This corresponds with the fact that in traditional Reformed worship the free choice of texts has often given the Old Testament a dominant position in preaching, and singing has been limited to an adaptation of biblical texts, particularly the Psalms. All this has tended to uphold a certain Old Testament orientation, also in worship. In the Lutheran church, on the other hand, the framework of the church year has tended to emphasize the New Testament—especially the gospel pericopes, but to some extent also the Epistles—and a greater freedom in hymnody has reduced the relative importance of the Old Testament Psalms. This corresponds to an even more substantial difference in biblical orientation, which may also serve to distinguish the traditions. In a way, Reformed theology, with its strong Old Testament commitment and its lesser emphasis on distinguishing between law and gospel, may be more inclined to see creation and redemption as an organic unity (whichever of the two may be the dominant point of orientation) than, in general, is Lutheran theology. With Calvin especially, it seems obvious that ''la gloire de Dieu'' as the global structure of theological reference favors such a unified vision.

It is precisely at this point that it becomes clear how also the ''opposite'' Reformed tradition—to recall Heron's classification—with the covenant people of God as the basic unifying vision, has essential traits in common with classical Calvinism. The history of the covenant people is understood not so much as a progress from one distinctive phase of revelation to another, for the formation of a chosen people under the word of God took final shape already in the Old Testament. Rather, the covenant way is the one in which the word of God takes expression in history. This may involve a notable softening of the doctrine of predestination, for the concept of covenant is not easily reconciled with the idea of certain members of the covenanting community being for some reason secretly excluded from the promises of the covenant.

---

[146]I.XI.8, ibid., 97 (67).

[147]I.IV.1, ibid., 46 (12).

In Karl Barth's doctrine of election the Abrahamic motif is renewed and re-iterated: election to confer blessing on humankind as a whole, election for the sake of the "rejected."[148] In both cases, the Anselmian vision of salvation (atonement) as a restoration of damaged creation—which in somewhat different ways has pro-foundly influenced also the Roman Catholic and Lutheran traditions—is some-what modified, salvation being understood either as part of the creation decree (which may draw the orientation slightly in an Eastern Orthodox direction[149]) or as the concrete event that alone throws appropriate light on creation. Having stated the diversity of Reformed creation theologies in such a comprehensive manner, it might be fruitful to contemplate further on these obvious trends of commonal-ity.[150] Above all, such a consideration of more comprehensive ecumenical rela-

---

[148]Karl Barth, "The Elect and the Rejected," *Church Dogmatics,* vol. II/2 (Edinburgh: T. & T. Clark, 1957) 340-409. *Kirchliche Dogmatik* II/2, 391; cf. 1-563!

[149]On particular affinities between the Reformed tradition and Eastern Ortho-doxy, see also *The Theological Dialogue Between Orthodox and Reformed Churches,* ed. Thomas F. Torrance (see n. 2), which contains the main papers presented at three bilateral dialogue consultations (1979, 1981, and 1983). The most interesting feature here is probably Torrance's own presentation on "Ortho-dox/Reformed Relations" (3-18), which focuses on what he sees as their sharing of "a Trinitarian understanding of creation" as represented by the Alexandrian school (Athanasius, Cyril) over against the Cappadocian slant toward a submis-sive Trinitology resulting in an undue separation between the Father Creator, on the one hand, and the Son (and Spirit) Redeemer(s), on the other—and thus be-tween creation and redemption. "This line of approach opens up classical Greek theology to fresh appreciation in the context of the modern scientific world, which makes it clear that theology is the most relevant of all for our modern scientific world, as well as for the union of the whole Church in Christ today." (17) How-ever, the official Orthodox respondent, Metropolitan Emilianos Timiados, does not immediately accept this rapprochement, insisting on including all the pre-Chalcedonian Fathers in his vision of an undivided "consensus patrum" (21). He does however accept certain modifications of the impressions of a metaphysical dualism, which he admits could arise from the adaptation of Aristotelian termi-nology by some Fathers (45-48). A certain fellowship-in-arms against a static Scholastic conceptuality and in favor of a more unified personalistic concept of Creator/creation thus seems to be reciprocally admitted, even if the Orthodox re-sponse to Torrance is an unmistakable "Festina Lente!"

[150]And it goes without saying that most of what we observed earlier to be characteristic of the relation between Western and Eastern theology applies to the Reformed tradition as much as to the Roman Catholic and the Lutheran. Likewise, what has been said about the Lutheran confrontation with Rome is by and large equally valid for the Reformed.

tions might serve to liberate Reformed/Lutheran conversation from focusing too narrowly on the two kingdoms/kingship of Christ polarization, and thus maybe also from the remaining traumas of the *Kirchenkampf.*

5.5 The Anglican contribution

When one starts to coordinate impressions from Anglican theology with the observations we have made so far, one rather promising difficulty is the obvious lack of discussion between British (though a certain exception can be made for Scottish) and Continental theology over the last 400 years. (It was considerably better in the days of Anselm, William of Ockham and Henry VIII!) This means that there may be unexpected discoveries to be made in the course of a renewed encounter, even if a synchronization of concepts and idioms may demand some patience. In addition, Anglicanism can be said to have its identity in a unified theology to a far lesser extent than any of the traditions dealt with so far. And in its ecumenical relations it is inclined to focus on issues of order and worship more than on questions of doctrinal controversy. In the context of our project, therefore, there is an obvious difficulty in integrating the Anglican voice—if such there be—into the chorus we have already heard. But some impulses toward renewal may promise to emerge through the well-known affinities of Anglican theology to patristic thought, on the one hand, and to the wide world of science, on the other.

In the planning of the 1983 Strasbourg consultation, there was no doubt that the topic "Incarnation and Sacrament—A Key to Creation?" should be entrusted to the main Anglican spokesperson, commissioned by Lambeth Palace, the Rev. J. Michael Langford (Hartlepool, England). The formulation of this topic anticipated that a particularly close coordination of creation, incarnation, and sacrament would be the specific Anglican contribution to our research, and this assumption was very much confirmed. However, it was observed that the absence of an Anglican low church profile in the discussion may have excluded a slightly more complex impression, as the speaker made no secret of his high church orientation. Langford's paper did not pretend to outline average Anglican thought; rather he presented a trend that is more characteristic of Anglicanism than of any other confessional family, and more distinctive of Anglican creation thought than any other comparable trend.

As point of departure Langford took the vision of St. Athanasius—Christ, the incarnate Logos, as revelation and fulfillment of the mystery of the entire cosmos—following this through from the early Greek Fathers, to medieval Western sacramental theology (particularly St. Thomas Aquinas), and on to two distinguished British authors of the present century. In so doing, he did not intend to speak of Anglicanism as a particular branch of the Christian tradition; rather to present a common Catholic tradition as seen and sensed by a high church Anglican, in basic solidarity with the orientation of the Old Fathers as well as with the underlying vision of Latin sacramental theology—an orientation presumably more characteristic of high Anglicanism than some insistence on a particular Anglican profile would have been!

The two 20th-century Anglican authors referred to were J.N. Figgis (*Civilization at the Cross Roads,* 1912, an answer to G. Tyrrell's *Christianity at the Cross Roads* of 1909) and V.A. Demant (*Religious Prospects,* 1939). In a profound analysis of modern civilization, with its inner emptiness and stress, Figgis sees the cure to spiritual vacancy not in the Puritan vision of personal existence as a purgatory but in a sacramental view of creation as a miracle, with a past, a present, and a future. Only in the sacramental fellowship of the church, can humankind find that it is the Creator's creation. One generation later, on the threshold of another world war, Demant sees that the failure of Christianity to find a remedy to the crisis of Western civilization was caused by its own disintegration in moralism or in liberal subjectivism and an insufficient idea of dogma as comprehensive historical and social orientation. "The full-blooded doctrine of the incarnation presupposes a radical doctrine of creation, the utter dissimilarity of Creator and creation related by the icon of God in man." The "fundamental fact of life, creation, and society is revealed in the incarnation, and celebrated and affirmed in the sacraments."

Against the background of these observations, Langford went on to describe a sacramental ontology:

> The ontological abyss between the Creator and his creation is bridged through the icon, the created, mirror image and likeness of God in man . . . revealed in the incarnation of the Logos, and preserved, celebrated, and experienced in the sacraments, chiefly in the eucharist. The eucharist restores and renews the lost interior vision of the Creator and the cosmos.[151]

The most representative and influential Anglican voice that can be quoted on this topic is obviously that of the late Archbishop of Canterbury, William Temple, and especially in his Gifford Lectures (1933–1934), *Nature, Man and God.*[152] In

---

[151]J. Michael Langford, "Incarnation and Sacrament—A Key to Creation?," 1983 manuscript, 26.

[152]William Temple, *Nature, Man and God* (London: Macmillan & Co., 1964 [1934]).

this book, the chapter that has exercised the most remarkable influence, particularly in recent years, is the one on "The Sacramental Universe."[153] Even if this series of lectures represents a conscious effort to stay within the limits of "natural theology" and makes no claim to any (and depends on no) presupposition founded in special revelation, this chapter very much focuses on aspects that are more specific to Christianity than to any other religion. However, Temple remains faithful to his enterprise in that he does not see it as his task to preach the gospel of incarnation and sacramental presence; rather he intends to show how these claims relate meaningfully to a rational contemplation of the cosmos. In the meantime, however, and particularly during the last 15 years, the very concept of a "sacramental universe," introduced for the first time by that book, has acquired tremendous influence not only in Anglican theology but throughout ecumenical theological reflection.

Man and Nature (1975) quotes the following statement from an official working group of the Church of England: "The Christian sacramental understanding of the material universe is congruent with the contemporary scientific perspective on the evolution of the cosmos."[154] Here, "the Christian sacramental understanding" is referred to as something that is generally known and accepted. In the same book, Arthur Peacocke, one of the leading contemporary Anglican specialists on creation theology, presents "A Sacramental View of Nature,"[155] in which he sketches the emergence and development of the term. On Temple's approach of a good 40 years earlier, Peacocke says that he "writes in somewhat Hegelian terms" and himself calls for "a contemporary elaboration of Temple's penetrating insight into the relevance of the Christian sacraments for providing the basis for a unified view of matter and of 'spirit.'" Peacocke also notes an essentially related attempt in L.S. Thornton's *The Incarnate Lord* (1928). In addition, he offers a bibliographical review on the theology of nature in the Eastern Fathers and among Anglican theologians. From the Anglican side he cites the works of F.J.A. Hort, an outstanding New Testament scholar with a pronounced Johannine orientation; of the particularly influential Bishop Charles Gore of Oxford; and of Bishop H.R. McAdoo (*The Spirit of Anglicanism*, 1965).

Temple introduces his famous formula as follows:

> We are trying to frame a conception which is not identical with any of
> the commonly offered suggestions concerning the relation of the eternal

---

[153]Lecture XIX, ibid., 473-95.

[154]*Man and Nature*, ed. Hugh Montefiori (London, 1975) 60.

[155]Ibid., 132-42, 202-204.

to the historical, and are now extending its application so as to include the relation of the spiritual and the material . . . and there is in some religious traditions an element which is . . . so close akin to what we want that we may most suitably call this . . . the sacramental conception.[156]

We are now . . . concerned . . . to vindicate the principle on which belief in sacraments reposes, in order that we may be secure in using it as a clue to the understanding of the relation of spirit to matter in the universe.[157]

Thus the view of the universe which I have called sacramental asserts the supremacy and absolute freedom of God. . . . Matter exists in its full reality but at a secondary level. It is created by spirit—the Divine Spirit—to be the vehicle of spirit and the sphere of spirit's self-realization in and through the activity of controlling it.[158]

It is obvious that Temple views the sacraments not as contingent historically established events but as expressions of a formative ontological orientation. As Peacocke points out, there is a philosophical dimension to this that has to be toned down in order for the theological point to come clearly across. The connection between creation, incarnation, and sacrament is viewed in a genuinely theological setting in one of Temple's earlier books, *Christus Veritas* (1924). Also here, the incarnation and the sacraments are the centers of gravitation, and a theological exposition is intended; but in the framework of a rather peculiar paraphrase of "natural" relatedness. The work is structured as progress and return, in five stages: outer circle, inner circle, core, inner circle, outer circle—the "core" being incarnation belief. Already here, the core event of Christianity is seen in the framework of universal relatedness, which is not designated as that of creation or a sacramental universe but that of "a value-metaphysic which finds its center in the historic incarnation of God in Jesus Christ."[159] We can already distinguish the theme that is emerging: incarnation and sacrament—clues to reality. But this reality is not yet projected as spatial world but—in a more idealistic conceptuality—

---

[156]William Temple, *Nature, Man and God* (see n. 152) 481-82.

[157]Ibid., 485.

[158]Ibid., 493.

[159]William Temple, *Christus Veritas: An Essay* (London: Macmillan & Co., 1962 [1924]) 253-54.

figured as value. This should not, however, distract our attention from the role here ascribed to the intended interrelatedness of the three Articles of the Creed.[160]

Forty years after Temple's proposition concerning the "sacramental universe," Peacocke, oriented less toward philosophy and more toward natural science, arrives at a more concise theory than the late archbishop:

> The created world is seen by Christians as a symbol because it is a mode of God's revelation. . . . It is also valued by them for what God is effecting instrumentally through it, what he does for men in and through it. But these two functions of matter, the symbolical and the instrumental, also constitute the special character of the use of matter in the particular Christian sacraments. Hence there is, in each particular sacrament, a universal reference to this double character of created physical reality and, correspondingly, meaning can be attached to speaking of the created world as a sacrament or, at least, as sacramental. However, it must be recognized that this sacramental character is only implicit, and that it is obscure and partial both because of man's limited perception and sensitivity and because of evil. The significance of the incarnation of God in a man within the created world is that in the incarnate Christ the sacramental character of that world was made explicit and perfected. In this sense, it may seem legitimate to regard the incarnate life of Christ as the supreme sacrament.[161]

In his contribution at the 1984 Klingenthal consultation (a consultation concentrating on transconfessional tensions in contemporary creation theology and not primarily geared to confessional divisions) Peacocke went a good deal further toward integrating the sacramental vision of creation into a (somewhat modified) process model of thought. Above all, the sacramental universe becomes an

---

[160]There seems to be no connection between this Anglican development and the striking fact that in 1928 Paul Tillich held his lecture on "Nature and Sacrament" at the Berneuchener Conference. In this presentation there is a richness of observation that might still give motifs for fruitful ecumenical reflection. The reasons for not dealing with it in this study are: 1. that it does not seem to have exercised any immediate influence on subsequent ecumenical terminology; 2. that Tillich himself does not really reflect on the ecumenical implications of his findings—apart from arranging them into the framework of his rather abstract construction of *The Protestant Era* (1948), an approach that we do not see as being ecumenically helpful. His presentation may deserve to be reviewed again, but certainly within a different and more contemporary framework of orientation.

[161]Arthur Peacocke, "A Sacramental View of Nature," *Man and Nature*, ed. Hugh Montefiori (see n. 154) 133-34.

expression of the awe we owe to the universal presence of the Creator in the evolutionary event of creation:

> God the Creator is immanent in a world that he is still creating. God is everywhere and at all times in the processes and events of the natural world. . . . This immediately suggests that man should respond to nature with a respect of the same kind as a man accords to his own body . . . a respect that is transmuted into reverence at the presence of God in and through the whole of the created order, which thereby has, as it were, a derived sacredness or holiness. But this is tantamount to saying that the world is sacramental, to use the traditional term in Christian theology. . . . This complex of proper responses of man to nature at once suggests that man's role may be conceived as that of a *priest of creation,* as a result of whose activity the sacrament is reverenced; and who, because he alone is conscious of God, himself and nature, can mediate between the insentient nature and God.[162]

Peacocke seems to be oriented more by his background in natural science (a background shared by several Anglican theologians) than by some high church sacramental preoccupation, and from his reflections it seems rather clear that incarnation (and subsequently the sacraments) does not retroactively confer on creation some dignity that it did not already possess; rather, with regard to creation, the importance of incarnation is to reveal what is already there. The sacramentality of the universe basically means a disclosure of the Creator's permanent presence in his work. With Temple a double orientation is apparent, but the consequences of this are not clarified theologically. He refers to a twofold meaning of the sacrament: one symbolic (communication of a spiritual content by means of concrete illustration) and one *ex opere operato* (an external event liberating us from captivity to internal psychological processes).[163] Even if the full theological implications of a "sacramental universe" in light of this distinction are not spelled out, it is not easy to see how Temple could have avoided translating his *ex opere operato* along the lines of the incarnation event substantially changing and enriching the character of divine presence in the universe. The consequence, then, would probably be as follows: through the incarnate Christ and the sacraments in-

---

[162]Arthur Peacocke, "Man's Relation to God in the Created," 1984 manuscript, 22. The topic of humankind as the priestly "mediator of creation" is particularly impressively developed by Paul Gregorios in *The Human Presence* (see n. 11) and *Cosmic Man* (see n. 9). See also our quotation from Thomas F. Torrance, *The Ground and Grammar of Theology* (see n. 127), here, p. 221.

[163]William Temple, *Christus Veritas* (see n. 159) 482-86.

stituted to actualize the lasting reality of his incarnation, also creation acquires an additional meaning, and thus a new dignity, reflecting, revealing, and communicating salvation as the final event of universal importance. If Temple's attempt in this regard seems to be lacking in explicitness as well as in clarity, this may be due, first, to the conscious theological limitation of his enterprise and, second, to the speculative trend in his Platonic- and Hegelian-inspired value philosophy.

With Peacocke such trends are swept aside, and the position portrayed is fairly unambiguous. But at the same time some rather intriguing aspects of the Temple approach seem to be lost: The *real presence* of the sacramental aspect is not being noticeably weakened, but to a certain extent its dependence on the incarnation as a unique historical event seems to be toned down in favor of an evolutionary vision of creation as an ongoing process—and the main distinction of the incarnation is to provide us with and consciously integrate us into the full meaning of this ongoing process.

One should be careful about labeling these features as "typically Anglican"—although it was Peacocke at the Klingenthal consultation who recalled that Whitehead, the father of modern process thought, was raised in an Anglican vicarage and that this coincidence should by no means be seen as insignificant.[164] Also at Klingenthal, German Lutheran Professor Sigurd M. Daecke strongly recommended a similar sacramental approach and gave full support to the positions of Peacocke. In addition, he recalled the contributions of the famous Jesuit scientist and thinker Pierre Teilhard de Chardin. No one has made a more moving description of the unity of sacrament (eucharist) and creation than we find in Teilhard's poetic and expressive language:

> At every moment the Eucharistic Christ controls . . . the whole movement of the universe. . . . The sacramental action of Christ, *precisely because it sanctifies matter,* extends its influence beyond the pure supernatural, over all that makes up the internal and external ambience of the faithful. . . . As our humanity assimilates the material world, and as the Host assimilates our humanity, the eucharistic transformation goes beyond and completes the transubstantiation of the bread on the altar. Step by step it irresistibly invades the universe. . . . The sacramental Species are formed by the totality of the world, and the duration of the creation

---

[164]Incidentally, the same applies to Whitehead's student and main theological "translator," Charles Hartshorne. See *Existence and Actuality: Conversations with Charles Hartshorne,* ed. John B. Cobb, Jr. and Franklin J. Gamwell (Chicago/London: University of Chicago Press, 1984) ix-xvii, 124.

is the time needed for its consecration. "In Christo vivimus, movemur et sumus."[165]

There is some justification for quoting the famous Jesuit, a controversial figure in his own church, in a review of the Anglican contribution to creation, not because of his affect on the Anglican tradition or vice versa but because a remarkable coincidence in basic vision links his contribution with that of contemporary Anglicanism. Also, there is an obvious fellowship in the inspiration of a eucharistic spirituality and in the attitude of non-Scholastical Johannine incarnational devotion. Even if the full breadth of Anglicanism would not feel at home in his style of expression, it might have given a broader echo to his visionary statements than his own church did in, at least, the pre-Vatican II period. In his undogmatic way of identifying with dogmatic Christianity, Teilhard may indeed be labeled an Anglican spirit. But it should not be concealed that the vision quoted above goes beyond the Anglican authors we have cited, including William Temple, in that it tends to identify creation and incarnation in a poetic language that makes it hard to distinguish whether and to what extent one of these concepts may be reduced to some metaphorical illustration of the other.

It is regrettable that Sigurd M. Daecke's most instructive study *Teilhard de Chardin und die evangelische Theologie* (1967) is limited to German Protestant theology and thus fails to take into account the rather obvious affinity between Teilhard and modern Anglican development. At Klingenthal, 17 years later, Daecke did extend his scope to include Anglican contributions, not only his fellow lecturer Arthur Peacocke but also William Temple and the working group "Man and Nature" (1975). Daecke was concerned to broaden the ecumenical fellowship of contemporary sacramental approaches to creation and, in addition to his Oriental Orthodox fellow lecturer Paul Gregorios, quoted several authors of various Roman Catholic and Protestant observances, including the neo-Barthian presentation of "the world as parable."[166]

---

[165]Pierre Teilhard de Chardin, *Le Milieu Divin: An Essay on the Interior Life* (New York: Harper & Row; London: Collins, 1960) 114-15. (French: *Oeuvres* 4 [Paris: Editions du Seuil, 1957 (1926-1927)] 153-54.) Cf. also Sigurd M. Daecke, "Säkulare Welt—sakrale Schöpfung—geistige Materie," *Evangelische Theologie* (May/June 1985): 261-76, esp. 272 n. 36.

[166]Christian Link, *Die Welt als Gleichnis* (see n. 43). More recently, Link has also given emphatic support to the concept of a "sacramental [neatly distinguished from a "sacred"] universe," as he sees that idea prefigured in the Reformed tradition by Calvin's *Institutio:* see Christian Link, "Der Mensch als Geschöpf und als Schöpfer," *Versöhnung mit der Natur?*, ed. Jürgen Moltmann

To Daecke the concept of a sacramental universe is one attempt—perhaps the most consistent attempt—to formulate the reconciliation that is so badly needed today between the Christian vision of a sovereign God, who should by no means be pantheistically identified with the world as such, and that of creation as the authentic expression of the Creator's presence in and within his creature. In this connection, Daecke does not shrink from combining it positively with other programmatical catchwords such as "panentheism,"—"process," and "evolution." Even if he is conscious of standing in a Lutheran tradition of "real presence"—and, in that regard, owes much to Roman Catholic and Anglican precursors—Daecke uses the "sacramental" language with less eucharistic orientation in the strict sense than, say, most Anglican reflectors.

Ecumenically, it is also interesting to note the straightforward way in which Carl E. Braaten integrates "A Sacramental Vision of the Creation" in his *Principles of Lutheran Theology*, without paying any particular tribute to the Anglican roots of the language—the only reference being to quote C.S. Lewis' "God likes matter; he invented it." More than any of the other authors quoted, Braaten succeeds in establishing an explicit theological balance between faith, worship, and ethic.

> The sacrament of the body and blood of Christ has a deep set of roots in the soil of the Incarnation, but it has another set of roots deeply embedded in the Christian doctrine of creation. . . . There is continuity between creation and incarnation, and so it is fitting that the sacrament of salvation should use as its means of expression the same earthly kind of stuff from which humanity emerged in its evolutionary journey. . . . A sacramental vision of life reacts positively to the contemporary search for an ecologically sound theology and ethic.[167]

That Braaten adopts this terminology and can expound it with so little reference to its origins is a testimony to the acceptance it has found in the course of the past 50 years mainly, of course, among churches with a traditional emphasis on

---

(Munich: Christian Kaiser Verlag, 1986) 15-47, 34-35. But in that Calvin reference we find no tendency to elucidate creation from the side of sacramental theology or vice versa.

[167]Carl E. Braaten, *Principles of Lutheran Theology* (see n. 66) 99-100. Cf. from the Roman Catholic side, the observation of Alexandre Ganoczy in *Theologie der Natur* (see n. 50) 102: "Herrenmahl . . . erfasst die materiellen, leiblichen und gemeinschaftlichen Lebensbedingungen der Teilnehmer. Es ist Feier ihrer Arbeit und der durch sie— liebevoll—bearbeiteten Natur. Es ist Realpräsenz des Todes und der Auferweckung des einen eigentlichen Retters dieser Welt.''

sacramental theology and "real presence." Historically, it must above all be understood in light of the "ecological crisis" (of, especially, the last 15 to 20 years) and the lack of modern theologies (liberal, neoorthodox, existential, and secular) to provide a vision fit to fight the conspicuous destruction of creation. In recent ecumenical reorientation another formula that basically says the same may have become even more influential than the "sacramental universe," namely that of a "eucharistic vision." In part, the breakthrough of this recent terminology seems to be due to the presentation of the "eucharist" in the Faith and Order convergence document *Baptism, Eucharist and Ministry*.[168] Heretofore of limited consequence in Protestant traditions other than Anglicanism, "eucharist" here received focal attention:

> The eucharist embraces all aspects of life. It is a representative act of thanksgiving and offering on behalf of the whole world. . . . Solidarity in the eucharistic communion of the body of Christ and responsible care of Christians for one another and the world find specific expression in the liturgies. . . . The eucharist opens up the vision of the divine rule which has been promised as the final renewal of creation, and is a foretaste of it.[169]

The Vancouver Assembly of the World Council of Churches (1983) took a step further forward when it proclaimed:

> Indeed the aspect of Christian unity which has been most striking to us here in Vancouver is that of a *eucharistic vision*. Christ—the life of the world—unites heaven and earth, God and world, spiritual and secular. His body and blood, given us in the elements of bread and wine, integrate liturgy and diaconate, proclamation and acts of healing. . . . Our eucharistic vision thus encompasses the whole reality of Christian worship, life and witness, and tends—when truly discovered—to shed light on Christian unity in its full richness of diversity.[170]

---

[168]The "Lima Document." Faith and Order Paper no. 111 (Geneva: World Council of Churches, 1982).

[169]Ibid., §§20-22.

[170]Report of Issue Group 2, II.4. *Gathered for Life: Official Report, VI Assembly, Vancouver, Canada, July 24—August 10, 1983*, ed. David Gill (Geneva: World Council of Churches, 1983) 44-45. Cf. Per Lønning, "Die 'Eucharistische Vision': Vancouvers Beitrag zum ökumenischen Weiterdenken," *Ökumenische Rundschau* 33/1 (1984): 40-49.

One could say that the concept of a "eucharistic vision," as here unfolded, is less explicit about creation seen as comprehending "nature" in its existing givenness than is the concept of a "sacramental universe." To a large extent this may be due to the difference in orientation between "universe" as an objectifiable entity and "vision" as an expression of a subjectively motivating perception. It may be equally meaningful to change the terms around and talk of a "eucharistic universe" and a "sacramental vision." The difference is that "eucharistic" uses one of the sacraments (which becomes particularly illustrative through its striking symbolism and constant repetition) as a clue to a sacramental understanding of reality, whereas "sacramental" immediately refers to this very understanding. If "universe" has the advantage of expressing the whole as having a dignity that by far transcends the sum of its single components, then "vision" has the advantage of emphasizing illumination and commitment. In addition, as here developed, the concept of a "eucharistic vision" has an immediate ecumenical relevance: It refers to the unity of the Christian church in a way and with a fullness that can be only indirectly derived from the concept of a "sacramental universe." But due to the way the two concepts have developed there is no reason to elaborate on their differences, for their converging interests are sufficiently visible and fundamental: to focus on creation as highlighted by the sacraments—and vice versa—through the medium of incarnation. With equal justification, it could be said: to witness and explicate the unity of creation and incarnation by means of the sacramental representation of the "uncreated" offering itself through the created.

What has been shown here has a bearing on all fields of Christian theology; indeed it is the unifying principle underlying this theology as a whole. It pertains to Christology, ecclesiology, sacramentology, and eschatology as profoundly as to creation theology. This discovery takes us back to the tension between a simple "kingship of Christ" and a double "two kingdoms" approach to Christian existence.[171] What distinguishes the sacramental approach from what is sometimes criticized as a "Christo-monistic" theological model may be twofold: first, in claiming a unifying vision of faith, it does not establish a one-way drive from incarnation to creation but maintains a more dynamic interaction; second, it is essential that the mutual illumination of creation and incarnation takes place precisely through the representative element of the sacrament. Or, one might describe it as triangular: the interrelatedness of the three corners—creation, incarnation, sacrament—could and should be understood as being complementary, starting from any one of the three points and moving in both directions. It is impossible not to interpret this triangularity in light of Trinitarian belief: the Father (Creator), the

---

[171]Reviewed here, §§5.3 and 5.4.

Son (incarnate), the Spirit (sacramental presence)—but with the immediate understanding that the unity of the vision at the same time reflects the unity of God, and that an abstract division would contradict the unity of all things, a unity grounded in the unity of their provenance.

If many of our observations in this chapter have had immediate reference to constituencies other than the Anglican, they all nevertheless directly or indirectly apply to Anglicanism as the identifiable matrix of the concept under consideration. In order to assess the importance of this fairly recent feature it is, of course, desirable to see it in the full breadth of its ecumenical occurrence, but certainly not without paying particular attention to the soil from which it grew. What is interesting is not when and where a particular formula was first used but how it came about. What was there in the Anglican spiritual inheritance that particularly favored the emergence of a "sacramental" universe?

A particularly fitting guide for this exploration may be Archbishop Arthur Michael Ramsey's *From Gore to Temple*. By no means uncritical of his great Canterbury predecessor, Ramsey confirms Temple's own statement that Charles Gore was his most influential theological inspirator, but he also underlines a fundamental difference between the two, namely in connection with Temple's philosophical (Hegelian) preoccupations: "In the double fact of his immense debt to Gore and his difference from him we may find a clue to much which was happening in the movement of Anglican thought."[172] Ramsey's understanding of Temple is rather unambiguous:

> He felt that the philosophical climate of the time was friendly to a spiritual interpretation of the world, unfriendly to a particular revelation. It was credible that God and men could be united in the whole process of the world, scarcely credible that deity could do things in particular. Against such assumptions Temple set himself to vindicate, in idealism's own terms, the rationality of an Incarnation and a particular revelation. It has to be discussed whether . . . he retained modes of thought more Hegelian than were really compatible with a Christian view of God's relation to the world. . . .

> But what, then, of this sentence: "Even to the eternal life of God, His created universe is sacramental to Himself. If He had no creatures to redeem, or if He had not redeemed them, He would not be what He is." It is hard to doubt that this later statement shows a subordinacy of the Bib-

---

[172]Arthur Michael Ramsey, *From Gore to Temple: The Development of Anglican Theology Between "Lux Mundi" and the Second World War, 1889-1939* (London: Longmans, 1960) vii.

lical and patristic view . . . to the needs of idealistic metaphysics. It seems to be akin to the view which sees in the Blessed Trinity the description of God's relation to the world and identifies the creation of the world with the begetting of the Son, rather than the view which worships the Blessed Trinity as the perfection of Majesty and Love upon which the world utterly depends.[173]

It is remarkable that Ramsey, who is known as the spokesperson of a rather profiled sacramental theology, shows so little enthusiasm about his more "liberal" predecessor's unifying vision of sacrament and creation. With his chronological and ecclesial emplacement, Ramsey is very conscious of having left the epoch of theological liberalism and thus also the challenges to which Temple was responding.[174] Not yet faced with the ecological breakup of the 1970s, he obviously sees Temple's approach less as conferring a sacramental quality on the universe and more as universalizing the sacraments (and the incarnation they confirm)—thus eventually depriving them of their uniqueness, that is, of their historical contingency.

To what extent the "sacramental universe" (not the designation, but the motif) could be ascribed to a Hegelian influence and to what extent it might indicate some distant Lutheran origin cannot be discussed here. Hegel's relationship to Christian theology, and particularly his beloved Luther, is a constant topic of discussion. Not only Hegel but also some of his contemporary interpreters are inclined to see in him an authentic expression of a Lutheran vision of "real presence," of the eternal Logos integrated in temporal history.[175] It is obvious that the "sacramental universe" as developed by Temple (but not necessarily any occurrence of the term) shows parallels to Hegel's idea of the incarnation as a hermeneutical principle (not primarily to the universe, but) to history. However, also according to Ramsey, other and more specifically Anglican factors have been at work to produce Temple's vision, and this is where Charles Gore, the most influential single character in Anglican theology during the period 1880–1930, comes in.[176]

---

[173]Ibid., 148, 150.

[174]Ibid., viii.

[175]See particularly Ulrich Asendorf, *Luther und Hegel* (see n. 72).

[176]About Temple and Gore, see also David L. Edwards, *Leaders of the Church of England, 1828–1944* (London: Oxford University Press, 1971) 272. For a fuller historical understanding it would even be of interest to examine the second and third quarters of the 19th century, paying particular attention to the integration of creation and redemption motifs in the "broad church" tradition (Samuel Taylor

About the *Lux Mundi* group promoted by Charles Gore, Ramsey writes:

> . . . a school of theology so avowedly incarnational. . . . To all of them the Eucharist was a constant interpreter of doctrine, and the Eucharist enabled them to see the doctrine in terms cosmic and liturgical, no less than evangelical. Mankind's deliverance into salvation means the recovery of the creaturely adoration of the Creator. The song of the redeemed is the recapture of the song of creation.[177]

Turning to the amazingly unified collection of essays (almost a dogmatic), *Lux Mundi* (1889), a few quotations will clarify our theme:

> The great thinkers of the early Church . . . realized that redemption was a means to an end . . . the reconsecration of the whole universe to God. And so the very completeness of their grasp on the Atonement led them to dwell upon the cosmic significance of the Incarnation, its purpose to "gather together all things in one." . . . Creation was viewed as the embodiment of the Divine ideas, and therefore the revelation of the Divine character; manifesting its Maker with increasing clearness . . . till in the fulness of time He Himself became man, and thereby lifted human nature, and with it the material universe to which man is intimately linked.[178]

> The Sacramental principle has been most plainly adopted by our Lord: the spiritual forces with which He would renew the face of the earth were to be exerted through material instruments.[179]

> And so through Sacramental elements and acts Christianity maintains its strong inclusive hold upon the whole of life. The consecration of material elements to be the vehicles of Divine grace keeps upon earth that vindication and defence of the material against the insults of sham spiritualism which was achieved for ever by the Incarnation and Ascension of Jesus Christ. We seem to see the material world rising from height to height . . . yet only gradually laying aside the inertness of its lower forms . . .

Coleridge, Matthew Arnold, John Frederick Denison Maurice) as well as in the new "high church" movement (tractarianism; John Henry Newman, Edward Bouverie Pusey), and not least with an eye on the conciliatory influence emanating from the poetic work of John Keble. But that is impossible within our present context.

[177] Arthur Michael Ramsey, *From Gore to Temple* (see n. 172) 50.

[178] J.R. Illingworth, "The Incarnation in Relation to Development," *Lux Mundi: A Series of Studies in the Religion of the Incarnation,* ed. Charles Gore (London, 1892 [1889]) 134.

[179] Francis Paget, "Sacraments," ibid., 307.

till in humanity it comes within sight of that which God has been preparing for it, even the reception of His own image and likeness.[180]

One could therefore say that all the necessary elements for a concept of the
"sacramental universe" have already been prepared. As to the personal influence
of Gore, the editor, it may have been channeled even more by his Bampton Lectures (1891), "The Incarnation of the Son of God." According to Ramsey, we
see here "the opening up of a line of exposition of the Incarnation which was, in
the main, to be followed in Anglican theology for many years to come."[181] Ramsey finds:

> The Incarnation was the center of a theological scheme concerning na-
> ture and man, in which Christ is both the climax of nature and history
> and the supernatural restorer of mankind. It is significant that no small
> use is made of the current concept of evolution, and that the thesis is con-
> gruous with part at least of the view of world familiar in idealistic phi-
> losophy. But it is no less significant that, at the core of the argument,
> there is the prophetic view of the living God, the Creator and Redeemer,
> and the place of Christ in the cosmic order is understood only in terms of
> His redemptive work and claim.[182]

According to Ramsey, among the *Lux Mundi* group, Gore may have been the
one who was least influenced by idealistic philosophy, and J.R. Illingworth the
one who was most profoundly influenced. But however much he might criticize
this trend, Ramsey readily admits that it is one of the most powerful elements in
the Anglican inheritance.

> Thus it was that the Anglicanism of our era, constantly involved with
> many forces in contemporary thought and culture, was affected—often
> in the potent realm of the subconscious—by Platonism, by spirituality,
> by its traditional scholarship and by the care for *Via Media*. These influ-
> ences made for integrity and for depth at a time when facile and shallow
> syntheses were all too easy.[183]

In our quotations from *Lux Mundi* the Platonic influence may seem to be almost overwhelming, but it is integrated with a Johannine incarnation approach that
makes the sacramental emphasis on matter sound rather logical. The Platonic vi-

---

[180]Ibid., 309.

[181]Arthur Michael Ramsey, *From Gore to Temple* (see n. 172) 18.

[182]Ibid.

[183]Ibid., 166.

sion of eternal ideas reflecting themselves in temporal matter is, of course, open to interpretation in two opposite directions as far as the ontological status of matter is concerned: either an emphatic devaluation of matter as presenting *only* the imperfect projections of a reality that is essentially absent and totally different; or the celebration of matter as *the only* available—and, at the same time, sufficiently adequate—representation of that reality. Where a Johannine model of the Logos incarnate is allowed to mediate, the result will inevitably be the latter. Even though, in their specific theological meaning, neither incarnation nor sacrament was strongly emphasized among the old Cambridge Platonists of the late 17th century, the link to a particular Anglican Platonic tradition may be rather visible. Here is a characteristic quotation from 1660:

> Religion . . . spiritualizes material things and carries up the souls of good men from sensible and earthly things to things intellectual and divine. . . . Religion spiritualizes the creation to good men; it teaches them to look at any perfections or excellencies in themselves and others . . . as so many beams flowing from one and the same fountain of light; to love them all in God, and God in all—the universal goodness in a particular being.[184]

Even if there is a lack of references to incarnation and the sacraments, what is definitely here is the vision of the physical universe acquiring supreme dignity from radiating the universal mystery of creation. And even if this basic vision is by no means sufficient to characterize Anglican theological identity as such, it prefigures a philosophical approach and suggests a model of natural theology that must be seen as being more specific to Anglicanism than to any other confessional tradition.

In *The Spirit of Anglicanism,* Bishop H.R. McAdoo strongly underscores that "the distinctiveness of Anglicanism lies not in theology but in a theological method":

> The absence of an official theology in Anglicanism is something deliberate which belongs to its essential nature, for it has always regarded the teaching and practice of the undivided Church of the first five centuries as a criterion.[185]

---

[184]John Smith, *The Excellency and Nobleness of True Religion* (Glasgow: R. Foulis, 1745 [1660]). Quoted from: *The Cambridge Platonists,* ed. Gerald R. Cragg (New York: University Press of America, 1968) 126.

[185]H.R. McAdoo, *The Spirit of Anglicanism: A Survey of Anglican Theological Method in the Seventeenth Century* (London: Adam & Charles Black, 1965) vi.

McAdoo expresses the basic identity of Anglicanism, its "spirit," by quoting the words of Francis Paget in his *Introduction to the Fifth Book of Hooker's Ecclesiastical Polity:* "The distinctive strength of Anglicanism rests on equal loyalty to the unconflicting rights of reason, Scripture and tradition."[186] And McAdoo systematically pursues and develops this triple orientation in *The Spirit of Anglicanism.* This results in a description that, perhaps, does not render full justice to the particular spiritual emphases with which Anglicanism has enriched ecumenical fellowship; as such, the approach remains too exclusively formal. But, in spite of this, it may be useful as a guiding principle for those who try to understand the "sacramental universe" in relation to its Anglican origin, and it may also serve to unveil its ecumenical implications in general.

As to the "rights of reason" advocated by McAdoo, we have frequently touched upon certain trends that are worthy of observation. A *Platonic tradition,* channeled and theologically modified through the *Lux Mundi* group (Charles Gore), becomes the unifying frame of reference for elements that have each been amply emphasized in the history of Anglican spirituality: creation, incarnation, sacrament. The universe as such becomes transparent for the presence of the Creator, thus giving to the historically contingent event of revelation a meaning and a credential supported by universal, cosmic rationality. This philosophical perspective could and should by no means be seen in isolation from the image of the world reflected in worship and spirituality, and it is therefore equally important for the understanding of that dimension. A *Hegelian input* (not least through Temple) links up with this emphasis but adds to it an orientation of historicity: dynamic, divine presence in the events of history as such. A principal emphasis on *evolution* is very much present already in the *Lux Mundi* attempt to overcome the aftermaths of the Darwinian controversy, but it seems to be even more dominant in the contemporary approach of which Arthur Peacocke may be the most influential interpreter, an approach that to a certain extent seeks epistemological reference in the modern process philosophy founded by the (Anglican) philosopher Alfred North Whitehead and the (Anglican) theologian Charles Hartshorne.[187]

---

[186]Ibid.

[187]Teilhard de Chardin, who has also exercised so obvious an influence on this branch of evolutionary thought, makes us recall that the programmatical etiquette of Charles Gore and the *Lux Mundi* group, "liberal Catholicism," could be used on him with more right than perhaps on anyone else. A striking Anglican plea for "natural theology" in a rational, almost Aristotelian style, is the recent contribution by Hugh Montefiori, former bishop of Birmingham, in *The Probability of God* (London: SCM Press, 1985). For statements of principle, see esp. 2-7, 277.

"Rationality" in this context should not be confined to philosophical orientation. It must also include the strong affinity of Anglican theology to natural science, not only in terms of looking to science as an honored conversation partner,[188] but also in terms of the considerable presence of natural scientists in the Anglican clergy, including the ranks of church leadership, a fact too familiar to need documentation here.

Among the Anglican contributors to the Strasbourg creation project, two were formerly distinguished university teachers in science: Peacocke, who gave a paper on "Creation—Secularity or Sacrality of the Created?" at the 1984 Klingenthal consultation, and the Rev. Dr. J.C. Polkinghorne, who, in addition to delivering one of the "pre-reflections" at the 1983 consultation also lectured on "Creation and Science: Yesterday—Today—Tomorrow" at the July 1984 International Seminar. There is probably a less dualistic attitude to the faith and science issue within Anglicanism than in any other Protestant tradition. The reasons for this may have been partly stated in our previous discussion on philosophy, but they will be supplemented in the observations that follow.

Regarding the "rights of Scripture," we have already observed the particular Johannine orientation in much of Anglican theology. This orientation became particularly apparent in the work of the famous Cambridge School from around 1860 (F.J.A. Hort, Joseph Barber Lightfoot, Brooke Foss Westcott), and the link between Johannine Christocentricity and patristic incarnation theology was extensively exposed. The emphasis of this school has established itself as a remaining and powerful factor in the Anglican theological tradition, and its vitality was proved when John A.T. Robinson proclaimed in his last major work: "I believe that John represents in date, as in theology, not only the *omega* but also the *alpha* of New Testament development."[189] Simultaneously emphasizing reason and tradition, it

---

[188]In spite of an apparently very dramatic rupture in the days of the Darwinian controversy. In later years, the dramatic clash on evolution between Bishop Samuel Wilberforce and Thomas Huxley acquired almost mythical proportions. It should, however, be borne in mind that Charles Darwin, whose basic orientation was by no means so unambiguously antireligious as mythology has made it, was to a large extent inspired by Anglican natural theology, and that the theological reception process of his theories was well advanced already in the late 19th century. Cf. *Der Darwinismus: Die Geschichte einer Theorie,* ed. Günther Altner (Darmstadt: Wissenschaftliche Buchgesellschaft, 1981) and *Science and Religion in the Nineteenth Century,* ed. T. Cosslett (Cambridge: Cambridge University Press, 1984).

[189]John A.T. Robinson, *Redating the New Testament* (London: SCM Press; Philadelphia: Westminster Press, 1976) 311.

is obvious that Anglicanism must pay proportionately less attention to the Bible than those Reformation churches that unambiguously profess *sola Scriptura*. However, it is equally clear that Anglican tradition as a whole would contest the accusation that it takes biblical truths less seriously than those churches, and on some issues (especially divorce and remarriage) it has been basing its arguments on Scripture more insistently than some of the *sola Scriptura* churches. The Johannine approach to Scripture seems to accommodate both a certain plea to ''reason'' (the Logos) and a smooth transition from Scripture to the early church. In both regards, the Pauline approach to Scripture that is so dominant in the Lutheran and Reformed traditions favors a more exclusive insistence on scriptural uniqueness. As has been repeatedly confirmed in recent years, Pauline literature is not without reference to a ''cosmic'' Christ or to salvation as creation fulfilled,[190] and Johannine literature by no means neglects personal ''existential'' salvation.[191] But, historically, it is easy to distinguish the difference between a predominantly Johannine and a predominantly Pauline approach to Scripture in Christian theology. The ecumenical task for us today may be not so much to combine the two approaches indiscriminately as to make them enrich each other in a constructive dialectical interplay.

In Anglicanism, the ''right of tradition'' may also be a fairly complex term, in that generally, as in Eastern Orthodoxy, it emphasizes the testimony of the ancient ''undivided'' church of the first five centuries, with certain reservations (varying from one Anglican wing to another) as to the successive medieval Western development. There is also emphasis on the particular Anglican legacy (the 17th century more than the 16th, but also the last two-thirds of the 19th century and trends leading up to our own time). In the Anglican vision of tradition, theology is as little divided from spirituality as from philosophy and science, and as such the concept of tradition is fairly comprehensive—but again with the understanding that in reviewing history (with reverence and in solidarity) each of the main orientations within the Anglican community finds its own, if only slightly divergent, line of genealogy.

Identification with the Greek Fathers favors a particular feeling of solidarity with the Eastern churches. The first report from the bilateral dialogues between Anglicans and Orthodox, the 1976 Moscow Statement, contains two statements of particular interest to our present enquiry. In discussing the authority of the Ecumenical Councils, the report pays particular attention to the controversial Seventh Ecumenical Council and its decision on the veneration of icons:

---

[190]Particularly Romans 8:18-23, Colossians 1:15-20.

[191]John 3:1ff., 4:1ff., 1 John 1:5ff.

The Orthodox . . . understand its positive injunctions . . . as an expression of faith in the Incarnation. The Anglican tradition places a similarly positive value on the created order, and on the place of the body and of material things in worship. Like the Orthodox, Anglicans see this as a necessary corollary of the doctrine of the Incarnation.[192]

In the eucharistic celebration the Church is a confessing community which witnesses to a cosmic transfiguration. Thus God enters into a personal historic situation as the Lord of creation and of history.[193]

Here again, we find all the constituents of a "sacramental universe": creation, incarnation, the earthliness of the eucharistic elements, transfiguration of the cosmos. What may be said to be lacking is the term as such and—perhaps more important—a unifying ontological framework to state more precisely *how* the constituents relate to each other. Neither Hegelian dialectic nor the contemporary concept of evolution is particularly dear to Orthodox theology, but between Anglicans and Orthodox there may well be a fellowship of a "mild" pre-Scholastic, transfiguration type of Platonism, a topic that could have been developed. But above all there is fellowship in an integral vision of creation and salvation. This could be seen as Barthianism turned 180 degrees, in that it does not presuppose Christ, *Heilsgeschichte,* as an exclusive illuminating event in a world that was hitherto in unfathomable confusion; rather it endeavors to unify the universal meaning of creation, the epochal significance of the unique historical fulfillment (incarnation), and the persisting transfigurant representation (sacrament). Thus that "everything receives its meaning from and in Christ" becomes no less important than in Barthianism—but only when seen in conjunction with "everything receives its meaning from the Creator's design" and "everything receives its meaning through sacramental presence." Whereas the Barthian vision is exclusively Christocentric, the Anglican-Orthodox vision is inclusively Christocentric. This, of course, is in opposition to the traditional Reformed (iconoclastic) fear of an idolatrous relation with created "matter" and would be much more consistent with the Lutheran emphasis on "real presence"—an observation confirmed by the relatedness in expressions of worship. But, on the other hand, the pointed, almost monistic, Christocentricity of the Anglican orientation may in a way come closer to a Reformed covenant approach than to a Lutheran law and gospel dialectic. As

---

[192]Moscow Statement, 1976, §16. *Growth in Agreement: Reports and Agreed Statements of Ecumenical Conversations on a World Level,* ed. Lukas Vischer and Harding Meyer (Ramsey NY: Paulist Press; Geneva: World Council of Churches, 1984) 43.

[193]Moscow Statement, 1976, §28. Ibid., 46.

to the relative independence of creation faith, there may be indications of a tension: on the one hand, the Orthodox/Anglican/Reformed position; on the other, the Roman Catholic/Lutheran. Obviously, such a statement has to be considered with utmost care if it is to contribute to ecumenical clarification. But be that as it may, it should not be overlooked that—paradoxical as it may sound—the ambiguity of the Anglican approach might provide some assistance to overcoming what remains of the Lutheran/Reformed deadlock.

One element that should not be forgotten when talking of "tradition"[194] in Anglicanism is the influence of "traditional" spirituality. To Anglicanism, "tradition" is not primarily that certain things are bound to stay as they were; it is something considerably more reflected, namely to preserve the fellowship of worshipers as diachronic (as well as synchronic) communion, a vision that has too often been diminished in other Reformation churches. In a noteworthy study, Karl-Michael Dierkes calls attention to the role of the creation motif in Anglican hymnody and, having analyzed a series of examples, sums it up as follows:

> Bei allen diesen Liedern ist es typisch, dass in ihnen das Natürliche zu Stufen zum Übernatürlichen wird, dass die irdischen Dinge transparent sind und hinter ihnen die Ewigkeit aufleuchtet. Diese Haltung verhindert, dass die Schöpfungsfrömmigkeit im Naturalismus verflacht und bewirkt, dass der heilsgeschichtliche Aspekt zum Tragen kommt. Andererseits aber besteht bei der dichterischen Allegorisierung des Geschöpflichen die Gefahr, dass die Schöpfung in ihrem Eigenwert nicht genügend ernst genommen wird, wenn sie nur als Stufe und Übergang zum "Eigentlichen," zum Übernatürlichen angesehen wird. . . .

> Beachten wir, in welcher Kühnheit und fast radikal verkürzter prophetischer Perspektive Christus der Schöpfer und Christus der Erlöser als Einheit gesehen werden.[195]

Dierkes approaches the topic from a Roman Catholic perspective, which is particularly interesting in view of his criticism that Anglican creation hymns move too quickly from a natural to a supernatural orientation. Perhaps a Lutheran observer would have made a similar remark. In any case, comparison with, say, Paul Gerhardt, the prince of Lutheran hymnody and a great interpreter of incarnation as well as creation (albeit with less of an explicitly integrative approach), may give considerable assistance to further clarification.

---

[194]Quotation marks used to indicate that here "tradition" and "traditional" stand for something more than in everyday language.

[195]Karl-Michael Dierkes, *Anglikanische Frömmigkeit und Lehre im Kirchenlied* (1969) 79, 81.

With the importance it places on integral and integrative creation theology being constitutive of the "eucharistic vision," it is obvious that the Anglican contribution is of remarkable relevance for the contemporary discussion. Even if "sacramental universe" is not a strictly unambiguous term, and even if it has been criticized by authoritative Anglican spokespersons (e.g., Ramsey), it is still fair to characterize it as a challenging and inspiring expression of a distinctive Anglican contribution toward an ecumenical theology of creation.[196]

5.6 The Free church contribution

The term "Free church" raises a series of problems—both methodological and thematical—that are different from and in addition to those present in our dealings with the confessions in the previous sections. First, there are more denominations than we have examined up to now, and each has a special theological tradition that it might have been of interest to examine on its own. Where, then, since time and space force us to undertake some sort of rationalization, do we leave a scheme of single encounters and start grouping churches together? Should this be done according to size, to length of history, to estimated influence, to specific resources, or according to some other rationale? Quantitative implications may well have their weight, but at the same time one rather objective criterion should probably also be decisive. All the churches we have dealt with so far are, or at least have been, "folk churches," churches that are determined to comprehend—are indeed struggling to comprehend—the whole of the population in a given country or region, and in that aim they have, by tradition, even been assisted by public legislation. Even if in general the legal as well as the sociological position of these churches has been essentially modified, their structure and ecclesiological self-awareness is by and large still marked by a visible "folk church" comprehensiveness. This applies even to their self-presentation in nations where a "no" to

---

[196]Even if it brings no confessional aspect to the foreground, it can hardly be seen as accidental that, like process theology, the work of Grace M. Jantzen, *God's World, God's Body* (London: Darton, Longman & Todd; Philadelphia: Westminster Press, 1984) comes from an English background. The author concludes that "the model of the universe as the embodiment of God . . . clearly . . . injects new life into an understanding of the sacraments, especially the Eucharist" (157). The proposed model goes beyond the general ideas connected with a "sacramental universe," and the author thinks that even Peacocke is too reticent in terms of preserving "ontological otherness" (130). However, the correspondence in terms of the interrelatedness of universe and sacramentality is clear.

church establishment is a cornerstone of civil life, as in the USA or, in a different way, in France.

On the other hand, there are churches that have never been, and for theological reasons have never tried to become, folk churches; they have deliberately organized themselves as fellowships of individual believers. To what extent theological and nontheological factors may have combined to account for this may be a particularly intriguing topic for ecclesial self-understanding as a whole (as a counterpart to the similarly intriguing question about the interaction of theological and nontheological factors in the historical formation of established ecclesiality and folk church life). It may be rather simple to distinguish Free churches from the surrounding constituency of some folk church and also to trace the distinction in a country where, constitutionally, all churches are on the same footing. But the rest of the orientation may be more difficult. Although the major "classical" Free churches are easily identifiable and delineable (Baptists, Quakers, Methodists), others are more complex, almost impossible to survey in a structural way, and thus awkward to review as distinctive families (diverse Pentecostal and Holiness churches); still others may fall into the somewhat diffuse border zone between churches and sects (Unitarians, Adventists—although the latter, at least, seem to be moving in the direction of contact with the wider ecumenical fellowship). Mainly due to lack of resources, one particularly interesting question was not raised at the appropriate stage of the Strasbourg research process but must still be regarded as somewhat important: To what extent does the recent development of African Independent churches demand to be taken seriously as a new, but certainly not unauthentic, part of the historical Christian communion? Would their voice(s) be of particular interest in an ecumenical reflection on creation faith?

However, the main problem is this: The one characteristic that could link the Free churches together into one, albeit not very consolidated, classification group is certainly not a common theological inheritance. And least of all is it a creation theology, for ever since the Reformation this has not been a dominant factor in the tensions between the "established" and the "nonestablished" churches. What to a certain extent may join churches of the Free church tradition are certain ecclesiological assumptions about the integrity of the church as a holy community of believers, visibly distinguishable from the surrounding "world." In liberal Free church traditions such as left-wing Quakerism, Socinianism, and Unitarianism, the focus is on the free and responsible human personality as religious agent rather than on born-again individual holiness. But the formal parallel seems to remain sufficiently evident. However, even in terms of structure, there is an obvious distance between churches of the independent/congregational current and, say, the Methodist emphasis on centralized church government. How can such a theological and ecclesial multiplicity be taken as a block and have some effect on our deliberations on creation and ecumenism?

Two official Free church representatives attended the 1983 Strasbourg consultation, the same number as from each of the more established traditions previously presented. As in all other cases, one was invited as a "pre-reflector" on one of the other traditions, the other was given a topic that was formulated with particular reference to the virtues and weaknesses of the reflector's tradition. In this case, Professor J. Robert Nelson (United Methodist, USA), former secretary and later chairperson of the Faith and Order working committee, was invited to "pre-reflect" on Orthodoxy. Having been invited to approach the task with his own confessional commitments in mind, he made some rather striking ecumenical observations related to the Methodist orientation. Even if, in his opinion, to John Wesley the created world was primarily a stage for God's dealing with human beings according to their sin or to their faith—in other words, a rather otherworldly orientation—he stressed that it should not be forgotten that the optimism inherent in the Methodist understanding of sanctifying grace basically confirms the goodness of creation—in a way not too far apart from the Orthodox vision of *theosis*. It may, of course, be interesting to ask whether that observation applies also to other Free church traditions, and especially to those of the Holiness and Pentecostal families, which have obviously been deeply influenced by Methodism itself.

The question to what extent and how an optimistic doctrine of sanctification may in this way be indirectly indicative of a particular creation theology is certainly thought provoking. And the answer does not seem to be immediately obvious. The question that inevitably arises is the one posed to the Lutherans at the 1983 consultation: To what extent does "new creation" express continuity *and* discontinuity with the old? In some cases, an optimistic view of sanctification as the empirical renewal of human life may express a pronounced confidence in the renewability of (created) human nature; in others it may emphasize renewal as a need and a result of radical transformation (*Erneuerungsfähigkeit* versus *Erneuerungsbedürftigkeit*). It is not difficult to find a revival type of preaching in which the triumphant experience of transformed life appears against the background of undifferentiated corruptness:

> Amazing grace, how sweet the sound
> that saved a wretch like me!
> I once was lost, but now am found;
> was blind, but now I see.[197]

---

[197]John Newton in *The Lutheran Book of Worship* (1978) no. 448:1.

Such an expression should not immediately be taken as proof of a negative or lacking creation faith, but rather as a strong, situationally conditioned expression of a subjectively experienced lost-and-found-ness. But it certainly proves that a strong emphasis on transformation does not necessarily emphasize optimistic assumptions with regard to creational transformability. But this observation does not intend to refute Nelson's surprising statement; rather, it is intended as a plea that, in a wider setting, it receive the consideration it undoubtedly deserves.

Contemporary theology has been paying increasing attention to the topic "holiness of creation," especially within the framework of a sacramental or eucharistic vision.[198] Would it therefore be applicable to raise the issue about *creation and holiness* also in the framework of a revivalist (or, equally, a traditional Roman Catholic or an Orthodox ascetic) concept of individual sanctification? In what way and to what extent does a sanctified person testify to the sanctity of creation? Could this kind of a "theotic" approach lead to supporting and confirming the "eucharistic" approach, or is the inbuilt tension between a spiritual-individualistic and a sacramental-communal approach too deep-rooted to allow for that kind of coordination?

Obviously, the prevailing as well as the traditional assumptions in Orthodoxy and in Roman Catholicism would be strongly in favor of eucharistic earthliness and saintly humanhood mutually sustaining and confirming each other. But church history shows that such a coordination has too often disintegrated and has fostered confrontations within the respective churches. Indeed, in the Protestant segment of Christianity such tension seems to have been the rule rather than the exception. In the Free church traditions (as in revival movements within folk churches) the stress on personal "change" has usually been accompanied by a pronounced suspicion of sacramental emphases. In Roman Catholicism a similar tension became particularly apparent during the Jansenist-Jesuit conflict of the 17th century. With explicit reference to creation theology, an exciting area of hitherto practically unobserved questions could be suggested by the theme "The Saints—Guides to Creation," or "Reborn Christians—Authentic Witnesses of Creation."

The main Free church contribution at the 1983 consultation focused on the theme "'No' to the World as 'Yes' to Creation" and was entrusted to the English Baptist Dr. Michael Taylor. He began by demonstrating the inappropriateness of the theme if interpreted too simplistically, saying that it could provoke the impression that the Free churches represented some well-established system of world denial, an otherworldly orientation that was determined by the concern to give an appropriate witness to creation faith. This impression would not be correct. Tay-

---

[198]Cf. §5.5 on Anglicanism.

lor found no distinctive concern for creation in English Free church history, a fact he very much regretted and, in harmony with several contemporaries in Free church theology, was determined to counteract. But, as he admitted, this would have to be done with reference to common ecumenical sources as they appear in contemporary church life rather than with reference to particular Free church assets. He noted that a Free church "no" to the world was mainly a "no" to religious oppression and to social inequities arising from that oppression. He saw that Puritan abstention from normal social activities was to a large extent the result of being involuntarily excluded by and from the surrounding repressive society. But he rejected the more or less established Free church vision of the world being chiefly "a vale for soul-making," as this tended to empty creation belief of theological relevance.

What has been expressed through the Free churches on this point may be seen as a slightly caricatured image of Western Christianity as a whole. In profiled criticism of this tradition, Taylor went quite far in the direction of the view that "our theologies of atonement and redemption should be subsidiary to our theology of creation" (thus stressing the analogy between individual and cosmic fulfillment) and referred to "all the possibilities of the sacramental Body which is this world."[199] Although this phrase sounds as though it is loaded with comprehensive ecumenical consequences, these were not developed in the presentation. Such a formulation obviously reflects ecumenical influence in general and Anglican neighborship in particular, but with no explicit reference to the sacramental practice of the church. Used in this setting, it may not be appropriate to take it as an expression of a sacramental representation by a Baptist speaker (that is, as a statement endorsed by Baptists as a whole); rather, it should be seen as a proposal to use the word "sacramental" in a wider—and dogmatically less restrictive—sense than it is traditionally used. Such a proposal would, however, involve certain theological implications that are fairly symptomatic of recent ecumenical development in general.

A dominant trend in Taylor's presentation was the repeated elaborate assumption that what eventually distinguishes a Free church approach to creation from that of established Christendom is not so much a difference in theological orientation as a difference in social situation, an assumption that would also account for an obvious diminution of that difference in our time. This observation confronts us with one important issue: To what extent do the different social situations of the churches—not only as they vary from time to time and place to place

---

[199]Michael Taylor, " 'No' to the World as 'Yes' to Creation," 1983 manuscript, 27.

but also as they may distinguish different church neighbors in time and in space—affect or reflect (important distinction!) divergent theological positions? And how may creation theology be the cause of this, or at least indicative of this? Obviously, these questions do not arise from the particular situation of the Free churches as such; rather from comparing the Free churches with churches of the state church and/or folk church tradition. That their own relation with society at large not only *may* but inevitably *must* have theological implications becomes striking to the churches once they are confronted with other churches that have a different profile of social integration. In many historical situations—and in a way that was rarely apparent at the time—the state church/Free church encounter could have served to illuminate the interaction between an ecclesiological and a social polarization, both position and opposition being determined by their relationship to the same legal establishment and to the same set of social dynamics. Discovering the more or less unconscious sociopsychological dependence of one's discussion partner thus provides one with a mirror in which one very soon detects one's own.

It is clear that the situation here sketched is a reality that goes far beyond the simple alternative of legal establishment or nonestablishment—even though this question may be a crucial part of it in certain circumstances. In one way or another, attitudes toward the state-and-church issue will probably be indicative of orientations with regard to creation theology. A strong emphasis on creation is likely to favor human fellowship at large and thus embrace political structures that are expressive of such fellowship; whereas a one-sided emphasis on redemption will elevate the community of believers and thus reduce the relationship with the state (symbolic of human togetherness at large, or "world") to an alleged minimum. But there should be no uncritical formulation of such observations. In recent years, the issue of "civil religion" has attracted a good deal of attention in ecumenical studies,[200] and it has become increasingly clear how the question of legal establishment is but a minor part of the question as to how the churches integrate—or resist integration—into their social environments, for the interaction of theological reflection and sociological dynamics is generally exceedingly complex.

---

[200]E.g., see the study on this topic organized by the Lutheran World Federation Department of Studies, on which the following reports have appeared: "On Civil Religion," *LWF Documentation*, no. 12 (December 1982); "On Civil Religion in Asia," *LWF Documentation*, no. 20 (June 1986); *The Church and Civil Religion in Asia, Ichigaya Center, Tokyo, Japan, November 27–December 2, 1985*, ed. Béla Harmati (Geneva: LWF Studies, 1984). On America, see also *Creation and Culture: The Challenge of Indigenous Spirituality and Culture to Western Creation Thought*, ed. David G. Burke (New York: LWM Studies, 1987).

In several ways, the state-and-church problematic is much simpler and easier to review than the complex question of church-and-society, and the former reflects conscious options in a way that the latter does not. But a look at the simpler dilemma may provide certain insights for our dealing with the more complex problem, always provided that observations are transferred with the necessary amount of critical retrospection. As was clearly demonstrated in Taylor's presentation, the dealings of the Free churches with the political establishment throughout the centuries have to be understood in two different but interrelating perspectives: 1. As a matter of principle, how did their theological understanding of their own identity define their relationship with the human community at large and, thus, with political authority in particular? 2. As a matter of fact, how did undesired repercussions and political oppression (as well as various forms of official or unofficial exclusion from social life) contribute to shaping particular Free church patterns of polity, and, in turn, what imprints did such polity leave on Free church theological reflection? The importance of asking these question goes beyond their immediate and apparent interest, for the answers will also shed light on the corresponding but less surveyable question of how principal reflection and unreflected behavior relate in the opposite, that is, folk church, tradition.

The major difficulty is not to distinguish and describe the main trends at work; they have been sufficiently obvious up to our own day. Rather, the difficulty may be to distinguish their mutual force and, thus, to estimate their relative influence on the historical process. Differing images of history may arise through disagreement on the factual occurrence of certain trends as well as on their relative contribution to the final outcome. A promising methodological control, then, may be to compare the development in North America (where Free churches have enjoyed equal rights and where, through the U.S. constitution, the established system became one of "Free churches") with that of Europe (where, historically, the state church has been dominant). What differences emerge in the Free church attitudes to state, society at large, human fellowship? Or, even more to the point, what differences could be observed around 1900, before the great age of European disestablishment got under way?

However, we immediately see that this question is inadequate. As obvious as it is that Free church attitudes differ from each other, it is equally obvious that lines of geographical division between Europe and the USA are less clear than denominational differences. In general, the pattern of Free church divisions is the same on both sides of the Atlantic. European Free church communities were transplanted to America during the 17th and 18th centuries, but later, in the 19th and 20th centuries, the dominant trend was in the opposite direction. In this way, the contact between the American and European branches of a particular community has usually remained closer than that between different communities on the same continent, in terms not only of structural links but also of shared spirituality. It therefore follows that experiences in one continent may, generations later, have had considerable influence on orientations and attitudes in the other. One particular example: The heated debate over religious liberty in the USA is considerably affected by earlier and traumatic European experiences, experiences that have significantly less impact in present-day Europe. In the USA there still seems to be a widespread concern for reinforcing the separation between church and state, something that may be motivated less by experiences from the American Free church system than by recollections of the Pilgrim Fathers' experiences in 17th-century Europe.[201] It is thus not possible to quote indiscriminately from American Free church representatives, for they speak out of an uncontested Free church situation and have no direct experience of the state as oppressor. Apropos, it may be interesting to note that both the most consistent champions of and the most passionate opponents to the issue of prayer in public schools seem to come from a classical Free church background!

From viewing the vast American Free church scene—in part motivated theologically, in part moulded by historical circumstances—one must therefore conclude that in order to see the relation to creation theology it is necessary to go beyond the church-and-state issue and proceed to the wider question of church and "world." "Free churchliness" usually implies a rather definite rejection of "worldliness." And this worldliness can be viewed in different ways. This may include various degrees of suspicion directed toward dependence on political (and ecclesiastical) authorities, toward political involvement by churches and/or by individual Christians, or toward various fields of cultural activity, business, entertainment, or social contacts. But it is clear that a certain "'no' to the world" constitutes a kind of common Free church legacy. The founders generally split from the mainline church(es) of their day because—for reasons of principle and/or experience—they found that the identity of the church was endangered by too close a relationship with political powers and social establishments that were not genuinely illuminated by divine truth.

This did not necessarily imply a more pessimistic view of human nature in general—and thus of fallen creation—than in the mainline church(es); for such pessimism could also serve to present an optimistic view on the possible renewal of nature by grace, and even provoke a countercriticism of it being simply another illusion about human perfectibility. Martin Luther, spokesperson for a rather different ecclesiology than the average Free church type, may be the classic example

---

[201]Not least, I make this conclusion as a decade-long reader of the distinguished American (Adventist) magazine *Liberty*.

of how an optimistic view of creation and a pessimistic assessment of fallen humankind can be dialectically combined. Even if his practical conclusions may seem to be more critical of traditional Free church than traditional folk church orientations, there is obviously no reason why an equally dialectical approach could not be combined with a Free church type of ecclesiology.

Referring in his presentation to the obvious below-average interest historically shown by the Free churches in creation theology, Taylor briefly touched on the Unitarians as a possible exception. However, it may be difficult to pay very comprehensive attention to Unitarianism in a review of Free church theology, partly because they comprise a small and rather isolated segment of the international Free church world (traditionally having ecumenical affinity only with the left wing of Quakerism), partly because, doctrinally, they do not seek an integration of the First Article of the Creed with the following two articles in the traditional Trinitarian sense. To a large extent, the theological concerns reflected by Unitarianism coincide with those reflected in the left wing of the major established churches in the era of the Enlightenment, a trend with a Universalist accent that was strongly supportive of folk church comprehensiveness. Unitarian nonconformity may be due more to the rejection of Unitarian theological orientation by the mainline churches than to a basic Free church orientation on its own behalf. It may be difficult to tell to what extent we are reviewing a cause, an effect, or simply a corollary when, in the same context, we observe the urge for freedom of conscience as a particularly beloved Unitarian motif coupled with a theological accent rather different from what we find among Congregationalists, Baptists, or Adventists.

The variety of patterns of reflection at our disposal in considering the theme of creation faith and ecclesiosociological orientation becomes even more impressive when we include in our vision the vast spectrum of religious communities—both past and present—that have experimented with theological ideas beyond the horizon of what is generally seen to be ecumenically acceptable. For the sake of simplicity one could suggest the Docetic-Manichean tradition (Christian Science, Theosophy, Anthroposophy), which tends to let created matter evaporate in favor of a spiritualized universe, and in social life seems to favor a certain cultural elitist segregation that is critical of mediocrity and matter-relatedness. Or, in the opposite direction, one could suggest the Ebionitic-Immanental tradition (e.g., Jehovah's Witnesses, Children of God, Mormons), which imagines divine reality as some sort of extension of an objectified world of matter, and in social life opposes established power (political, economic, cultural) structures "from below" (with the striking exception of the Mormons, who succeeded in creating a sociopolitical establishment of their own that quickly led to the emergence of socioconservative attitudes), their natural enemies being the agents of established power positions. Again, we are not attempting here to give a balanced historical judgment of particular communities; rather to point out generally observable trends in order to illustrate the options available. And, above all, we are not suggesting that there are dogmatical links between the Free churches and the wide spectrum of religious communities outside the fellowship of the Ecumenical Creeds. Our glimpse behind the walls of traditional Christendom involves no attempt to assess these walls as such, simply to highlight the dynamics at work in the interactional field of creation/church/sociology.

It would therefore be most misleading if the question put to the Free churches at the 1983 consultation, "'No' to the World as 'Yes' to Creation?," was taken to suggest that the Free churches—if not as a solidly unified block, then at least by reason of statistically verifiable trends—should have their own concern for creation that would account for some joint rejection of the "world" (that is, of the extensive human community in its empirical "fallen" state) and thus help the world back to the perfection originally given in—or at least prefigured by—the great directive event of creation. To suggest that such a vision was constitutive of a somewhat common Free church orientation would be little more than sheer fantasy. But what does seem to make eminent sense is, first, to see that a certain "no" to universality is characteristic of the Free churches vis-à-vis established churches and, second, to ask how the positive affirmation implied in this negation (whether directly phrased or not) may be oriented in relation to creation as the primeval event, a belief solidly testified also in the Free church tradition. Only when an answer to this question has emerged is it meaningful to ask to what extent we may here be faced with insights that are of direct importance to the church as a whole.

This is certainly a more complex procedure than the one that arose regarding the—dogmatically as well as structurally—more unified traditions we have dealt with so far. Among the Free churches there is a much less identifiable complex of theology than there is in, for example, Orthodoxy, Roman Catholicism, and Lutheranism, and we would search in vain for spokespersons representing a "unified family" of Free churches. Likewise, what we have suggested about the role of creation theology does not refer to some unified theory that someone has proposed as a common theological denominator on behalf of this group of churches. What we are looking for is some general trend as to the actual function of creation faith, and we expect implicit rather than explicit dogmatical references. This means that we are not searching for some joint "doctrine" but for some credible theological interpretation of the average Free church attitude.

The common Free church alienation from the "world" cannot be understood in isolation from a firm support of creation as the basic event of the Bible. Even if in this tradition (or these traditions) creation has often been presupposed rather than preached (as in the New Testament), the average Free church renunciation of the "world" is not based on a Manichean denunciation of created matter as ungodly. There is always some implicit distinction between the ideal world as God's good creation and the actual world as created *and* fallen. To renounce the actual world with all its distractions is, then, essential to the confirmation of the real world as willed by the Creator. This vision may be shared by more or less all churches, but in the Free church tradition the deliberate distancing from establishment, political and social, underscores the antithesis with an extraordinary vigor, and also challenges some popular trends of wishful thinking that are too readily accepted by churches that may depend, functionally, on the friendship of the "establishment" at large.

This, again, makes the Free churches particularly sensitive to the illusion of vested interests simplistically advocating creation faith in support of established conditions as established. We touch on widely congenial concerns when we remember Ernst Bloch's polemic (so enthusiastically embraced by wide theological constituencies during the last generation) against the unreflected use of the biblical creation account's "Behold, it was very good" in support of leaving things as they are. That Bloch uses this observation to support a frontal attack on creation faith as a whole is a different matter, and has been regretted also by influential theologians who have received direct inspiration from him. But the general observation can be made that, for good reasons, the Free churches have been less exposed to the temptation of politically abusing the "Behold, it was very good" than have other major Christian traditions. In general, adherents of the Free churches have seen and clearly stated that God's creation is not simply identical with the world as it actually is, with its structures, institutions, and established patterns; the Creator's world is different, and it takes our free choice to change creation from what it *actually* is into what it *essentially* is.

Seen in this perspective, there is no doubt that a Free church approach to creation—however little or much the word "creation" may be on display—could serve as a permanent corrective to much of established creation theology. Its pervasive "'No' to the World" could contribute to supporting and purifying (or supporting *in* purifying) a common "'Yes' to Creation."

5.7 A preliminary summing up

The main impression gained from this "confessional" review may be what Professor Reinhard Slenczka emphasized so strongly in his contribution to the 1983 consultation: In the realm of creation theology there is no essentially dividing polarization between the churches; such divisions were essentially overcome during the doctrinal controversies in the ancient church, through which a pessimistic devaluation of creation was as resolutely eradicated as an optimistic elevation of the integrity of creation. Throughout the intervening centuries, the doctrinal decisions have remained basically unchallenged and are not behind these schisms persisting in Christendom today. If tensions in creation theology do represent a threat to church unity today, the issues are of a confessory, not confessional, nature, the fronts running not *between* but *across* the churches. Controversies such as those between politicized and apolitical Christianity, between process, existential, and more traditional models of thought, and between accents on divine transcendence versus immanence may in certain instances have comprehensive consequences for creation theology, seen as some particular dogmatical *locus,* as well as for theological orientation and ecumenical rapprochement as a whole. But even if some denominationally based trends of statistical correlation can be discerned, this still does not question the general conclusion: that the real divergences in contemporary creation theology are crossdenominational and not interdenominational. There is a limited degree of statistically detectable confessional interrelatedness, but this is by far not the most disturbing factor as far as ecumenically crucial confrontations are concerned.

In itself, this observation should recommend a relaxed exchange and encourage a mutual give-and-take between the churches as far as the First Article is concerned, and this should give rise to a willingness to explore one's own shortcomings in light of the biblical truth as seen by others. Through the wider perspectives thus opened up, creation faith may be expected to throw new, hopefully reconciliatory, light also on those theological issues that are still church divisive. Having said this, it is necessary already now to deal with the very concept of confessions/denominations in a more relaxed way, always bearing in mind that the theological identity of a communion is far more complex than one may assume from its official self-definition, and that the theological distinctiveness of one or the other church is never one solidly unified body of doctrine but rather the result of several historically detectable gravitational pulls. Against this background, mutual enrichment is not simply defensible but also recommendable; such enrichment is even an obligation between and among all churches as well as within each single church.

An *Orthodox* "theotic" vision should be greeted in that it stresses the primeval as well as the ultimate unity of creation and salvation and at the same time questions the actual being of all static ontological formulae. On the other hand, it should be questioned about its eidetic Neoplatonic assumptions as well as about the corresponding temptation to let the world of matter be so hastily absorbed by its celestial transfiguration that the earthly life—after all—loses in intrinsic validity. Is the icon a confirmation or a denial of created reality? This question should certainly not be kept beyond dispute.

A *Roman Catholic* "supernatural" orientation is to be recommended for its understanding of creation as givenness, meaning, and order, and for its concern to interrelate natural life and Christian worship without mistaking the one for the other. At the same time, Roman Catholicism should be questioned about the danger of (over-) constraining ''nature'' to a rigid cosmological-conceptual shell.

A *Lutheran* ''law and gospel'' approach should receive attention for its determination to confirm God's work in creation as well as in redemption, and for distinguishing his double mode of operation in a way that secures active human cooperation with the Creator without risking any confusion of saving faith and human self-assertion. But Lutheranism should be questioned about the risk of double ethical standards and the misuse of ethical realism as an excuse for practical indifferentism and political accommodation.

A *Reformed* ''gloire de Dieu'' program should be welcomed as a reminder of divine sovereignty eliciting a doxological response (including very concrete works of obedience) through creation. But it should be challenged on possible dualistic implications in the direction of an iconoclastic worldview, including also a certain ''Christo-monistic'' iconoclasm with regard to ''natural theology.''

An *Anglican* ''sacramental'' emphasis should be greeted, not least against the background of the contemporary ecological challenge, as an inspiring attempt to highlight the inner connection between creation, incarnation, and sacrament. But it should be questioned about the temptations of ontologizing contingent historical events or of seeing the world of nature exclusively through the spectacles of some Christianized sacramental transformation.

A *Free church* emphasis on Christian ''otherness'' from the ''world'' and its critical attitude toward any simplistic identification of created order and present establishment should likewise be hailed as a corrective to ecclesiastical and political attempts to exploit creation to the benefit of an unreflected defense of the status quo, and also as a true incentive to explore and criticize trends of social, cultural, and political captivity on the part of churches in various traditions. It should be critically examined with regard to the tendency to glorify some particular pattern of structural opposition and too quickly assume a prophetic brand of self-consciousness.

On the whole, it is not difficult to see how a renewed encounter in the domain of creation theology, especially in view of today's serious ecological challenges, might bring the churches closer together in common reflection and service. One can also see that each of the churches could be enriched from such a widening of its horizon; it might strengthen their awareness of belonging together and they might be richer in community than they are on their own. Already this might turn out to be a major ecumenical asset. But still more important is the question of the wider ecumenical implications. Have our tentative advances into a landscape that is close to unexplored on an ecumenical level taught us anything about the possible constructiveness of widening the horizons of ecumenical reflection into areas that have so far been considered to be ecumenically irrelevant and "practically" uncontroversial? Again, this presupposes a more concrete question: Does increased awareness of some already existing but latent common understanding—as, for example, in the domain of creation theology—contribute to a fuller mutual appreciation among churches in general? Including a more congenial assessment of doctrinal positions that may still be regarded as church dividing?

This reflection must move in two directions:

On the one hand, it must state the integral unity of any committed theological vision (a pattern of single, separated "loci" has no inherent motivating force) as well as the permeating impact creation will have on—and will receive from—a global theological vision. Against that background it is simply impossible that unity in creation faith—once adequately explored—would not have extensive consequences on church unity as a whole. The big issue would then be whether, through some traditional half-conscious awareness, our far-reaching creation consensus has already been discounted ecumenically, that is, some might say "in spite of their basic consensus on creation, the churches are not able to unite . . . and *that* testifies to the dominant influence of other theological or nontheological factors." Or do we still have the decisive exploration before us?—"*So far* the existing consensus on creation has not really been reflected in our ecumenical conversations; simple theological consistency demands that this be done and a new advance be made."

On the other hand, we must at the same time raise a question in the opposite direction: What are the issues that maintain the division among the churches today, and what possible consequences could a discovered oneness-in-variety of creation faith have for our further dealing with these divisions? To answer this would require a great deal of consideration and analytical effort and would certainly transcend the limits of our present research. But it should already now be noted as an important item on the agenda for tomorrow! It may, however, be useful to make a few fairly superficial suggestions.

Obviously, today as for the last 1,000 years, church divisive issues are mainly to be found in the domain of the Third Article of the Creed—generally speaking, in ecclesiology, with certain implications related to soteriology and sacramentology. Not only editorially (article-wise) but also substantially, these issues will at first glance seem to be modestly interrelated with creation faith. But several observations that have been made en route, along with our principal observation concerning the integrity of theology, demand that we question this immediate impression. To take one example, apparently as remote as can be imagined: What may creation theology have to do with, say, the infallibility of the pope? First, one would have to consider the wider ontological question of created being(s) as possible manifestation(s) of the Creator's presence in the world of his making. Second, there would be the question as to whether patterns of coordination—hierarchical or other—constitutionally inscribed in creation may also include the church. The question to what extent general structures of creation could and should be derived from, or possibly be applied to, the church would, therefore, obviously give rise to an issue within an issue. Third, a "sacramental vision" founded in incarnation *and* creation would have to be rethought with regard to and in light of the understanding of sacramental ministry, with all the theological implications such a doctrine may have. As we see, reflections on church primacy are by no means unrelated to creation faith!

This should be more than enough to suggest that a continued elaboration of the study hereby begun may also shed important light on issues of overt ecumenical disunity. But still more important than this direct contribution would be the exploration of a new and extended ecumenical perspective, a perspective that might lead to some reassessment of the relative significance of specific areas of concern, including the importance of ecclesiominiterial structures vis-à-vis issues of faith and/or ethics. This is not said in the pious "Protestant" hope that questions about structure could be relativized in relation to the "contents" of our common confession; a priori there is just as much of a risk that the outcome would be the opposite. But what we are suggesting is that conscious ecumenical reflection on the First Article would lead to a revitalization of ecumenical theology as a whole, and that, in light of the rather far-reaching unity testified by this First Article, this may entail a new and inspiring drive toward recognized theological unity in, between, and among all churches.

The condensed report of the 1983 Strasbourg consultation on creation and confessionality published in *The Ecumenical Review*[202] concluded by noting four groups of questions that lend themselves for further discussion. In the course of the further study process and during the elaboration of the present analysis, none of these questions has been thoroughly resolved, nor has the impression of their urgency diminished. They have been further spelled out, explained, and sustained, but by and large they will remain the main findings not only of that consultation but of the study project as a whole.

The first of the four observations mentioned further consideration in the direction anticipated in §5 of this study and concluded with a clear *recommendation for future studies*, a recommendation that can only be confirmed here: "The ecumenical issue is not creation per se, but how creation relates to history/revelation/salvation. Maybe the most fruitful way to formulate the issue would be: which are

---

[202]*The Ecumenical Review* 36/2 (April 1984): 204-13; reprinted in *LWF Documentation* no. 27 (October 1989).

the basic theological concerns separating the churches, how do they pertain to creation, and how could a reflective creation theology contribute to overcoming them?'' This indicates a methodological approach rather different from that of the present creation study, but it could provide a very helpful complementary reflection.

The second observation focused on the question: *creation fulfilled or restored*? For the sake of clarification, it contrasted two typical approaches, approaches that may, in the course of the centuries, have appeared together in various combinations rather than in purely paradigmatic and, thus, competitive forms. However, there are good historical reasons for referring to one as a particularly Oriental thrust, the other as a typical Occidental thrust. In a patristic ''recapitulation'' perspective—dominant as it has been in Eastern theology over the centuries—accent is on Christ as the cosmic Lord, the one who brings creation to fulfillment, his preincarnate presence in the primeval work of creation already foreshadowing his coming incarnation for the glorious consummation of the universe. In a Latin ''restoration'' perspective—an Anselmian orientation generally inherited also by the churches of the Reformation—the incarnation of Christ is generally seen as the reconquest of a ''Paradise Lost,'' as restitution of a creation that, had it not been for the Fall, might have achieved consummation without that kind of extraordinary intervention (a possibility usually not exposed to serious reflection). It is obvious that we are confronted here with an area of problems that have as basic a bearing on the theology of creation as on that of incarnation, and the interaction of these respective doctrines becomes particularly clear. We shall confine ourselves to suggesting the constitutive Christian convictions that may be at stake, namely: on the one hand, there is salvation leading precisely to the great, intended consummation of creation (a vision seldom sufficiently observed in Western theology); on the other, ''the Word of the Cross'' makes the recovery of a world otherwise lost totally dependent on a historical act of redemption (in the Eastern tradition sometimes swallowed up by a precipitate cosmic Easter triumph).

But the question that now arises is whether a more organic linkage of the two ''motifs'' could not secure a better resonance to the fullness of biblical truth and restrict the possibilities of deviation that we have seen to be connected to each of them separately. This might also have a bearing on the ''Barthian controversy'' (and on the post-Cartesian creation dilemma as a whole). How can creation faith be organically incorporated into our historically conditioned ''covenant'' relationship with Christ without implicitly ruling out that *in principio,* which is ultimately constitutive of ''creation'' faith? Could the Barthian Christological approach to creation—irrespective of the final theological judgment on the outcome—be seen, inter alia, as a legitimate step in the direction of the Eastern visionary and integrative approach to the global complex of creation and salvation? At least, this seems to be how Jürgen Moltmann views his own neo-Barthian approach. But as important as disagreement on emphases and priorities may be, the urge for an organic coordination must in itself be seen as sufficiently valid. And the invitation to such a coordination should be taken seriously, even if with a certain amount of reservation as to the paths hitherto proposed.

The third observation concerned the *sacramentality of creation*. By dialectically combining the doctrine of creation with one other particular area of theological concern (or rather two: incarnation *and* sacrament), this is obviously also an issue that raises a question of coordination, but automatically also a question of interaction and accent. Immediately we see two reciprocal questions: 1. Through their use of elements not only actually created but also visibly chosen as paradigmatic expressions of created life, what have the sacraments got to say about creation? Of creation as sheer creatureliness, and of creation as eventually consecrated and redignified through the incarnation event? 2. By the way in which it lends itself to serve as sanctifying sacramental "matter," what has creation got to say about the sacraments? How must incarnation as the crucial historical event be underlined in order to protect our reflection from a self-sufficient metaphysics of matter? Above all, there are two dangers to beware of: 1. a "sacramentalist" approach to creation that could reinstate a Gnostic *esse est salvari*, even if in a very cultic, high church fashion, and eventually include some echoes of the *religionsgeschichtliche* holiness approach of around 1920 (e.g., Otto, Heiler, Söderblom); and 2. a "natural" approach to sacramentality with an overemphasis on matter as the general expression of the Creator's presence (was William Temple himself quite free of this? Paul Tillich, obviously, was not). In both cases, it seems clear that a conscious insistence on incarnation as the mediating term may serve to prevent the one-sided orientations we fear.

The fourth observation relates to the nearly 200-year-old dilemma (Friedrich Schleiermacher) that was so spectacularly highlighted in the Barthian challenge to creation theology in the last two generations: Is there such a thing as a *"relative independence" of creation faith*, or does it belong to the framework of a strictly "Messianic theology" (the program of Jürgen Moltmann)? This question has limited confessional implications, although certain traces of confessional relatedness may be there. (After all, Schleiermacher was also Reformed, consciously so!) In general, it challenges contemporary theology in its transconfessional exchange. However, because of its basic importance for the definition of Christian involvement with the world of today, it has tremendous principal bearing also on patterns of ecumenical cooperation. Even discussions about a traditional Roman Catholic concept of "nature" and on a Lutheran "law and gospel" dialectic have certain implications here that should not be overlooked. At the same time, it is important that confessionally related tensions are not unduly "confessionalized" in a way that paralyzes ecumenical rapprochement instead of serving as an incentive.

In general, our survey confirms that the search for confessional orientation in creation theology may be useful to help uncover the roots and implications of theological differences in general, but that this in itself presupposes keeping an eye open for other and immediately more operative sources of theological diver-´ gence. The result of our study has been to de-confessionalize rather than confessionalize theological controversy, and thus to indicate avenues for a future rapprochement (of the churches more than of conflicting transconfessional "schools"). To be sure, avenues are useful only to the extent that they are used, and, for obvious reasons, the accomplishments of a pioneering exploration such as this must remain modest. An exploration such as this can open up a new terrain for ecumenical research, but it does not offer a substantial contribution to the research which, it is to be hoped, will follow. Others will have to take up the invitation in order to make something more out of what we have offered here: a modest extended preface. Even if we would like to think that the observations we have made en route show some promise, a promise is worth little without some further implementation.

At the same time, we feel it is important that this project—unprecedented as its line of orientation may be—is thematically linked with important ongoing ecumenical projects, such as the joint WCC Church and Society/Faith and Order project on "Justice, Peace, and the Integrity of Creation," and the Faith and Order projects "Towards the Common Expression of the Apostolic Faith Today"[203] and "The Unity of the Church and the Renewal of Human Community." Precisely because of their difference in general orientation, these projects may serve to supplement and emphasize each other, and also to introduce a new and important stage in the ecumenical exchange—not on creation as a theme per se, but on ecumenism in the light of creation, that is, in light of the event that is prior to and basic to all other "events" of our faith. "In the beginning God created heaven and earth." For the sake of ecumenical rapprochement, we have to look not simply for *a* beginning but for *the* beginning.

---

[203]Which pays equal attention to each of the three articles. Cf. "The Integrity of Creation in the Light of the Apostolic Faith," *Faith and Renewal: Reports and Documents of the Commission on Faith and Order, Stavanger 1985, Norway,* ed. Thomas F. Best, Faith and Order Paper no. 131 (Geneva: World Council of Churches, 1986). German: "Die Integrität der Schöpfung im Licht des apostolischen Glaubens," *Glaube und Erneuerung: Stavanger 1985. Sitzung der Kommission für Glauben und Kirchenverfassung, Berichte, Reden, Dokumente,* ed. Günther Gassmann (Frankfurt am Main: Verlag Otto Lembeck, 1986) 115-23.

Index of Names